LEADERSHIP
AND LEGACY

SUNY series on the Presidency: Contemporary Issues
———————
Robert P. Watson

LEADERSHIP AND LEGACY

The Presidency of Barack Obama

EDITED BY

Tom Lansford, Douglas M. Brattebo,
Robert P. Watson, and Casey Maugh Funderburk

SUNY PRESS

Published by State University of New York Press, Albany

© 2021 State University of New York

All rights reserved

No part of this book may be used or reproduced in any manner whatsoever without written permission. No part of this book may be stored in a retrieval system or transmitted in any form or by any means including electronic, electrostatic, magnetic tape, mechanical, photocopying, recording, or otherwise without the prior permission in writing of the publisher.

For information, contact State University of New York Press, Albany, NY
www.sunypress.edu

Library of Congress Cataloging-in-Publication Data

Name: Lansford, Tom, editor.
Title: Leadership and legacy : the Presidency of Barack Obama / edited by Tom Lansford, [and 3 others].
Description: Albany : State University of New York, [2021] | Series: SUNY series on the Presidency: contemporary issues | Includes bibliographical references and index.
Identifiers: LCCN 2020045638 (print) | LCCN 2020045639 (ebook) | ISBN 9781438481876 (hardcover : alk. paper) | ISBN 9781438481869 (pbk. : alk. paper) | ISBN 9781438481883 (ebook)
Subjects: LCSH: Obama, Barack—Influence. | United States—Politics and government—2009–2017.
Classification: LCC E907 .L42 2021 (print) | LCC E907 (ebook) | DDC 973.932092—dc23
LC record available at https://lccn.loc.gov/2020045638
LC ebook record available at https://lccn.loc.gov/2020045639

10 9 8 7 6 5 4 3 2 1

Contents

Introduction: Their Place in History   1
   Robert P. Watson

I. Executive, Administrative, and Party Leadership

1 The Vice Presidency of Joe Biden   25
   Richard M. Yon, Michael J. Ferro, and Jeremy Hunt

2 The Evolving Political Partnership of Barack Obama and Bill Clinton   47
   Douglas M. Brattebo

3 Barack Obama's Executive Orders   75
   Raymond Frey

4 Obama, Party Leadership, and Domestic Elections   87
   Tom Lansford

5 Michelle Obama's First Ladyship   103
   Elizabeth J. Natalle

II. Domestic Policy

6 Obama, Economic Recovery and Macroeconomic Policy   133
   Paul Burton and Joseph J. St. Marie

7	The Affordable Care Act: Obama and the ACA—Innovation by Tradition *Max J. Skidmore*	151
8	Obama and the Supreme Court *Sean J. Savage*	167
9	Obama and Congress *Sean D. Foreman*	185
10	The Obama Administration's Approach to Disaster Response and Recovery *David Harms Holt and Casey Maugh Funderburk*	205

III. Foreign and Security Policy

11	Obama and the Wars in Afghanistan and Iraq *Robert J. Pauly Jr.*	233
12	The Arab Spring and the Middle East *Wayne F. Lesperance Jr. and John M. Callahan*	251
13	Obama's Leadership in Addressing Climate Change *Wayne Law, Alanna Lecher, Jonathan Smith, and April Watson*	267
14	China, Russia, and U.S. Primacy in World Affairs *William Keeton*	289

IV. Conclusion

| 15 | Barack Obama: The Post-Presidency
Michael J. Devine | 317 |

| Appendix A: Grading President Obama | 327 |
| Appendix B: Barack Obama Biography | 328 |

Appendix C: The Obama Administration	329
Select Bibliography	333
About the Editors	341
About the Contributors	343
Index	349

Introduction

Their Place in History

ROBERT P. WATSON

The Rating Game

It is not surprising that presidential rankings and ratings generate enormous interest and debate. The president of the United States is, after all, the most visible leader in the world, with countless media outlets and online sources covering his (and one day *her*) every move. So too is there is a natural inclination to rate and rank all things, especially in America. The American public enthusiastically consumes the weekly polls of college football's "top 25" and the annual *US News and World Report* college rankings, lists of corporations in the Fortune 500 and the year's top-grossing movies, and all sorts of other ranking lists. Scholars have also been ranking and rating the presidents. Indeed, everyone with an opinion seems to get in on the action—whether it is a public opinion approval poll, a panel of commentators on a television talk show, co-workers huddled around the office water cooler, or even a group of professors working on a book. It is inevitable that we should ask, "How is the president doing?" (Pederson & McLaurin, 1987).

Americans have asked this question since the beginning. Indeed, the "cult" of the presidency was born shortly after George Washington's death in December 1799 when Parson Weems's imaginative book *The Life of Washington* lionized the Founder and created numerous legends about the first president. Perhaps the first effort to rate the chief executives occurred nearly a century later in 1888 when the Irish-born diplomat and writer James Bryce published *The American Commonwealth*. In his ambitious account of the United States, Bryce placed the presidents into categories based on their achievements. His groupings included those whose deeds will be remembered in "the history of the world" such as Washington, Jefferson, Lincoln, and Grant, while dismissing those presidents serving after Andrew Jackson and before Lincoln as "mere politicians." In this latter respect, his assessment generally reflects the consensus of modern scholars (Brinkley, 2019).

Perhaps the first systematic and scholarly effort to assess the presidents occurred in 1948 when the noted Harvard professor Arthur M. Schlesinger surveyed a group of fifty-five of the nation's leading historians. In his poll, Schlesinger asked the participants to rate the presidents by placing them into categories such as "great," "near great," and so on, all the way to "failure." The results of this groundbreaking poll were published in *Life* magazine to much fanfare; and so the enterprise of ranking presidents was born (Schlesinger, 1948).

Interest in such ratings and polls has only increased over the years. Accordingly, several major presidential ranking polls have been commissioned and released since the 1948 study. New polls have been done every few years to update assessments and include recent presidents. Likewise, as more archival documents are released and new biographies written, further information becomes available to scholars, all of which creates more accurate assessments.

The passing of time also allows history to see the wisdom or error of presidential decisions, not only with enhanced accuracy, but in a more dispassionate and objective manner. What may once have seemed foolhardy and unpopular, for instance, may have ended up helping the nation and the world. Take Harry Truman's role in the Marshall Plan, Berlin Airlift, desegregating the armed forces, and planning for the establishment of NATO, all of which once faced political opposition but now seem to be nothing less than visionary and bold.

There is clearly the need for early and continued assessment of the presidents. And so it was when Schlesinger conducted a second poll in 1962. This time, he surveyed seventy-five leading historians and published the results in the *New York Times Magazine*. The popularity of the rankings were given an added boost when it was learned that President John F. Kennedy, who was in office at the time of the poll, expressed interest in the new poll (and, it should be noted, also took satisfaction in the fact that his predecessor, Dwight Eisenhower, was not rated very highly). Over the ensuing years, the rating polls grew to be something of a "cottage industry" which continues to the present time (Schlesinger, 1962; Schlesinger Jr., 2003).

As is evident in Table I.1 on page 4, polls have been conducted every few years and several scholars and organizations have participated in the rankings, including C-SPAN, the Siena Research Institute, the American Political Science Association, both Schlesinger and his son Arthur Jr., and others. The results generate an ever-increasing interest from scholars and the public (and likely the presidents themselves). The more recent polls also continue the practice of surveying professional historians and political scientists with expertise on the American presidency. However, the recent polls have added two twists—they sometimes employ larger numbers of respondents and often rate the presidents on specific aspects of the roles and responsibilities of the president. This latter point includes such factors as the quality of appointments, state of the economy, handling of foreign policy, ethical leadership, public speaking, crisis leadership, moral authority, relations with Congress, and so on (C-SPAN, 2000; Murray & Blessing, 1994; Schlesinger Jr., 1996; SRI, 2010).

The popularity of these presidential rankings has even translated to polls on the first ladies and presidential cabinets. Like the presidential rating polls, these rankings also survey leading scholars of the presidency and first ladyship, and typically ask respondents to either rank their subjects from best to worst or place them into categories similar to those used by Schlesinger and other pollsters (Watson, 2003; Watson, 2000; Watson, 1999).

Obviously, the task of ranking or rating presidents is both important and an ongoing endeavor. The same is true for assessing individual presidents such as Barack Obama, although it is an undertaking marked by challenges and controversy.

Methodology

The noted Lincoln scholar David Herbert Donald used to tell the story of visiting with President John. F. Kennedy in 1962. During their conversation, the president expressed his concern about the methodology behind the rankings, maintaining, "No one has a right to grade a president—not

Table I.1. Leading Presidential Ranking Polls

PRESIDENT	1948	1962	1982	1996	1996	2000	2010	2017	2018
Washington	02	02	03	02	03	03	04	02	02
J. Adams	09	10	09	11	14	16	17	19	14
Jefferson	05	05	04	04	04	07	05	07	05
Madison	14	12	14	17	10	18	06	17	12
Monroe	12	18	15	15	13	14	07	13	18
J. Q. Adams	11	13	16	18	18	19	19	21	23
Jackson	06	06	07	05	08	13	14	18	15
Van Buren	15	17	20	21	21	30	23	34	27
W. Harrison	X	X	X	X	35	37	35	38	42
Tyler	22	25	28	32	34	36	37	39	37
Polk	10	08	12	09	11	12	12	14	20
Taylor	25	24	27	29	29	28	33	31	35
Fillmore	24	26	29	31	36	35	38	37	38
Pierce	27	28	31	33	37	39	40	41	41
Buchanan	26	29	33	38	40	41	42	43	43
Lincoln	01	01	01	01	01	01	03	01	01
A. Johnson	19	23	32	37	39	40	43	42	40
Grant	28	30	35	33	38	33	26	22	21
Hayes	13	14	22	23	25	26	31	32	29
Garfield	X	X	X	X	30	29	27	29	34
Arthur	17	21	23	26	28	32	25	35	31
Cleveland	08	11	17	13	16	17	20	23	24
B. Harrison	21	20	26	19	31	31	34	30	32
McKinley	18	15	18	16	17	15	21	16	19
T. Roosevelt	07	07	05	06	05	04	02	04	04
Taft	16	16	19	22	20	20	24	24	22
Wilson	04	04	06	07	06	06	08	11	11
Harding	29	31	36	39	41	38	40	40	39
Coolidge	23	27	30	30	33	27	29	27	28
Hoover	20	19	21	33	24	34	36	36	36
F. Roosevelt	03	03	02	02	02	02	01	03	03
Truman	–	08	08	08	07	05	09	06	06
Eisenhower	–	21	11	10	09	09	10	05	07
Kennedy	–	–	13	12	15	08	11	08	15
L. Johnson	–	–	10	14	12	10	16	10	10
Nixon	–	–	34	36	32	25	30	28	33
Ford	–	–	24	28	27	23	28	25	25
Carter	–	–	25	27	19	22	32	26	26
Reagan	–	–	–	25	26	11	18	09	09
G. H. Bush	–	–	–	24	22	20	22	20	17
Clinton	–	–	–	20	23	21	13	15	13

PRESIDENT	1948	1962	1982	1996	1996	2000	2010	2017	2018
G. W. Bush	–	–	–	–	–	–	39	33	30
Obama	–	–	–	–	–	–	15	12	08
Trump	–	–	–	–	–	–	–	–	44
Total N	29	31	36	39	41	41	43	43	44

Key: The president was not ranked (x)
The president did not yet serve his full term (–)
There are also a few ties in the polls

Polls: 1948 Arthur M. Schlesinger Poll
1962 Arthur M. Schlesinger Poll
1982 Robert K. Murray & Tim H. Blessing Poll
1996 Arthur M. Schlesinger Jr. Poll
1996 William J. Ridings Jr. & Stuart McIver Poll
2000 C-SPAN Poll
2010 Siena Research Institute Poll
2017 C-SPAN Poll
2018 American Political Science Association Poll

Table I.2. Leading First Lady Ranking Polls

FIRST LADIES	1982	1993	1999	2003	2003	2008	2014	2018
Washington	9	12	4	13	5	9	9	10
A. Adams	2	3	2	2	4	2	2	6
Jefferson	X	X	X	X	X	X	X	X
Madison	4	4	3	3	2	6	4	4
Monroe	23	23	24	31	31	29	30	31
L. Adams	14	16	22	12	26	21	18	23
Jackson	X	X	X	X	X	X	X	X
Van Buren	X	X	X	X	X	X	X	X
A. Harrison	22	X	39	X	X	X	X	40
L. Tyler	31	30	30	34	35	35	37	36
J. Tyler	24	27	28	26	28	28	27	32
Polk	21	20	6	10	11	26	23	19
Taylor	29	33	31	35	36	34	35	37
Fillmore	25	31	15	29	25	32	32	33
Pierce	33	34	37	38	37	38	39	41
Lane	X	X	7	X	X	X	X	X
Lincoln	37	37	38	36	33	36	31	30
E. Johnson	20	24	16	22	32	33	38	39

continued on next page

Table I.2. Continued.

FIRST LADIES	1982	1993	1999	2003	2003	2008	2014	2018
Grant	19	26	7	18	18	24	22	24
Hayes	12	15	21	14	12	18	20	26
Garfield	27	28	14	30	X	27	28	34
Arthur	X	X	X	X	X	X	X	X
Cleveland	13	22	9	23	15	20	26	25
C. Harrison	30	29	25	25	16	30	29	28
McKinley	35	32	32	32	34	31	34	35
Ed. Roosevelt	10	14	12	9	10	11	13	16
Taft	18	25	35	21	22	22	25	22
El. Wilson	16	21	10	19	19	13	19	17
Ed. Wilson	7	10	28	11	13	10	14	14
Harding	36	35	36	37	29	37	36	29
Coolidge	17	19	26	17	23	17	21	20
Hoover	11	13	27	16	14	14	17	13
El. Roosevelt	1	1	1	1	1	1	1	1
Truman	15	11	18	20	27	16	16	27
Eisenhower	28	17	33	27	30	19	24	21
Kennedy	8	7	11	4	8	3	3	7
C. Johnson	3	6	17	7	3	5	7	5
Nixon	32	18	23	33	24	25	33	18
Ford	6	9	4	8	9	7	8	8
Carter	5	5	20	6	7	8	10	9
Reagan	34	36	34	28	21	15	15	15
B. Bush	–	8	19	15	17	12	11	12
Clinton	–	2	13	5	6	4	6	3
L. Bush	–	–	–	24	20	23	12	11
Obama	–	–	–	–	–	–	5	2
Trump	–	–	–	–	–	–	–	38
Total N	37	37	39	38	37	38	39	41

Key: The first lady was not ranked or was deceased (x)
The first lady did not yet serve in office (–)
There are also a few ties in the polls
James Buchanan never married; his niece Harriet Lane served as his hostess

Polls: 1982 Siena Research Institute Poll
1993 Siena Research Institute Poll
1999 Watson Poll
2003 Siena Research Institute Poll
2003 Watson Poll
2008 Siena Research Institute Poll
2014 Siena Research Institute Poll
2018 Watson Poll

even poor James Buchanan—who has not sat in his chair, examined the mail and information that came across his desk, and learned why he made his decisions" (Donald, 1995). On the other hand, President Theodore Roosevelt viewed the matter simply. In the opinion of the "Bull Moose," presidents could be placed into one of two broad categories—they were either the "Lincoln type" or the "Buchanan type." Of course, Roosevelt dominated his contemporary political stage as a Lincolnesque leader (Smith, 2019). Yet, the rankings are rarely so obvious.

Methodologically, one of the inherent problems in assessing presidents is the small "N" (limited number of presidents). As of this writing, only forty-four men have served in forty-five presidencies (Grover Cleveland was both the twenty-second and twenty-fourth president). The problem of the sample size is simply one of the limitations facing any effort to rank or rate the presidents, but a shortcoming that does not hinder an assessment of a single president such as Barack Obama. It is also exceedingly difficult to compare presidents across time, as the nature of the office and events facing the country when John Adams governed were quite different than those that marked Obama's presidency. Moreover, there is much variation among the presidents. Each has had his own style and challenges, as well as his successes and failures. Therefore, it is exceedingly difficult to even compare presidents.

Not all the presidents are ranked in all the polls. For instance, some scholars omit William Henry Harrison, who served just one month in office before his untimely death, and James Garfield, who was assassinated during his inaugural year in the presidency. Because both men died early in their presidential terms it is next to impossible to rank them in the same polls with presidents who served the full four or eight years. The same might even be said for Zachary Taylor, who passed away halfway into his second year in office, making it difficult to judge his performance. As a result, few scholars have attempted to offer detailed assessments of these three presidents (Pious, 2003).

The ranking polls do not include the pre- or postpresidential years. While some presidents have continued their public service after leaving the White House, such as John Quincy Adams and Andrew Johnson, who were elected to the U.S. House and U.S. Senate, respectively, and William Howard Taft, who served on the U.S. Supreme Court, this service is not factored in to the assessments. Relatedly, some former presidents have distinguished themselves in other ways after leaving office that ended up improving their public image. This includes Richard Nixon, who wrote a number of successful books after his presidency, Jimmy Carter, who was tireless in his work with Habitat for Humanity and efforts to monitor elections around the world, and Bill Clinton, whose presidential center has run a number of global initiatives (Skidmore, 2004).

However, even if such service helps to offset the impact of Nixon's Watergate scandal, Carter's 444-day Iranian hostage crisis, or Clinton's affair with an intern, the postpresidential years are not factored into the ratings. Only presidential performance while in office is considered. On the other hand, much like biographies, assessments of individual presidents do concern themselves with the president's early years, entire career, and postpresidencies. That is the case with the present book.

It is not just *whom* to assess, but the matter of *when* to rate them that proves problematic. For instance, there are convenient milestones in a presidency—the end of the "first hundred days" and the midterm election, for instance—which naturally lend themselves to examining a president's progress in office. But, such assessments are only initial assessments, as it often takes years to get a full appreciation for a presidential legacy. Consider the cases of Harry Truman and Dwight Eisenhower, both of whom were seen in modest terms during the initial years after their presidencies. The standing of both presidents, however, has risen dramatically with the passing of time. Therein is the challenge of assessing not only presidents who are still in office, but also those who only recently completely their presidencies, as is the case for Obama.

To be sure, there has always been movement in the rankings and no presidential reputation has suffered more in recent years than that of Andrew Jackson. While Old Hickory used to enjoy a spot just outside the "great" tier and was heralded as being the first "populist" president and a champion for the common folk, recent scholarship has focused on his role as an "Indian killer," brutal slave owner, and something of a contrary, knee-jerk reactionary. The Seventh President's standing continues to fall, while his future on the twenty dollar bill seems doomed. So too is his protégé's standing undergoing reassessment. James K. Polk is no longer seen simply as the leader behind the Mexican-American War of 1846–1858. Rather, Young Hickory's legacy now includes his unfettered pursuit of war in the name of Manifest Destiny and continental imperialism. This movement in the rankings also includes those at the bottom. A new appreciation for Ulysses Grant's role in promoting rights for all and his principled decision making has elevated the former Civil War general out of the "failure" category. Yet, hapless Warren Harding and James Buchanan seem destined to remain as cellar dwellers in the rankings (Smith, 2019).

Indeed, a president's standing is not fixed; rather, it varies as new information comes to light, new biographies are written, additional archival documents are available to scholars, and as we look back at history from the vantage point of hindsight. The National Archives and Records Administration (NARA) releases presidential papers through the presidential libraries it administers, but it often takes ten or more years before all the documents are available. Therefore, it can take years before a firm rendering of a legacy can be offered. We will likely not have the full picture of the Obama presidency for some years, even if a compelling argument can be made to begin the enterprise now. Either way, it will certainly be a contentious and ongoing affair (Pederson & McLaurin, 1987).

As is the case after one hundred days or at the midterm, there are other occasions when scholars come together to reassess certain presidents. One example was in 1999, when Washington scholars took advantage of the bicentennial of the great general's passing to reassess his standing. The "Father of His Country" had, during the 1990s and 2000s, slipped a position or two from his lofty ratings in some of the polls, which compelled historians to reexamine Washington. Traveling museum exhibits, academic conferences, and numerous publications during the bicentennial celebration restated the case for Washington and led to a flurry of new scholarship. Likewise, the year 2009 marked the bicentennial of Lincoln's birth, and Lincoln scholars celebrated with a variety of bicentennial programs and festivities and numerous publications seized the opportunity to reexamine the Great Emancipator's legacy (Watson, Pederson, & Williams, 2010).

As such, there is the need not only for an initial assessment soon after the conclusion of a president's time in office, but for frequent reevaluations in the years to come. This may be especially true for Obama, a president who evoked strong and mixed feelings from Democrats and Republicans. Paradoxically, he was, after all, a president who was celebrated as one of the better presidents, yet decried as being one of the worst. It is certainly hard to think of another president before him who received media coverage running the full gambit from great to failure, depending on the particular news outlet and the day of the week. Obama was the subject of relentless social media movements designed to discredit his every policy, question his patriotism, assert that he was not even an American citizen, and allege ties to and support for terror organizations. It remains unclear how these occurrences will ultimately factor into an assessment of his legacy.

There are also considerations as to who should be charged with assessing the presidents. Countless opinion polls conducted by an array of polling organizations, universities, and major media outlets routinely examine the president's approval and disapproval numbers. Even though these polls offer a helpful snapshot of public opinion, they are limited in what they offer history in terms of a president's legacy and rating. They are also too narrow in their scope and far too temporary in their resonance to be of much use to scholars trying to weigh a president's legacy (Pious, 2003).

For instance, C-SPAN, Gallup, and other organizations have polled the American public and asked them to evaluate the presidents, indicate their favorite presidents, or list the greatest and worst presidents. The results tend to reflect popular and contemporaneous political preferences and are appallingly ahistorical. For example, such polls have listed John F. Kennedy and Ronald Reagan ahead of George Washington and Abraham Lincoln, results no serious scholar of the American presidency would support. One recent poll revealed that 13 percent of the public listed Bill Clinton as the top president, while 20 percent of the respondents felt Clinton was the worst president. It is, of course, interesting that any president could be considered as both the best *and* worst president concurrently. But such results merely reflect the public's focus on the most recent presidents and lack of knowledge about earlier commanders in chief (C-SPAN, 2011).

Therefore, only professional historians and political scientists with expertise in the presidency are asked to participate in the ranking polls or books such as this one. As to the number of scholars polled, the range varies from the thirties to the seventies, however, one of the Siena Research Institute polls had 238 participants and the Murray-Blessing poll employed a whopping seventeen-page instrument and polled 953 scholars (Murray & Blessing, 1982; SRI, 2010).

One other valuable resource for assessing presidents is the president's own writings. Fortunately, all presidents serving from Herbert Hoover onward have presidential libraries. Administered by NARA, these libraries house the president's papers. These papers are made available to scholars and the public a few years after the president leaves office, in compliance with the 1978 Presidential Records Act. There are also numerous edited and published collections of presidential papers and many excellent biographies for most of the presidents.

So too did several presidents pen memoirs. Scholars are in general agreement that among the most insightful are those by Ulysses Grant and Harry Truman. Sadly, some of the great presidents such as Abraham Lincoln and Franklin Roosevelt did not survive their terms in office and history has been denied their memoirs. Other presidents chose not to pen accounts of their time in office, while still others wrestled with imperfect and selective memories in producing accounts of their presidencies. All presidents have worried about or at least been conscious of their standing in history. Several, most notably Thomas Jefferson, Theodore Roosevelt, Richard Nixon, and Bill Clinton, have been quite aware of how their legacies might be understood and shaped over time, while Ronald Reagan's supporters continue to actively promote his legacy. James Buchanan, who wrote his memoir shortly after the Civil War said of his failed term in office that he hoped history would not be too harsh in its judgment. It was.

Going forward, a number of methodological challenges surrounding the polls will remain. Likewise, the increasingly divided and partisan nature of the times in which Bill Clinton, George W. Bush, Barack Obama, and Donald Trump served will pose additional problems (Pious, 2003; Watson, Covarrubias, Lansford, & Brattebo, 2012). What is clear is that there are inherent limitations in attempting to assess—and especially in attempting to rank—presidents. Such is the case for Obama who, as of this writing, has only been out of office a few years and was a president who was seen in radically different ways by the American public. It is also inescapable that, as the first African American and bicultural president ever to serve, race will factor in to future assessments of his presidency.

Controversies

Even when leading scholars have been employed in the effort to rank the presidents, methodological criticisms exist. For instance, some pundits have suggested a "Harvard yard bias." These critics maintain that the professors who rate presidents are liberals with a natural preference for activist presidents and an inability to approach the task professionally or objectively (Bailey, 1967; Felzenberg, 1997; Felzenberg, 2003). They point to the fact that several Republican presidents in the twentieth century fared poorly in the polls while, conversely, several Democrats were rated highly. To counter this alleged bias, some conservative organizations began polling groups of conservatives. An Intercollegiate Studies Institute ranking, for instance, polled thirty-eight scholars with a conservative bent and, not surprisingly, found that Democratic presidents fared far worse than in other polls, with Clinton and Lyndon B. Johnson even listed as "failures" and Reagan as one of the nation's greatest presidents (Pierson, 1997). Of course, such results are nonsense and it does not help the enterprise by stacking a poll or study one way or the other.

Tim Blessing, who has both rated presidents and written about the polls, argues that bias is not an issue in most scholarly polls (Blessing, 2003). He points to the poor presidencies of such Republicans as Warren G. Harding, Calvin Coolidge, and Herbert Hoover, who served consecutive terms in the 1920s, and the scandalous presidencies of other Republicans including Ulysses Grant and Richard Nixon as accounting for the reason why a cumulative average ranking of Republicans tends to be somewhat lower than the Democratic average. Of course, Democratic averages have benefited by such impressive presidents as Franklin Roosevelt, Harry Truman, John Kennedy, and Lyndon Johnson, who served from 1933 to 1969 with the exception of Eisenhower's two terms in the middle of that streak. It should also be noted that the scholarly ranking polls have placed early Democratic presidents—James Buchanan, John Tyler, and Franklin Pierce—toward the bottom of the polls, while such Republicans as Theodore Roosevelt and Abraham Lincoln are nearly always in the top five spots.

It is difficult to use present-day party labels for early presidents, as the parties of the nineteenth century had nearly polar opposite platforms of those in the subsequent century and today. Yet, at the same time, recent presidents of both parties such as Gerald Ford and Jimmy Carter have been ranked as average in the polls, and there is wide agreement by nearly all of the scholars as to this placement and those discussed in the aforementioned paragraphs (these results are supported by the editors of this book).

Criticisms of the ratings have also centered on concerns of "maleness." The celebrated scholar James MacGregor Burns noted that presidents were assessed by males, from male perspectives, and according to male traits. Matters such as war, law and order, and other "force" issues have been prioritized in some of the polls and ratings. Fortunately, recent polls have included several female participants and women are comprising an ever-increasing presence among the ranks of presidential scholars (Burns, 1984; Burns, 1973).

Another issue pertains to the age-old question of whether the "times makes the man" (or, it might be said, whether the president makes the times). Did Washington, Lincoln, and FDR, for example, have the opportunity to achieve greatness because of the momentous events thrust upon them? Teddy Roosevelt, for instance, even worried whether his presidency would be seen in positive terms because he believed he did not have the requisite war or crisis to allow him to achieve a lofty status. However, TR ended up commanding his times and transforming the office and nation. On the other side of history was James Buchanan who had a looming war and national crisis but severely mishandled both.

Perhaps the main challenge to assessing presidential performance is the vagueness of the roles and responsibilities outlined in Article II of the Constitution. As a result, the approach to the office has varied over time as much as have the presidents themselves. Perhaps the late, great scholar Clinton Rossiter summed it up best, when he quipped, "The president is not a Gulliver immobilized by ten thousand tiny cords, nor even a Prometheus chained to a rock of frustration. He is, rather, a kind of magnificent lion who can roam widely and do great deeds so long as he does not try to break loose from his broad reservation" (Kutler, 1990, p. 607).

Accordingly, some of the same behaviors that earn a president praise can also undermine his administration. How is John Adams to be assessed? He implemented the Alien and Sedition Acts, which chiseled away basic freedoms, yet he also acted boldly to prevent an expanded war with France, even though going to war was popular and his hesitancy ended up devastating his Federalist Party. Or, take the case of Lyndon Johnson who advocated for the 1964 Civil Rights Act and followed it up by signing Medicare into law the following year. It is difficult to balance these efforts with his penchant for bullying behavior and his expansion of the Vietnam War. How are such presidents as Adams and Johnson to be ranked?

Not surprisingly, there are many disagreements among scholars about how to attempt to rank presidents. While Schlesinger and his son favored asking scholars to place the presidents into categories such as "great," "near great," and so on, other polls have used a "holistic" approach by asking respondents to simply list the presidents chronologically from best to worst. Others have used a "mechanistic" approach by rating the president according to several categories that pertain to the major roles and responsibilities of the office. As to which categories should be used, it will likely not surprise the reader to learn that different scholars use different criteria. There are, however, some similarities across the students. Barbara A. Perry, Director of Presidential Studies and Co-Chair of the Presidential

Oral History Program at the University of Virginia's Miller Center, notes that historians consider roughly ten key "characteristics" in assessing a president's legacy. These include winning election/reelection, legislative record, management of the economy, handling of crises, Supreme Court appointments, international leadership, communication skills, scandals, approval ratings, and political legacy (Rothman, 2017).

Stephen J. Wayne, a leading voice in presidency studies, suggests several frameworks for assessing a president, including constitutional, legislative-based, quantitative, and public opinion (Wayne, 2003). Other leading scholars have also weighed in with their own approaches to the task. This includes Richard Neustadt who advocated a power-based approach (Neustadt, 1991; Neustadt, 1980), James MacGregor Burns and Fred Greenstein who used a president's leadership style and the notion of democratic leadership (Burns, 1984; Burns, 1973; Greenstein, 2000; Greenstein, 1988), and Sydney Milkis and Michael Nelson, who recommended focusing on political leadership (Milkis & Nelson, 2007). Other, more recent and creative approaches have been recommended such as examining how well presidents overcame the paradoxes inherent within the challenging office (Cronin & Genovese, 2009), considering the historic and cyclical periods in which presidents have served (Skowronek, 2011), and the rhetorical style used by presidents to motivate people (Kernel, 2006).

Table I.3. Major Approaches to Assessing Presidents

Political (Wayne)	Historical (Rothman)	Rankings (SRI)
Use of Power	Winning Election/Reelection	Party Leadership
Leadership Style	Legislative Record	Communication
Democratic Leadership	Management of Economy	Relations with Congress
Political Leadership	Handling of Crises	Court Appointments
Overcoming Paradoxes	Supreme Court Appointments	Handling of Economy
Historical Cycles	International Leadership	Ability to Compromise
Rhetorical Style	Communication Skills	Executive Appointments
	Scandals	Risk Taking
	Approval Ratings	Imagination
	Durability of Policies	Foreign Policy
		Domestic Policy
		Executive Ability
		Intelligence
		Avoiding Crucial Mistakes

It is often said that, in the presidency, character is king (Shogun, 1999). And so, one of the more popular approaches in assessing presidents is character, whereby both a president's leadership qualities and personality traits are examined. Character transcends personality insofar as presidents such as Kennedy and Reagan benefited from their charm and likeability. But it is an altogether more challenging task to try and define character and examine its impact in the White House. Character includes judgment, disposition, worldview, and personal style; but it is much more. The noted presidency scholar James David Barber proposed using political psychology to determine a president's fitness for office, predict behavior, and, ultimately, assess performance. While Barber's methods received mixed reviews from scholars, his basic premise remains useful (Barber, 1992; Renshon, 1975).

In terms of character, would the fact that George H. W. Bush violated his main campaign pledge—"Read my lips, no new taxes"—be a betrayal and personality flaw? Or would it be better understood as being flexible in the face of the realities of the situation? In the latter scenario, adaptability is a positive personality and leadership trait. Nor is character simply a matter of being ethical. Jimmy Carter and Calvin Coolidge were ethical individuals but neither one is rated highly by scholars or has been said to have been made of the "right stuff" for presidential greatness.

Indeed, character transcends a lack of scandal or a penchant for honesty. Yet, many presidents, such as Nixon, have been ruined by scandal. Others such as Clinton and Reagan had their legacies blemished by scandal, but remained rather popular, and scholars are still debating how to assess Clinton's affair involving an intern and Reagan's Iran-Contra scandal. For instance, how should the admittedly impressive budget surpluses and economic growth of the Clinton years be considered against the lies surrounding his affair with a young intern? Marital infidelity did not ruin the ratings for other presidents such as FDR or Eisenhower, just as the horrific practice of owning slaves has not denied Washington and Jefferson their lofty rankings. How should Reagan's considerable popularity be judged relative to the fact that he violated international norms and laws against trading weapons to an enemy such as Iran and subverted governments in Central America, all the while lying and trying to cover up the scandals? The answers to all these questions remain elusive.

Indeed, questions of character and scandal are complicated. FDR could be both coldly calculating and disingenuous but also compassionate and charismatic, revealing a vastly complex character. He is rated as one of the nation's greatest presidents and is sometimes held up as the standard by which all presidents in modern times are judged.

To be sure, not all scandals are created equal; a case in point is the nature of the differences between the scandals associated with President Nixon—which were crimes of *commission*—and the scandals of President Grant—which were crimes of *omission*. A case can be made that Nixon's scandals were not only worse but more indicative of a lapse of character. Not all mistakes are created equal; it is hard to imagine the elder Bush's verbal miscues being equivalent to his son's mismanagement of two long wars or Clinton's marital peccadilloes rising to the level of Reagan's complicity in attempting to trade armaments to rogue regimes in the Middle East.

There is no clear answer to how best to approach the task of assessing a president. Accordingly, this book adopts an array of frameworks to assess Obama's presidency including all the aforementioned approaches—holistic, categories based on the major roles and responsibilities of the president, and the frameworks used in some of the leading books on presidential performance and leadership and ranking polls.

Assessing Obama

As of this writing, Obama's presidential library has not yet opened and the collection of Obama papers and documents is still being organized. However, some of the Obama papers are beginning to be made available to scholars and the former president has written books including autobiographies. At the same time, numerous historians are also now working on books about the forty-fourth president. All of these resources will play a role in shaping both the initial assessment of his presidency and his ultimate legacy. Of course, at the same time, television pundits and both the blogosphere and social media are ripe with all sorts of colorful perspectives on Obama.

The Obama presidency is noteworthy for many reasons; most obviously, he was the first African American president and he was reelected to a second term. However, another prominent aspect of his legacy was the devastating defeats his party endured in the midterm elections of 2010 and 2014. While it is the historical case that the president's party has generally fared poorly in midterms over the past century, the

Democratic Party lost a whopping sixty-three seats in the House and six in the Senate in 2010. In the next midterm they lost thirteen seats in the House and nine in the Senate. For context, it is worth noting that the average size of the midterm losses for the party in power since 1862 has been two seats in the Senate and thirty-two seats in the House of Representatives.

The Obama years were also noteworthy for what did not happen. President Obama managed to avoid a serious scandal and the closet full of ethical brouhahas that were a part of some recent White Houses. With respect to the role that scandal plays in shaping a presidential legacy, as listed in Table 1.3, Obama's presidency was, in the words of Professor Perry, "remarkably free" from scandal. He also avoided major political and policy mistakes and crises.

On the policy front, Obama passed landmark measures on healthcare and climate change, is generally given high marks for his court appointments, was able to pass an economic recovery package and preside over a remarkable resurgence of an economy in recession, and remained rather popular after leaving office, all of which will likely boost his legacy. However, in terms of some of the other criteria used by historians, Obama's relations with Congress were, at best, strained, irrespective of whether the fault rests with him or not, and he suffered some foreign policy missteps. He was unable to muster support for a comprehensive gun control bill and some of his treaties and appointments stalled in a hostile Congress. It also remains to be seen whether his policies will survive the aggressive dismantling during the initial years of the Trump administration.

Another aspect of Obama's legacy will likely be that the size, scope, and roles of the federal government grew under his presidency, largely in response to the extraordinary array of domestic, fiscal, and international challenges he faced upon assuming the office, and in part due to his personal philosophical and ideological views on governance. This growth must be understood from the standpoint of one of Obama's main accomplishments. When he was sworn in as president, the nation was in the grips of the Great Recession, the worst economic downturn since the Great Depression. The stock market had dropped precipitously, unemployment numbers were growing, reaching 10 percent in October of his first year in office, and the annual budget deficit had skyrocketed to 1.6 trillion dollars. However, by the end of the Obama years, the stock market and economy had enjoyed seven consecutive years of expansion, unemployment had fallen to 4 percent, and the budget deficit had been reduced by two-thirds according to nonpartisan government reports by the Bureau of Labor Statistics and Office of Management and Budget (BLS; OMB, 2018). Still, debate raged over the president's decision to bail out the failing U.S. auto manufacturers, promote an economic stimulus package, and his Troubled Asset Relief Program (TARP). Although all three efforts appear, by any objective measure, to have succeeded, they required an aggressive role for the federal government, which was controversial.

Yet, long before Obama was inaugurated, the office had grown to the point where it scarcely resembled the office held by Washington, Lincoln, or most of the presidents for that matter. In spite of the limitations imposed on the presidency by the cautious Framers, the office has grown to become the most dominant force in the American political system. The evolution of the presidency has been in response to crises and changes in society, as well as presidential character and viewpoints. The growth under Obama was no exception to this history.

Three other factors make it even more challenging to makes sense of the Obama years. First, Obama's presidency occurred during the explosion of new social media and communications technologies, from FaceBook and Twitter to iPhones and tablets, all of which impacted the nature of politics in far-reaching ways, both good and bad. Second, one of the dilemmas in assessing Obama is the current political climate, spawned in part by these very advances in telecommunications. With the nation in the throes of hyperpartisanship, incivility, and what might politely be deemed political dysfunction, the assessment of any president has become increasingly problematic and contentious in recent years. Many readers would probably admit that having an honest and objective discussion with office mates or even family members about Presidents Obama and Trump has been, at best, elusive and, at worst, a shouting match. Sadly, both the truth and civil discourse are threatened by the current climate of division, anger, and fact-optional politics.

Take, for example, Obama's policies to expand health care coverage, regulate assault weapons, and defer action on immigrants brought to the country as children, or his efforts to forge international alliances to deal with Iran's nuclear ambitions, expand trade in the Pacific, and address global climate change. All of these policies have been both enthusiastically celebrated and anxiously condemned, depending on whether one is a Democrat or Republican. Subsequently, the same was true when Trump did the opposite of his predecessor—limit funding for "ObamaCare," oppose gun regulations, and promote the deportation of illegal children. So too were his efforts to withdraw from treaties and agreements on Iran's nuclear ambitions, trade in the Pacific, and global climate change met with both applause and gasps. Of course, differing political perspectives have always produced debate and varying levels of support or opposition to policies and presidents.

Third, so too has Obama faced unrealistic expectations from the public and the legacy of the "imperial presidency" described by Schlesinger, whereby the sheer array of interest groups, rising expectations, and the complexity of challenges pose nearly insurmountable obstacles for the president (Schlesinger Jr., 2004). As President Carter once admitted, "When things go bad you get entirely too much blame. And I have to admit that when things go good, you get entirely too much credit" (Hodgson, 1980, p. 25). As professors Cronin and Genovese noted, the public has impossible expectations, wanting the president to address every problem while distrusting the centralized power necessary for him to do so (Cronin & Genovese, 2009, 1998). The inherent paradoxes of the presidency seem to be more challenging than ever.

Ironically, the clamor for nonpartisan and bipartisan approaches is more prevalent than ever while society struggles with the most bitter partisanship and venomous political tone in decades; and the "damned if you do, damned if you don't" aspect of the Oval Office is more pronounced than ever. The editors and contributors fully expect that this book will arouse debate, which is a good thing. Every effort was made to mitigate such pitfalls by having multiple editors and contributors, all with diverse academic backgrounds, and by employing an array of theoretical frameworks and approaches to assess Obama.

It is difficult to evaluate a president who only recently left office. Accordingly, this evaluation does not pretend to be the definitive word. Far from it, as years will pass before a conclusive account can be forwarded. However, it is time for the assessment to begin and this book provides a relatively comprehensive account of numerous significant policy issues faced by Obama, a dispassionate historical examination of the events surrounding the Obama presidency, and a preliminary assessment of the major facets of his presidency, character, and administration. Neither Obama nor this book will have the final word on his legacy.

References

Bailey, T. (1967). *Presidential greatness*. Stanford University Press.

Barber, J. D. (1992). *The presidential character: Predicting performance in the White House*. 4th ed. Prentice-Hall.

Blessing, T. H. (2003). Presidents and significance: Partisanship as a source of perceived greatness. *White House Studies, 3*(1).

Brinkley, D. (2019). A brief history of presidential rankings. In Brian Lamb & Susan Swain (Eds.), *The presidents: Noted historians rank America's best—and worst—chief executives*. Public Affairs.

Bureau of Labor Statistics. (2018, February 20). Labor force statistics from the current population survey. http://www.bls.gov.

Burns, J. M. (1984). *The power to lead: The crisis of the American presidency*. Simon & Schuster.

Burns, J. M. (1973). *Presidential government: The crucible of leadership*. 2nd ed. Houghton Mifflin.

C-SPAN. (2000, February 21). Survey of presidential leadership: How did the presidents rate? http://www.americanpresidents.org/survey/.

C-SPAN. (2011). Viewer Poll. http://www.americanpresidents.org.

Cronin, T. E., & Genovese, M. A. (2009). *The paradoxes of the American presidency*. Rev. ed. York: Oxford University Press.

Donald, D. H. (1995, December 24). Interview on C-SPAN's Booknotes. www.booknotes.org/watch/68638-1/david-herbert-donald.

Edwards, G. C. III, & Wayne, S. J. (2009). *Presidential leadership: Politics and policy making*. 8th ed. Wadsworth.

Felzenberg, A. (2003). Partisan biases in presidential ratings: Ulysses, Woodrow, and Calvin, "We hardly knew Ye." *White House Studies, 3*(1).

Felzenberg, A. (1997). There you go again: Liberal historians and the *New York Times* deny Ronald Reagan his due. *Policy Review* (March–April).

Greenstein, F. I. (2000). *The Presidential difference: Leadership style from FDR to Clinton*. Free Press.

Greenstein, F. I. (1988). *Leadership in the modern presidency*. Harvard University Press.

Hodgson, G. (1980). *All things to all men: The false promise of the modern American presidency*. Simon & Schuster.

Kernell, S. (2006). *Going public: New strategies of presidential leadership*. 4th ed. CQ Press.

Kutler, S. I. (1990). *The wars of Watergate: The last crisis of Richard Nixon*. W. W. Norton.

Milkus, S. M., & Michael, N. (2007). *The American presidency: Origins and development, 1776–2007*. 5th ed. CQ Press.

Murray, R. K. (1994). *Greatness in the White House: Rating the presidents*. 2nd ed. Pennsylvania State University Press.

Neustadt, R. (1991). *Presidential power and the modern presidency: The politics of leadership from Roosevelt to Reagan*. Free Press.

Neustadt, R. (1980). *The politics of leadership from FDR to Carter*. John Wiley & Sons.

Office of Management and Budget. (2018, February). Summary of receipts, outlays, and surpluses or deficits. http://whitehouse.gov/omb.

Pederson, W., & McLaurin, A. (1987). *The rating game in American politics*. Irvington.

Pierson, J. (1997, September 29). Historians and the Reagan legacy. *The Weekly Standard*, 22–24.

Pious, R. M. (2003). Reflections of a presidency rater. *White House Studies*, 3(1).

Renshon, S. A. (1975). *Psychological analysis and presidential personality: The case of Richard Nixon*. Atcom.

Rothman, L. (2017, January 18). 10 criteria future historians will use to rate Obama's presidency. *Time*. time.com/4632126/presidential-legacy.

Schlesinger, A. M. (1962, July 29). Our presidents: A rating by 75 historians. *New York Times Magazine*, 12–13, 40–41, 43.

Schlesinger, A. M. (1948, November 1). Historians rate the U.S. presidents. *Life Magazine*, 65–66, 73–74.

Schlesinger, Jr., A. M. (2004). *The imperial presidency*. Mariner Books (reprint from 1974).

Schlesinger, Jr., A. M. (2003). Commentary. *White House Studies*, 3(1), 75–77.

Schlesinger, Jr., A. M. (1996, December 15). The ultimate approval rating. *New York Times Magazine*, 46–47.

Shogun, R. (1999). *The double-edged sword: How character makes and ruins presidents; From Washington to Clinton*. Westview.

Siena Research Institute. (2010). Siena poll: American presidents. www.siena.edu/pages/179.asp?item=2566.

Skidmore, M. J. (2004). *After the White House: Former presidents as private citizens*. Palgrave Macmillan.

Skowronek, S. (2011). *Presidential leadership in political time: Reprise and reappraisal*. University Press of Kansas.

Smith, R. N. (2019). The magnificent lion. In Brian Lamb & Susan Swain (Eds.), *The presidents: Noted historians rank America's best—and worst—chief executives*. Public Affairs.

Watson, R. P. (2003, Fall). Ranking the first ladies: Polling elites to evaluate performance. *PRG Report* (Presidency Research Group of the American Political Science Association, now renamed the Presidents and Executive Politics section), 26 (1), 15–22.

Watson, R. P. (2000). *The presidents' wives: Reassessing the office of First Lady*. Lynne Rienner.

Watson, R. P. (1999). Ranking the presidential spouses. *The Social Science Journal*, 36(1), 117–136.

Watson, R. P., Covarrubias, J., Lansford, T., & Brattebo, D. M. (2012). *The Obama presidency: A preliminary assessment.* State University of New York Press.

Watson, R. P., Pederson, W. D., & Williams, F. J. (2010). *Lincoln's enduring legacy.* Lexington Books.

Wayne, S. J. (2003). Evaluating the president: The public's perspective through the prism of pollsters. *White House Studies, 3*(1), 35–40.

I

Executive, Administrative, and Party Leadership

1

The Vice Presidency of Joe Biden

RICHARD M. YON, MICHAEL J. FERRO, AND JEREMY HUNT

Introduction

The office of the vice president has grown considerably since the post-Watergate era, and the influence exercised by the occupants of the office has expanded as well. This is exemplified by the vice presidencies of Walter Mondale, Al Gore, Dick Cheney, and Joe Biden. Cheney's vice presidency, in particular, represents the height of influence, which precipitated discussions regarding the scope of vice presidential influence. When the Obama-Biden ticket campaigned for office in 2008, the candidates promised a more restrained executive branch, partially in response to the ascendancy of the vice presidency and executive power, which critics argued was characteristic of the Bush years. Acknowledging current national sentiment at the time, Joe Biden stressed the importance of returning the vice presidency back to its historical roots. During the 2008 vice presidential debate, Biden stated:

> The vice president of the United States of America is to support the president . . . and to preside over the Senate, only in a time when in fact there's a tie vote. The Constitution is explicit. The idea he's part of the Legislative Branch is a bizarre notion invented by Cheney to aggrandize the power of a unitary executive and look where it has gotten us. It has been very dangerous. (*New York Times*, 2008)

However, Biden's vice presidency demonstrated little progress in attaining that standard. Instead, Biden's tenure in office mirrored other vice presidents of the modern era. He was an instrumental figure in the day-to-day activities of the Obama administration, a trusted advisor and confidant of the president, and ranks among Mondale, Gore, and Cheney as one of the most influential vice presidents.

Biden was a critical advisor, and sometimes indispensable confidant, within Obama's administration. His hard-hitting approach to public office provided President Obama with a truly unique vice president. This chapter analyzes Vice President Biden's tenure in office in order to understand how his role evolved. Through his successes and failures, this chapter assesses Biden's impact on the Obama administration and compares the vice president to his contemporary counterparts. In order to understand the evolution of Joe Biden's role, one must view the ascent of the modern vice presidency in light of the historical context.

Historical Role of the Modern Vice President

The rise in vice presidential power stems from major changes to society and the responsibilities required of modern presidents. With the president responsible for tackling multiple issues a day, a vice president is frequently expected to alleviate some of the demands on the president, thus providing him or her with new and expanding roles. This has paved the way for the vice president to assume a new role as chief advisor to the president, cementing his or her position as a close presidential confidant (Light, 1984). No longer is the vice president solely a figurehead for ceremonial occasions, but rather a strategic player on both political and policy issues.

At one point, the term "vice presidential influence" served as an oxymoron, as this role was a mere afterthought of the founding fathers. With no legitimate power designated by the founders, the vice presidency was an underused institution. However, the twentieth century witnessed a reevaluation of the office. The vice presidency began to grow in two respects. First, the office began to attract strong-willed individuals with seasoned careers. Great personalities, such as Theodore Roosevelt, were no match for the historically constraining vice presidential office. Second, the vice presidency began assuming modest tasks outside the realm of its constitutional authority to include new informal advisory roles, which helped ease the burden on presidents and provided an outlet for the political talents of the nation's vice presidents (Goldstein, 2008, p. 375). Aside from acting as the tiebreaking vote in the Senate (one of the few explicit duties listed in the Constitution), the individuals occupying the office became instrumental in decision making, lobbying Congress, and realizing a president's legislative agenda.

The modern vice presidency relies on three pillars: ceremonial, political, and policy duties (Light, 1984, p. 22). The Great Depression–World War II era launched the policy/political vice presidency. With a multitude of new responsibilities, the president had to rely on his second-in-command in order to accomplish these new tasks. A keystone event happened "in 1947, [when] Congress acknowledged this change by making the vice president a statutory member of the National Security Council" (Goldstein, 2008, p. 375). This was a central shift from the vice presidencies of yesteryear. As presidents were required to be a focal figure on an influx of domestic and international issues, the vice president began assisting the president with the demanding responsibilities he faced. This change provided the vice president with a formal executive duty and permitted him or her to be a key player in foreign policy and national security issues (Light, 1984). The political and policy vice presidency, which began to evolve over the latter part of the twentieth century, helped usher in the advisory role of the vice presidency, perhaps its most important role and one from which it derives most of its influence.

Biden and His Predecessors

Regardless of the new heights it reaches, vice presidential power or influence remains a presidential construct. Even Biden acknowledged that "there is no inherent power in the office of the vice presidency . . . zero. None. It's all a reflection . . . of your relationship with the president" (Trujillo, 2014). Yet, the office of the vice president continues to build an everlasting legacy on the way executive power is perceived. Over the last forty years, the vice presidency has morphed into a position that the president requires, needs, or demands it to be. With no fixed job description, the president utilizes the office to serve his needs and each vice president uses the office to advance themselves through their own unique approach and style.

The vice president also has flexibility in defining their role. Since Mondale's term, the vice president began to assume projects that would define their stance on important issues as a way of bolstering popularity and providing critical experience for a future potential presidential run. "Al Gore pursued niche projects (the environment, Reinventing Government), and Cheney guarded what an aide called the 'iron issues' (defense, energy, and national security)" (Osnos, 2014). We now see a reinvented vice president who accepts line item assignments, in order to be a strategic player in the White House's decision-making process, while creating a springboard for their own presidential ambitions. Still, vice presidents are cautious when it comes to line assignments, fearing that these assignments will distract them from their wider involvement in day-to-day activities and decision making in the White House (Goldstein, 2016; Baumgartner & Crumblin, 2015).

Of recent vice presidents, Walter Mondale in 1984, George H. W. Bush in 1988, and Al Gore in 2000 were able to successfully secure their party's presidential nomination. In many ways, the vice president is seen as the natural successor for the incumbent president. On the other hand, some vice presidents maintain no political aspirations after serving, such as Cheney who declared from the very beginning zero interest in running for the Republican nomination at the conclusion of the Bush administration. Vice President Dan Quayle was an outlier among recent vice presidents as he "was unable to win a presidential nomination after serving as vice president, and he withdrew early from the race in 1996 and 2000" (Goldstein, 2012). Vice President Biden also appears to be an outlier among recent vice presidents as well. A decision to run for president, in 2016, was dramatically delayed well into the presidential contest, despite the intense pressure he received from supporters to announce his bid and the speculation it drew in the media. After many months of flirting with the idea of a run, Biden announced he would not be a candidate for the presidency due to the tragic and untimely death of his son, Beau Biden (Baker & Haberman, 2015). Despite sitting out the contest in 2016, Biden declared his candidacy for president on April 25, 2019, in which he cast his decision to run as an answer to a "national emergency," and implored Democrats to "put the task of defeating Mr. Trump above all their other ambitions" (Burns & Martin, 2019). The Biden campaign messages his candidacy in 2020 as "a stabilizing statesman in a tumultuous time" (Flegenheimer, 2019).

From start to finish, Mondale may very well be one of the most important vice presidents because he set the tone for all future occupants of the office. Mondale was not only a critical component in Jimmy Carter's election victory, but it was his philosophy on the vice presidency that helped Carter advance his policy initiatives and made it possible for other vice presidents, such as Gore, Cheney and Biden, to emerge as strategic players (Goldstein, 2016). "He viewed his role as an advisor, not a decider, and as someone who would help implement the decisions Carter made by persuading various constituencies and governmental figures of their merit" (Goldstein, 2008, p. 379). On international issues, Mondale became the linchpin in promoting Carter's foreign policy. Mondale understood his role, advancing the causes of the president while never overstepping his boundaries. He worked toward ending racial discrimination in South Africa and promoted peace in the Middle East. Many foreign diplomats considered Mondale a trusted statesman, due to the credentials and contacts he built while in the Senate. His stirring speech to the UN conference on Indochinese refugees in July 1979 won international support. He was well traveled and worked to advance U.S. bilateral cooperation (Goldstein, 2008). His trip to China in 1979 was widely hailed as an important foreign policy venture, normalizing relations and easing tensions between the two powers (Goldstein, 2008, p. 379).

While Mondale may well have been one of the most well-rounded vice presidents, Dick Cheney greatly expanded vice presidential influence. Cheney had the luxury of such increased influence due to his lack of ambition to seek future office (Baker, 2013). Without those constraints, Cheney took on roles from which other vice presidents would have shied away and responsibilities that presidents would be reluctant to give their vice presidents. In an unprecedented move at the time, Cheney led the presidential transition, became the point person for the U.S. government's response to 9/11, forcefully advocated for greater executive authority to prosecute the war on terror, and was the chief architect of many controversial programs associated with the war on terror, such as the Terrorist Surveillance Program (Yon, 2017). No one could mistake the nature of Cheney's role in the Bush administration. He was a thoroughly engaged vice president who exercised extraordinary influence.

Biden emulated the style of Lyndon Johnson, taking advantage of his similarly long tenure in Congress, however, he sought to avoid some of the difficulties that Johnson faced (Osnos, 2014). Considering that both served under much younger presidents, Biden and Johnson understood that political relevance was about "getting and staying in the deal." "In reading 'The Passage of Power,' the 2012 volume of Robert Caro's biography of Johnson, Biden realized just how frustrated Johnson had been: 'His opinion wasn't asked on anything, from the Bay of Pigs, to the Cuban missile crisis. He just wasn't in the deal'" (Osnos, 2014). As a result, Biden was determined to be involved in every major decision, and the president ensured that he was included in critical deliberations (Hornick & Levs, 2008). As a result, "He advised on all important decisions from foreign and domestic policy to congressional relations, judicial appointments, and legislative strategy" (Yon, 2017, p. 530).

Biden's contributions are marked by reinforcing the president's supremacy rather than maneuvering around it. This is in contrast to Cheney, who was not concerned about his national popularity. Functionally, Cheney had carte blanche to be a key player on an array of domestic and international policy decisions, without concern for a future presidential contest, which was rather liberating for him and President Bush (Osnos, 2014). Biden, on the other hand, infamously moved ahead of President Obama on the issue of gay marriage prior to the 2012 Democratic National Convention, forcing the president's hand. "He probably got out a little bit over his skis, but out of his generosity of spirit," Obama told ABC News (Sink, 2012). However, "Biden demonstrated that a vice president can be loyal without surrendering his public identity and becoming lost in the president's shadow" (Goldstein, 2017).

Public perception has become an important factor in charting vice presidential success. With the rise of vice presidential influence, it is no surprise that the office faces a new level of scrutiny. Since Vice President Mondale, more polls attempt to quantify approval of the vice president. "The growth in polling on the vice president is consistent with the enhanced policy role of the post, as well as its placement in the ambition hierarchy for the presidency" (Cohen, 2001, p. 143). More importantly, the number of polls referencing only the vice president (and excluding the president) illustrates how the office is becoming its own political entity. According to Cohen, from 1977 to 1999 there has been an increase by 41.1 percent of polls dedicated solely to vice presidential matters. The upward trend in vice presidential polls has continued at a steady pace over the last three decades (Cohen, 2001, p. 144). Jody Baumgartner, however, contends that vice presidential approval is not formed independent of the president; rather is heavily influenced by presidential favorability (Baumgartner, 2017).

There is good a priori reason to suspect that people do not make judgments

> of the vice president independent of the president. For example, a sizable minority of Americans are unable to identify who

> the vice president is at any given time. A Gallup poll from January 2000 found that 10 percent of the sample could not identify Vice President Al Gore, then in the eighth year of his vice presidential tenure and running for the Democratic presidential nomination. A 2008 poll found that 15 percent could not name Vice President Dick Cheney in his seventh year in office. In a 2012 poll, 21 percent could not identify Joe Biden as vice president. (Baumgartner, 2017, p. 4)

While vice presidential legacies and public opinion might be inextricably linked to their respective presidents, the continuing trend of increased responsibility, roles, visibility, and influence provides vice presidents with a political stature that escaped many of their predecessors prior to the modern vice presidency.

Nonetheless, vice presidential approval ratings tend to be higher than their presidential counterparts. Looking at Al Gore, "his ratings ranged from a low of 60.7 to a high of 76.2; all are extremely high compared to Bill Clinton's job approval ratings during the same time period, even though Clinton's ratings were then quite strong" (Cohen, 2001, p. 145). His contributions to the administration and high public approval gave him the tools necessary to run for president in 2000. Equally important, it is imperative for the vice president to receive the blessing of the president and his party in order to move forward with his or her presidential ambitions. "While a president cannot unilaterally kill a vice president's chances for the nomination because of the primary system, lack of support will surely undermine the vice president's chances of securing the party's nomination" (Cohen, 2001, p. 143). Although Biden decided not to run in 2016, his vice presidential approval rating prior to leaving office makes him a formidable candidate in 2020. According to McCarthy, Biden garnered a 61 percent approval rating prior to leaving office, his highest favorability rating in eight years, while Obama received a 58 percent favorability rating (McCarthy, 2017).

Biden as Vice President

Who is Vice President Biden? Much can be said about one of the most vibrant figures ever to grace the vice presidency. Biden continues to garner similar attention to when he was in office. There is a fascination with Biden, the man, with many comparisons made to an endearing uncle who is not averse to speaking his mind. Although previous polls pointed to him being an "idiot" or "incompetent" (Pew Center, 2012), public perception on Biden has become more upbeat. In a Suffolk University/ *USA Today* poll in 2015, one thousand potential voters were told to define the potential presidential nominee. "Favorable" and "like" tallied 12.1 percent and "honest" garnered 7.3 percent of votes. However, 4.7 percent of respondents defined Biden as an "idiot" or "joke" (Campbell, 2015). Unfortunately, this moniker was a label often attributed to the vice president. Even Osama Bin Laden advised assassins to spare Biden and target Obama, telling them, "Biden is totally unprepared for that post, which will lead the U.S. into a crisis" (Osnos, 2014). Despite these derogatory labels, Biden endeared himself to many Americans who found his down-to-earth persona and candor refreshing. For instance, at a speaking engagement in 2014 while visiting the Harvard Institute of Politics during an event discussing foreign policy, a questioner was introduced as the student body *vice president*, to which Biden commented: "Isn't that a bitch?" (Bradner, 2014). Given Biden's popularity, it is not surprising that he has remained in the public's mind unlike other vice presidents. And as of this writing, he is the 2020 Democratic presidential nominee from a field of twenty-two other candidates (Scherer, Uhrmacher, & Schaul, 2019).

Biden's candor and willingness to ask the tough questions and challenge advice given to President Obama made him an instrumental figure within the president's inner circle. Obama relied heavily on Biden's judgment and candor to assist in decision making, and their professional relationship forged one of the closest personal relationships between a president and vice president in history. In fact, several media outlets reported on the apparent "bromance" between the two—especially due to their matching "friendship bracelets" (Lang, 2016). Biden's style as vice president fused blunt charisma with decades of political insider experience. Despite his unique personality, the nation came to accept Biden's eccentricity, and his style produced countless memes and satire, which have become known as Bidenisms (Baker, 2014). While these gaffes were difficult for the administration from a public relations standpoint, they became part and parcel of the vice presidency during the Obama years. Even satirical websites, such as *The Onion*, dedicated significant space to poking fun at Vice President Biden. Examples of "Bidenisms" abound. At a September 2014 question and answer session at Harvard, the vice president alluded that our allies, including Turkey, Qatar, and the United Arab Emirates, had extended unconditional financial and logistical support to Sunni fighters trying to oust the Syrian government of President Bashar al-Assad. "Our allies poured hundreds of millions of dollars and tens of thousands of tons of weapons into anyone who would fight against al-Assad, including jihadists planning to join the Nusra Front and Al Qaeda" (Arsu, 2014). Biden quickly apologized, stating, "The United States greatly values the commitments and sacrifices made by our allies and partners from around the world to combat the scourge of ISIL, including Turkey" (Arsu, 2014). While his apology was swift, the damage had been done.

Still, one of the most difficult hurdles between President Obama and Vice President Biden arose during the 2012 election. Biden's repeated gaffes proved problematic for the campaign and the media often discussed the possibility of dropping him from the ticket. In fact, the president's campaign team began referring to Biden's gaffes as "Joe Bombs" (Yon, 2017). One such "Joe Bomb" occurred during a *Meet the Press* interview with the vice president. Speaking openly, Biden confessed that the president had voiced his support for gay marriage. During this conversation, Biden broke a cardinal rule: the vice president should do no harm (Warshaw, 2009). In this case, Biden forced the president to publicly address an issue he was not prepared to deal with at that time. Many insiders felt this would drastically change the landscape of the relationship. In a later interview, Biden clarified:

> We sometimes disagreed on tactics as to how to proceed to try to get what he wanted done, which I've agreed with, but we've never disagreed on policy. And even the so-called discussion about, you know, my saying I was comfortable with gay and lesbians and relationships, I knew his positions. (Bohn, 2013)

As a result of Biden's various missteps, his standing in the administration changed. For example, Obama's senior advisor David Plouffe once dismissed Biden's favored candidate for the job of his own vice presidential chief of staff. The veto reportedly infuriated Biden and further exacerbated his relationship with Obama's closest advisors (Edelman, 2014). Eventually, Vice President Biden received his second pick, but only after a personal appeal to the president and assurances on the soundness of his choice (Thrush, 2014).

While the Obama-Biden relationship remained personally strong throughout their tenure, and in fact has been one of the strongest in comparison to other postpresidential relationships, Biden's influence in the administration waned due to his repeated gaffes and his on again/off again flirtation with a presidential run. Nonetheless, President Obama always valued Biden's candor. When Obama notified Biden that he would be his running mate, he pronounced, "I [Obama] want you to say exactly what you think. And I want you to ask the toughest questions you can think of. . . . [I]n that sense I think Joe served an enormously useful function" (Woodward, 2010, p. 160).

Foreign Policy

There is no denying that Biden's most important contributions were in the foreign policy arena, despite sometimes being regarded as wrong on major foreign policy issues (Gates, 2014). Nonetheless, his foreign policy expertise was one of the reasons that President Obama asked him to join the ticket in the 2008 election (Heilemann & Halperin, 2010). In his first term, Obama called on the former chairman of the Senate Foreign Relations Committee to assist in efforts to restore U.S. diplomatic relations. His relationships in Congress and exceptional rapport with prominent foreign figures made him a suitable running mate for a president deficient in international relations and foreign policy experience. Outside the secretary of state, Biden has been a critical insider in helping voice President Obama's foreign policy platform. The president, on multiple occasions, allowed Vice President Biden to speak directly on foreign policy (Witcover, 2010). Robert Gates, former secretary of defense, discussed in his memoir how Biden was tasked to carefully lay out foreign policy directions on behalf of the president. Biden traveled to Iraq and Afghanistan prior to the inauguration in 2009, and his message to Nouri al-Maliki and Hamid Karzai, respectively, was that Obama would not engage with them nearly as often as President Bush had previously done (Gates, 2014, p. 336). Clearly, Obama placed a great deal of trust in Biden in regard to international relations, and this was perpetuated through their time in office. Biden helped craft President Obama's foreign policy stratagem and was outspoken about it in the process (Traub, 2012). He was an integral actor in the clash between the Pentagon and White House regarding more troops on the ground in Afghanistan. In 2009, Biden made his thoughts known on how the Obama administration should handle requests for more military troops in the Middle East. "Biden had told the press that he wasn't going to let the military 'bully' the White House into making decisions about more troops for Afghanistan because of 'artificial timelines'" (Gates, 2014, p. 338). Throughout Obama's presidency, Biden's efforts provided a unique voice on an array of foreign policy concerns.

Biden's first term was dedicated to rebuilding and restructuring a strategic plan for America. Obama and Biden adhered to a restrained foreign policy, to avoid errors. Obama has stated, "You take victories where you can. You make things a little bit better rather than a little bit worse" (Groll, 2015). Many observers have defined this approach as an example of the president's lack of leadership on foreign policy. But those in the administration viewed this more of a realistic, cautious approach. Even Obama, through the "Obama Doctrine," has defined his foreign policy methods in baseball terms, where, "You hit singles, you hit doubles; every once in a while, we may be able to hit a home run" (Osnos, 2014). With this philosophy in mind, Biden was an integral part of securing those small victories. Biden was called upon by the Obama administration to travel on behalf of the country and rekindle diplomatic relations with regional powers, especially since most of those partnerships were strained due to the United States' predominate focus on the Middle East. While traveling to the Balkans, Afghanistan, and Pakistan on the president's behalf, Biden reiterated the administration's willingness to rebuild allegiances, resolve conflicts, and establish strategic partnerships. It was Biden's speech in Munich, Germany, "where [he] coined the term 'reset' to describe the administration's plan to restore relations with Russia as part of the new paradigm of 'engagement'" (Traub, 2012).

Biden was also the voice of skepticism on many foreign policy issues facing the administration. His tenure on the Senate Foreign Relations Committee prompted him to question action, perhaps even to a point of overanalysis. Biden has preached the implementation of a diplomatic foreign policy, only advocating force in dire situations. There were multiple issues over which Biden had adamantly disagreed with then-secretary of state Hillary Clinton and defense secretary Leon Panetta. "Biden opposed intervention in Libya arguing that the fall of Muammar Qaddafi would result in chaos" (Osnos, 2014). When the need to use military force was apparent, Biden was stridently opposed to putting more boots on the ground. Even in his deliberations on securing Afghanistan in 2009, Biden refused to support sending more troops. In the administration's first National Security Council (NSC) meeting in January 2009, General

David McKiernan pushed for the approval of an additional thirty thousand troops to thwart a Taliban offensive. Even before the strategy was constructed, Biden objected to any proposal that required the use of more military forces (Gates, 2014, p. 338). Biden tends to tread lightly when risk is involved. He argued for a more modest, counterterrorism-focused effort, however, the president generally went along with the generals' recommendations, approving a surge (Golan-Vilella, 2012).

In contrast to those more hawkish on U.S. military intervention, Biden's contributions to foreign policy took a more passive and diplomatic approach, in hopes of carefully handling future challenges. In a July 2014 interview, Biden stated: "We no longer think in Cold War terms, for several reasons. One, no one is our equal. No one is close. Other than being crazy enough to press a button, there is nothing that [any nation] can do militarily to fundamentally alter American interests" (Osnos, 2014). This logic is another reason why Biden was against the Osama bin Laden raid. Although both individuals (Obama and Biden) enjoyed a mutual respect on an array of issues, Biden did not agree that the timing of the mission to kill Osama bin Laden was right. In his opinion, the mission was far too risky for the administration to absorb in the event of failure (Bohn, 2013). Dismissing Biden's qualms, Obama proceeded with the mission, ultimately marking one of the president's greatest foreign policy achievements. Unfortunately, those close to the administration have been consistent in their critical assessment of Biden's judgment on foreign affairs. One of his more outspoken critics was former secretary of defense Robert Gates. Speaking candidly, Gates disclosed, "I think he [Biden] has been wrong on nearly every major foreign policy and national security issue over the past four decades" (Gates, 2014, p. 288).

While Biden continued to be a contributing member of Obama's foreign policy team, his influence noticeably changed during the latter part of the administration. In contrast to his first term, "Obama leans less visibly on Biden for foreign-policy advice than he once did" (Osnos, 2014). Much of this can be attributed to Biden's views, which sometimes run contrary to those of the president. Regardless, there was a noticeable shift in Biden's style on foreign policy issues in the final term of the Obama administration. Some insiders commented that he "kind of disappeared behind the foreign-policy curtain" (Osnos, 2014). He even became less vocal in the principal's meetings of the National Security Council (Osnos, 2014). As the wars in the Middle East scaled back, Biden shifted his focus to smaller foreign policy priorities (Fuller, 2014).

His efforts in Ukraine were viewed as an assignment with little political upside. In 2014, Biden spent considerable time in Ukraine, observing elections and, more importantly, tasked with closely monitoring security in eastern Ukraine, now controlled by pro-Russian separatists. But even the president has acknowledged that, although he has been important to long-term U.S. foreign policy, Biden may not be gaining the recognition necessary for long-term exposure:

> You know, when I sent him to Ukraine for the recent inauguration of Poroshenko, and he's there, a world figure that people know, and he's signifying the importance that we place on the Ukrainian election. And then world leaders can transmit directly to him their thoughts about how we proceed. That's not necessarily helping him in Iowa. (Osnos, 2014)

Regardless, the vice president was committed to assisting the administration, even if it did not necessarily help him politically. In 2013, Biden commented: "I have traveled over 640,000 miles since I've been vice president, and most of the time the President sends me to places that he doesn't want to go" (Goldfarb, 2013). But how did this shift develop? Many point to the stark difference between Biden's and Obama's foreign policy ideologies; however, "some senior leaders at the Pentagon blamed Biden for stoking distrust between the White House and the military" (Osnos, 2014). Many questioned Biden's judgment on Middle Eastern issues, especially regarding Iraq and Afghanistan. His views to divide Iraq into three provinces, in his presidential bid of 2008, caused many to question the vice president's ideas on foreign policy. Biden's persistent questioning of the military and the harsh assessments that he received from several of the president's inner circle of advisors may have exacerbated the divide and led to his diminished influence in foreign policy.

Domestic Policy

Although consumed by a flurry of foreign policy issues, the Obama administration, since day one, built its legacy on domestic policy. The passage of the Affordable Care Act, a package of economic reforms, and an emphasis on equal rights (most notably the repeal of Don't Ask, Don't Tell) will all be regarded as important accomplishments during Obama's eight years in office. Although less visible on domestic issues, Vice President Biden left an enduring mark on many of the president's domestic policy successes and in many ways helped usher them through Congress.

Biden's domestic engagement fell more in line with his ceremonial responsibilities, his role as political party surrogate and a principal liaison on Capitol Hill. With thirty-five years of experience on Capitol Hill, Biden successfully leveraged his relationship with Congress to promote President Obama's agenda. Even as vice president, Biden continued his workouts in the Senate gym—strengthening his relationship with old colleagues (Baumgartner & Crumblin, 2015). His clout at the Capitol helped pass the economic recovery plan, convince Republican Senator Arlen Specter to run for reelection as a Democrat, push the Senate to ratify the START treaty, craft a tax bill to extend Bush-era tax cuts, raise the debt ceiling, and set spending limits (Yon, 2012; Baumgartner & Crumblin, 2015; Dovere & Samuelsohn, 2012).

In 2009, Biden's involvement in implementing the American Recovery and Reinvestment Act's sweeping economic recovery packages, in an effort to stimulate the economy, placed the administration's focus on fixing a troubled financial situation. Inheriting a flailing economy, the administration allowed Biden to spearhead the tracking of the $787 billion stimulus, as it pertained to the creation of jobs, state by state. In 2009, *The Hill* reported Biden stating that the stimulus package must succeed, because, "If it fails, I'm dead" (Youngman, 2009). Biden has been by the president's side, promising to "assist the governors with any help they needed in understanding the guidelines and rules for reporting saved and created jobs from stimulus funds" (Youngman, 2009).

Despite the fact that President Obama stood in the limelight of controversy for most of his administration, Biden was steadfast in his support of the president. Specifically, Biden was a critical player in the administration's goal of bolstering contributions in order to improve the struggling economy. The successful passage of the stimulus package was one of many hotly debated domestic policies embraced by Democrats and vehemently contested by Republicans. For example, the state of Illinois was the recipient of $12.2 million in federal funds, yet only received $9.44 million (Fitzgerald, 2014). Still, in February 2014, the vice president visited southwestern Illinois to defend the successes of the Recovery Act—even in the face of controversy.

In an effort to focus on his own initiative, Biden continued working on promoting awareness and stricter laws in regard to domestic abuse.

Biden's efforts to reduce the prevalence of violence against women was at the forefront of his political career. "On June 20, 1990, then-Senator Joe Biden introduced the Violence Against Women Act (VAWA) in the United States Congress . . . since the passage of the Violence Against Women Act in 1994, rates of domestic violence have decreased by over 50 percent" (obamawhitehouse.archive.gov, 2014). Biden continued this work as vice president where he focused on strengthening efforts to reduce violence against women. The Obama administration used Biden's expertise on the topic and he became the chief advocate for the administration's work on sexual assault. "On January 22, 2014, the Vice President joined President Obama when he created the White House Task Force to Protect Students from Sexual Assault. Biden co-chaired the interagency taskforce along with the White House Council on Women and Girls," and his office published the "Rape and Sexual Assault: A Renewed Call to Action" report (obamawhitehouse.archive.gov, 2014). This report brought awareness to the issue and gave the vice president a voice on an issue that was not only a dominant focus of the news media but had been of great importance to him during his entire political career.

It is apparent that President Obama stopped relying on Biden the same way he did in his first term, especially in regard to foreign policy. While Biden's contributions were essential early on, one could make the assumption that Biden's direct input became less necessary once Obama was comfortable in his position. Although Biden seemingly drifted into obscurity, this does not mean the vice presidency diminished its powers. The fact remains: the vice presidency has grown into an office that modern politics requires it to be.

Biden in 2020

The first rumblings of a potential Biden presidential campaign came in 2012 when officials working on the Obama-Biden campaign noticed that Biden was aggressively courting Obama's donors (Allen, Martin, & VandeHei, 2013). He even held strategy sessions with key family members and long-time loyalists entertaining the possibility of a potential run (Osnos, 2014). All this despite telling Obama in 2008, "The good news is, I'm sixty-five and you're not going to have to worry about my positioning myself to be president" (Witcover, 2014, p. 496). In 2016, however, Vice President Biden found himself well positioned for a presidential bid and seemed to flirt with the idea on several occasions. At his son Beau's wake, he told friends that his son in his final days had said he hoped his father would run for president (Baker & Haberman, 2015). At one point, he even called a collection of potential campaign staffers and left them with the impression that he was going to run (ibid.). Nevertheless, in October 2015, the vice president announced in a speech in the Rose Garden that the window for a successful campaign had closed (Collinson, 2015).

Given the dramatic losses in the 2016 elections, where Democrats lost the White House and failed to win back either chamber in Congress, the former vice president continued to stoke speculation on a potential run in 2020. Many Democrats were particularly disappointed that he decided against a run in 2016; perhaps he might have been able to garner the same populist momentum that was partly responsible for President Donald Trump's victory in 2016 (Hagen, 2017). In its first six months, the Trump administration has been plagued by scandals, struggled with public approval, and has suffered several high-profile staffing setbacks (Levitz, 2017), causing many to look back kindly on Obama's eight years in the White House (Revesz, 2017). As a result, Biden admitted that he regrets not being president during an interview at Colgate University, in March 2017 (Nunez, 2017). Although he delayed an announcement, on April 25, 2019, Biden joined twenty-two other contenders to announce his candidadcy. Biden's vice presidential approval rating demonstrates the type of appeal he is capable of drawing, which has translated to his nomination as the Democratic candidate in 2020.

"Vice presidents with progressive ambition for the presidency hope that the public associates them with the successes of the administration in which they serve. This naturally leads a vice president to become a loyal member of the administration, at least in public, in part as a way to increase the likelihood that the public will make such a connection [which may benefit them come election time]" (Cohen, 2001, p. 143). Biden is no exception. His candidacy is attempting to demonstrate that Biden is best positioned to be the political heir to President Obama. However, this association of good public sentiment toward an administration and positive approval of a vice president's candidacy is currently being challenged. Biden's previous political positions and involvement in historical events are being reassessed by commentators and the public. For instance, his role as chairman of the Senate Judiciary Committee during the Clarence Thomas nomination hearings for the Supreme Court is being reevaluated against the backdrop of the #MeToo movement and his handling of the sexual harassment claims made by Anita Hill against Thomas (Bowden, 2019). Anita Hill publicly stated, "If the Senate Judiciary Committee, led then by Mr. Biden, had done its job and held a hearing that showed that its members understood the seriousness of sexual harassment and other forms of sexual violence, the cultural shifts we saw in 2017 after #MeToo might have began in 1991" (Bowden, 2019). Similarly, Biden's approach to politics, that of an "old-school backslapper" with a "tactile style of retail politicking" has garnered significant attention against the backdrop of the #MeToo era, to the point that the vice president has had to address the issue and has caused some in the Democratic Party to wonder if he is best positioned to go head-to-head against President Trump as the nominee (Stolberg & Ember, 2019).

Biden had time to weather these issues and a lot changed between the primaries and the presidential election in 2020. However, as his performance in the first Democratic debate indicated, he did not have an easy ride to the nomination. His lackluster performance in the debate and the attack by a rival (Senator, and later Biden's running mate, Kamala Harris), in which Biden was taken by surprise, emboldened his critics and opponents and caused others to question his ability to mount a successful campaign (Forgey, 2019). Biden's place in history and his performance in subsequent Democratic debates solidified his frontrunner status and eventually led to the presidential nomination.

Conclusion

The history of Joe Biden's vice presidency will reside in books and his contributions to the office will be examined by scholars for years to come. The vice presidency remains an ever-evolving political enigma. Those who have served as second in command embraced the office through difficult times and their pride and perseverance allowed them to quietly make significant contributions. Joe Biden is no different. His tenure in office will be remembered for assisting the president in ending two wars in the Middle East and advancing the administration's foreign policy. Like Quayle before him, Biden will also be remembered for his gaffes. But, as history has shown, the vice presidency is slowly coming into its own. Hiding in the shadows of the presidency, the vice presidency has proven its worth in the modern era. And although those serving have been frustrated at times, the service to country outweighs any negative implications. Biden said of the vice presidency, "For all my skepticism about taking the job, it's been the most worthwhile thing I've ever done in my life" (Osnos, 2014).

References

Allen, M., Martin, J. & VandeHei, J. (2013, January 23). Biden "intoxicated" by 2016 run. *Politico*. http://www.politico.com/story/2013/01/no-joke-joe-biden-makes-2016-moves-086600.

Arsu, S. (2014, October 4). Biden apologizes to Turkey president. *The New York Times*. http://www.nytimes.com/2014/10/05/world/europe/turkish-leader-demands-biden-apology.html?_r=0.

Baker, B. (2014, March/April). Joe being Joe: The best Biden gaffes, slip-ups, uncomfortable truths, and plain old bloopers. *Politico*. http://www.politico.com/magazine/story/2014/02/joe-biden-bidenisms-103689.

Baker, P. (2013). *Days of fire: Bush and Cheney in the White House*. Doubleday.

Baker, P., & Haberman, M. (2015, October 21). Joe Biden concludes there's no time for a 2016 run. *New York Times*. https://www.nytimes.com/2015/10/22/us/joe-biden-concludes-theres-no-time-for-a-2016-run.html.

Baumgartner, J. C. (2017). Polls and elections: Under the radar: Public support for vice presidents. *Presidential Studies Quarterly, 47*(1): 1–12.

Baumgartner, J. C., & Crumblin, T. F. (2015). *The American vice presidency: From the shadow to the spotlight*. Rowman & Littlefield.

Bohn, K. (2013, January 22). Biden on Obama at start of second term: "Totally simpatico." CNN. http://www.cnn.com/2013/01/21/politics/borger-biden-intv/.

Bowden, J. (2019, May 9). Anita Hill: "Me Too" could have started long ago if Biden-led panel had "done its Job." *The Hill*. https://thehill.com/homenews/campaign/443055-anita-hill-metoo-could-have-started-long-ago-if-biden-led-panel-had-done.

Bradner, E. (2014, October 3). Joe Biden gets colorful on being VP—and it rhymes with glitch. CNN. http://www.cnn.com/2014/10/02/politics/joe-biden-vp-remark/index.html.

Burns, A., & Martin, J. (2019, April 25). Joe Biden announces 2020 run for president, after months of hesitation. *The New York Times*. https://www.nytimes.com/2019/04/25/us/politics/joe-biden-2020-announcement.html.

Campbell, C. (2015, October 1). 1,000 voters were asked to describe the democratic candidates with a single word. http://www.businessinsider.com/poll-hillary-clinton-bernie-sanders-joe-biden-suffolk.

Cohen, J. E. (2001). "The poll": Popular views of the vice president: Vice presidential approval. *Presidential Studies Quarterly, 31*(1), 142–149.

Collinson, S. (2015, October 21). Joe Biden won't run for president. CNN. http://www.cnn.com/2015/10/21/politics/joe-biden-not-running-2016-election/index.html.

Dovere, E., & Samuelsohn, D. (2012, September 5). The Biden factor. *Politico.* http://www.politico.com/blogs/media/2015/08/the-biden-factor-211758.

Edelman, A. (2014, February 27). Relationships between Vice President Biden, President Obama frosty during 2012 campaign: Report. *Daily News.* http://www.nydailynews.com/news/politics/relationship-vice-president-biden-president-obama-grew-frosty-2012-campaign-report-article-1.1704514.

Fitzgerald, M. (2014, February 18). Did stimulus really work? Biden in town to trumpet recovery act success. *BND.com.* http://www.bnd.com/2014/02/18/3065462_biden-to-appear-in-granite-city.html?rh=1.

Flegenheimer, M. (2019, June 3). Biden's first run for president was a calamity. Some missteps still resonate. *The New York Times.* https://www.nytimes.com/2019/06/03/us/politics/biden-1988-presidential-campaign.html.

Forgey, Q. (2019, June 28). Joe Biden's rivals pummel him after shaky debate performance. *Politico.* https://www.politico.com/story/2019/06/28/joe-biden-debate-performance-1388071.

Fuller, J. (2014, July 21). Joe Biden is the most interesting politician who has no chance of becoming president. *The Washington Post.* http://www.washingtonpost.com/blogs/the-fix/wp/2014/07/21/joe-biden-is-the-most-interesting-politician-that-has-no-chance-of-becoming-president/.

Gates, R. (2014). *Duty: Memoirs of a secretary at war.* Random House.

Golan-Vilella, R. (2012, October 11). The Biden counter-doctrine. *The National Interest.* http://nationalinterest.org/blog/the-buzz/the-biden-counter-doctrine-7582.

Goldfarb, Z. A. (2013, February 2). Biden: President "Sends me to places that he doesn't want to go." *The Washington Post.* http://www.washingtonpost.com/blogs/post-politics/wp/2013/02/02/biden-president-sends-me-to-places-that-he-doesnt-want-to-go/.

Goldstein, J. K. (2008). The rising power of the modern vice presidency. *Presidential Studies Quarterly, 38,* 374–389.

Goldstein, J. K. (2012, June 14). Debunking myths about vice presidential selection. *Center for Politics.* http://www.centerforpolitics.org/crystalball/articles/debunking-some-myths-about-vice-presidential-selection/.

Goldstein, J. K. (2016). *The White House vice presidency: The path to significance, Mondale to Biden.* University Press of Kansas.

Goldstein, J. K. (2017, January 18). Why Joe Biden was a most unusual—and effective—vice president. *The Washington Post.* https://www.washingtonpost.com/news/monkey-cage/wp/2017/01/18/why-joe-biden-was-a-most-unusual-and-effective-vice-president/?utm_term=.1af743119e54.

Groll, E. (2015, February 9). Obama's foreign policy summed up in one quote. *Foreign Policy.* http://foreignpolicy.com/2015/02/09/obamas-foreign-policy-summed-up-in-one-quote/.

Hagen, L. (2017, March 22). Biden fuels 2020 speculation. *The Hill.* http://thehill.com/homenews/campaign/334324-biden-fuels-2020-speculation-with-remarks-schedule.

Heilemann, J., & Halperin, M. (2010). *Game change*. HarperCollins.
Hornick, E., & Levs, J. (2008, December 11). What Obama promised Biden. CNN. http://www.cnn.com/2008/POLITICS/12/21/transition.wrap/index.html?eref=ib_to.
Lang, C. (2016, November 16). Barack Obama and Joe Biden's great American bromance. *Time*. http://time.com/barack-obama-joe-biden-friendship-photos/.
Levitz, E. (2017, May 20). Trump's scandals are making his administration impossible to staff. *New York Magazine*. http://nymag.com/daily/intelligencer/2017/05/scandals-are-making-the-white-house-impossible-to-staff.html.
Light, P. C. (1984). *Vice-presidential power: Advice and influence in the White House*. Johns Hopkins University Press.
Martin, J. (2017, May 31). Biden to create a political action committee, a possible signal for 2020. *The New York Times*. https://www.nytimes.com/2017/05/31/us/politics/biden-to-create-a-political-action-committee-a-possible-signal-for-2020.html?_r=0.
McCarthy, J. (2017, January 16). President Obama leaves White House with 58 percent favorable rating. *Gallup*.http://www.gallup.com/poll/202349/president-obama-leaves-white-house-favorable-rating.aspx.
No Author. (2008, October 2). Transcript: The Vice-Presidential debate. *New York Times*. https://www.nytimes.com/elections/2008/president/debates/transcripts/vice-presidential-debate.html.
No Author. (2012, September 5). Biden in a word: "Good," "idiot." *Pew Research Center*. http://www.people-press.org/2012/09/05/biden-in-a-word-good-idiot/.
Nunez, E. (2017, March 27). Biden says he could've won if he ran for president in 2016. CNN. http://www.cnn.com/2017/03/27/politics/joe-biden-president-2016/index.html.
Osnos, E. (2014, July 28). The Biden agenda. *The New Yorker*. http://www.newyorker.com/magazine/2014/07/28/biden-agenda.
Revesz, R. (2017, February 2). Barack Obama: Most Americans want him back as president, poll shows. *Independent*. http://www.independent.co.uk/news/world/americas/donald-trump-barack-obama-president-white-house-poll-public-policy-polling-muslim-ban-obamacare-a7560256.html.
Scherer, M., Uhrmacher, K., & Schaul, K. (2018, May 26). Who is hoping to challenge Trump for president in 2020? *The Washington Post*. https://www.washingtonpost.com/graphics/2018/politics/2020-presidential-hopefuls/?noredirect=on&utm_term=.03c5a4529893.
Sink, J. (2012, May 10). Obama: Biden forced timing of gay-marriage announcement. *The Hill*. http://thehill.com/video/administration/226589-obama-would-have-preferred-to-have-done-gay-marriage-announcement-in-my-own-way.
Stolberg, S., & Ember S. (2019, April 2). Biden's tactile politics threaten his return in the #MeToo era. *The New York Times*. https://www.nytimes.com/2019/04/02/us/politics/joe-biden-women-me-too.html.

Traub, J. (2012, October 10). The Biden doctrine: How the vice president is shaping President Obama's foreign policy. *Foreign Policy.* http://www.foreignpolicy.com/articles/2012/10/10/the_biden_doctrine.

Trujillo, M. (2014, February 10). Biden: VP has no inherent power. *The Hill.* http://thehill.com/blogs/blog-briefing-room/197921-biden-vp-has-no-inherent-power.

Warshaw, S. A. (2009). *The co-presidency of Bush and Cheney.* Stanford University Press.

White House. (N.D.). About Vice President Biden's efforts to end violence against women. *ObamaWhiteHouse.archives.gov.* https://obamawhitehouse.archives.gov/1is2many/about.

Witcover, J. (2010). *Joe Biden: A life of trial and redemption.* William Morrow.

Witcover, J. (2014). *The American vice presidency: From irrelevance to power.* Smithsonian Books.

Woodward, B. (2010). *Obama's war.* Simon & Schuster.

Yon, R. (2012). The Biden vice presidency: Perpetuating influence or restoring historical insignificance? In R. P. Watson, J. Covarrubias, T. Lansford, & D. M. Brattebo (Eds.), *The Obama presidency.* State University of New York Press.

Yon, R. M. (2017). *Emerging from the shadows: Vice presidential influence in the modern era.* Doctoral Dissertation.

Youngman, S. (2009, September 24). VP Biden: If stimulus fails, "I'm dead." *The Hill.* http://thehill.com/homenews/administration/60251-biden-if-stimulus-fails-im-dead.

2

The Evolving Political Partnership of Barack Obama and Bill Clinton

DOUGLAS M. BRATTEBO

Introduction

Rare are the occasions when American presidents and first ladies, current and former, gather at an important national event televised for the wider world. Such was the case on December 5, 2018, when former presidents Jimmy Carter, Bill Clinton, George W. Bush, and Barack Obama, along with President Donald Trump, attended the state funeral of George H. W. Bush at the Washington National Cathedral. The Obamas provided a physical buffer between the Clintons and Trumps, to avert potential awkwardness between the Republican president and the Democratic adversary he had defeated, in the most unconventional of elections, to claim the White House in 2016. The Obamas' gesture, undoubtedly a sensible bit of stage management, may also have been a subtle testament to the genuine connection between Barack Obama and Bill Clinton that had developed across the previous decade and had cured into something solid and sustainable. The two men are very different, but as Pulitzer Prize–winning author David Maraniss, biographer of both Clinton and Obama, has noted, they have more in common than generally is appreciated: "Both came out of geographic isolation, Hawaii and southwest Arkansas, far from the center of power, in states that had never before offered up presidents. Both came out of troubled families defined by fatherlessness and alcoholism. Both at various times felt a sense of abandonment" (Maraniss, 2016a). Maraniss has also noted the commonality of Clinton and Obama "drawing on uncommon will, Ivy League training, mental agility, innate adaptability, and the symbolism of hope to reach the heights of American politics" (Maraniss, 2008a). The two men developed in contrasting ways from the experience of these common challenges, with Clinton becoming an extroverted glad-hander who thrived by skittering past his own flaws and finding his way out of messes often of his own making, and Obama becoming an introverted analyst of his own identity who sought to confront problems directly, while not always appreciating why others could not appraise matters in a similar fashion (Maraniss, 2016a).

Despite the ways in which Obama and Clinton diverged as they grew to political maturity, it is nevertheless natural that an American president would seek out the perspectives and the assistance of his predecessors, since so few men (and soon, women) have had the incomparable experience of leading the world's oldest and most powerful republic. There is a need to seek the opinions of others who know the burdens of the job. At any given moment, however, the relationships between the incumbent president and former holders of the office are inherently complicated and even fraught. Most often the barriers to full cooperation are those of party, ideology, and generation. Yet, the dynamic between Barack Obama and Bill Clinton was burdened at its inception by an additional, central factor: their status as bitter rivals when Obama emerged as the main and ultimately victorious competitor to Hillary Clinton in her 2008 bid for the Democratic presidential nomination. Overlaid upon that unique rift have been additional, more standard impediments to their evolving relationship: contrasts in their governing styles and policy ambitions in the White House, which signal competing visions for the Democratic Party as an electioneering and governing entity; societal and cultural currents that have sometimes brought the two men together and other times pushed them apart, as Americans' feelings about the two presidents have fluctuated; and an intense, if often unspoken competition, common to all former presidents, whereby each works to enlarge his own historical standing and legacy in comparison to those of his peers. Altogether, though, the ever-evolving relationship between the forty-fourth and forty-second American presidents has been one containing equal measures of genuine mutual respect and reciprocal strategic advantage.

This chapter explores the stages of the political partnership of Barack Obama and Bill Clinton, tracing its arc from a rancorous inception during the internecine 2007–08 nomination battle between Obama and Hillary Clinton, through a political "bromance" during Obama's 2012 reelection campaign and then on to the association they have today. The analysis concludes with projections on what their future interaction might look like and how their inevitable twilight competition for top billing in the history books might turn out, while fully acknowledging the uncertainties of such conjecture. The hope is to encourage appreciation for the importance of these relationships to the functioning of American politics and as object lessons in how Americans may overcome dissimilarities to collaborate on worthwhile undertakings.

Bad Blood

First-term U.S. senator Barack Obama (D-IL), had become, by early 2008, the thing that second-term U.S. senator Hillary Rodham Clinton (D-NY) and former president Bill Clinton dreaded most: a credible challenger to Hillary for the party's presidential nomination. The Clintons, like most political analysts, believed right up to the start of the primary contests that the nomination was Hillary's for the taking, because she had earned it by her public service as first lady during her husband's tumultuous presidency and her two subsequent victories in Senate contests. Underappreciated at the time was the fact that the Obama phenomenon was every bit as substantial a threat to Bill Clinton's future as to Hillary Clinton's, as the former president's immediate political relevance and also his ultimate historical legacy hinged on whether he would succeed in seeing his wife elected president, and thus get to serve another term (or two) as the country's first First Gentleman. Obama's unique life story, soaring political rhetoric, appeal across demographic lines, and the alluring prospect that the United States might have its first African American president made Hillary seem more an outgrowth of establishment politics and less an avant-garde breaker of gender barriers. Sensing the political stakes, Bill Clinton's campaign rhetoric in support of his wife's candidacy became increasingly shrill throughout the first few months of 2008, to such an extent that he crossed lines of propriety and became, if not an outright liability, then a factor of limited net value, in Hillary's struggle for the nomination. An important side effect of Bill's escalating behavior was that it poisoned the air between Hillary Clinton and Obama, and also between Bill Clinton and Obama, which created a dynamic in the new relationship between them that the two men struggled to overcome.

Never one to step outside the spotlight, Bill Clinton's central but increasingly problematic role in Hillary's campaign manifested fully during 2007. Early that year, Bill's outward disposition was sunny as he contemplated a return to the hustings on behalf of his wife, when he wrote, "I can't wait to join Hillary on the campaign trail and talk to people about what a great president she's going to be" (Kamen, 2007). The former president's equanimity, however, proved fleeting. By the end of the year, as Obama's campaign gained velocity, Bill Clinton became cranky, chastising the media for focusing less scrutiny on Obama's campaign than on his wife's (Pappu, 2007). Columnist David Ignatius pointed out something that had been widely discussed in public opinion polls and media coverage of the Clintons—the "two presidents" problem—about which he observed, "Whatever you think of the Clintons, it's hard to get your mind around having a current and former president in the White House" (Ignatius, 2007). Columnist Eugene Robinson concurred, asking, "Since the Constitution provides for one president, not two, could [Bill] find a way to live in a White House that wasn't all about him?" (Robinson, 2007). The rebuttal by the Clintons was to remind voters of the successes of Bill Clinton's administration, a presidency that he had stated before Election Day in 1992 would offer voters "two for the price of one" and to portray the policy accomplishments as products of the Clintons' joint labor (Kornblut & MacGillis, 2007). A *Washington Post* article observed, "At times, [Clinton's] pitch for his wife is focused so much on his own accomplishments as president that it almost sounds as if he himself is running for reelection" (Kornblut & MacGillis, 2007). Indeed, things were becoming personal for Bill Clinton and soon he would publicly act out in ways counterproductive to his wife's candidacy, his own high standing with the American public, and the establishment of an effective relationship with Obama.

After his wife had lost the Iowa caucuses and was positioning herself for what ultimately would be a comeback victory in the New Hampshire primary, Bill Clinton swiped at what he considered the lack of substance beneath the hope-and-change glow of Obama's candidacy, telling Granite State voters: "You have to decide what this election is about. Do you want a feeling of change, [or] do you want the facts of change? Do you want the words that sound good, or do you want the actions that change your life for the better?" (Murray, 2008a). Soon thereafter, while campaigning in South Carolina, a primary contest Obama later won, Bill Clinton appeared to question whether there was any substance to Obama's rise. Characterizing the widespread perception that Obama had consistently opposed the Iraq war as "the biggest fairy tale I've ever seen," many voters interpreted Bill Clinton's wording and intense body language as a broadside at the very legitimacy of Barack Obama (Kornblut & Murray, 2008). Bill Clinton tried to walk back the comments, but the damage was done. In a debate with Hillary in South Carolina, Obama observed, "I can't tell who I'm running against sometimes" (Balz, 2008a).

Three more incidents would make matters considerably worse. The first episode grew out of a comment Obama made in an interview with *The Reno Gazette-Journal*. Although analytically correct and not unfairly critical of Bill Clinton when taken in its totality, Obama's observation incensed both Clintons:

> I think it's fair to say that the Republicans were the party of ideas for a pretty long chunk of time there over the last 10–15 years in the sense that they were challenging conventional wisdom. . . . I think Ronald Reagan changed the trajectory of America in a way that Richard Nixon did not and in a way that Bill Clinton did not. He put us on a fundamentally different path because the country was ready for it. . . . I think he tapped into what people were already feeling, which was: We want clarity, we want optimism, we want a return to that sense of dynamism and entrepreneurship that had been missing. I think we are in one of those times right now where people feel like things as they are going aren't working, that we're bogged down in the same arguments that we've been having, and they're not useful. And the Republican approach, I think, has played itself out. (Dionne, 2013; Suarez, 2008.)

Two things about Obama's musings no doubt hit way too close to home for the Clintons. First was the fact that Bill Clinton had been willing to question Democratic orthodoxy and even praise Reagan for certain policies and actions during his own 1992 presidential campaign—and now Obama was doing the same thing, but to the detriment of the Clinton brand (Dionne, 2008). Second, Obama's remarks portrayed Bill Clinton's emerging legacy as being less imposing than that of another modern president—a Republican, no less—causing Bill Clinton to worry that, if "the dream of a Clinton Restoration" were to go unrealized, his legacy would have little chance to grow and ripen in the course of time (Robinson, 2008).

The second episode had its genesis in remarks made by Bill Clinton, who characterized Obama's victory in the South Carolina primary as being like those of the erstwhile Democratic presidential candidate Jesse Jackson in 1984 and 1988 (Cohen, 2008). Bill Clinton's loyalists claimed he was merely observing that the coalition of voters Obama had stitched together to win in the Palmetto State had resembled that which Jackson had assembled decades earlier. However, African Americans perceived Bill Clinton's remarks as painting Obama's candidacy as a symbolic effort rather than the victorious force it increasingly appeared to be (Cohen, 2008). Adding insult to injury was Bill Clinton's allegation against the Obama campaign, in a radio interview weeks later, wherein he stated: "I think they played the race card on me" (Kornblut, 2008b).

Third, after having become steadily more impressed with Obama, and increasingly convinced that Bill Clinton had riled up racial animosities in the nomination campaign, Senator Edward "Ted" Kennedy (D-MA), President John F. Kennedy's only surviving brother and patriarch of a Democratic political dynasty, endorsed Barack Obama. In a joint public show of support at American University, alongside JFK's only surviving child, Caroline Kennedy, and his own son, Representative Patrick Kennedy (R-RI), Ted Kennedy passed the torch of Camelot, not to the woman with whom he had collaborated on healthcare and other issues her time as first lady and as a fellow senator, but to the insurgent freshman senator whom the Clintons considered an interloper (Kurtz, 2008). For Bill Clinton, in the midst of seeking to burnish his own place in history through a Clinton dynasty of sorts, it is hard to imagine a more painful repudiation.

By early March 2008, campaigning ahead of the Texas primary, it was Hillary Clinton who claimed of Obama, "His entire campaign is based on one speech he gave at an antiwar rally in 2002" (Kornblut, 2008a). Bill Clinton, however, having been burned by his own abiding ambition and hot rhetoric, kept things upbeat as he campaigned on Hillary's behalf in Ohio, seemingly having "morphed from the angry husband of January to the proud partner of March" (Bacon, 2008). It might be an overstatement to posit that Bill's excesses and miscalculations in the early phases of the nomination battle with Obama were enough to sway the final outcome away from Hillary. The truth, as columnist Kathleen Parker mused five years later, might be that the outcome was determined more by "the most unexpected thing of all—this man Obama, this *deus ex machina* who descended from some distant star to blind the masses with his light. His destiny, alas, was greater than hers and so . . . Hillary had to wait"

(Parker, 2013). But what could not wait in the spring of 2008 was an answer to a vexing question: With Obama marching steadily forward to clinch the nomination, how would Bill Clinton find a way to work with him, after everything that had transpired, to harmonize the interests of Hillary and himself with those of the man who might become the next president, and thus his equal in the world's most select club?

Rapprochement

From early June 2008, when Hillary Clinton formally conceded the nomination race to Barack Obama, until Election Day in early November, Bill Clinton and Obama interacted sparingly and coolly, continuing to size each other up and seeking to identify a way to work together. Obama's inner circle did not entertain deeply the notion that Hillary Clinton would become his running mate, and so the big question looming over this period of tentative détente was what formal role, if any, she would have in the Obama administration. From the time of the Democratic National Convention in Denver, in late August, deliberations about Hillary Clinton's role explored the likely complications that Bill Clinton's status as a highly paid global speaker and prominent philanthropist guiding the efforts of the sizeable William J. Clinton Foundation might pose for his wife and, by extension, an administration in which she served. By the time Hillary Clinton's future was formally decided, at the start of December with Obama's announcement that she would be his secretary of state, the relationship between Bill and Obama increasingly stabilized. There was no warmth between them, but the bad blood began to dissipate and they gradually came to see each other as reliable partners. Ultimately, they became more willing to expand the scope or their mutual reliance. It seems improbable that either foresaw just how closely their futures would be interwoven by the spring of 2012, as Barack Obama was heading into the homestretch of his first term and doing everything within his power to ensure that he would have a second one.

During June 2008, following Hillary Clinton's concession to Obama, the presumptive nominee encouraged his major campaign donors to help retire a $10 million vendor-related chunk of Hillary's total $22.5 million campaign debt. Soon after, Hillary Clinton introduced Obama to her biggest donors at a joint event in the nation's capital (Murray, 2008b). Not long thereafter, Bill Clinton spoke by phone with Obama and accepted his invitation to campaign for the Democratic ticket in the fall, and an Obama spokesperson praised the former president as "one of this nation's greatest leaders and most brilliant minds," adding that Obama "looks forward to seeing him on the campaign trail and receiving his counsel in the months to come" (Weisman, 2008). Obama's team members knew only too well that no other figure in American politics could communicate as well as Bill Clinton with voters worried about the economy, and they wanted him to take up that task in the general election campaign (Murray and Balz, 2008).

But Bill Clinton, still smarting from the nomination battle and its outcome, was stinting in praise of Obama at the start of August, less than a month away from the Democratic National Convention, offering that Obama was "smart" and "a good politician," while expressing confidence that national demographic trends "would work in any Democrat's favor" (Kornblut, 2008d.) Bill Clinton also held out the prospect that he would be content to fade back into the world of philanthropy, proclaiming with a dash of disingenuity, "This is my life now, and I was eager to get back to it, and I couldn't be happier" (Kornblut, 2008c). Nonetheless, both Clintons delivered dutifully in their addresses at the convention, with Hillary Clinton telling a national television audience on August 26, 2008: "Barack Obama is my candidate. And he must be our president" (Balz, 2008b). Bill's endorsement the next night was even stronger, calling Obama "the man for the job," while noting he possessed a "remarkable ability to inspire people," "intelligence and curiosity," and a "clear grasp" of foreign policy (Maraniss, 2008b). It was good political theater, but it also signaled something more important: perhaps for the first time in his political career of storied ups and downs, Bill Clinton was seeking to redeem himself, while helping Obama in the process (Maraniss, 2008b). Bill Clinton was doing so—despite an adviser's admission that "Obama does not like Clinton, and Clinton knows it"—in hopes that Obama would come to see the full utility of working together (Maraniss, 2008a). Obama paid Bill Clinton a visit for lunch at his Harlem headquarters on September 11, 2008, and Bill Clinton reiterated his willingness to hit the hustings for Obama and his ticket mate, Senator Joseph Biden (D-DE) (Heilemann, 2012). Both Clintons campaigned conscientiously for the Democratic Obama-Biden ticket that fall, with Bill seeking to keep margins in rural southwestern Virginia close (Staff Writer, 2008), the former first couple campaigning together with Biden in Pennsylvania (Barnes, 2008), and Bill appearing jointly with Barack in Kissimmee, Florida, in late October (Heilemann, 2012).

After Election Day, as Obama sought to identify his Cabinet secretaries, much national media coverage centered on how Bill Clinton's role—"as something akin to the world's philanthropist in chief"—might open up a slough of actual and potential conflicts of interest for Hillary Clinton, if she were to become secretary of state (Shear & Rucker, 2008). The former president had become wealthy by landing high-paying speaking gigs, many with foreign companies, as a result of his networks emanating from the William J. Clinton Foundation and its Clinton Global Initiative, which annually convened a conference of "hundreds of corporate chiefs, heads of state, humanitarians and celebrities" (Shear & Rucker, 2008). Indeed, in less than eight years since departing the White House, Bill and Hillary together had earned a staggering $109 million, with almost half of that coming from Bill's speaking engagements (Mosk, Grimaldi, & Stephens, 2008). With so much money sloshing about, there seemed to be an immensely complicated web of interconnections and mutual backscratching among individual and corporate donors who, at various times, contributed to the presidential campaigns of both Clintons, paid Bill Clinton to give speeches and/or hired him as a paid corporate consultant, donated to the Clinton Global Initiative, and donated to the William J. Clinton Presidential Library (Mosk, Grimaldi, & Stephens, 2008). Making the process murkier was the fact that many of the donors to the foundation and the library had never been disclosed (Shear & Rucker, 2008). The editorial board of *The Washington Post* posed a fair hypothetical: "When Mr. Clinton exhorted a foreign government to provide funding or cooperation, would he be carrying the implicit support of the U.S. government?" (Editorial Board, 2008).

Since Bill Clinton thought his wife should take the job if the president-elect offered it, and because Hillary Clinton came to the same conclusion, the Obama and Clinton teams were able to work out an agreement about how to handle potential conflicts of interest emanating from Bill Clinton's complex professional activities (Abramowitz, Murray, & Kornblut, 2008). Through public statements, the former president signaled his determination to do whatever was necessary in the eyes of the incoming administration and whatever government protocol would require, to ensure an absence of entanglements (Mosk & Stephens, 2008). Bill subsequently moved to separate himself from the foundation and pass the leadership of the organization to daughter Chelsea Clinton. Remarkably, Bill Clinton did not overshadow Hillary Clinton during her full term as secretary of state (Rucker & Kane, 2010). Moreover, he appreciated deeply the respectful, professional working relationship that the president built with Hillary Clinton (Heilemann, 2012). Obama, for his part, had to be both relieved and delighted that Hillary Clinton worked relentlessly at executing the country's diplomacy with no need to encroach upon the limelight. All of this made for a stable, functional arrangement that undoubtedly appealed to a president who had always loathed drama in the workplace—and it enabled the relationship between Obama and Bill Clinton to transform into something bigger than a bond borne of defensive necessity.

By the spring of 2010, Obama was increasingly putting Bill Clinton to work on a host of admittedly low-profile, but important political errands, as sort of "a roving, always on-call fixer who lends his political skills to help Obama and Democrats in tough spots" (Rucker & Kane, 2010). If Democratic candidates in places where Obama was not popular needed a powerful fundraiser and campaign surrogate, Bill Clinton was up for the task. The former president also was willing to speak with prospective Democratic congressional candidates, prior to the 2010 primary season, and encourage or discourage their candidacies, based on the White House's analysis of who would make the strongest nominee for a particular office in the fall (Rucker & Kane, 2010). With Obama's approval ratings running low as the midterm elections approached, Bill Clinton could show up across the map and be welcomed in states as diverse as Arizona, Georgia, Massachusetts, New Mexico, New York, and Pennsylvania (Rucker & Kane, 2010). The ever-gregarious former president was still puzzled why Obama did not phone him to shoot the breeze, though, since that was the way he had operated in the White House (Heilemann, 2012). What Bill Clinton failed to appreciate was that Obama, an inveterate introvert, did not want or need to spend his evenings talking on the phone (Heilemann, 2012). The wipeout that the Democratic Party suffered in the 2010 midterms changed Obama's threshold for tending to key political relationships, however, and soon Bill Clinton would find himself not only on Obama's regular call list, but back in the White House at the president's side. This marked a turning point in their relationship.

Bromance

The tea party tsunami of the 2010 midterm elections cost Democrats a whopping sixty-three House seats (and control of that chamber) as well as six Senate seats (resulting in a slimmed majority). Obama appreciated with new urgency that he would have to find his way back to political vitality in time for reelection in a span of twenty-four months. Among recent presidents, Bill Clinton had engineered just such a revival, in the wake of the disastrous 1994 midterm elections, to win reelection in 1996. There was no one better to enlist in Obama's political recovery than Bill Clinton himself, and Obama began to reach out to him regularly over the phone. Obama's approval rating was hurting, ironically, from some of the same kinds of charges Bill Clinton had faced during his presidency, hurled by the left wing of the Democratic Party, which considered Obama too centrist and pragmatic. The sticking point that crystallized progressives' objections was Obama's postelection deal with congressional Republicans to retain tax cuts for high-income households (a holdover from George W. Bush's presidency) in exchange for extending unemployment benefits, as the country continued to recover from the Great Recession that had begun in 2008. Obama invited Bill Clinton to meet with him in the Oval Office on December 10, 2010, but neither man appreciated, at the time, what a watershed it would be for their political partnership (Heilemann, 2012).

Obama and Clinton spoke in the Oval Office for more than an hour, "the longest talk they'd had since Obama took office" (Heilemann, 2012). Their conversation, which centered on Clinton's analysis of how to explain the president's policy positions and accomplishments, prompted Obama to hold a spontaneous joint press conference in the White House's press briefing room (Maraniss, 2012). The two men entered the room together, with Obama noting affectionately, "I thought I'd let the other guy in," and Clinton then provided a seminar of sorts that showcased his analysis of the economy, the thesis being that Obama was leading the country back from the Great Recession with skill and consistency, as Obama chimed in sparingly (Maraniss, 2012). Obama soon had to excuse himself to attend a Christmas party, lest he incur the displeasure of the first lady, and then things got a bit strange: "Clinton said, 'I feel awkward being here, and now you're going to leave me all by myself'—and then proceeded to demonstrate that awkwardness by fielding questions for 23 minutes after Obama bailed" (Heilemann, 2012). The episode garnered national attention and earned a deserved place among the most compelling and downright strange joint appearances by American presidents in the nation's history.

The immediate effect of the memorable press conference was that the intraparty spat died down, but far more important was that Obama moved—slowly at first, but with increasing urgency—to make his relationship with Clinton the centerpiece of his 2012 reelection effort. After another standoff with congressional Republicans in August 2011, as Obama's approval rating reached its nadir at 38 percent, the White House stepped up outreach to Clinton (Heilemann, 2012). The two men golfed at Andrews Air Force Base, in late September, and Obama made certain not to let the phone lines cool. The president also dispatched the most important members of his campaign team to meet with Clinton at his Harlem headquarters in November to provide a full overview of the strategy that would be used to take on the probable Republican presidential nominee, former Massachusetts governor Mitt Romney (Heilemann, 2012). In early December, the two men appeared together at an exposition on green buildings, one of Clinton's many philanthropic interests, in Washington, D.C. They praised each other effusively, with Clinton talking up his own track record on stewardship of the national economy and taking visible enjoyment in Obama's reply to a reporter, who asked what economic advice Clinton might have for Obama: "Oh, he gives me advice all the time" (Heilemann, 2012). Obama had come to fully acknowledge and act in accord with a verity about the forty-second president: "Flattery will carry you a long way in life, and even further with Bill Clinton" (Heilemann, 2012).

Clinton now had become amenable to doing whatever Obama requested in service to Obama's reelection. The willingness was a product of two things: Clinton's sense that Obama's prudent policymaking was unfairly criticized by fringe elements in his own party, just as Clinton's efforts had been in the 1990s, and Obama's purposeful decision to jettison any criticism of Clinton's economic centrism and political slipperiness (Heilemann, 2012). Crucial in deepening the two presidents' personal rapport was a series of three joint fundraising events they held in Virginia starting in late April (Pace 2012). One of those gatherings gave Obama and Clinton an opportunity to spend more than an hour together over dinner without any advisors present (Tumulty, 2012). After a busy Spring 2012 season of fielding other assignments in support of Obama's reelection bid, Clinton received a call from Obama in late July, just over a month before the Democratic National Convention in Charlotte, North Carolina: Obama asked Clinton to give an evening address placing the president's name in the nomination, and Clinton accepted (Heilemann, 2012). Clinton's assignment would be to explain why Obama had been and would continue to be a better steward of the national economy than

Romney, a task senior White House adviser David Plouffe considered more important than Obama's own address, because "Clinton is an economic arbiter like no other" (Heilemann, 2012). Clinton got to work immediately, focusing on the need to explain economic complexities in a way that regular Americans could understand, thereby redressing the one aspect of presidential leadership on which Clinton had always found Obama wanting: describing policy achievements so that he could take credit for them (Heilemann, 2012).

Clinton's speech was a thing of beauty, akin to an artist's or athlete's peak performance on the best outing of a career. He took the stage as his 1992 theme song, Fleetwood Mac's "Don't Stop (Thinking About Tomorrow)," boomed through the venue (Balz & Rucker, 2012). When the bedlam had calmed a bit, Clinton opened by talking about why he wanted to nominate Barack Obama for a second term, intoning, "I want to nominate a man who's cool on the outside, but who burns for America on the inside" (Transcript, 2012). He expressed gratitude to Obama "for the relationship of respect that [Hillary Clinton] and the president have enjoyed and the signal that sends to the rest of the world, that democracy does not have to be a blood sport, it can be an honorable enterprise that advances the public interest" (Transcript, 2012). From there on, Clinton got down to business, characterizing the Republican Party's main argument against Obama thusly: "We left him a total mess. He hasn't cleaned it up fast enough. So fire him and put us back in" (Transcript, 2012). The commanding core of the speech found Clinton recounting his own hard experience of working to resuscitate the economy during his presidency, while playing up the fact that "President Obama started with a much weaker economy than I did" (Transcript, 2012). Then came the most important words Clinton spoke that night: "Listen to me, now: No president—no president, not me, not any of my predecessors, no one—could have fully repaired all the damage that he found in just four years. But he has laid the foundation for a new, modern, successful economy of shared prosperity. And if you will renew the president's contract, you will feel it. You will feel it" (Transcript, 2012). Obama appeared with Clinton at the close of the speech, and the two presidents "embraced in a bear hug. Obama, his hand on Clinton's shoulder, then tried to lead his Democratic predecessor off stage—but Clinton kept returning to the crowd for more hugs and handshakes. Finally, Obama decided to wait backstage for a few moments until Clinton finished enjoying his night" (Milbank, 2012). Then began the rollcall of states to formally renominate Barack Obama.

Michelle Obama would later refer to the onstage embrace as "the public display of the bromance" between Obama and Clinton (Access Online, 2012). The hug, however, was a flourish to the rhetorical performance by Clinton. By the time both Obama and Romney made September cameo appearances at the Clinton Global Initiative's annual conference in New York City, it had become clear that Clinton's convention speech had achieved its political objective: Polls showed significant increases in the percentage of the American people who (1) thought the country was headed in the right direction, (2) were optimistic about the economy, and (3) considered the president better suited than Romney to manage the economy (Heilemann, 2012). This improvement in Obama's overall strategic position heading into the final weeks of the campaign provided a valuable cushion when Obama stumbled in the first of three televised debates with Romney and also when Romney brazenly tacked toward the ideological center in the remaining debates and closing days of the contest (Heilemann, 2012). The morning after the third debate, Clinton met with Obama adviser Jim Messina and declared he was at the president's disposal for the final weeks of the campaign, which saw the former president campaign frenetically in swing states on behalf of the Obama-Biden ticket (Leibovich, 2012). Appearing jointly at a rally outside the state capitol in Concord, New Hampshire, on the final Saturday evening of the campaign, the duo's chemistry was on display for the masses, and it was moving to hear them heap laurels on each other, especially when the older, white man, with his vocal chords failing him, stated to his younger, black successor in the Oval Office: "I gave my voice in the service of my president" (Walsh, 2012).

Seeking a Common Successor

Electing a successor to a two-term president is an uphill enterprise, even in the best of circumstances, as the electorate grows tired of a particular approach to governance and becomes eager for something different. Nonetheless, President Obama and Bill Clinton found themselves enlisted in this inherently challenging project in 2016. The effort was complicated by the fact that Obama really had not groomed a designated successor (Eilperin, 2014). The causes for this were several, but an especially important one was that Obama owed the Clintons much, particularly for his 2012 reelection. This created an awkward dynamic for the president, whose closest political and personal friendship across his presidency had developed with Vice President Joe Biden, and Obama presumably did not want to get at cross purposes with either Hillary Clinton or Biden by favoring one over the other. The death of Biden's oldest son Beau, in late May 2015, precipitated a period of reflection by Biden about whether he should seek the presidency once again (in addition to his 1988 and 2008 candidacies). Ultimately, the vice president decided to focus attention on his family rather than run. Other factors hindered the effort to ensconce Hillary Clinton as the Democratic successor to Barack Obama. Chief among these were: the evolving sensibilities of rank-and-file Democrats about the Clintons, plus nascent ideological and generational fissures within the Democratic Party; Hillary Clinton's weaknesses as a politician and candidate; and the undeniable pluses and minuses that Bill Clinton brought to his wife's campaign, as a political surrogate and would-be first First Gentleman.

As early as the first months of 2014, political analysts noted that the base of the Democratic Party had become more progressive during the Obama presidency, with the center of energy and ideas shifting to a younger, more populist core (Balz and Rucker 2014a). In the wake of the 2008 financial collapse and grudging economic recovery that followed, many Democrats were uneasy with Bill Clinton's policy record of financial deregulation and free trade, which they saw as having exacerbated economic inequality (Goldfarb, 2014). This posed a challenge to a 2016 Hillary Clinton candidacy because she would have to craft a new economic pitch that would alienate neither the establishment New Democrat contingent nor the nascent reformist wing of the party (Balz & Rucker, 2014a). Interestingly, there was, at that time, no sign of an emerging progressive candidate with the wherewithal to seriously challenge Clinton for the nomination, with polls finding that nearly three-quarters of Democrats describing themselves as liberals and moderates, men and women, whites and nonwhites supported her candidacy (Balz & Rucker, 2014a). Moreover, as late as the summer of 2014, polls also showed that Bill Clinton had reclaimed his standing as the most popular political figure in America, with substantial positive ratings among both independents and Republicans in addition to near-unanimous support among Democrats (Clement & Craighill, 2014). Should that consensus hold, there appeared to be a clear way forward for Hillary Clinton, to both the party's nomination and also the White House. However, if the atmosphere were to shift unpredictably, Clinton was, in the words of one columnist, "no ingénue. She's been around for a very long time" (Cohen, 2013). Therefore, Hillary Clinton had the difficult task of seeking to become the successor to a two-term president whose 2008 candidacy was the textbook definition of an outsider crusade and which had galvanized a newly diversified coalition of Democratic voters, while deploying as a campaign surrogate her spouse, the living embodiment of the party's late-twentieth-century middle-of-the-road temperament. Senator Tom Harkin (D-IA), a longtime ally of the Clintons, expressed confidence in September 2014 that she could pull off the balancing act: "If she does what she did last time, she'll be in great shape, because I don't think there's another phenomenon out there like Barack Obama that would upset everything" (Balz & Rucker, 2014b). Yet, his words carried dark and prescient undertones. Months earlier, Stuart Stevens, who had served as chief strategist for Republican presidential nominee Mitt Romney's 2012 presidential campaign, had stated: "I think the parallels of 2008 are pretty apt here. What started out as being a coronation ended up in an extraordinarily negative, tough race" (Rucker & Goldfarb, 2014).

Concerns about the general strategic terrain confronting Hillary Clinton's 2016 bid for the White House dovetailed with equally serious concerns about her managerial acumen, political instincts, and communication skills—all of which persisted from her ill-fated 2008 presidential campaign and proved to be farsighted. Democratic memories were vividly colored by how she had gone from being "most likely the first female president in American history to a perceived stumblebum out of touch with the political moment" (Gearan, 2015). By the spring of 2015, newly released communication records from her time at the State Department portrayed a picture of Hillary Clinton as anything but an efficient manager of a large entity. Instead, she was too willing to attach weight to the advice of longtime personal loyalists rather than hew closely to the input of officials in a formal advisory system (Tumulty, 2015). The critiques underlying such lingering narratives undercut Hillary Clinton's credibility when she made understandable efforts to differentiate herself from her former boss on policy matters, as when she criticized Obama's foreign policy mantra, "Don't do stupid stuff," as something less than "an organizing principle" for international relations (Eilperin, 2014). Neither the party's liberal base nor Obama's inner circle appreciated the broadside, even if the latter understood its necessity, and the episode demonstrated how tricky it was for an administration to concentrate on "running the country while one of its own campaigns in part on what it's doing wrong" (Eilperin, 2014).

Indeed, key current and former Obama intimates were working diligently to get Hillary elected, viewing her successorship as a structural linchpin to Obama's long-term legacy (Eilperin, 2015). But bad optics about the Clintons' wealth accumulation and philanthropic endeavors continued to reappear as Hillary Clinton became as highly paid a speaker as Bill Clinton (Gold, Helderman, & Narayanswamy, 2015). Also, the Clinton Foundation announced that in the event of a new Clinton administration, "the foundation would no longer accept contributions from foreign governments or corporations" (Balz, 2016). This statement understandably elicited wonderment about why such a practice had ever been acceptable in the first place. Emblematic of how Hillary Clinton frequently did not help herself in public forums, while positioning herself for the nomination, was her tone-deaf statement in June 2014 claiming that she and Bill Clinton had been "dead broke" by the time they left the White House and were not among the "truly well off" (Balz, 2014a). Increasingly, some within and outside Clinton's campaign sought comfort in the hope that the country's morphing demography, along with the prospect of the first female president, would be enough to deliver her to the White House, but her personal capacities never seemed quite up to the task of making the most of either factor (Balz, 2014b).

At the Democratic National Convention in Philadelphia, in late July, Barack Obama repaid his political debt to Bill Clinton with a full-throated endorsement of Hillary as his successor. Obama offered an across-the-board defense of his own administration, painted an optimistic portrait of the American experiment and its horizons, condemned the "darkly pessimistic vision" of Republican presidential nominee Donald Trump, and proclaimed himself "ready to pass the baton" to Hillary Clinton (Maraniss, 2016b). Obama's Wednesday evening address, coming after Joe Biden's speech earlier that same evening and remarks by Michelle Obama and Bill Clinton capping the first two nights of the convention, showcased Obama's rhetorical prowess as he said of Hillary: "I can say with confidence there has never been a man or woman—not me, not Bill, nobody—more qualified to serve as President of the United States of America." With applause filling the convention hall, Obama added, "I hope you don't mind, Bill, but I was telling the truth, man" (ABC News, 2016). Bill Clinton's address, by contrast, had taken on an uncharacteristically modest mission the previous evening: painting a human portrait of Hillary Clinton as the heart of the Clinton family, "first and foremost" a parent and "the best mother in the whole world" (Romano, 2016), whose love of her daughter gave additional fuel to her lifelong work as a "change maker" who has "never been satisfied with the status quo" (Gerson, 2016). It was an important speech, but much more limited in its ambitions than his 2012 endorsement of Obama. Like the text of the speech, the mien of the speaker also seemed to promise more modest things than four years earlier. Bill Clinton appeared visibly aged, his voice was less robust, and his capacity to command the country's gaze seemed to have ebbed. In this sense, the address both presaged a more limited mission for the fall general election campaign and also sought to avert the prospect that he might become a liability for his wife in the general election campaign.

From the get-go in Hillary's quest for the 2016 nomination, Bill had, with rare exception, conducted himself abstemiously while making a case for his wife to become president. However, he picked up sooner than the others that the political environment in 2016 mighty deny her—and his—ultimate objective. While campaigning in Iowa in late 2015, Bill Clinton joked, "I am tired of the stranglehold that women have had on the job of presidential spouse" (Tumulty & Rucker, 2015). It was a good line and well received, in part because it playfully acknowledged his own ceaseless ambitions. More ominous, though, was the banner towed by a circling plane overhead that day: "REVOLUTON [sic] STARTS NOW! FEEL THE BERN!" (Tumulty & Rucker, 2015). Bill Clinton was received positively in parts of the country where President Obama himself seemed to have worn out his political welcome by the fall of 2016; thus, he could be deployed on discrete missions, as could Joe Biden and even the extremely popular first lady Michelle Obama, to places where the incumbent president could not (Milbank, 2014). Bill Clinton seemed—at least for a time, and at least to an extent—to have put the lie to Obama strategist David Axelrod's observation that "Bill Clinton is an incomparable genius when it comes to politics—except when it comes to his wife" (Phillip, 2016). But the former president's past history of sexual indiscretions proved particularly awkward in 2016, for as Hillary Clinton was deploying Bill Clinton on the campaign trail, she was also calling out Trump on his track record of misogyny, which made the former president an inviting target for Trump's ripostes (Marcus, 2015). To his credit, Bill Clinton resisted getting drawn into fisticuffs with Trump over this issue (Tumulty, 2016). The inescapable fact remained, though, that the Clintons were not the right people to criticize Trump's misogyny, given Bill Clinton's checkered treatment of women across the decades. Also problematic was Bill Clinton's spur-of-the-moment decision on the tarmac at the Phoenix airport in late June 2016 to board Attorney General Loretta Lynch's plane to hobnob with her, despite the fact that Hillary Clinton was under investigation for her use of a private email server during her time as secretary of state (Schultheis, 2016).

On Election Night 2016, as the fact and magnitude of Hillary Clinton's defeat manifested themselves, Barack Obama called her to say, "You need to concede" (Ginsburg, 2017). After she spoke briefly with Trump to do so, Obama phoned again to console her and she offered him an apology: "Mr. President, I'm sorry" (Ginsburg, 2017). The political partnership of Barack Obama and Bill Clinton had not been adequate to the task, in 2016's too-late-appreciated environment of destructive revolt, of electing the country's first female president. As the 2016 Democratic National Convention had concluded and Hillary Clinton had embarked upon the general election campaign, columnist Michael Gerson offered one of the most insightful summaries of what was to come: "If this is a normal election—in which the composition of the electorate and the turnout of various groups roughly match recent presidential elections—[Hillary] Clinton's argument should be enough. If this is an anti-establishment wave election, she has the worst possible political profile—boasting of her royal resume during the French Revolution" (Gerson 2016). The much-anticipated Clinton Restoration was not to be, unless perchance it should involve Chelsea Clinton some distant year.

Members of the Club

Barack Obama, like Bill Clinton, has now made the constitutionally mandated transition to postpresidential life and work, with a presidential library and center coming to fruition. Both men are members in good standing in the club of former presidents. They quite likely will have occasion to work in common cause, in person and remotely, on political and other matters, in 2020 and beyond. A relationship that was at times "confrontational, co-dependent" (Lozada, 2014) during Obama's presidency is apt to be predicated less on mutual calculation and more on what they would enjoy teaming up to do. As they collaborate, history will continue its inexorable sifting and reappraisal of their contributions, seeking to identify their places in the hierarchy of legacies. What must be appreciated, early in that process, is that the two leaders, although quite different as people, have greater ideological congruence than often is grasped. Their records of governance are more complex and nuanced than the tropes that their defenders and critics bandy about. Not only their policy contributions, but also their personal auras, will settle out in the coming decades as American society evolves in myriad ways, the political party they both led—and the one that opposed them—develops in substance and sensibility, and the political institutions of the country rise to meet urgent challenges and also fail to do so. It is worth remembering that, in addition to what history records a president as having accomplished, there is also the fact that scholars and the multitude remember how a president made them feel.

It behooves a president to retain an identity that is separate from the rush that comes from both the adulation of the masses and the exercise of presidential power. If a president does not cultivate the appearance of some remove between his sense of self and the public's sense of him, it is hard to see how the chief executive might leave office with the public wanting more. Clinton's hyper-social neediness made presidential power a drug that was hard to quit, whereas Obama experienced a return to private life with relief rather than painful withdrawal. When Clinton left the presidency on January 20, 2001, he could hardly bring himself to depart Andrews Air Force Base and fly off into a new life, so he lingered for more than an hour and assured loyalists, "I'm still here. We're not going anywhere" (Tumulty, 2017). Obama, by contrast, was ready to move on, telling the crowd on January 20, 2017, "You know, Michelle and I have really been milking this goodbye thing, so it behooves me to be brief" (Eilperin & Thompson, 2017). It was not quite like Harry Truman's return to Independence, Missouri, in 1953, but it signaled that Obama was more sanguine than Clinton about turning over the reins of power, even to such an obstreperous personage as Donald Trump, because the quotidian satisfactions of normal life beckoned. History, therefore, may limn Obama as a reluctant servant-statesman who kept just enough distance between his inner life and the public arena to retain some mystery, and Clinton as an always-accessible but exhibitionistic and compulsive climber, even if he was most often driven toward noble ends.

The Democratic Party in the coming decades appears likely to reflect the views and preferences of the nation's diverse, progressive, ascendant demographic majority. In this sense, it probably will in broad strokes resemble the Obama coalition of 2008 and 2012 more than the New Democrat coalition of Bill Clinton in 1992 and 1996. A perplexity accompanies this future scenario: despite what their champions and detractors say, both Clinton and Obama were decidedly centrists, with Clinton being less of an apologist for the Reagan Revolution than often is alleged and Obama being more hospitable to market capitalism than frequently claimed. Clinton may have deregulated Wall Street, "reformed" welfare in 1996 in ways that had the effect of undermining the social safety net, energized the forces of globalization through NAFTA, postured rhetorically to proclaim big government a relic of the past, and exacerbated the rise of economic inequality, but he also kept his promise to appoint a Cabinet that "looks like America" (featuring more powerful roles for women and minorities), raised the minimum wage by 20 percent, facilitated greater minority home ownership, stood for reproductive choice and equal pay for equal work, and put in place the "don't ask, don't tell" policy for gays in the military (even if he was cowed into signing the Defense of Marriage Act in 1996) (Fromer, 2016). Obama, for his part, was more consistently progressive across the waterfront of economic and social issues, as borne out by standard measures of policy preferences during his time in the U.S. Senate and the White House, but he also pursued free-trade agreements (unsuccessfully, due to changing base politics within both political parties) and enacted an Affordable Care Act predicated on market forces rather than universal entitlement (Ehrenfreund, 2017), while working to reduce unsustainable budget deficits as the economy recovered from the Great Recession.

These acknowledgments of ideological similarity take nothing away from Clinton's formidable years-long recentering and revitalization of the Democratic Party from the leftist no man's land it had consigned itself to by the early 1980s, a comeback that took more protracted aforethought and grand strategy than Obama's reactivation of the 1968 Robert Kennedy electoral coalition in 2008. However, Clinton's reorientation of the Democratic Party may be permanently underappreciated by the public, precisely because it is harder to understand than a barrier-breaking campaign of "hope and change." Obama's legacy will be his status as the first African American president in a country that decidedly was still majority-white, a milestone of the kind history tends to smile on. Columnist Eugene Robinson has put this point well: "Obama ran rings around both Clintons in 2008. A black man with the middle name Hussein who gets elected president twice should be in the all-time-all-world Politics Hall of Fame" (Robinson, 2014). This was despite the fact that popular culture, taking a cue from author Toni Morrison, had bestowed, only half-jokingly, the title of "first black president" on Clinton (Parker, 2010). For Clinton, there will never be so indelible a moment in the collective consciousness as Obama in Grant Park on November 4, 2008, declaring that "change has come to America."

Two other factors, having to do with the perception of closeness to the sensibilities of regular Americans and the zeitgeist, will also play a part in determining how the former presidents will wear with the American people over the long run. It seems probable that the Obamas, undoubtedly aware of the complications that the unbridled postpresidential pursuit of wealth has produced for the Clintons, will avoid creating an air of covetousness in the coming years. Having signed with Penguin Random House soon after leaving the White House a dual book deal estimated by some sources at $65 million, it may well be that the Obamas will not feel compelled to hit the big-donor speaking circuit (Thompson, 2017). Thus, former president Obama may resist the temptation of entering "a world where it seemed natural that Chelsea Clinton's apartment in New York would cost $10 million and that Hillary Clinton would be paid $225,000 for a speech to Goldman Sachs executives" (Ignatius, 2017). It seems equally likely that Obama, who has no track record of sexual peccadillos, is a far better fit than Bill Clinton for the Me Too era, ushered in by the rapid proliferation of the anti–sexual harassment and abuse movement in late 2017. In the 2018 midterm elections, Clinton found himself with very few invitations to campaign with Democratic candidates across the country, a stark contrast to his in-demand status in both 2012 and 2016 (Lerer, 2018). Soon thereafter, a joint speaking tour by the Clintons, in late 2018, found many vacant seats in arenas around North America, a direct symptom of the revulsion that younger people in particular expressed in light of harsh societal reappraisals of Bill Clinton's behavior toward Monica Lewinsky and other women across the course of his political career (Dowd, 2018). Bill Clinton has often faced crises in his public standing and managed to recover handily, but at the age of seventy-two (compared to Obama's fifty-seven), this one felt like it contained a dash of irreparability.

Presidential legacies are mercurial things, going through unanticipated ups and downs that sometimes reveal as much about the changing state of America and Americans as they do about the presidents being evaluated. It is improbable that either Obama or Clinton will fall into the tiers of lowly-regarded presidents, and it seems likely that both of their legacies will come to be regarded as at least several cuts above the median. But if pressed for a prognostication, one suspects that the inheritance of the Obama legacy is better positioned to catch the winds of the American future—even if it first must pass through the doldrums of the Trump presidency, a far harsher crossing than George W. Bush's two terms were for emerging appraisals of Clinton. Perhaps Obama's openness to collaborating with Clinton will be enhanced by a sense of confidence that, although their ultimate standings are at the mercy of the currents of history, his own time horizon as an active curator of his own legacy likely will be longer, and bear fewer self-administered blemishes, than Clinton's. There are, of course, no guarantees. As Carlos Lozada has written: "Obama has written his paragraph. The fact that Trump gets to edit it suggests that the arc of history is indeed long, but any bend toward justice can prove merely coincidental" (Lozada, 2017).

References

ABC News. (2016, July 28). Full text: President Barack Obama's 2016 Democratic National Convention speech. *ABC News.* https://abcnews.go.com/Politics/full-text-president-barack-obamas-2016-democratic-national/story?id=40949231.

Abramowitz, M., Murray, S., & Kornblut, A. E. (2008, November 22). Obama close to naming Clinton and Gen. James Jones to key cabinet posts, sources say. *The Washington Post.* http://www.washingtonpost.com/wp-dyn/content/article/2008/11/21/AR2008112103981.html?noredirect=on.

Bacon, P. (2008, March 2). Campaigning in Ohio, Bill Clinton stays upbeat. *The Washington Post* at LexisNexis.

Balz, D. (2008a, September 15). The other Clinton is an absent presence. *The Washington Post* at LexisNexis.

Balz, D. (2008b, September 15). "Barack Obama is my candidate." *The Washington Post* at LexisNexis.

Balz, D. (2014a, June 29). The non-reinvention of Hillary Clinton. *The Washington Post* at LexisNexis.

Balz, D. (2014b, November 23). Democrats are ready when Clinton is. *The Washington Post* at LexisNexis.

Balz, D. (2016, August 21). Trump's turbulent week bumps Clinton's new issues. *The Washington Post* at LexisNexis.

Balz, D., & Rucker, P. (2012, September 6). Clinton lays out a stark choice. *The Washington Post* at LexisNexis.

Balz, D., & Rucker, P. (2014a, February 16). Democrats' next leaders will grapple with schism. *The Washington Post* at LexisNexis.

Balz, D., & Rucker, P. (2014b, September 13). Looking to 2016, Running from '08. *The Washington Post* at LexisNexis.

Barnes, R. (2008, October 13). Clintons join Biden to campaign for Obama in Scranton. *The Washington Post*.

Clement, S., & Craighill, P. (2014, May 29). Poll shows Clintons' popularity is strong. *The Washington Post* at: LexisNexis.

Cohen, R. (2008, April 29). Words heard differently. *The Washington Post*.

Cohen, R. (2013, December 31). Clinton's bad timing. *The Washington Post*.

Dionne, E. J. Jr. (2008, January 25). The ideas Bill forgot. *The Washington Post*.

Dionne, E. J. Jr. (2013, September 15). The Reagan model. *The Washington Post* at LexisNexis.

Dowd, M. (2018, November 2). Curtains for the Clintons. *The New York Times*.

Editorial Board. (2008, November 19). Secretary Clinton?: Sen. Hillary Rodham Clinton should get fair consideration, but Bill Clinton's role would have to change. *The Washington Post* at LexisNexis.

Ehrenfreund, M. (2017, July 11). Democrats' internal debates over white working class are coming to a head. *The Washington Post*.

Eilperin, J. (2014, August 13). Obama has spent little time preparing to pass the baton. *The Washington Post* at LexisNexis.

Eilperin, J. (2015, April 7). For president's loyalists, a chance to shape a legacy. *The Washington Post*.

Eilperin, J., & Thompson, K. (2017, January 21). Quietly moving on as another couple moves in. *The Washington Post*.

Fromer, Y. (2016, February 14). Radical today, mainstream tomorrow. *The Washington Post* at LexisNexis.

Gearan, A. (2015, January 20). Democrats fear Clinton has not learned all the lessons of her last failed campaign. *The Washington Post* at LexisNexis.

Gerson, M. (2016, July 31). A choice between the uninspiring and the unfit. *The Washington Post*.

Ginsburg, S. (2017, April 23). A quotidian telling of a dramatic collapse. *The Washington Post* at LexisNexis.

Gold, M., Helderman, R. S., & Narayanswamy, A. (2015, May 19). Clinton was paid by firms with a 2016 stake. *The Washington Post* at LexisNexis.

Goldfarb, Z. A. (2014, May 30). Hillary Clinton's new challenge: 1990s economy. *The Washington Post*.

Heilemann, J. (2012, October 14). Bill and Hillary forever. *New York Magazine*.

Ignatius, D. (2007, December 9). Hillary's ex factor: The "two presidents" issue isn't going away. *The Washington Post*.

Ignatius, D. (2017, May 5). How Democrats can do their part. *The Washington Post* at LexisNexis.

Kamen, A. (2007, February 23). A presidential candidate Bill Clinton can publicly embrace. *The Washington Post*.

Kornblut, A. E. (2008a, March 2). On the ground and in the air with the Democrats. *The Washington Post* at LexisNexis.

Kornblut, A. E. (2008b, April 23). Bill Clinton insists he is the victim. *The Washington Post*.

Kornblut, A. E. (2008c, August 3). Clinton embraces return to ambassador role: After the bitter primaries, he calls charity "my life." *The Washington Post*.

Kornblut, A. E. (2008d, August 8). Democratic aides working on plan to keep the peace at the convention. *The Washington Post*.

Kornblut, A. E., & MacGillis, A. (2007, December 22). Hillary Clinton embraces her husband's legacy. *The Washington Post*.

Kornblut, A. E., & Murray, S. (2008, January 12). Clintons move to ease some racial friction. *The Washington Post* at LexisNexis.

Kurtz, H. (2008, February 4). For Obama, a most congenial spot. *The Washington Post*.

Leibovich, M. (2012, Novermber 4). Voice is strained, but support on the trail unstinting. *The New York Times*.

Lerer, L. (2018, November 2). No one wants to campaign with Bill Clinton anymore. *The New York Times*.

Lozada, C. (2014, November 9). A daily rundown of the Obama years. *The Washington Post* at LexisNexis.

Lozada, C. (2017, September 15). Yes he did? *The Washington Post* at Lexis Nexis.

Maraniss, D. (2008a, August 27). Obama, Bill Clinton remain distant: Despite similar stories, a complex relationship. *The Washington Post*.

Maraniss, D. (2008b, August 28). Clinton, thinking about tomorrow. *The Washington Post*.

Maraniss, D. (2012, September 4). Bill Clinton, eagerly stepping in. *The Washington Post* at LexisNexis.

Maraniss, D. (2016a, May 1). The content of his presidency. *The Washington Post* at LexisNexis.

Maraniss, D. (2016b, July 28). Obama hands back a baton—and seeks to cement legacy. *The Washington Post* at LexisNexis.

Marcus, R. (2015, December 29). Trump is right: Bill is fair game. *The Washington Post*.

Milbank, D. (2012, September 6). Clinton takes spotlight—for a night. *The Washington Post* at LexisNexis.

Milbank, D. (2014, October 21). Barack Obama, the pariah president. *The Washington Post*.

Mosk, M., Grimaldi, J. V., & Stephens, J. (2008, April 5). Clintons earned $109 million in 8 years: Senator releases tax returns as part of presidential battle. *The Washington Post* at LexisNexis.

Mosk, M., & Stephens, J. (2008, November 22). A complex knot of conflicts: Husband's charity would raise issues for a Secretary Clinton. *The Washington Post*.

Murray, S. (2008a, January 6). In backing his wife, Clinton recalls his legacy, but New Hampshire voters may have outgrown even his outsized charm. *The Washington Post* at LexisNexis.

Murray, S. (2008b, June 25). Obama asks his top donors to help Clinton with debt. *The Washington Post*.

Murray, S., & Balz, D. (2008, June 28). New campaign for Democrats: Unity—Clinton, Obama take public step toward solidarity. *The Washington Post*.

No Author. (2012, September 21). Michelle Obama dishes on the president's "bromance" with Bill Clinton. *Access* at https://www.accessonline.com/articles/michelle-obama-dishes-on-the-presidents-bromance-with-bill-clinton-123366.

Pace, Julie. (2012, April 30). Once rivals, Obama and Bill Clinton teaming up. *The Washington Post* at LexisNexis.

Pappu, S. (2007, December 19). The Magic & Bill Show, providing the charisma assist. *The Washington Post*.

Parker, K. (2010, June 30). Our first female president. *The Washington Post*.

Parker, K. (2013, March 24). Hillary's time at last? *The Washington Post* at LexisNexis.

Phillip, A. (2016, February 16). Bill Clinton on campaign trail: A help and a headache. *The Washington Post* at LexisNexis.

Robinson, E. (2007, December 21). A problem like Bill. *The Washington Post*.

Robinson, E. (2008, January 22). What's gotten into Bill? *The Washington Post*.

Robinson, E. (2014, May 9). A transformational presidency. *The Washington Post*.

Romano, L. (2016, July 29). The quiet Clinton. *The Washington Post* at LexisNexis.

Rucker, P., & Goldfarb, Z. A. (2014, May 15). Clintons take on critics in GOP. *The Washington Post* at LexisNexis.

Rucker, P., & Kane, P. (2010, May 29). Bill Clinton has evolved into Obama's Mr. Fix It. *The Washington Post*.

Schultheis, E. (2016, June 29). Bill Clinton, AG Loretta Lynch meet on tarmac in Phoenix. CBSNews.com at LexisNexis.

Shear, M. D., & Rucker, P. (2008, November 17). One cabinet job would put focus on two Clintons: In ex-president's global reach, pluses, minuses for a wife at State. *The Washington Post* at LexisNexis.

Staff Writer. (2008, October 12). Va. Democrats' surprising plan: Call Bill Clinton—Once-shunned former president to shore up support for Obama. *The Washington Post* at LexisNexis.

Suarez, F. (2008, January 19). Clinton hits Obama on His Reagan comments. CBSNews.com at LexisNexis.

Thompson, K. (2017, March 2). Obamas sign an 8-figure book deal. *The Washington Post* at: LexisNexis.

Transcript. (2012, September 5). Transcript of Bill Clinton's speech to the Democratic National Convention. *The New York Times* at LexisNexis.

Tumulty, K. (2012, June 7). For Obama, a double-edged sword. *The Washington Post* at LexisNexis.

Tumulty, K. (2015, May 23). Clinton's management style under scrutiny. *The Washington Post* at LexisNexis.

Tumulty, K. (2016, May 23). Clinton finds voice in supporting role. *The Washington Post* at LexisNexis.

Tumulty, K. (2017, January 21). Obama hands off presidency—and burdens—to Trump. *The Washington Post* at LexisNexis.

Tumulty, K., & Rucker, P. (2015, October 25). Guess who's coming to dinner in Democratic battleground? *The Washington Post* at LexisNexis.

Walsh, J. (2012, November 5). "In the service of my president": Bill Clinton is campaigning tirelessly because a second Obama term cements his legacy—and rebukes racism. *Salon* at https://www.salon.com/2012/11/05/in_the_service_of_my_president/.

Weisman, J. (2008, July 1). Obama meets with Bill Clinton. *The Washington Post* at LexisNexis.

3

Barack Obama's Executive Orders

RAYMOND FREY

Introduction

The U.S. Constitution states that "all legislative powers" are the province of the Congress. The president, however, plays a prominent role in formulating public policy, which often resembles a legislative role. The chief executive has the power to veto any congressional legislation, and it does not become law unless a successful two-thirds vote by both houses of the legislature overrides it. In addition, legislation drafted by Congress is frequently the result of presidential influence to pass new laws (University of Groningen, 1991). But when Congress and the chief executive disagree on policy, the president has additional implied powers at his or her disposal: memoranda, proclamations, and executive orders.

These actions are not specified in the Constitution, but all presidents have used them. In the early twentieth century, the presidency of Theodore Roosevelt began a period of more frequent use of these unenumerated executive powers. University of Chicago presidential scholar William G. Howell noted that "the capacity to 'go it alone' is a key characteristic of the modern presidency" (Major, 2016).

When Barack Obama was a presidential candidate, he criticized the previous Bush administration for trying to bring more power into the executive branch in order to bypass Congress. After assuming office, and facing what presidential scholars called the "uncompromising opposition" of the Republican Party, Obama began to see it differently. He recalled the words of John F. Kennedy: "Many things can be done by the stroke of the presidential pen" (Major, 2016).

An executive memorandum is, in effect, an executive order. At times they are used to interpret legislation and establish precedent, or to advise federal agencies on how to act. Unlike executive orders, there is no established process for how a president can use or publish a presidential memorandum (Coble, 2017). President Obama used the executive memorandum more than four hundred times, the most notable being the Deferred Action for Childhood Arrivals (DACA), immigration policy, policies on federal gun control, and a clarification of the Fair Labor Standards Act on overtime rules (Percha, 2017).

Proclamations are announcements of policy from the president (Georgetown Law Library). Most presidential proclamations announce ceremonial events, such as Black History Month. Yet there is no clear line between an executive order and a proclamation (Penn State Law). Since proclamations generally address people outside of the government, they tend to be legally weaker than executive orders. Proclamations can be directed at the entire nation, as in the declaration of a federal holiday, or applied to specific individuals, as in the issuing of a presidential pardon. In 2016, President Obama issued a presidential proclamation on Martin Luther King Day, reminding Americans to "observe this day with appropriate civic, community, and service projects in honor of Dr. King" (Penn State Law). During his presidency, Obama issued 212 pardons to individuals.

An executive order is different from a law. Presidents have used executive orders to direct and manage government operations. Executive orders have much of the same power of a federal law, and are subject to Congress passing a new law to override an executive order, although the president retains the right to exercise his veto power (National Constitution Center, 2016). Unlike memoranda and proclamations, executive orders must be consecutively numbered and recorded in the Federal Register. Presidents Obama, Bush, and Clinton "all used executive orders most frequently to make changes related to government commissions, boards, or committees" (Bialik, 2017).

Presidential executive orders can be compared to written orders issued by the CEO of a corporation. The federal government's official website explains how an executive order is different from a law passed by Congress: "[P]residents use executive orders to direct and manage how the federal government operates." They are part of the chief executive's implied powers derived from Article II of the Constitution. This gives a president semi-legislative authority to use his or her discretion to enforce laws and manage national affairs. As the head of the executive branch and commander-in-chief of the armed forces, the president must ensure that the laws are "faithfully executed." As long as they are constitutional, executive orders have the full force of law, but none of the permanence (Cameron, 2019). Congress can pass a new law to override an executive order, but the president can veto it, making it subject to a congressional override. In addition, the U.S. Supreme Court has ruled that it has the authority to block an executive order if it determines that it exceeds the constitutional limits of presidential power, or addresses an issue more properly addressed by legislation. As with all branches of federal government, the Court can subject executive orders to judicial review, and overturn them if they are found to be unconstitutional (Murse, 2019).

In 2017, President Trump signed a "sweeping executive order" temporarily banning entry for refugees, including immigrants from seven mostly Muslim countries. This resulted in dozens of lawsuits from several states. Some states took the Trump administration to court, arguing that the immigration order "harms their economies and residents." (Kaleem, 2017). Some of the lower federal and state courts were successful in delaying or blocking the order, but a full interpretation of the constitutionality of Trump's executive action in this case ultimately needs be determined by the U.S. Supreme Court.

The ability of a president to issue executive orders raises some profound questions concerning the constitutional separation of powers. Some legal scholars have gone so far as to question the authority of a president to issue executive orders, as it seems to delegate Congress's legislative power to the executive branch. A case in point is President Kennedy's civil rights agenda. Early in his term, the president was convinced that Congress was not prepared to pass a comprehensive civil rights bill. In turn he tried to address the issue through a series of executive orders addressing discrimination in federal housing projects, establishing a Presidential Commission on Equal Employment Opportunity, and prohibiting discrimination in federally aided libraries and hospitals, among others. Presidential scholar Larry Berman noted that Kennedy's seeking to address racial discrimination through his "prerogative powers" had little overall effect. Not until a few years later, when civil rights became a national issue through the work of Martin Luther King Jr. and the Freedom Riders, was Congress ready to act (Berman, 1986). Additionally, a future president can cancel a predecessor's executive orders. On his second day in office, President Obama signed an executive order revoking President George W. Bush's order that allowed the use of "waterboarding" by the CIA to gain information from suspects (Cameron, 2019).

On January 21, 2009, one day after being sworn in as the forty-fourth President of the United States, Barack Obama signed Executive Order 13489. Like many presidents before him, Obama used his early executive orders to reinforce the fundamental philosophies of his campaign platform. This first order established a new process for handling claims of executive privilege on records of present or former presidents (Brown Political Review, 2014). It revoked an executive order issued by President George W. Bush, which placed restrictions on access to presidential records. Some political pundits claimed that Obama's intent was to conceal some of his own records from public view, such as his controversial birth certificate, after he left office. Obama explained that his action "was consistent with pledges he had made as a presidential candidate to conduct an open administration" (Rozell & Sollenberger, 2015).

In his first one hundred days in the White House, President Obama signed nineteen executive orders. Among the orders was a review of individuals retained at the Guantanamo Bay Naval Base and the possible closure of the facility, ensuring lawful interrogations, the establishment of a White House Office of Urban Affairs, removing barriers to responsible scientific research involving human stem cells, and the establishment of the White House Office of Health Reform. There were also four executive orders revising or amending previous executive orders, and the revocation of "Certain Executive Orders Concerning Regulatory Planning and Review" (Guzman, 2017). On average, President Obama issued fewer executive orders per year than any U.S. president since Grover Cleveland. He issued 277 executive orders in all, averaging thirty-five per year. In comparison, Franklin Delano Roosevelt averaged 307 executive orders per year, and Harry S. Truman averaged 117. Obama ranked sixteenth among presidents in total number of executive orders issued (Bialik, 2017).

In his second term, frustrated by Republican opposition in Congress, Obama accelerated his use of executive actions to carry out his agenda. "I've got a pen and I've got a phone," he declared (Fox News, 2016). In 2014, Speaker of the House John Boehner told reporters that he was considering suing President Obama over his use of executive actions (CNN, 2014). Conservative Republican lawmakers argued that Obama had "overstepped his authority," and was "breaching his constitutional power by side-stepping the legislative process" (CNN, 2014). They cited an executive order directing the Department of Labor to extend family leave to same-sex couples, and another order that would raise the minimum wage for federal contractors (CNN, 2014). In response, the Republican-controlled House of Representatives passed two bills attempting to limit Obama's use of executive orders; neither was taken up by the Democrat-controlled Senate (CNN, 2014).

Using executive orders when faced with an uncooperative legislature, Obama was acting no differently from many chief executives before him who needed to get things done. As the clouds of war gathered over Europe, Franklin Roosevelt, on September 8, 1939, proclaimed a "limited national emergency" enabling him to authorize the transfer of fifty mothballed destroyers to Great Britain, in exchange for leasing rights to British military bases and possessions (Berman, 1986, p. 65). This flew in the face of 1930's Neutrality Acts, passed by Congress to limit U.S. involvement in future wars. Having won the support and trust of the majority of Americans, FDR continued to use executive orders, proclamations, and memoranda to carry out what he believed was his implied constitutional authority and responsibility—to mobilize America for war. Likewise, Obama, dealing with a gridlocked government, took his case to the people through proclamations and executive orders. He faced the same criticisms that FDR did, from those who saw it as an abuse of power. Lincoln, FDR, and Obama would most likely respond that it shows the flexibility of the Constitution when the country is confronted with issues, problems, and threats that need immediate action.

Most presidential executive orders deal with mundane or procedural issues and attract little public attention. At times, however, an executive order can usher in sweeping changes and affect millions of Americans. On February 19, 1942, President Roosevelt issued Executive Order 9066, which gave the United States broad military powers to relocate and intern hundreds of thousands of American citizens of Japanese ancestry living on the West Coast of the United States (History Matters, NDa). The order was challenged in the U.S. Supreme Court case *Korematsu v. United States*. In 1944, the Court ruled that the president had the right to order the relocation of American citizens in the event of a wartime emergency (History Matters, NDb).

In the spring of 1952, while American troops were mired in the cold and mud in Korea, the United States faced a major strike by steel mill workers. After considering several legal alternatives, including the activation of the Taft-Hartley Act (which Truman felt only applied in peacetime situations), and after last-minute efforts to end the strike ultimately failed, the president issued Executive Order 10340, directing the secretary of commerce to take federal possession of the privately owned steel mills and keep them running (Constitutional Rights Foundation). On June 2, 1952, the Supreme Court ruled that Truman's seizure order was unconstitutional, arguing that the president did not have the power to seize private property without authorization from Congress; and that Truman was, in effect, "making law," which exceeded his constitutional authority (Constitutional Rights Foundation).

By 2010, President Obama was increasingly facing pressure to implement immigration reforms. Throughout most of his first term, he insisted to supporters that he did not have the constitutional authority, as president, to change the immigration laws by executive order. In 2011, he reiterated that with "respect to the notion that I can just suspend deportations through executive order, that's just not the case." He further acknowledged that he could not "bypass Congress and change the law myself . . . that's not how democracy works" (Von Spakovshy, 2017). But in June 2012, Obama changed his mind. Frustrated with congressional inaction, and uncertain whether he had the authority to change the current law, he went ahead and issued an executive memorandum to shield millions of undocumented immigrants from deportation. The use of a memorandum rather than an executive order was deliberate, because an executive order would have required the president to cite a specific constitutional authority or power (National Constitution Center, 2017).

Obama was hoping that a future president would not want to face the criticism of reversing his decision. He defended his action by saying that it was not his intent to overreach his authority. "In the absence of any immigration action from Congress to fix our broken immigration system," he explained, "what we've tried to do is focus our immigration resources in the right places" (Greenberg, 2018). He admitted that this would not be a permanent fix, and that Congress should move to pass the Development, Relief, and Education for Alien Minors Act, popularly known as the "DREAM" Act. In November 2015, the U.S. Circuit Court of Appeals blocked the Obama memorandum. Thus, the core policy initiative of his administration was struck down. Its ultimate fate would now be decided by his presidential successor.

The 2,136 official signed statements by President Obama—memoranda, proclamations, and executive orders—have the force of law, unless repealed by another president (Cameron, 2019). In many cases, Obama deftly made use of memoranda to influence policy in subtle ways. By reinterpreting existing laws rather than appearing to legislate from the Oval Office, Obama could inform and suggest how federal agencies could creatively approach and implement certain policy decisions. Presidential researcher Kenneth S. Lowande, who made a careful study of Obama's executive actions, said, "I think he was pretty aggressive in thinking about ways you could apply old laws to new situations and extract the last ounce of presidential preference out of prior laws" (Cameron, 2019).

In a way, especially concerning the DACA immigration issue, Obama's use of the executive order is reminiscent of its use by Abraham Lincoln. Article 2, Section 3 of the U.S. Constitution states that it is the president's responsibility to "take care that the laws be faithfully executed." Lincoln interpreted this "Take Care Clause" to mean that he was authorized to issue the Emancipation Proclamation (Chambers, 2013). Even though it essentially ignored legislation regarding slaves and slavery passed by Congress after the beginning of the Civil War, Lincoln cited the "crisis of slavery" and the need to eradicate it to be a "necessary and proper" use of his executive power. Similarly, the "crisis of immigration" spurred Obama to risk a constitutional confrontation to carry out the spirit of the laws if Congress would not act. Obama's action was subsequently overturned.

The confrontation Obama was expecting through his aggressive executive actions came not from the U.S. Supreme Court, but from Republicans in the House of Representatives, who were preparing to use the Constitution's "Take Care Clause" against him. In committee hearings, they crafted an argument that claimed that Obama had failed to "faithfully execute" laws in three major areas: waivers to the No Child Left Behind education law, the delay of the employer mandate in the Obamacare legislation, and the blocking of deportations for the children of unauthorized immigrants (Prokop, 2014). But Obama remained defiant. "Where Congress is unwilling to act," he said, "I will take whatever administrative steps that I can in order to do right by the American people" (Prokop, 2014). On July 30, 2014, Republican speaker of the house John Boehner made good on his threat and initiated a lawsuit against the president over the Affordable Care Act, claiming that Obama was deliberately delaying the payment of subsidies to private medical insurers as required by the new law. The U.S. District Court for the District of Columbia ruled that the House could proceed with the lawsuit, but later decided that the House of Representatives could not sue the executive branch (Ballotpedia). Like Lincoln before him, President Obama pushed the implied powers of the executive branch into new and uncharted constitutional waters.

Barack Obama's ambitious agenda was blocked by Congress for most of his two terms in office. In his mind, he had no choice except to use the implied executive power that his predecessors such as Lincoln and Theodore Roosevelt exercised. "Once Mr. Obama got the taste for it," a *New York Times* article stated, "he pursued his executive power without apology, and in ways that will shape the presidency for decades to come" (Appelbaum & Shear, 2016).

Recent presidents, including Barack Obama, have begun their first day in office by canceling some of their predecessor's orders. Early in his campaign, candidate Donald Trump said he would reverse all of Obama's "unconstitutional" executive orders (Cameron, 2019). Once he became president, Trump wasted no time in commencing to reverse Obama's policies "with a vehemence and an order of magnitude that is different from previous modern administrations," wrote a reporter for the *Boston Globe* (McGrane, 2017). On Inauguration Day, January 20, 2017, the new president's first executive order was to "minimize the economic burden" of the Affordable Care Act (Quingle, 2017). Three days later, Trump issued a presidential memorandum prohibiting government agencies from hiring any new employees, except for the military, national security, or public safety needs. The following day, another executive order "directed the Chairman of the White House Council on Environmental Quality to create expedited procedures and deadlines for environmental reviews and approvals for high-priority infrastructure projects" (Quingle, 2017). These executive orders were quickly followed by a series of new orders—directing the secretary of homeland security to begin planning, designing and constructing a wall along the U.S.-Mexico border, the pursuit of undocumented immigrants, the hiring additional immigration officers, and reevaluation of visa and refugee programs (rescinded March 6) (Quingle, 2017).

During the presidential debates with Hillary Clinton, candidate Trump promised "to unravel Obama's accomplishments" (Smith, 2018). Clearly, Trump was obsessed with tearing down Obama's legacy as chief executive. It seemed more than just him taking the nation in a new direction; it was also personal.

Before Barack Obama left the Oval Office, he offered his successor some presidential advice: pursue policy changes through Congress, not by executive orders. "Going through the legislative process is always better, in part because it's harder to undo," he told the president-elect (Fox News, 2016). If he wants to reverse some of those rules, that's part of the democratic process. "That's, you know, why I tell people to vote—because it turns out elections mean something" (Detrow, 2016).

What will be the legacy of Barack Obama's executive actions? Although as with most presidents, the majority of executive orders and memorandums were part of the routine business of governing the country, Obama's executive orders addressing greater inclusiveness for LBGT Americans, gun control, climate change, and immigration will be long remembered for improving the lives of all Americans.

References

Appelbaum, B., & Shear, M. D. (2016, August 13). Once skeptical of executive power, Obama has come to embrace it. *New York Times.* https://www.nytimes.com/2016/08/14/us/politics/obama-era-legacy-regulation.html.

Bialik, K. (2017, January 23). Obama issued fewer executive orders on average than any president since Cleveland. Pew Research Center. http://www.pewresearch.org/fact-tank/2017/01/23/obaba-executive-orders/.

Ballotpedia. Boehner's lawsuit against the Obama administration. Ballotpedia.org. https//ballotpedia.org/Boehner%27slawsuit-against-the-Obama-administration.

Berman, L. (1986). *The new American presidency.* Little, Brown.

Brown Political Review. (2014, February 28). Executive privilege, politics, and the separation of powers. *Brown Political Review.* http://www.brownpoliticalreview.org/tag/executive-order-13489/.

Cameron, D. (2019, January 31). What President Obama's executive actions mean for President Trump. *Washington Post.* https://www.washingtonpost.com/graphics/politics/executive-action/.

Chambers, H. L. Jr. (2013). Lincoln, The Emancipation Proclamation, and executive power. 73 Md.L.Rev.100.

Constitutional Rights Foundation. Seizure! Truman takes the steel mills. CRFUSA.org. http://www.crf-usa.org/bill-of-rights-in-action/bia-4-4-b-seizure-truman-takes-the-steel-mills.html.

CNN. (2014, June 24). Boehner plans lawsuit over executive orders. CNN.com. http://policalticker.blogs.com/2014/06/24/boehner-considering-lawsuit-against-obama-over-executive-orders/.

Coble, C. (2017). What's the difference between executive orders, memoranda, and proclamations, legally speaking? Findlaw.com. https://blogs.findlaw.

com/law_and_life/2017/01/whats-the-difference-between-executive-orders-memoranda-and proclamations-legally-speaking.html.

Detrow, S. (2016, December 19). Obama warns Trump against relying on executive power. *National Public Radio*. htpps://www.npr.org/2016/12/19/505860058/obama-warns-trump-against-relying-on-executive-power.

Fleishman, J. L., & Aufes, A. H. (1976, Summer). Law and orders: The problem of presidential legislation. *Law and Contemporary Problems, 40*(5).

Fox News. (2016, December 20). Obama's advice to Trump: Maybe don't use executive orders so much. Foxnews.com. https://www.foxnews.com/politics/obamas-advice-to-trump-maybe-dont-use-executive-orders-so-much.

Georgetown Law Library. Presidential Guides. http://guides.ll.georgetown.edu/c.php?g=365454&p=2468883.

Greenberg, J. (2018, January 9). Did Obama say he didn't have the right to issue DACA? Politifact.com. https://www.politifact.com/truth-o-meter/statements/2018/jan/09/Donald-trump/obama-hedged-didnt-say-he-lacked-legal-right-daca/.

Guzman, N. (2017, January 25). How many executive orders did Obama issue in his first 100 days? Donald Trump might outpace him. Bustle.com. https://www.bustle.com/p/ how-many-executive-orders-did-obama-issue-in-his-first-100-days-donald-trump-might-outpace-him-33176.

History Matters. (NDa). Executive Order 9066: The president authorizes Japanese relocation. Historymatters.gmu. http://historymatters.gmu.edu/d/5154.

History Matters. (NDb). *Korematsu v. United States*: The U.S. Supreme Court upholds internment. History Matters.gmu. http://historymatters.gmu,edu/d/5151.

Kaleem, J. (2017, February 6). Dozens of suits have been filed against Trump's sweeping travel ban. Here are the most important ones. *Washington Times*. https://www.latimes.com/nation/la-na-trump-travel-ban-story-so-far-20170206-story.html.

Major, M. (2016, October 17). How does Obama's use of unilateral powers compare to other presidents? *The Conversation*. http://the conversation.com/how-does-obamas-use-of-unilateral-powers-compare-to-other-presidents-65773.

McGrane, V. (2016, December 16). Trump's greatest mission: Erasing Obama's legacy. *Boston Globe*. https://www.bostonglobe.com/news/nation/2017/12/16/trump-greatest-mission-erasing-obama-legacy/OA9M4qwS2hHlOj3MGLxGxK/story.html.

Murse, T. (2019, January 26). President Obama's first executive order. Thought Co. http://www.thoughtco.com/president-obamas-first-executive-order-3322189.

National Constitution Center. (2016, August 5). President Obama's use of executive orders in historical terms. https://constitutioncenter.org/blog/president-obamas-use-of-executive-orders-in-historical-terms.

National Constitutional Center. (2017, January 23). Executive Orders 101: What are they and how do presidents use them? https://constitutioncenter.org/blog/executive-orders-101-what-are-they-and-how-do-presidents-use-them/.

Penn Sate Law. Presidential proclamations: Questions and answers. Center for Immigrants' Rights Clinic. https://pennstatelaw.psu.edu/sites/default/files/Proclamations%20Memo%20Final.pdf.

Percha, J. (2017, January 27). Your cheat sheet for executive orders, memorandums, and proclamations. PBS News Hour. https://www.pbs.org/newshour/politics/cheat-sheet-executive-orders-memorandums-proclamations.

Prokop, A. (2014, September 9). How Barack Obama is expanding presidential power—And what it means for the future. Vox.com. ttps://www.vox.com/2014/9/9/5964421/obama-lawsuit-republicans-abuse-of-power.

Quingle, A. (2017, March 8). All of Trump's major executive actions so far. *Politico*. https://politico.com/agenda/story/2017/01/all-trump-execytuve-actions-000288.

Rozell, M. J., & Sollenberger, M. A. (2015). Presidents: Executive privilege. In *Encyclopedia of public administration and public policy*. 3rd edition. Taylor & Francis.

Smith, D. (2018, May 11). The anti-Obama: Trump's drive to destroy his predecessor's legacy. *The Guardian*. https://www.the guardian.com/us/news/2018/may11/donald-trump-barack-obama-legacy.

University of Groningen. (1991). American revolution from Revolution to Reconstruction. "Presidential Powers." http//www.let.rug.nl/usa/outlines/government-1991/the-executive-branch-powers-of-the-presidency/presidential-powers.php.

Von Spakovshy, H. A. (2017, September 8). DACA is unconstitutional, as Obama admitted. Heritage Foundation.org. https://www.heritage.org/immigration/commentary/daca-unconstitutional-obama-admitted.

4

Obama, Party Leadership, and Domestic Elections

TOM LANSFORD

Introduction

Barack Obama's election was a transformational event. However, his presidency failed to transform the essential nature of U.S. politics, outside of the healthcare reform that unofficially carried his name. Elected with a massive mandate after a campaign that promised "hope and change," Obama was unable to secure his major legislative goals after 2010, following a series of electoral reverses. Although Democrats secured control of the White House and both houses of Congress in 2008, Republicans reclaimed the House in 2010 and held the chamber for the remainder of Obama's presidency. The GOP also gained a majority in the Senate in 2014. Republicans had even greater success at the state and local level. By the time Obama left office in 2017, Democrats had lost approximately 1,030 seats at the local, state, and federal levels.

Obama moved the national Democratic Party to the political left and embraced policy positions that resonated with the party's left wing, while distancing his presidency from centrist Democrats, especially rural voters. Moderate Democratic officeholders, including Southern Blue Dog Democrats and suburban centrists, found themselves increasingly isolated and vulnerable to Republicans at the ballot box as the White House abandoned attempts to capture the political center of the nation. Instead, the administration seemed to believe that it could move that center to the left. Concurrently, progressive Democrats became increasingly critical of Obama for not moving even farther to the left and chastised the president for not being more bold and assertive in policy formulation and implementation.

The trends reflected the rising partisanship in U.S. politics, especially at the federal level. Obama remained fiercely popular among one portion of the U.S. population, but reviled by another, while a third group admired the president without embracing many of his policy aims. Meanwhile, Republicans enhanced their electoral successes through effective gerrymandering following the 2010 midterm elections and campaigns that solidified their ascendency in the South and highlighted renewed competitiveness in the Midwest and Rust Belt. This combination of factors resulted in a presidency that struggled to achieve its legislative agenda after 2010, as it was hamstrung by significant party losses both in Congress and at the state level. Ultimately, Obama left office with a significantly weakened Democratic Party, at the federal, state, and local levels.

The Obama-era Elections

It is difficult to overstate the weight of Obama's 2008 victory. Democrats enhanced their control in both houses of Congress, including securing a filibuster-proof majority in the Senate for the first time since 1937 after Pennsylvania Senator Arlen Spector switched parties in April 2009. Indeed, the success of the party in the 2008 balloting, made its later losses all the more significant. In the 2010 midterms, Democrats lost sixty-three seats in the House, six Senate seats, six governorships, and its total control of state legislatures fell from to twenty-seven to sixteen. After the balloting, Republicans controlled 242 seats in the House to 193 for the Democrats. In addition, Republicans gained control of an additional nineteen state legislative chambers, bringing their total to fifty-four of the ninety-nine total.

Historically, the party in power loses seats in the midterm. The Democratic losses in 2010 were historic. For instance, the University of Virginia's Center for Politics reported that Republicans received 51.7 percent of the House vote, securing 42,672,135 votes to 36,581,023 (44.9 percent) for the Democrats (Sabato, 2010a). The Center also found that after the elections, Republicans held 53.7 percent of all state legislative seats (3,890), the highest number for the party since 1954, compared with 46.3 percent for the Democrats (3,374), the lowest number for that party since 1946 (Sabato, 2010a). The reversals prompted the president to admit that the party took a "shellacking."

In the 2012 balloting, on November 6, Obama was reelected with 51.1 percent of the vote, while his Republican opponent, former Massachusetts governor Mitt Romney, secured 47.2 percent. In the House, Democrats gained an additional eight seats, bringing their number up to 201, compared with 234 for the GOP. Significantly, Democratic House candidates won 48.8 percent of the vote, to 47.6 percent for Republicans. In the Senate, Democrats won two additional seats, bringing their total to fifty-three. Republicans secured one additional governorship, for a total of thirty, to nineteen for the Democrats (with one independent). Among state legislatures, Democrats regained eight of the chambers they lost in 2010. Republicans won control of the Arkansas legislature, giving the party control of all legislative chambers in the South for the first time since Reconstruction, and picked up other chambers, including the Wisconsin Senate, so that the net gain for the Democrats was only five chambers. Democratic results were in line with past elections when incumbents were reelected.

The 2014 midterms provided the Democrats with another series of significant defeats. In that balloting, the Republicans regained control of the Senate for the first time since 2006. The party won an additional nine seats, with 51.7 percent of the popular vote to 43.8 percent for the Democrats. The incoming 114th Congress had fifty-four Republican senators, with forty-four Democrats and two independents that caucused with the Democrats. In the House, the GOP added thirteen seats to its majority (247 seats). Democrats fell from 201 seats to 188. In the elections, Republican House candidates secured 51.2 percent of the vote to 45.5 percent for the Democrats. In gubernatorial races, Republicans secured two additional posts (thirty-one state governorships), with 50.3 percent of the overall vote, to 46.2 percent for Democrats (eighteen governorships). There was one independent governor, Bill Walker of Alaska. Among state legislatures, Republicans gained eleven chambers, bringing their total to sixty-eight of ninety-nine, including two legislative bodies in New York and Washington where the GOP ruled through a coalition with other parties. Democrats held fewer state chambers than at any time since 1860.

Autopsies on the Losses

Presidential scholars, political pundits, Obama, and leaders in the Democratic Party offered a range and variety of explanations and rationales for the 2010 and 2014 losses, and the inability of the party to replicate its 2008 success in 2012 when Obama again headed the ticket. Republicans asserted that they were able to nationalize the voting, with GOP candidates running against their Democratic rivals, against Obama, and, in some cases, polarizing figures such as Nancy Pelosi, the Democratic Speaker of the House or Harry Reid, the Senate Majority leader, both of whom had very low public approval ratings. For instance, Pelosi's approval rating was just 29 percent on the eve of the 2010 balloting, while Reid's was 36 percent. Approval of Congress itself hovered near 20 percent, prompting assertions that the 2010 balloting was really just an anti-incumbency election. However, only two Republican incumbents in the House lost their seats in the polling, thereby undermining that anti-incumbency argument.

As noted, the party in power in the White House traditionally loses seats in Congress and at the state level during midterm balloting. Ronald Brownstein argued strongly in an essay in the *Atlantic* that Democratic reversals under Obama were generally in line with historical precedents. Brownstein contended that the best way to judge a president's electoral impact on his party is to compare seat distribution before the chief executive enters office and in the last election in which he leaves office, in this case, the 2006 polling and 2016 (Brownstein, 2017). The author noted that when Obama left office, the Democrats had "39 fewer House seats (233 to 194), three fewer Senate seats (51 to 48), and 12 fewer governorships (28 to 16). . . . Those losses are formidable, but hardly unique" (Brownstein, 2017). However, Brownstein failed to adequately address the substantial losses by the party at the state level and likely overestimated the importance of Obama's legacy on the 2016 balloting. As Jay Cost (2016) noted, "[D]uring the postwar era, no two-term president has lost more U.S. House seats and state legislative seats than Obama." Why? What factors led to the dramatic legislative losses suffered by Democrats? Especially given that Obama remained personally popular. His average approval rating in 2018 was third among recent presidents, behind John F. Kennedy and Ronald Reagan, but ahead of Bill Clinton and George H. W. Bush (UVA Center for Politics, 2018).

Party Leadership and the Permanent Campaign

Modern presidents serve as the face of their party and its titular head. Successful or popular chief executives typically provide coattails for their respective parties to gain seats at all levels of government during presidential elections. In election years, presidents become campaigners-in-chief and fundraisers-in-chief. They set national goals and messages and become the focal points of campaigns, as midterm or off-year elections often serve as referendums on their presidency. Presidents can also be used to rally the electoral base and serve as a focal point to raise money for the party or for individual candidates. One result has been the emergence of the "permanent campaign" whereby one of the key functions of the White House is to continuously provide electoral assistance to the party and to ensure a nexus between policy, official statements and functions, and electoral strategy (see Blumenthal, 1980 or Corrado & Tenpas, 2004).

The Obama White House ran a highly effective permanent campaign, but it was an effort that focused on the reelection of the president, not building the party. In this effort, the campaign emphasized Obama's personality and personal popularity more than his record, a tactic that can be highly effective, as personality often matters more to voters (see Popkin, 1994). However, this emphasis on presidential popularity can leave congressional and state candidates with little in terms of policy accomplishments upon which to campaign.

In writing about the 2012 election, John Dickerson noted that Obama "won because he ran a permanent campaign, keeping his offices open in the battleground states from his 2008 campaign, tending his coalition assiduously" (Dickerson, 2012). Indeed, some Democrats were highly critical of Obama's campaign organizations, Obama for America (2008 OFA) and the Organization for America (2012 OFA), because those bodies focused intensely on the election and reelection of the president, but not on broader efforts to elect Democrats at the state level. Senior party members charged that the groups became a "shadow party because Obama operatives had no faith in state parties" (Debenedetti, 2017). Even during the 2008 cycle, Democrats charged that the Obama campaign did little to raise funds for party candidates at all levels and that the 2008 OFA often failed to coordinate with party campaigns on matters as central as Obama's appearances in districts or efforts to develop joint statements on issues (Bresnahan, 2008). In a *Politico* article, John

Bresnahan (2008) quoted a senior Democratic staffer who declared that at the time the Obama campaign "think[s] they know what's right and everyone else is wrong on everything. . . . They are kind of insufferable at this point." Obama developed a significant fundraising advantage over his 2008 opponent, Arizona Senator John McCain. The Obama campaign raised more than $778 billion, while McCain took in over $383 billion. Some Democratic candidates would charge that Obama's success in 2008, and later in 2012, starved down-ballot efforts, especially at the state level.

The Obama campaign organizations centralized campaign funds. Some state and local Democratic leaders maintained that the two OFAs specifically deprived state parties of resources in order to bolster Obama's electoral efforts in 2008 and 2012 (Debenedetti, 2017). One result was that the 2012 OFA overtook the Democratic National Committee (DNC) as the president's main campaign vehicle, relegating the DNC to a minor role in the 2012 balloting.

The strategy reflected a desire on the part of the White House to tightly control the messages and themes of the 2012 election and to highly centralize the campaign. The Obama campaign also believed that it was much more efficient at fundraising and better able to secure dollars from small donors. Ryan Grin (2017) contended that "Obama . . . reasoned that he could become the party, his dynamic and charismatic personality carrying it at the national level" and building the kind of coalition that brought the party its massive gains in 2008. Obama's personal popularity, especially among the base, was seen by his senior campaign staff as the party's best asset to bolster turnout and cement a more urban coalition in both midterm and presidential balloting.

The Economist argued in a 2008 editorial that "Obama owe[d] his victory to blacks, Hispanics, the young, women of all ages, the poor, and the very rich" (*The Economist*, 2008). Following the massive Democratic wave of 2008, predications were that demographics were on the side of Obama's coalition, which was on its way to creating a permanent Democratic majority. But the coalition that elected Obama developed in support of the former Illinois senator and not specifically to back the Democratic Party. When Obama was not on the ballot, Republicans proved highly competitive between 2010 and 2018.

Obama was not a candidate in 2010 and 2014, and the OFA proved incapable of coordinating a strong campaign in the midterm balloting because of a lack of state and local infrastructure. In addition, state party officials in battleground states often clashed with the White House over strategy and resources. This rift accelerated in the 2014 balloting and would impact the party in 2016. Grin argued that the problems that emerged with the DNC in the 2016 polling were the result of its marginalization in the 2008 and 2012 elections and the legacy of the 2012 OFA (Grin, 2017).

Policy Versus Process

In reflecting on the 2010 balloting, Obama and his closest advisors contended, at least publicly, that the losses reflected the president's failure to transform politics at the federal level. After campaigning on "Hope and Change," Obama and his aides pursued policy in much the same manner as previous administrations. Thus, the president declared that "we were in such a hurry to get things done that we didn't change how things got done . . . that frustrated people" (Obama, 2010). Obama lamented that he had not made more of an effort to cooperate with Republicans or cultivated a better relationship with the business community, and pledged not to spend the remainder of his term "refighting the political battles of the last two [years]" (Obama, 2010). However, the next six years would be exactly that.

By the time Obama left office, the partisan divide in the United States was at its highest level in almost seventy years. At the end of his second term, Obama's partisan approval gap (the difference between support from Republicans and Democrats) was 73 percent, compared to 54 percent for George W. Bush, 50 percent for Clinton, 59 percent for George H. W. Bush, and 55 percent for Reagan (Pew Research Center, 2016). Obama certainly was not solely at fault for the rise in partisanship. Republicans framed much of their electoral campaigns in opposition to Obama and his policies.

Obama made a strategic decision not to move to the political center after the 2010 balloting, unlike Clinton, whose 1994 losses prompted a dramatic recalculation of his political priorities (Jacobson, 1996). Instead, after his reelection in 2008, Obama's second inaugural address emphasized overtly partisan themes, ranging from immigration to gun rights, in what columnist E. J. Dionne called a "combative" and "unapologetic" speech and one that made "a case for a progressive view of government" (Dionne, 2013). This contrasted sharply with Obama's first inaugural address which emphasized bipartisanship and unity (Neal, 2018, p. 46). Obama's second term would be marked by an even greater rise in partisanship, especially after the 2014 balloting as both parties moved farther away from the center. Obama's partisanship reflected what Morris

Fiorina (2018) described as "sorting," a top-down process by which the two parties moved away from efforts to be "big tent" organizations, and instead focused on alignment with their political class—"office seekers, donors, party and issue activists, and partisan media commentators." These were groups that continued to rate Obama very highly, even as the electorate rewarded the Republicans.

Republicans routinely charged, fairly or unfairly, that they were shut out of the policymaking process. Just as Obama did not particularly enjoy or engage in political wrangling with Democrats, he was even less inclined to work with Republicans if he could avoid it. Moderate Republicans complained that the president did not reach out to them, but White House officials argued that Republicans presented a fairly united front in refusing to work with the president. This provided the GOP with an ability to blame Obama and congressional Democrats for unpopular policies. Obama and Democrats charged Republicans were simply obstructionist and unwilling to compromise on any point. The result was that Obama increasingly turned to the use of executive actions, instead of trying to negotiate or cut deals with GOP leaders on the Hill. Speaking about unilateral executive action, Republican Senator John Thune of South Dakota uttered these prophetic words in 2016: Obama's "power and authority will be increasingly marginalized, because anything he does on the executive or regulatory side will last less than a year" (Everett & Sherman, 2016). Thune's comments proved fairly accurate following the election of Donald Trump in 2016 and the rollback of many of Obama's executive actions.

Party Building and Congress

Obama and his administration also faced criticism over relations between the White House and Congress. Many congressional Democrats asserted that Obama remained aloof and unwilling to engage in the politicking usually associated with chief executives. A succession of articles and editorials highlighted the vexation congressional Democrats felt throughout Obama's tenure. For instance, in a 2011 editorial entitled "Obama's Aloofness Irks Democrats," *Investor's Business Daily* declared that the president's "aloofness is frustrating members of his own party and staff" and quoted California senator Dianne Feinstein that "one of the problems with the White House is that it's been too set apart. It needs to get out" (*Investor's Business Daily*, 2011). Writing in the *Atlantic* in 2016,

George E. Condon Jr. noted that Obama's "dealings with Congress over the past seven years have bred few affectionate memories" (Condon, 2016). Stephanie Kirchgaessner, in an article in the *Financial Times* in 2013, analyzed how the president's unwillingness to engage in personal politicking had endangered both his legislative agenda and his legacy (Kirchgaessner, 2013).

At the electoral level, congressional Democrats routinely complained about the lack of support the White House provided for their campaigns. Jake Tapper noted in July 2010 that "after months of growing frustration, Congressional Democratic leaders exploded this week, saying the president isn't giving them the support they need ahead of the coming mid-term elections, despite their tough work on his behalf" (Tapper, 2010). Tapper further relates a common irritation among congressional Democrats that the president often "hog[ged] credit for their work" (Tapper, 2010), reflecting a sense among some that Obama held himself above the normal, and often ugly, partisan wrangling in Congress, but then sought to claim any accolades that resulted from policy victories or developments. One ramification was that Democratic members of Congress had a hard time conveying to constituents the importance of the roles they played in achieving legislative victories or, later, in blocking Republican efforts. This, in turn, weakened their reelection bids.

Party Building and Policy

Congressional Democrats also voiced concern over their lack of inclusion in policy development and formulation on various issues. For example, House Democrats complained bitterly about Obama's 2011 budget deal with Republican leaders in the chamber. That agreement raised the debt ceiling, but cut federal spending by $38.5 billion. Henry Cuellar, Democratic House member from Texas, and vice chair of the party's Steering and Policy Committee in that chamber, declared that "a lot of us feel like we're almost being ignored" by the White House during such policy negotiations (Lillis, 2011). On multiple other occasions, Democrats again criticized the president. In 2014, Democrats joined with Republicans to question the administration's policy toward the growing threat from the Islamic State and chided the president for being "too cautious" in his reaction to Russian aggression in Ukraine (Shalal, 2014). At the same time, more progressive Democrats criticized Obama for being too timid on policy and not moving more to the left. In an essay on the debate over Obama's legacy, T. A. Frank argued that when faced with policy choices between centrist Democrats and progressives in the party, "it was predictable that Obama, when forced to choose, would side with the establishment" (Frank, 2019).

To some extent, the criticism of Obama not working with Democrats on the Hill reflects the normal degree of disenchantment that builds between a chief executive and his party. Especially during periods of divided government, which Obama faced from 2011 until the end of his term, presidents must craft deals with the opposition that may not completely integrate the priorities of the chief executive's party. George W. Bush faced criticism from his party for working with Democrats in an ill-fated effort at immigration reform. Bill Clinton angered Democrats on the Hill for his 1998 budget deal with Republicans, among other examples (Galvin, 2009). However, the degree to which congressional Democrats perceived the White House to be aloof and unresponsive to their priorities seemed to go beyond past instances of friction. Especially troublesome for party building were the instances when moderate Democrats perceived that their concerns were not fully appreciated by the White House. This sentiment was echoed by moderate to conservative Democrats at the state level who increasingly believed the party was moving too far to the left for their constituents.

As noted, the Obama tenure was highlighted by dramatic losses by Democrats in the South and Midwest, especially in states such as West Virginia and Wisconsin. These reversals for the president reflected broader shifts in party alignment, especially in the South, which came under GOP dominance (although the Obama era also witnessed an acceleration of the decline of the New England Republican). Republicans in 2010 were able to nationalize the election and turn it into a referendum on the Obama presidency to that point. Some Democrats endeavored, with limited success, to "localize" their contests and create some distance between themselves and the president. Even the most conservative Democrats proved vulnerable to attacks linking them with Obama and House Speaker Pelosi (Pelosi emerged as a favorite target for Republicans in moderate to conservative districts in that electoral cycle, with multiple GOP candidates arguing that a vote for an incumbent Democrat was a vote for Pelosi as speaker). For instance, in Mississippi, two conservative Democrats, Travis Childers and Gene Taylor, were defeated in the 2010 balloting (Taylor had represented South Mississippi since 1989 but was defeated by GOP newcomer Steven Palazzo whose campaign slogan was "Fire Pelosi!").

It is also important to note that while Obama's approval ratings remained fairly constant in his second term, they were 43 percent at the time of the 2014 balloting (Motel, 2014). Meanwhile, 59 percent of the public did not think the president would accomplish much in his remaining time in office (Motel, 2014). Americans were split over whether they wanted the president to "take the lead in solving the country's problems" (40 percent) or the Republican-led Congress (41 percent). These figures suggest that the ability of Obama to attract independent voters or motivate cross-party voters was compromised.

Gerrymandering

The 2010 balloting proved to be especially punishing for the Democrats, as the election coincided with the decennial census, allowing Republicans at the state level to use their new control to redraw district lines in competitive states, ranging from Wisconsin to Pennsylvania to Florida. Elections scholar Tim Story noted that in the aftermath of the election, the "GOP, in dramatic fashion, finds itself now in the best position for both congressional and state legislative line drawing than it has enjoyed in the modern era of redistricting" (National Conference of States Legislatures, 2010). The new electoral boundaries in the post-2010 balloting would bolster the GOP at the congressional, state, and local levels.

A succession of articles and books emerged after the 2010 elections that argued that Republican gains were mainly due to partisan gerrymandering through a strategic effort known as the Redistricting Majority Project (REDMAP) first articulated by GOP strategist Karl Rove (Daley, 2016). However, these analyses tended to oversimplify the role of redistricting in the Obama elections. Republicans regained control of the House and made major inroads into state legislatures in 2010, before they were in a position to significantly redraw districts in many states (as had been the case for the GOP in 1994). Also, at the congressional level, the GOP secured more votes than the Democrats in both 2010 and 2014 (Kiley, 2014).

Studies from the 2010 and 2014 balloting suggest that geography was a major issue in the Obama elections. The urban base of the Democratic Parties tends to live in more compact, denser districts, while Republican rural voters dwell in more sparsely populated regions. The result is that it is easier to draw electoral districts for Democrats that are more compact. Computer simulations run by Jowei Chen and Jonathan Rodden (2014) found that "in the vast majority of states, our nonpartisan simulations produced Republican seat shares that were not much different from the actual numbers in the last election [2012]." Chen and Rodden went on to write that "the Democrats' geography problem is bigger than their gerrymandering problem" (Chen & Rodden, 2014). This suggests that the Obama coalition needed to expand its appeal to moderate rural and suburban voters, outside of safe Democratic districts.

Of course Democrats were not adverse to gerrymandering. Democrat-controlled Maryland's post-2010 electoral map produced a seven-to-one advantage in U.S. House seats for the party and was ordered to be redrawn by federal judges in 2018 (Shepard, 2018). Nevertheless, Republican gerrymandering outnumbered that of Democrats simply because of the number of states controlled by the GOP. In the end, gerrymandering certainly was one factor in Republican electoral gains during the Obama era. An analysis by the Associated Press found that the GOP secured an additional twenty-two House seats in the 2016 elections, giving the party "a comfortable majority that stood at 241–194 over Democrats . . . a 10 percentage point margin in seats, even though Republican candidates received just 1 percentage point more total votes nationwide" (Lieb, 2017).

Conclusion

The losses suffered by the Democratic Party under Obama were due to a variety of reasons. Some were the fault of Obama and his aides, other factors were outside of the president's control. The party in power in the White House typically loses seats in midterm balloting, but the Democratic Party faced serious reversals, especially at the state level where the party failed to dedicate more resources and efforts. The concentration of effort and resources around Obama's presidential campaign organizations weakened the broader party and provided Republicans with opportunities at the congressional and state levels.

During Obama's tenure, the Democratic Party moved to the left, while the GOP moved to the right. One consequence was the continued ascension of the Republicans in the South, a trend that really began with Richard Nixon's Southern strategy, and culminated in the 2010 balloting. Republicans easily swept the region, as the midterms marked the demise of the Southern Democrat. Combined with GOP victories among rural and suburban voters in the Midwest, the stage was set for Republicans to redraw districts after 2010 in such a way as to enhance their future electoral success.

Obama's reluctance to engage in the traditional political interactions between the White House and the legislature or to build relationships with both members of his party in Congress and Republicans on the Hill undermined his policy efforts. While the rise of partisanship certainly contributed to this, the president clearly demonstrated an aversion to the coalition building that might have resulted in more policy successes. Democratic electoral losses under Obama culminated in the 2016 balloting in which Republicans were able to gain control of both the White House and Congress.

References

Brownstein, R. (2017, January 12). What happens to the Democratic Party after Obama? *The Atlantic*. https://www.theatlantic.com/politics/archive/2017/01/the-post-obama-democratic-party/512885/.

Blumenthal, S. (1980). *The permanent campaign: Inside the world of elite political operatives*. Beacon Press.

Bresnahan, J. (2008, July 15). Hill Democrats miffed at Obama. *Politico*. https://www.politico.com/story/2008/07/hill-democrats-miffed-at-obama-011750.

Chen, J., & Robben, J. (2014, January 24). Don't blame the maps. *New York Times*. https://www.nytimes.com/2014/01/26/opinion/sunday/its-the-geography-stupid.html.

Condon, G. Jr. (2016, January 14). Why Obama has so few friends on the hill. *The Atlantic*. https://www.theatlantic.com/politics/archive/2016/01/why-obama-has-so-few-friends-on-the-hill/459084/.

Corrado, A., & Tenpas, K. D. (2004, March 30). Permanent campaign brushes aside tradition. Brookings Institute. https://www.brookings.edu/opinions/permanent-campaign-brushes-aside-tradition/.

Cost, J. (2016, November 28). Democratic losses in the age of Obama. *The Weekly Standard*. https://www.weeklystandard.com/jay-cost/democratic-losses-in-the-age-of-obama.

Daley, D. (2016). *Ratf**ked: Why your vote doesn't count*. Liveright.

Debenedetti, G. (2017, February 9). Obama's party-building legacy splits Democrats. *Politico*. https://www.politico.com/story/2017/02/obama-democrats-party-building-234820.

Dickerson, J. (2012, November 7). How Obama won four more years. *Slate*. https://slate.com/news-and-politics/2012/11/how-obama-won-he-had-a-better-team-that-ran-a-first-rate-campaign.html.

Dionne, E. J. Jr. (2013, January 21). Obama's unapologetic inaugural address. *The Washington Post*.

The Economist. (2008, November 8). Signed, sealed, and delivered.

Everett, B., & Sherman, J. (2016, January 11). Obama, GOP Congress near end of long, ugly relationship. *Politico*. https://www.politico.com/story/2016/01/obama-gop-congress-ugly-relationship-217550.

Fiorina, M. (2018, May 2). Polarization is not the problem. *Stanford Magazine*. https://medium.com/stanford-magazine/morris-fiorina-stanford-polarization-is-not-the-problem-cbb411a57a67.

Frank, T. A. (2019, January 9). Hope vs. change: Why some Democrats are turning on Obama's legacy. *Vanity Fair*. https://www.vanityfair.com/news/2019/01/why-democrats-are-turning-on-obamas-legacy.

Jacobson, G. C. (1996). The 1994 House elections in perspective. *Political Science Quarterly*, 111(2), 202–223.

Galvin, D. J. (2009). *Presidential party building: Dwight D. Eisenhower to George W. Bush*. Princeton University Press.

Graham, D. A. (2013, February 4). Congressional Democrats are angry at Obama . . . again. *The Atlantic*. https://www.theatlantic.com/politics/archive/2013/02/congressional-democrats-are-angry-at-obama-again/272844/.

Grin, R. (2017, November 3). Angry about the DNC scandal? Thank Obama. *Intercept*. https://theintercept.com/2017/11/03/dnc-donna-brazile-hillary-clinton-barack-obama/.

Investor's Business Daily. (2011, December 16). Obama's aloofness irks Democrats. https://www.investors.com/politics/editorials/obama-avoids-personal-contact-democrat-lawmakers/.

Kiley, J. (2014, November 5). As GOP celebrates win, no sign of narrowing gender, age gaps. Pew Research Center. http://www.pewresearch.org/fact-tank/2014/11/05/as-gop-celebrates-win-no-sign-of-narrowing-gender-age-gaps/.

Kirchgaessner, S. (2013, June 3). Global insight: Obama's frosty relationship with Congress bodes ill. *Financial Times*. https://www.ft.com/content/51f49574-c9fc-11e2-af47-00144feab7de.

Lieb, D. (2017, June 25). AP analysis shows how gerrymandering benefitted GOP in 2016. Associated Press. https://www.apnews.com/e3c5cc51faba4b7fb67d8a3f996bdaca.

Lillis, M. (2011, June 28). House Democrats feel jilted by the President in budget, debt talks. *The Hill*. https://thehill.com/homenews/house/168713-house-democrats-feel-jilted-by-the-president.

National Conference of State Legislatures. (2010, November 3). Republicans exceed expectations in 2010 state legislative elections. *NCSL News*. http://www.ncsl.org/press-room/republicans-exceed-expectations-in-2010.aspx.

Neal, A. (2018). *The oral presidency of Barack Obama*. Lexington Books.

Obama, B. (2010, November 3). President Obama's press conference: "Let's find those areas where we can agree." White House. https://obamawhitehouse.archives.gov/blog/2010/11/03/president-obama-s-press-conference-lets-find-those-areas-where-we-can-agree.

Popkin, S. L. (1994). *The reasoning voter: Communication and persuasion in presidential campaigns*. 2nd ed. University of Chicago Press.

Pew Research Center. (2016, December 14). Obama leaves office on high note, but public has mixed views of accomplishments. http://www.people-press.org/2016/12/14/obama-leaves-office-on-high-note-but-public-has-mixed-views-of-accomplishments/#obamas-approval-rating.

Sabato, L. J. (2010a, November 11). 2010 by the numbers. University of Virginia, Center for Politics. http://crystalball.centerforpolitics.org/crystalball/articles/ljs2010111102/.

Shahal, A. (2014, August 14). Obama faces bipartisan criticism over his foreign policy. *Reuters*. https://www.reuters.com/article/us-usa-obama-foreignpolicy-idUSKBN0GV0TJ20140831.

Shepard, S. (2018, November 7). Federal judges toss Maryland congressional map for partisan gerrymandering. *Politico*. https://www.politico.com/story/2018/11/07/federal-judges-toss-maryland-congressional-map-for-partisan-gerrymandering-973245.

Tapper, J. (2014, July 10). House Democrats furious with President Barack Obama over lack of support for reelection campaigns. *ABC News*. https://abcnews.go.com/WN/house-democrats-furious-president-barack-obama-lack-support/story?id=11174124.

UVA Center for Politics. (2018, February 15). Public rates presidents: Kennedy, Reagan, Obama at top, Nixon, Johnson, Trump at bottom. Ipsos/UVA Center for Politics Poll. http://www.centerforpolitics.org/crystalball/articles/public-rates-presidents-jfk-reagan-obama-at-top-nixon-lbj-trump-at-bottom/.

5

Michelle Obama's First Ladyship

ELIZABETH J. NATALLE

Introduction

Michelle Obama served as the First Lady of the United States from January 2009 to January 2017. By all accounts she can be assessed as a very successful modern first lady in popularity, persuasive effect, inclusivity, and development of the office supporting the first lady. She entered the White House with an approval rating of 67 percent ("The First Ladies," 2009), and she departed with a 72 percent favorability rating ("Obama Leaves Office" 2016). Although she polarized Americans on the basis of partisan politics (Burrell, Elder, and Frederick, 2010), Mrs. Obama's high ratings in the polls speak to her consistency in the role. Her agenda built around the public persona of "Mom-in-Chief" included a new twist on old expectations for what a first lady should symbolize and what she should engage in in her daily activities. Her success among Democrats, Independents, Black and Hispanic citizens, women, and young people came as a result of using rhetorical strategies based in youth, modern technology, popular culture, and healthy living. Mrs. Obama had more success transcending the difficulty of partisan politics than her husband, but she was criticized on a daily basis in racist and sexist messages that made it a challenge to carry out the duties of being the first African American first lady in the United States. Mrs. Obama serves as a role model for how to successfully navigate the role of first lady in a rapidly changing social and political environment, and she goes down in history as a first. Being the first black woman in the role symbolically and practically changes the criteria for who qualifies as First Lady in America.

This chapter provides a report card on Mrs. Obama's achievement by examining her campaign strategies, the structure of the First Lady's Office under her leadership, her use of social media and popular culture activities, her persuasive agenda for change and the legacy of her role as the first lady who modeled a work-life balance for all contemporary women. In the process of attempting to provide a fair assessment of her effectiveness in a role that has no job description or constitutional requirement, this chapter will employ a method that triangulates the research question on effectiveness through rhetorical analysis of her speaking, descriptive history, inclusion of media response, and polling numbers. In addition to published primary and secondary academic sources, materials available through the Internet and a collection of speeches from the Obama White House website, research is drawn from a personal vertical file of approximately four hundred newspaper and magazine articles.

Political Life and Campaigning

Michelle LaVaughn Robinson was born in Chicago on January 17, 1964, to working-class parents Fraser Robinson and Marian Shields Robinson (Slevin 2015). She grew up alongside her older brother Craig, in a household that emphasized the importance of education, strong family values, and the strength of community action. These uplift themes guided Michelle Robinson throughout her life and can be traced in her decisions to attend Princeton University and Harvard Law School, to marry fellow lawyer Barack Hussein Obama, to work as a community organizer in public health, to support her husband's bid for the United States Senate while mothering two daughters and to ultimately agree to campaign for Barack Obama as President of the United States in 2008 and again in 2012.

Emerging as the first African American first lady of the United States, her deeply rooted family history from Southern slavery to South Side Chicago and post–Jim Crow society produced a personal politics based in a deep belief that family is the center of American agency in successful civil society. Her continuous through line in her own politics and in her support of the Obama Presidency was that personal responsibility to family and the education of oneself provides the means for success and the betterment of community. In her experience as a Black woman growing up in a racist society, she never forgot the context of social circumstances, but she practiced a philosophy of political transcendence where race can move away from its divisive mechanism and toward its role for opportunity of difference in a world that can benefit from diversity and inclusion (Natalle, 2015; Stolberg, 2014). However, the race politics of being the first African American first lady of the United States often challenged her own authenticity and ability to assist her husband to enact the platform of the Democratic Party.

Mrs. Obama is not intrinsically a political person and she has publicly said, "I don't like the back and forth of the political process" (Obama, 2016e). However, because she was America's first Black woman seeking her husband's place in the White House, her role in presidential campaigning was fraught from the beginning with racism directed toward her. Campaign advisor David Axelrod said it best in his memoir, *Believer*: "Thrown out on the campaign trail without adequate staffing or preparation in 2007, she quickly became fodder for the right-wing noise machine, which seized on every opportunity to cast her as the angry, militant Black woman behind the affable candidate" (Axelrod, 2015, p. 4). American voters interpret messages literally and tend not to function well in the nuances of irony and satire. The multiple interpretations of Mrs. Obama's campaign speech during the February 2008 Wisconsin primary where she said, "For the first time in my adult lifetime I am really proud of my country" (2008a), was misconstrued as unpatriotic when, in fact, much of the misinterpretation beyond sheer racism can be attributed to media analysis of sound bites rather than complete sentences in proper context. The satirical cover of *The New Yorker* in July 2008 that depicted her as a black militant totally misfired, and the public then absurdly thought of her as the anti-American, angry Black woman capable of terrorism. These incidents set the stage for eight years of personal insults that went well beyond the initial campaign period, and scholars across disciplines (e.g., Jeffries, 2013; Moffitt, 2011; Scott, 2017; Taylor, 2011) wrote essays to deconstruct stereotypes and argue against racist assumptions behind the explicit and implicit accusations that Mrs. Obama might be less fit for the role of first lady than a Caucasian woman. No other modern first lady has been vilified like Mrs. Obama, but she endured comments about her body ("Moochelle"), her race (an "ape in heels"), and her health agenda (a "nanny state") by using her ethos as First Lady to transcend the daily onslaught of misogynistic disrespect directed at her. Not once did Michelle Obama lose her temper under these circumstances in eight years in the White House. Even when she finally addressed some of the insults (or, "the noise" as she called it) in her Tuskegee University commencement speech, she did so in the context of advice to the graduates: "Stay true to the most real, most sincere, most authentic parts of yourselves" (Obama, 2015). Being true to herself during the White House years brought Michelle Obama through to the other side as the authentic person that she was and still is.

Mrs. Obama quickly learned from the initial experience on the campaign trail. Her image, according to Robert Watson (2012), turned from the negative frames of "angry black woman," "un-American," "Marie Antoinette," and "another Hillary" to a positive brand characterized by "first fashionista," "mom-in-chief," and "first volunteer." Jeffries's (2013) analysis of her public image, centered on her body and sexuality, reinforces the conclusion that America is sociologically stunted in its (in)ability to fully accept a Black woman as a first lady, but Michelle Obama's consistent behavior in office demonstrated her skill in shattering stereotypes along a wide demographic range. By the time of the 2016 election results, when she was polling a 64 percent positive popularity rating (Chozick, 2016), *The New Yorker* online ran a Benjamin Schwartz cartoon with a therapist sitting in a session with a very young client saying, "My advice? Skip denial, anger, bargaining, depression, and acceptance, and go straight to Michelle in 2020" (Schwartz, 2016). Indeed, Mrs. Obama's performance in the role of campaigner had changed that significantly. She will be remembered as a poised first lady with excellent public speaking skills who served as "the closer" (Davis, 2016) when Hillary Clinton trailed Donald Trump by five points in the polls (CNN/ORC, 2016) only ten days before election day. In spite of Mrs. Obama's arguments in favor of preserving the dignity of all Americans, voters chose the Republican candidate.

In a deep analysis of Michelle Obama's two Democratic National Convention (DNC) speeches as the candidate's wife (Obama, 2008b; 2012b), rhetorical critic Tammy Vigil (2015) demonstrates how Mrs. Obama transcended race in 2008 by using conventional strategies to talk about family while at the same time using her own family narrative as the example of the American Dream, thus subverting the idea that a white, middle-class configuration is the only possible model of family. Her youth orientation and the family model that included her mother signaled to Americans that family values and children are important building blocks of society.

By the 2012 DNC, Mrs. Obama had morphed into the "Mom-in-Chief" as her version of Republican Motherhood (Parry-Giles & Blair, 2002). The American family itself was presented as not just ethnically diverse, but she advocated for gay marriage and equality for all in her description of what the American Dream (Vigil, 2015) could be with the reelection of Barack Obama, his values, and the policies that could fulfill the ambition of citizens for a higher quality of life. What Michelle Obama accomplished so well in almost fifty campaign speeches in 2012 was to demonstrate that her husband's character and policies reflected moral principles based on the politics of inclusivity (Natalle, 2019; Sheckels, 2014). In fact, it was Mrs. Obama who advocated first for gay marriage and persuaded her husband to join her stance (Becker, 2014). When the Supreme Court in June 2015 handed down the ruling that gave legal protection for same-sex marriage in the United States, this only enhanced the Obama administration's ethos as fair-minded and open to a wider definition of equality.

Michelle Obama's role as campaigner developed so quickly that her presence on the campaign trail extended to the 2016 general election where she became the voice of America's moral conscience (Natalle, 2019) as candidate Donald Trump's treatment of women took center focus in the most vicious presidential campaign in modern history. At the DNC in Philadelphia in July 2016, Mrs. Obama gave a speech that surprised the electorate with her now memorable line "when they go low, we go high" (Obama, 2016c) as the defense mechanism against all untoward behavior. In an unusual move for a sitting first lady, during the last month and half of the general election campaign Mrs. Obama stepped in to assist Hillary Clinton by giving eight powerful speeches to counteract Donald Trump's rivetingly negative accusations against Clinton. The major contribution of Michelle Obama to the 2016 election was to assist Hillary Clinton in altering the political landscape for women in the United States. Since Clinton's loss, women have engaged "women's marches," significant numbers of women are running for political office, and the #MeToo movement has emerged in response to the sexual misbehavior of men in power.

The Office of the First Lady

Officially, a first lady supports the president's administration based on the White House Personnel Act of 1978 (Public Law 95-570, 105e), but there is no actual Office of the First Lady. Her structural location is the East Wing of the White House, but her staff is paid by shared budget with the president's staff. Sometimes, staff members' duties (e.g., social secretary) are carried out for the first lady and the president because the job is a White House appointment. There is no separate budget to fund any programs or policy that the first lady might wish to implement, thus creating an odd situation where a productive work environment is left in a place of uncertainty. Nevertheless, Michelle Obama has continued the specialized development of her office that reflects Borrelli's (2011) analysis detailing the sophistication and interconnection of East and West Wing since the days of Rosalynn Carter.

East Wing Staff Demographics

Michelle Obama is known as an organized person who appreciates control and attention to detail. When the new first lady of New York City, Chirlane McCray, asked First Lady Obama for advice, Mrs. Obama was absolutely pragmatic and told McCray to employ trustworthy people in the positions of chief of staff, scheduler, and communications director (McCray, 2017). Michelle Obama followed Laura Bush by employing a similar number of staff—around two dozen—but Obama added new demographics in terms of race, sexuality, gender, and experience. Mrs. Bush employed both long-time Bush staffers and newer, younger professionals eager to take on the rigors of White House work (L. Bush, 2010). Michelle Obama had a similar staff profile. Valerie Jarrett, senior advisor to the president and First Lady and longtime friend from Chicago, is the person who provided stability and wise counsel throughout the Obama administration. The original, immediate team for Mrs. Obama included a chief of staff and two deputies, a director of policy and projects, a director of communications, a director of logistics, and the White House social secretary. Most of the staff were comprised of well-educated young professionals in their twenties and thirties and many were Harvard educated or had Chicago roots.

The original team reflected the Obama inclusivity principle: four white women, two Black women, and one Hispanic man. By 2016, the social secretary's position had turned over four times in eight years, including the first two Black women to hold the job, Desirée Rogers and Deesha Dyer, and the first gay male to perform the role, Jeremy Bernard. During the second term, the White House photography staff hired Amanda Lucidon to specifically cover the First Lady's activities. Lucidon's visual portrait of Mrs. Obama in her book, *Chasing Light* (2017), documents the diversity and inclusivity of people all over the world who interacted with the First Lady. New staff positions such as Lucidon's and those of social media advisors are evidence of the increasing specialization needed to complete the work of the FLOTUS office.

Support staff—such as deputies and assistants—were numerous, and Mrs. Obama's staff included four men who worked on logistics, correspondence, speech writing, and trip coordination (Nelson, 2017). There were few gaffes during the Obama first ladyship, but the biggest occurred when the first social secretary, Desirée Rogers, was held responsible for the security breach at the state dinner for the Indian Prime Minister. Two television actors were admitted to the dinner and managed to get through the receiving line to shake hands with President and Mrs. Obama. Ms. Rogers resigned and was replaced by staff member Julianna Smoot ("Julianna Smoot," 2010).

The Speech Writer and Public Speaking

Mrs. Obama's primary speechwriter was Harvard lawyer Sarah Hurwitz, who worked with Mrs. Obama through both terms. Hurwitz had previously written for Al Gore, Hillary Clinton, John Kerry, and Barack Obama before hitting her stride with Michelle Obama. They were an extremely effective team, producing more than six hundred speeches in the first six years and a couple hundred more by 2016. Lauren Wright (2016) demonstrated in her study of first ladies Clinton, Bush, and Obama that the wives of presidents are now integral elements of communication policy because they enhance the president's image and support for policy. According to Wright's evidence, Mrs. Obama has eclipsed all former first ladies in her ability to use public appearances to increase favorable public opinion of the presidency. Mrs. Obama's speaking skills are so effective that her ability to create audience rapport is unmatched by most women on the public platform today, and she has been called an American rhetor for our time (Natalle & Simon, 2015).

As speechwriter Hurwitz told *The Washington Post*, "[S]he's given me so much feedback over the years and [is] so clear about what she wants. . . . Michelle Obama knows who she is, and she always knows what she wants to say" (Thompson, 2016a). Indeed, the First Lady was always well rehearsed, in control, and usually delivering a speech that included the constant narrative of family, upbringing, and the potential for personal success. Like other former first ladies, Michelle Obama made public appearances for campaign speeches, graduation speeches, advocacy for her agendas (health, education, and the military), and miscellaneous speeches in the context of women, children, volunteerism, and the role of first ladies. In addition to her well-received DNC speeches in 2008, 2012, and 2016, the First Lady will be particularly remembered for her 2014 eulogy of Maya Angelou (Obama, 2014b) and her 2015 graduation speech at Tuskegee University. In both these speeches, Mrs. Obama reinforced the value of African American lives and the legacy of Black people in American history while confronting the demons of racism. In that sense, she became the first American first lady to actively speak about race, racism, and equality from the point of view of a Black feminist intellectual. Certainly, Mrs. Obama's personal rhetorical success can be attributed to her own speaking skill, her ability to connect with a wide range of audiences and the mutual collaboration on content with her speechwriter. However, what remains in question is how much political success she was able to bring to Barack Obama's presidency. No matter how high her poll numbers, the systematic resistance to both President Obama's policies and his person made it very difficult for her to serve as "substantive representation" of the presidency, to use Borrelli's (2011) concept about the power of her office. Rather, her symbolic representation, Borrelli's notion that first ladies use symbols such as White House events to provide meaning for the presidency, is very clear in Mrs. Obama's success as a role model for young people and her use of the White House to promote inclusive events from poetry slams to Seders to enhance the emotional appeal of the Obama philosophy.

Collaboration with the Second Lady

Additionally, beyond the dynamic and inclusive staff, Michelle Obama created space for her office to use the one person who is virtually never mentioned as part of the team: the so-called second Lady, or the wife of the vice president. No other first lady in modern times has showcased the presence and expertise of the second lady like Michelle Obama has done with Dr. Jill Biden, the wife of Joe Biden. In this relationship, First Lady Obama established what I have termed elsewhere "co-rhetors" (Natalle, 2015), where Obama and Biden worked together in their *Joining Forces* public campaign to support military families. Their collaborative ethos persuaded others to take social responsibility for the care and welfare of military families; thus, Obama and Biden created communal agency to get things done. In April 2011, the Obamas and the Bidens together launched the initiative that bridged the unsuccessful military policy, which was not resolving conflict in Iraq and Afghanistan, to ways that the Obama presidency *could* support the families of military personnel in a constructive manner to gain popular approval.

Dr. Biden, a military mother, enhanced the ethos of Mrs. Obama, who only knew about the traumatic aftereffects of war service through the stories of constituents. Both women used their friendship and communication expertise to enlist the aid of companies such as Walmart and Best Buy, and organizations such as Major League Baseball and NASCAR, to create awareness and provide voluntary services to help military families in need. Together, Jill Biden and Michelle Obama gave interviews, visited military bases as a team, sponsored White House events and made public service announcements. They spoke in public separately and together to persuade America to voluntarily care for and honor our military. By the end of the Obama presidency, the *Military Times* reported (Shane, 2016), the five-year effect of the initiative was the hiring of 1.25 million veterans and spouses, and legislation across all fifty states enabled certification transfers for spouses to continue working. It was very successful as a bipartisan initiative, including public support from George and Laura Bush.

In April 2010, Mrs. Obama chose to share leadership with Jill Biden when they traveled to Haiti to demonstrate the commitment of the Obama administration to helping that country recover from a devastating hurricane. Acting as surrogates for the president and vice president, Mrs. Obama and Dr. Biden observed relief efforts and thanked American, UN, and relief agency employees for their help. As the two spoke to the media, Mrs. Obama (2010) said of the total destruction and need to rebuild from the ground up:

> [I]t was important for Jill and I to come now because we're at the point where the relief efforts are underway but the attention of the world starts to wane a bit . . . it was important for us to come and shed a light . . . but as the President sees it [rebuilding], it's also an incredible responsibility. But it's going to take all of us.

Clearly, the partnership between Michelle Obama and Jill Biden was mutual and demonstrated multiple ways that a first and second lady can use their power together to create agency and persuade through social responsibility and volunteerism. Inviting the second lady in to fully participate as a member of the office of the first lady is a new precedent set by Michelle Obama and one worth continuing as the roles of both spouses develop in the future.

Social Media, Popular Culture, and First Lady "Coolness"

Barack Obama's success with social media as a campaign tool was the first of its kind, and he continued to use various forms of social media during the presidency. Katz, Barris, and Jain (2013) claim that the "Obama Administration primarily used social media as a way to put out its message and viewpoints and mobilize the public in support of Administration objectives" (Katz, Barris, & Jain 2013, 7) while being less successful in promoting public participation in policymaking. As the first social media first lady, Michelle Obama navigated the double-edged sword of using this form of communication as a persuasive tool while also being scrutinized 24/7 as the object of social media activity.

Although she used social media during the campaigns, Mrs. Obama had one primary goal during her first ladyship tenure: to reach American citizens (primarily young people and families), to promote her agendas for healthy living (*Let's Move!*), education (*Reach Higher* and *Let Girls Learn*), and support for the military (*Joining Forces*). Residually, she also created positive ethos for Barack Obama and his policies. In a 3-D interview with the technology network *The Verge*, the first lady claimed that she and her husband knew pop culture and could respond by being nimble, even "cool," in an ever-changing environment (Obama, 2016a). She said, "We are always striving to be cutting edge" and to come across to audiences as "authentic and natural" (Obama, 2016a). She had no problem projecting an ethos of cool because much of her social media imagery included action shots of her with young people or engaging in activities such as shooting hoops with Miami Heat players—a technique that deliberately uses "collaborations with non-news media celebrities" to enhance her status and "keep breaking through" (Thompson, 2016b). Mrs. Obama's effectiveness at "cool" is, so far, both a first and unmatched by any other first lady—this would be in addition to her unparalleled use of hugging to put people at ease and create rapport (Adichie, 2016). Unlike Jacqueline Kennedy, the nation's first television first lady and media celebrity, Mrs. Obama was even more known across a range of ages. Michelle Obama quickly eclipsed the fashion comparisons to Jacqueline Kennedy and took on the meaning of cultural icon that especially appealed to African American women (Chambers, 2017). Part of Michelle Obama's unique attraction can be explained by her adept use of both celebrity and her own youth in the Mom-in-Chief persona. While Mrs. Kennedy rejected the role of celebrity, Mrs. Obama embraced it. Her five-woman media team targeted messages carefully and pushed the use of digital media to reach audiences.

Of all the roles identified for first ladies (Gonnella-Platts & Fritz, 2017; Watson, 2014), Michelle Obama was known to most Americans as a celebrity mom with a great wardrobe and a love of music. She is a fan of popular culture herself, she likes to have fun, and much of her fun during the White House days was embedded in popular culture and social media use. She enjoyed driving around the compound singing Carpool Karaoke with James Corden of the *Late Late Show*, SoulCycling with friends and staff at a local gym, dancing the "mom dance" on *Late Night With Jimmy Fallon*, hula-hooping on the White House South Lawn, jumping rope in China, dressing in colorful fashion from hip designers while simultaneously buying from J. Crew, watching Nickelodeon's *iCarly* with her daughters and then appearing on the show, inviting Broadway musical stars from *Hamilton* to entertain at the White House, promoting healthy eating with Big Bird, reading Christmas stories at a children's hospital with Ryan Seacrest, sharing Beyoncé's workout using Instagram, posting messages on Twitter and keeping up with all the fads that her two growing daughters, Malia and Sasha, brought home from school and their social networks.

Reaching Americans through popular media outlets paralleled the use of social media, allowing Mrs. Obama's brand to serve as a positive influence on the president and promote her agenda. The First Lady was on the cover of magazines that cut across race, age and class, including: *Ebony, Essence, Vogue, Glamour, Ladies Home Journal, AARP The Magazine, Parade Magazine, The New York Times Magazine*, and *Children's Health*, to name a few. The Obama White House website was connected to Facebook, Twitter, Flickr, YouTube, Vimeo, iTunes, LinkedIn, Instagram, Vine, Tumblr, and Google, and a blog (authored by the press office) where the First Lady was featured along with her husband, daughters, and family dogs. Mrs. Obama met regularly with her social media advisors so that tweets and videos were released constantly. As she left the White

House, her Twitter account had 6.9 million followers, and today she is up to 12.8 million. She currently has 17 million Facebook "likes" and her Instagram account has 30.9 million followers. Her ability to use social media increased her role as a celebrity first lady (Wright, 2016), but what Mrs. Obama gained in return was access to young people to promote her causes and engage as a role model; her outreach capability significantly increased just given the structure of platforms such as Facebook and Instagram where sharing and reproducing messages is possible. Her effective use of social media contained content that was both informative and persuasive as she tried to promote health and education to the youth of America.

In a study analyzing her Twitter presence, Paul and Perreault (2018) found that Michelle Obama's most popular images contained the themes of "an activist mother" and the Obamas as a "normal American family." Thus, her controlled imagery reinforced the Mom-in-Chief persona that she used to frame herself throughout the Obama administration and feeds into Paul and Perreault's claim that her imagery "largely aligns with the media and public's perception of the ideal image of first ladies" (Paul & Perreault, 2018, p. 173). Although the first lady's Twitter imagery reinforced the traditional approach to Republican Motherhood that is a common trope in first lady research (Parry-Giles & Blair 2002), for Mrs. Obama this may also have been a safe bet to mitigate the racism and sexism she often faced. Her strategic choices could also reflect "respectability politics" (Gatison, 2017/18), or the use of cultural rules for self-presentation that make a Black woman acceptable to a Eurocentric audience. Her consistently high ratings in public opinion polls might have benefited both from the respectability effects and her neoliberal narrative of success, which Meyers and Goman (2017) argue diminished much of the systemic discrimination she had to navigate.

Political scientist Lauren Wright (2016) observed that Mrs. Obama's staff expanded communication expertise to control social media presence while simultaneously selecting traditional news venues in the First Lady's brand development. Additionally, Wright's analysis demonstrated the way "the administration's policy interests [were] artfully woven" (Wright, 2016, p. 69) through Michelle Obama's speeches. For example, health care policy was referenced in *Let's Move!* speeches so that Mrs. Obama was effectively promoting the Affordable Care Act without actually mentioning it by name. Such a strategy also served to bolster the ethos of her husband.

Mrs. Obama was the object of blog coverage in fashion and food on the Internet. The eating habits of the Obama family and the healthy eating events related to Mrs. Obama's *Let's Move!* campaign were documented on websites such as Food Network (foodnetwork.com) and Obama Foodorama (obamafoodorama.com) blog sites. Of the half-dozen fashion blogs, the most popular was Mrs-O, (mrs-o.com) a blog that ran from September 2008 through February 2014 and served as a daily chronicle of the First Lady's clothes while encouraging conversation among the blog users. Although judging her fashion was a popular theme among Michelle Obama watchers throughout her eight years in the White House (Horyn, 2012; Friedman, 2017), Americans seemed to appreciate the First Lady's sense of style in addition to her substance. Thus, Mrs. Obama leveraged fashion as a visual argument to reflect the ethos of the Obama administration and to express her philosophy of inclusion and diversity based on the designers whose clothes she wore. And, in the end, clothes for Michelle Obama, as she told *Vogue*, after comfort level and the ethics of the designer, is really a matter of, "Is it cute? . . . Don't take it all so *seriously*" (Van Meter, 2016, p. 291). Cute notwithstanding, Michelle Obama's economic impact on the fashion industry was enormous. *Harvard Business Review* reported that NYU finance professor David Yermack (2010) found that after 189 public appearances, Michelle Obama's clothes created $2.7 billion of value for the twenty-nine companies that manufactured the clothes she wore and that each public appearance was worth $14 million in public purchases. Such significant and abnormal market value continued throughout the Obama first ladyship. Yermack attributed the impact to her position as first lady, her authentic interest in fashion, and the power of social media combined with e-commerce.

There were countless YouTube videos of the First Lady documenting her public activities, from campaigning to college signing speeches to her travel abroad and her guest interviews on television shows. She even created a FLOTUS Travel Journal with blog entries and daily videos that covered her Africa trip in 2013 (Hanson & Osei-Hwere, 2015). However, much of the social media coverage was neither authorized nor controlled by the Obama administration, so the effects of such coverage were both positive (e.g., likes and followers) and negative (e.g., racist comments and criticism of her health objectives). Americans and the media spent a disproportionate amount of time metacommunicating about the First Lady's image and not enough time following her behavior as a role model, which was her actual objective. Persuit and Brunson's (2015) study of Mrs. Obama's brand development through epideictic speaking reinforces the conclusion that a first lady's role in constructing and preserving community requires a relationship between speaker and audience that goes beyond social media image. Navigating the many forms of communication now available to a first lady will be the future challenge of the East Wing, but as the first social media first lady, Michelle Obama, and her staff, can be given high marks for reaching target audiences with consistent and positive messages to promote causes.

Persuasive Agenda

As policy advocates, first ladies have slowly developed in proportion to the power exerted by the particular woman in the White House. Hillary Clinton and Michelle Obama both hold law degrees and Laura Bush holds a master's degree. Mrs. Bush had policy advisors on staff, and Mrs. Obama continued that practice. Policy and politics are now present in the agendas of first ladies, and Michelle Obama carefully linked her agenda that fostered health, education, and family to President Obama's policies; she ran parallel campaigns that synchronized with his initiatives. She also joined with co-rhetors, such as opinion leaders, government agencies, and corporations, to persuasively move her goals into broader law, policy, and practice. Given the fact that first ladies have no budget or legal authority to implement agendas, Mrs. Obama was an innovator who used collaboration with others to create communal agency and get things done. For example, she joined with her husband in 2009 to launch *United We Serve* as a way to give volunteer time to the community and honor the mission of the Corporation for National and Community Service—the federal agency responsible for service. Mrs. Obama initiated *Let's Move!* in 2010, *Joining Forces* in 2011, *Reach Higher* in 2013, and *Let Girls Learn* in 2014. Her primary rhetorical strategy involved using her Mom-in-Chief persona to persuade young people through participatory activities to want to move, learn, and serve community. As she revealed her target audience for all she did, Mrs. Obama said, "I am powerfully moved by children. I need them in my life. They keep me focused; they keep me directed" (Steinhauer, 2013b, p. A11).

First Lady Obama initiated *Let's Move!* in 2010 as her signature campaign. *Let's Move!* was a successful parallel to the president's Patient

Protection and Affordable Care Act (ACA) (Natalle, 2015). She reinforced the legislation by homing in on a campaign to eliminate childhood obesity and simultaneously encourage physical activity and healthy eating. *The New York Times* referred to *Let's Move!* as her "policy agenda" (Steinhauer, 2013a), demonstrating that politics and policy are more difficult to tease out today from what used to be known as a first lady's "pet project." Although *Let's Move!* was structurally messy, the persuasive effects were substantial. It consisted of two interconnected sets of strategies: one for physical activities and one for food. The labels *campaign* and *initiative* are somewhat confusing, but the constant and multiple rollouts, often with the president and Mrs. Obama together in the East Room of the White House for the announcement, meant more people could become involved, and more slogans for healthy living could saturate the nation. The fast pace also kept up with social media demands for new topics to cover, even if the message was ultimately the same.

The White House itself served as a rhetorical strategy in getting people to move and eat healthy. Mrs. Obama, together with the National Park Service and chef-advisor Sam Kass, established the White House Kitchen Garden in March 2009. She used it consistently as the site for food education, demonstrations of healthy eating, and a reward for all the school children and White House visitors who worked in, knew about, and admired the garden. Rather than a coffee table book about the family pets (B. Bush, 1992) or White House traditions (Clinton, 2000), Michelle Obama produced *American Grown: The Story of the White House Kitchen Garden and Gardens Across America*. She said she hoped the garden would serve as a catalyst for "conversation about the food we eat, the lives we lead, and how all that affects our children" (Obama, 2012a, p. 9). Through pictures, garden plans, recipes, and the documentation of events, *American Grown* was the philosophy behind the events and partnerships to encourage healthy eating and the wise choice of foods. Schoolchildren helped plant and harvest the garden. In 2012, the First Lady hosted the first of her annual Kids State Dinners where children who had won the "Healthy Lunchtime Challenge" recipe contest (co-sponsored with Epicurious, the U.S. Department of Education, and the Department of Agriculture) came to the White House to celebrate eating their own dishes made with plants from the garden. By 2014, *Drink Up* encouraged kids to drink more water, and in 2015 the *Eat Brighter* campaign advocated adding fruits and vegetables to everyone's daily menu. Meanwhile, the White House chefs assisted in creating the *Chefs Move! to Schools* program sending 3,400 chefs out to volunteer in schools across America to rework cafeteria menus and plant school gardens.

Mrs. Obama influenced thinking about obesity in America that resulted in government policy and agency programs. President Obama signed the Healthy, Hunger-Free Kids Act in 2010 with Mrs. Obama standing at his side. The U.S. Department of Agriculture (USDA) initiated a Healthier US School Challenge and had three thousand schools participating in food changes and physical activity. In 2011, the USDA introduced its $2 million *Choose MyPlate Project* (www.choosemyplate.gov) to replace the food pyramid, and by 2013 the Partnership for a Healthier America was in full swing. Mrs. Obama unveiled *MyPlate* along with the agriculture secretary and the surgeon general, and it was reported (Neuman, 2011) that the First Lady's "anti-obesity team" gave advice to the USDA during the creation of the plate. The White House itself had issued nutritional guidelines in 2012, and the USDA adopted rules for healthier lunches in its subsidized school lunch program. There was pushback from some congressional representatives and some schools wanted out (Eng, 2011; Nixon, 2014), but most schools met the guidelines even as kids complained about less tasty food. Mrs. Obama went on the offense in May 2014 with an op-ed contribution to *The New York Times* arguing that millions of kids were getting better nutrition and that obesity rates in children were falling. Her overtly political statement ended with, "And when we make decisions about our kids' health, we rely on doctors and experts who can give us accurate information based on sound science. Our leaders in Washington should do the same" (Obama, 2014a).

Less controversial was the physical activity domain of *Let's Move!* The annual Easter Egg Roll turned into a coveted invitation to participate in multiple sports and meet both professional and Olympic athletes. Photographs of the First Lady hula-hooping on the South Lawn were just as popular as shots of kids in blue *Let's Move!* T-shirts. Olympian Dominique Dawes co-chaired the President's Council on Fitness, Sports & Nutrition, and the activities crystallized into the *South Lawn Series* and the *Gimme Five* challenge where celebrities, kids, and athletes shared their exercise regimes in person and over social media. In her "victory speech" (Obama, 2016b) to the Partnership for a Healthier America (PHA) in May 2016, the First Lady reported that "childhood obesity rates have stopped rising for the first time in decades" and that her work laid "the groundwork for that change" which is the total elimination of obesity:

And since we first launched *Let's Move!*, PHA has brought together partners like you in more than 50,000 locations across all 50 states. . . . Let's just look at the stats. Because of you, 1.6 million kids are now in healthy daycares, eating more than 225 million healthy snacks and meals a year. . . . Thirty million kids are eating healthier school breakfasts and lunches. Ten million kids are getting 60 minutes of physical activity at a Let's Move! Active School. . . . Eighty million Americans are living in a Let's Move! City, Town or County with summer meal programs, and athletic leagues, and new parks and playgrounds. Eight point one million people in underserved areas finally have somewhere to buy groceries, including 1,000 convenience stores that are now selling fresh food. (para. 7)

Today, the PHA, a nonprofit inspired by *Let's Move!*, continues the goal to eliminate childhood obesity, and Michelle Obama serves as its honorary chair.

The president and Mrs. Obama believed in their personal responsibility to mentor youth, particularly African American teens, and to serve as role models. There had never been an opportunity like this before, so the Obamas used their position in the White House to practically demonstrate and enact what it means to be successful. They used their own personal stories as the basis for inspiring others. The president established *My Brother's Keeper* as a racial justice initiative to mentor boys and young men in 2014, but Mrs. Obama began her work with women and girls within her first year in the White House. There was a White House Council on Women and Girls and, as early as March 2009, a Women of Excellence event was held to bring girls and celebrity women together to talk about life goals and success. But within the White House, First Lady Obama established another first: a mentoring program where she and her staff were paired in a mentoring relationship with high school girls chosen from local schools, the Girl Scouts, and military families ("Obama's Mentoring," 2009). Over time, these one-on-one relationships were efforts to successfully move young people ahead and to encourage higher education.

By the end of 2013, *Reach Higher* had become a way for the First Lady to assist the 2020 North Star Goal to increase college graduation rates, particularly among low-income and disadvantaged youth. *The New York Times* headlined, "Michelle Obama Edges Into a Policy Role on

Higher Education" (Steinhauer, 2013c), and indeed Mrs. Obama planned to work with the U.S. Department of Education (DOE) to help her achieve the motto of *Reach Higher*: "Complete your education. Own your future." Her rhetorical strategies included working with school counselors and the American School Counselor Association, giving commencement speeches at strategically selected high schools and colleges, attending and speaking at *College Signing Day*, sponsoring *Beat the Odds* summits to hear from students who graduated from high school, engaging students in conversation about college through *Better Make Room* and figuring out new ways to use social media to help provide resources for students. *Reach Higher* "convenings" occurred all around the country so that stakeholders could bring resources together and prepare more students for college. By 2016 there were forty-two *Reach Higher* state teams in place bringing school counselors, state agencies, and college personnel together (*Reach Higher Progress Report*, 2017). Metrics were set up and policy interventions followed. A number of best practices emerged, from high school counselor training to using data to improve high school graduation rates.

Social media played an integral role in the success of *Reach Higher*. For example, in October 2015 the First Lady partnered with the DOE to launch a mobile app competition "to promote the development of mobile solutions that will help students navigate education and career options" ("Launched Today," 2015). With a prize pool of $465,000, Mrs. Obama found a way to team with a government agency, fund her initiative, and reach a youthful target audience known for using mobile apps as a lifestyle. By August 2016, *ThinkZone Games* won the $100,000 grand prize for its career exploration mobile app Hats & Ladders, they and rolled out the app in 2017 to fifty middle schools where students would explore careers with the app Hats & Ladders (www.hatsandladders.com). Today the Hats & Ladders app is going strong. It is not clear what immediate effects *Reach Higher* has had on its target audience given how early it is in the initiative, but in his farewell address President Obama (2017) said about his wife, "And the new generation sets its sights higher because it has you as a role model."

Michelle Obama told Oprah Winfrey in her farewell interview (2016e) that it was difficult to say what her biggest impact had been, but perhaps being a role model for young women, especially Black women, was her strongest achievement. Inspired by education activist and role model for girls Malala Yousafzai, the First Lady and President Obama initiated a global girls' education program in 2015 called *Let Girls Learn*. It is the strongest collaboration among American and global government agencies and may be the most effective of Mrs. Obama's efforts over the long term. Her foray into global advocacy even opened the door for what *The New York Times* called "a rare adventure into foreign policy" (Shear, 2014, p. 9), when she linked the right to education to terrorism policies and spoke out for the safety of the Nigerian schoolgirls kidnapped by Boko Haram.

Agencies involved in *Let Girls Learn* included: The Department of State, the U.S. Agency for International Development (USAID), the Peace Corps, the U.S. Department of Labor, the U.S. Department of Agriculture, the Millennium Challenge Corporation (MCC) and the U.S. President's Emergency Plan for AIDS Relief (PEPFAR). It was clearly policy-oriented and is the result of what the website calls "the necessary political will, diplomacy, grassroots organizing, and development expertise to create lasting change" (https://letgirlslearn.gov/about/). This initiative brought together everything Michelle Obama values: family and children, education, and community growth and stability. Even much of her international diplomacy was devoted to meeting with girls in countries such as Cambodia, Cuba, Argentina, Liberia, and Morocco. In 2016, she reported to a United Nations audience the following:

> And that's really the mission of our Let Girls Learn initiative—to give girls worldwide the education they need to fulfill their potential and lift up their families, their communities and their countries. Now, I want to be clear, as may be true for many of our first ladies who are here, as First Lady of the United States, I have no budget of my own for programs. I have no authority to make or pass laws. I cannot issue any kind of executive orders. But in just a year and a half, through Let Girls Learn, we've established partnerships with nearly 80 companies and organizations that are committing money, resources and expertise. We're collaborating with countries like Canada, Mexico and the Nordic countries on girls' education efforts. Countries like Japan, South Korea, and the UK have invested nearly $600 million. The U.S. is investing over half a billion dollars more, and running Let Girls Learn programs in 40 countries. And the World Bank Group will be investing $2.5 billion over the next five years. (Obama, 2016d)

Let Girls Learn is a continuing United State government program. It is a demonstration of Mrs. Obama and her staff's competence and ability to address the problem of undereducated citizens on a global scale. For a first lady with no budget or legal authority, *Let Girls Learn*, *Reach Higher*, and *Let's Move!* model the way in which a first lady agenda is now expected to be multilateral, local, and global, and it should be aimed at solving serious social problems. The Obama Foundation (www.obama.org) does not directly carry forward any of the four initiatives discussed in this essay, but structures are in place for others to continue the work of Mrs. Obama. She even raised $2.5 million in private funding before leaving the White House to continue the Kitchen Garden in conjunction with the garden's custodians, The National Park Service (Van Meter, 2016). Overall, her persuasive agenda as First Lady should receive high marks for importance, effect, and relevance.

Legacy

If Michael Eric Dyson (2016) is correct that race defined the Obama presidency, then Michelle Obama's legacy as the first African American first lady of the United States will be what she is remembered for in the history books. It has been argued elsewhere (Natalle & Simon, 2015) that Mrs. Obama was exactly the right person for the historical moment to demonstrate that an American first lady may very well be nonwhite *and* the symbol of the story of the United States. Her brand of motherhood and model of family was consistently popular with Americans. It is arguable that she brought "American ideals and practices . . . closer to perfection," according to Dyson (2016, p. 125). Through her sheer presence and unrelenting presentation of a woman true to herself, Michelle Obama made significant contributions toward changing sociological perceptions of who should lead in the White House and how that should be done.

Her philosophy of inclusivity meant that she opened the White House to welcome the widest range of guests ever invited—young and old, black and white, Jewish and Muslim, domestic and international, gay and straight. The Obamas employed the most demographically diverse staff of any prior administration. Although Mrs. Obama was known for her empathy and ability to relate to a wide range of constituents, not all citizens were pleased. In fact, a vocal demographic of women in the Black community often felt that the First Lady did not do enough to eliminate racism and sexism because she was not vocal enough about the oppression of Black women (Huggins, 2018). Michelle Obama made no apologies in her memoir (Obama, 2018) for who she is as a person or how she made decisions to advocate for Black citizens while in the first lady role.

Measuring the effectiveness of a first lady often comes down to looking at how well she performed the typical roles expected of her and her agenda to help the American people. Michelle Obama accomplished many "firsts." She was the first to consider holistically in the White House the role of children. She actively cultivated their presence in all the events she created and attended because she truly believes in children as the future of a stable democracy. She hugged them, she danced with them, she admired their performances, she inspired their goals, and she emulated behavior for kids. While other first ladies were mothers during their time in the White House, Mrs. Obama put forth the image and will be remembered as our "Mom-in-Chief." In making this choice, she became the surrogate mother of all American children and she demonstrated a family model of work-life balance that included her own mother living in the White House. In linking moms and family as concepts, the notion of a family's healthy lifestyle guided by a thinking mom was a central argument in her *Let's Move!* campaign. She will be remembered as one of the most physically active first ladies in history. If Mrs. Obama inspired Americans to eat healthy, move, and lose weight, then she contributed to the resolution of one of our most serious health problems.

Michelle Obama forces first ladies scholars to rethink what it means to be effective in the role. Understanding a person who is not Caucasian requires different theoretical frameworks to fully explain the person and her values as she attempts to carry out the job. Natalle and Simon (2015), for example, employed feminist rhetorical theory, Black feminist theory, and cultural studies to frame an analytical approach to Mrs. Obama. Additionally, the social media context in which first ladies must now act creates cultural meaning beyond the traditional scope of assessment that we previously applied. Poll numbers and rankings may not be enough to judge the impact of a given first lady—Twitter and Facebook metrics may be part of the equation in determining first lady effectiveness. Nevertheless, traditional polls and rankings still provide solid indicators of a first lady's role and impact in the presidential administration. Michelle Obama enjoyed high favorability rankings throughout her time as first lady. The Pew Research Center ("Michelle

Obama's," 2010) reported after her first year that Mrs. Obama had a 71 percent favorability rating compared to Laura Bush's 64 percent and Hillary Clinton's 60 percent. By the time she was ready to leave the White House, Mrs. Obama still maintained a high 72 percent favorability rating, according to Pew ("Obama Leaves Office," 2016), but Gallup data indicated she was rated a 72 percent in 2009 and had a final rating of 68 percent in January 2017 (McCarthy, 2017). Gallup's numbers showed Michelle Obama's final favorability rating below Laura Bush's 76 percent, but significantly higher than Hillary Clinton's 56 percent when she left the White House in 2000. Regarding her place in history, the most recent Siena ranking (2014) has Michelle Obama in fifth place behind the venerable Eleanor Roosevelt, Abigail Adams, Jacqueline Kennedy, and Dolley Madison. The 2018 Gallup Poll (Jones, 2018) of most admired women in the world placed Mrs. Obama first.

From a popular culture perspective, it would be easy to say she was a fashionista who left social and economic impact as a result of her clothes (Givhan, 2016), or that she was the country's first social media first lady who loved popular culture and gave hugs to everyone—including the Queen of England! She was the first to have a White House garden since Eleanor Roosevelt's victory garden, and she was the first to work with her own staff to mentor young girls. Michelle Obama certainly should be remembered for her work in education, health, support for the military, and community service. Education, above all else, was the key in the First Lady's plan for citizens to achieve success. The Obama Foundation, launched in 2014, continues the work of the Obamas through the mission "to inspire, empower, and connect people to change their world" (www.obama.org). Eight projects are currently in the works to accomplish the mission, however Barack Obama is more visible than Michelle on the website and in project descriptions that center, mostly, on leadership development. This does not readily help us to see Michelle Obama's legacy. And, although the First Lady emerged as the moral conscience of the nation during the 2016 election campaign in a way no other first lady ever has (Natalle, 2019), the clamoring for her to run for office will not materialize into anything concrete. What she has left in the popular lexicon is the motto "when they go low, we go high" as a way to combat meanness, prejudice, and all the forms of "ism" now present in the national conversation.

While the 2016 Pew Survey ("Obama Leaves Office," 2016) showed that more Americans would remember Barack Obama for the Affordable Care Act than for being the first Black president, no polls asked about

Michelle Obama's legacy. Academic assessments of the first lady are largely missing from the books coming out on the Obama administration (e.g., Rich, 2019; Schier, 2016). Why? First ladies are now integral members of a presidential administration and they contribute substantially to the modern presidency. They are "elected" as part of a package when a candidate stands for office, and first ladies are expected to demonstrate leadership. If we look at standards for evaluating presidents, it is now possible to generalize to first ladies. Greenstein's (2009) six criteria apply as well to Mrs. Obama. As a first lady demonstrating leadership, she exhibited excellent public communication skills; she was extremely well organized; her political skills manifested in a successful agenda; her vision supported the president's; she engaged a cognitive style that marked her decision making as intelligent and detail oriented; and her emotional intelligence reflected empathy and an even temper.

As academic analyses locate Mrs. Obama in first lady history there are implications for significant reevaluation of: who can serve in the role; how a first lady symbolizes the story of the United States; which audiences she can reach to achieve social change; what "difference" means when achieving inclusion and diversity of opportunity; how family and relationships are culturally valued; and what the direction will be in this country regarding the divisive factor of race. For scholars of American first ladies, we need to continue to construct the long-term legacy of First Lady Michelle Obama in the context of the Obama presidency.

References

Adichie, C. N. (2016, October 23). Michelle Obama: A thank-you note to the woman who has spent the past eight years quietly and confidently changing the course of American history. *T: The New York Times Style Magazine*, 150–153.

Axelrod, D. (2015). *Believer: My forty years in politics*. Penguin.

Becker, J. (2014, April 16). How the president got to "I do" on same-sex marriage. *The New York Times Magazine*. https://www.nytimes.com/2014/04/20/magazine/how-the-president-got-to-i-do-on-same-sex-marriage.html.

Borrelli, M. A. (2011). *The politics of the president's wife*. Texas A&M University Press.

Burrell, B., Elder, L., & Frederick, B. (2010). From Hillary to Michelle: Public opinion and the spouses of presidential candidates. *Presidential Studies Quarterly*, 41(1): 156–176.

Bush, B. (1992). *Millie's book: As dictated to Barbara Bush*. Harper Perennial.
Bush, L. (2010). *Spoken from the heart*. Scribner's.
Chambers, V., ed. (2017). *The meaning of Michelle: 16 writers on the iconic first lady and how her journey inspires our own*. St. Martin's Press.
Chozick, A. (2016, October 7). Michelle Obama, the closer for Clinton. *The New York Times*, A16.
Clinton, H. (2000). *An invitation to the White House: At home with history*. Simon & Schuster.
CNN/ORC International Poll. (2016, October 20–23). http://i2.cdn.turner.com/cnn/2016/images/10/24/cnn.poll.pdf.
Davis, J. H. (2016, November 6). The Closer. *The New York Times*, ST1, 14, 16.
Dyson, M. E. (2016). *The Black presidency: Barack Obama and the politics of race in America*. Houghton Mifflin Harcourt.
Eng, M. (2011, August 8). Government role in fight against obesity debated. *Chicago Tribune* (reprinted in *News & Record*, Greensboro, NC), A1, 4.
Friedman, V. (2017, January 15). How clothes defined her. *The New York Times*, ST1, 3.
Gatison, A. M. (2017–18). Michelle Obama and the representation of respectability. *Women & Language*, 40(1): 101–110.
Givhan, R. (2016, December 11). Michelle Obama leaves style legacy. *Chicago Tribune*. https://search-proquest-com.libproxy.uncg.edu/usnews/docview/1847625331/fulltext/5DF3F18FCB2F459CPQ/11?accountid=14604.
Gonnella-Platts, N., & Fritz, K. (2017). *A role without a rulebook: The influence and leadership of global first ladies*. George W. Bush Institute.
Greenstein, F. I. (2009). *The presidential difference: Leadership style from FDR to Barack Obama*. Princeton University Press.
Hanson, T. L., & Osei-Hwere, E. (2015). Michelle Obama speaking in Africa on education, family, and the African legacy. In E. J. Natalle & J. M. Simon (Eds.), *Michelle Obama: First lady, American rhetor* (pp. 85–102). Lexington.
Horyn, C. (2012, December 30). First in fashion. *The New York Times*, ST1, 7.
Huggins, Y. (2018). Michelle Obama: Flight vs. fight. In M. Duster, P. M. Seniors, & R. C. Thevenin (Eds.), *Michelle Obama's impact on African American women and girls* (pp. 31–42). Palgrave/Macmillan.
Jeffries, M. P. (2013). *Paint the White House black: Barack Obama and the meaning of race in America*. Stanford University Press.
Jones, J. M. (2018, December 27). Michelle Obama ends Hillary Clinton's run as most admired. https://news.gallup.com/poll/245669/michelle-obama-ends-hillary-clinton-run-admired.aspx.
Julianna Smoot: Desiree Rogers' social secretary replacement. (2010, April 28). *The Huffington Post*. https://www.huffingtonpost.com/2010/02/26/julianna-smoot-desiree-ro_n_478717.html.

Katz, J. E., Barris, M., & Jain, A. (2013). *The social media president: Barack Obama and the politics of digital engagement*. Palgrave Macmillan.

Launched today: The Reach Higher Career App challenge. (2015, October 7). Reach Higher Blog. https://www.reachhigherchallenge.com/blog/page/5/.

Lucidon, A. (2017). *Chasing light: Michelle Obama through the lens of a White House photographer*. Ten Speed Press/Crown Publishing.

McCarthy, J. (2017, January 16). President Obama leaves White House with 58% favorable rating. *Gallup News*. https://news.gallup.com/poll/202349/president-obama-leaves-white-house-favorable-rating.aspx.

McCray, C. (2017). Two black first ladies walk into a room. In V. Chambers (Ed.), *The meaning of Michelle: 16 writers on the iconic first lady and how her journey inspires our own* (pp. 73–84). St. Martin's Press.

Michelle Obama's strong personal image: Views of recent first ladies. (2010, January 21). *Pew Research Center*. http://www.pewresearch.org/2010/01/21/michelle-obamas-strong-personal-image/.

Meyers, M., & Goman, C. (2017). Michelle Obama: Exploring the narrative. *Howard Journal of Communications*, 28(1), 20–35.

Moffitt, K. R. 2011. Framing a first lady: Media coverage of Michelle Obama's role in the 2008 presidential election. In C. R. Squires, K. R. Moffitt, & H. E. Harris (Eds.), *The Obama effect: Multidisciplinary renderings of the 2008 campaign* (pp. 233–249). State University of New York Press.

Natalle, E. J. (2015). Michelle Obama's ethos and *Let's Move!* In E. J. Natalle & J. M. Simon (Eds.), *Michelle Obama: First lady, American rhetor* (pp. 61–83). Lexington.

Natalle, E. J. (2019). The moral conscience of the nation: Michelle Obama and the 2016 presidential election. In J. S. Sacco (Ed.), *Women and the 2016 election* (pp. 85–104). Lexington.

Natalle, E. J., & Simon, J. M., eds. (2015). *Michelle Obama: First lady, American rhetor*. Lexington.

Nelson, R. (2017, January 19). The bros of Michelle Obama's office. *GQ*. https://www.gq.com/story/the-bros-of-michelle-obamas-office.

Neuman, W. (2011, June 3). Nutrition plate unveiled, replacing food pyramid. *The New York Times*, B3.

Nixon, R. (2014, May 30). House panel advances bill on school lunch options. *The New York Times*, A15.

Obama, B. (2017, January 10). Remarks by the president in farewell address. *Los Angeles Times*. http://www.latimes.com/politics/la-pol-obama-farewell-speech-transcript-20170110-story.html.

Obama leaves office on high note, but public has mixed views of accomplishments. (2016, December 14). *Pew Research Center*. http://www.people-press.org/2016/12/14/obama-leaves-office-on-high-note-but-public-has-mixed-views-of-accomplishments/.

Obama, M. (2008a). Michelle Obama campaign speech in Wisconsin. https://www.c-span.org/video/?204114-1/obama-campaign-event&start=663.

Obama, M. (2008b, August 25). Michelle Obama's one nation, speech at the Democratic National Convention, Denver, CO. *CNN*. http://www.cnn.com/2008/POLITICS/08/25/michelle.obama.transcript/.

Obama, M. (2010). First Lady Michelle Obama and Dr. Jill Biden hold a media availability, as released by the White House. https://search-proquest-com.libproxy.uncg.edu/usnews/docview/356962872/fulltext/7B2F601468B04715PQ/1?accountid=14604.

Obama, M. (2012a). *American grown: The story of the White House kitchen garden and gardens across America*. Crown Publishers.

Obama, M. (2012b, September 5). Remarks by the first lady at the Democratic National Convention. https://obamawhitehouse.archives.gov/the-press-office/2012/09/05/remarks-first-lady-democratic-national-convention.

Obama, M. (2014a, May 28). The campaign for junk food [Op-Ed]. *The New York Times*. http://www.nytimes.com/2014/05/29/opinion/michelle-obama-on-attempts-to-roll-back-healthy-reforms.html?_r=0.

Obama, M. (2014b, June 7). Remarks by the first lady at memorial service for Dr. Maya Angelou. http://www.whitehouse.gov/the-press-office/2014/06/07/remarks-first-lady-memorial-service-dr-maya-angelou.

Obama, M. (2015, May 9). Remarks by the first lady at Tuskegee University commencement address. https://www.whitehouse.gov/the-press-office/2015/05/09/remarks-first-lady-tuskegee-university-commencement-address.

Obama, M. (2016a, March 14). Michelle Obama 360. Interview with Caroline Adler on *The Verge*. https://www.youtube.com/watch?v=0QY72R3ZDzw&feature=youtu.be.

Obama, M. (2016b, May 20). Remarks by the first lady at Partnership for a Healthier America's Building a Healthier Summit. https://www.whitehouse.gov/the-press-office/2016/05/20/remarks-first-lady-partnership-healthier-americas-building-healthier.

Obama, M. (2016c, July 25). Remarks by the first lady at the Democratic National Convention. https://www.whitehouse.gov/the-press-office/2016/07/25/remarks-first-lady-democratic-national-convention.

Obama, M. (2016d, September 19). Remarks by the first lady at the United Nations General Assembly Spousal Program. https://www.whitehouse.gov/the-press-office/2016/09/19/remarks-first-lady-united-nations-general-assembly-spousal-program.

Obama, M. (2016e, December 19). A farewell interview with Michelle Obama by Oprah Winfrey. *CBS Television News*.

Obama, M. (2018). *Becoming*. Crown.

Obama's mentoring program will be historic for a first lady. (2009, November 2). *News & Record* (Greensboro, NC), A8.

Parry-Giles, S. J., & Blair, D. M. (2002). The rise of the rhetorical first lady: Politics, gender ideology, and women's voice. *Rhetoric & Public Affairs*, 5(4), 565–600.
Paul, N., & Perreault, G. (2018). The first lady of social media: The visual rhetoric of Michelle Obama's Twitter images. *Atlantic Journal of Communication*, 26(3), 164–179.
Persuit, J. M., & Brunson, D. A. (2015). First lady brand in the epideictic rhetoric of Michelle Obama. In E. J. Natalle & J. M. Simon (Eds.), *Michelle Obama: First lady, American rhetor* (pp. 39–57. Lexington.
Reach Higher Progress Report. (2017, January 6). U.S. Department of Education. https://www2.ed.gov/documents/press-releases/reach-higher-progress-report.pdf.
Rich, W. C., ed. (2019). *Looking back on President Barack Obama's legacy*. Palgrave/Macmillan.
Schier, S. S., ed. (2016). *Debating the Obama presidency*. MD: Rowan & Littlefield.
Schwartz, B. (2016, November 10). Daily Cartoon. *The New Yorker* https://www.newyorker.com/cartoons/daily-cartoon/morning-thursday-november-10th-michelle-2020.
Scott, K. D. (2017). *The language of strong Black womanhood: Myths, models, messages, and a new mandate for self-care*. Lexington.
Shane, L. III. (2016, November 12). Michelle Obama's signature military initiative faces an uncertain future under Donald Trump. *Military Times*. http://www. militarytimes.com/ military-honor/salute-veterans/2016/11/12/michelle-obama-s-signature-military-initiative-faces-an-uncertain-future-under-donald-trump/.
Shear, M. D. (2014, May 11). Mrs. Obama speaks out on schoolgirl abductions. *The New York Times*, A9.
Sheckels, T. F. (2014). The rhetoric of a campaigning first lady. In R. E. Denton Jr. (Ed.), *Studies of communication in the 2012 presidential campaign* (pp. 71–94). Lexington.
Siena Study of First Ladies. (2014). https://scri.siena.edu/first-ladies-study/.
Slevin, P. (2015). *Michelle Obama: A life*. Alfred A. Knopf.
Steinhauer, J. (2013a, February 28). New attention to first lady as she presses ahead with healthy eating drive. *The New York Times*, A18.
Steinhauer, J. (2013b, March 1). Dismissing her critics, Mrs. Obama forges ahead. *The New York Times*, A11.
Steinhauer, J. (2013c, November 12). Michelle Obama edges into a policy role on higher education. *The New York Times*, A16.
Stolberg, S. G. (2014, May 16). A decision that helped shape a first lady. *The New York Times*, A16.
Taylor, U. Y. (2011). Too black and too strong: First lady Michelle Obama. In C. P. Henry, R. L. Allen, & R. Chrisman (Eds.), *The Obama phenomenon:*

Toward a multiracial democracy (pp. 236–249). Southern Illinois University Press.
The First Ladies. (2009, January 20). The New York Times/CBS News Poll. *The New York Times*, A19.
Thompson, K. (2016a, June 13). What's on Michelle Obama's mind? Meet the speechwriter who puts it into words. *The Washington Post.* https://www.washingtonpost.com/lifestyle/style/whats-on-michelle-obamas-mind-sarah-hurwitz-knows-how-to-put-it-in-words/2016/06/13/440d2130-3103-11e6-8ff7-7b6c1998b7a0_story.html?utm_term=.48a3a7a8f927.
Thompson, K. (2016b, December 18). In the homestretch, the Michelle Obama PR machine goes into overdrive. *The Washington Post.* https://www.washington post.com/lifestyle/style/in-the-homestretch-the-michelle-obama-pr-machine-goes-into-overdrive/2016/12/17/32164670-c210-11e6-8422-eac61c0ef74d_story.html?utm_term=.a362f6fd3d04.
Van Meter, J. (2016, December). Unforgettable. *Vogue*, 219–228, 290–291.
Vigil, T. (2015). Conventional and unconventional rhetorical strategies in Michelle Obama's Democratic National Convention addresses. In E. J. Natalle & J. M. Simon (Eds.), *Michelle Obama: First lady, American rhetor* (pp. 15–37). Lexington.
Watson, R. P. (2012). First Lady Michelle Obama. In R. P. Watson, J. Covarrubias, T. Lansford, & D. M. Brattebo (Eds.), *The Obama presidency: A preliminary assessment* (pp. 379–397). State University of New York Press.
Watson, R. P. (2014). *The presidents' wives: The office of the first lady in US politics*. 2nd ed. Lynne Rienner.
Wright, L. A. (2016). *On behalf of the president: Presidential spouses and White House communications strategy today*. Praeger.
Yermack, D. (2010). How this first lady moves markets. *Harvard Business Review*, 88(11), 38–39.

II

Domestic Policy

6

Obama, Economic Recovery, and Macroeconomic Policy

PAUL BURTON AND JOSEPH J. ST. MARIE

Introduction

On November 4, 2008, Barrack Obama defeated John McCain in the United States presidential election. When Obama took office on January 20, 2009, he inherited an economy that had been in recession since December 2007 (National Bureau of Economic Research, 2018). The economy would not return to growth until 2010, and it would take through 2011 for the economy to deliver an aggregate economic output greater than it had produced in 2007 (World Bank, 2018a).

The "Great Recession" was the worst the United States had experienced since World War II and it was only the second time since the war that the United States had posted a decline in economic output for two consecutive years (the other period was 1974–75). Nevertheless, the economy during the Obama administration did grow each year from 2010 onward, so is President Obama's economic legacy adequately characterized by this achievement alone? Or should President Obama's economic legacy be judged by other factors too? What role did partisan politics play in the economic performance of the United States during the Obama presidency? In leading the United States economy out of recession, was President Obama an innovator, or did he adhere to economic orthodoxy?

To answer these questions we will look at how the Obama administration impacted the economic freedom of Americans. Economic freedom is the ingredient that allows individuals to seize control of their well-being and prosper commensurate with their ability and work ethic. In section 1 we will define and analyze economic freedom and look at an index of economic freedom and how it registered during the Obama administration. This anaylitical tool provides a lense to view domestic policy in an unconventional and unique manner.

In section 2 we will look at the specific, salient initiatives of the Obama administration and how they contributed to the economic freedom of the American people. As we will see, it is not easy to adjudge good or bad the economic policies of the Obama administration because there is no consensus on what good, or bad, is. Finally, in the conclusion we will offer answers to the above questions, as well as offering a rationale for Obama administration policies other than the promotion of economic freedom.

Economic Freedom

Economic freedom can be defined as the "absolute absence of coercion or constraint of economic liberty beyond the extent necessary for citizens to protect and maintain liberty itself" (Miller & Kim, 2014). When government actions influence the economic actions of an individual, it acts upon the liberty of the individual. Whether the action is positive or negative is often a topic of hot debate. Resolving the debate one way or another is not possible absent agreement beforehand on the proper role of government, especially as relates to the tradeoff between economic freedom and notions of social justice and economic equity or equality. Nevertheless, it cannot be denied that any action by government that impacts the control an individual exerts over his labor or his property impacts the amount of economic freedom experienced by that individual.

With this definition in hand, the question at bar can be stated simply: Did the Obama administration increase or decrease the economic freedom of the American people while President Obama was in office? According to the conservative Heritage Foundation, the Obama administration decreased the economic freedom of the American people while President Obama was in office. Conversely, the center-left Brookings Institution characterized the Obama administration's agenda as "[h]eavy on technology and climate change and civil rights, light on concrete measures to boost working- and middle-class income, [which] appealed much more to coastal elites than to the rest of the country (Galson, 2017).

In the next section we lay the foundation for an answer to this question. We will examine the major economic policy initiatives of the Obama administration. Do these initiatives and their purported effects suggest a greater or lesser involvement of government in the economic life of Americans, beyond what is necessary for the maintenance of economic liberty itself?

Economic Policy Accomplishments of the Obama Administration

President Obama signed into law the American Recovery and Reinvestment Act in February 2009. Originally the law authorized $787 billion in federal spending. The law as passed cut taxes by $288 billion, spent $224 billion on extended unemployment, education, and healthcare benefits, and it authorized $275 billion in federal contracts, grants, and loans. In the fiscal year (FY) 2012 budget Congress extended the program to $840 billion (Amadeo, 2010a). The law was a direct response to the Great Recession and it was intended to stimulate consumer spending and save jobs. The law was in effect a massive Keynesian stimulus whereby the government attempted to offset a reduction in private spending with an increase in government spending.

The impact of the law remains difficult to ascertain and, therefore, in dispute. This is because the law was intended to save jobs that "would have been" lost and mitigate the "worst" of the economic effects of the ongoing recession. Did the law succeed? Experts come down on both sides of this question and it really is impossible to conclude one way or another. This is because it is impossible to determine how many jobs would have been lost and how much worse the recession would have been for economic growth without the stimulus. It is also impossible to say what the effect of a different stimulus would have been. Consequently, it is impossible to offer a cost-benefit analysis with any reasonable level of confidence. Consequently, as Rauchway writes, "Obama's decision to deemphasize stimulus in favor of pressing for health insurance reform was a gamble of immense, if unknowable, magnitude and consequence" (Zelizer, 2018).

What *can* be said with some level of confidence, however, is that the American people expected the government to act boldly in the face of the economic crisis and President Obama did exactly that, just as President George W. Bush had done in the final days of his administration when he signed the Economic Stimulus Act of 2008. As a result, in 2010, the second full year of the Obama administration, the United States economy returned to growth. Moreover, there is a consensus among economists that the benefits from the stimulus probably outweighed its costs and that without the stimulus more jobs would have been lost in total (IGM Forum, 2012). With hindsight, it appears that government power was appropriately used to impact the private sector in a time of nearly unprecedented economic emergency. This conclusion is supported by Robert Samuelson who writes that "the [Obama] administration's greatest achievement was, in its first year, stabilizing a collapsing economy and arguably avoiding a second Great Depression" (Samuelson, 2017).

Nevertheless, if there is a criticism of the Obama administration and how it acted to remediate the Great Recession with fiscal policy, the criticism is rooted in how President Obama prioritized the spending of the fiscal stimulus. Instead of spending on "shovel ready" projects that would have had an immediate and direct impact on employment and consumer spending, the Obama administration instead directed money at policy initiatives in clean energy, education, and healthcare, in addition to tax cuts and funding unemployment (Worstall, 2013). While important, and certainly part of the policy agenda he campaigned on, none of these initiatives would have the short-term economic effect of, as an example, an infrastructure project (Worstall, 2013). President Obama's choices in this instance seemed to cater to his ideological convictions. This pleased his liberal supporters (though they complained about the meager size of the stimulus), but it also subjected him to criticism from Republicans who perceived that he was exploiting an economic crisis to generate funding for an economic agenda that should be developed in collaboration with Congress and follow a normal legislative process. In the end, the Federal Reserve Bank of Phadelphia's research indicated that "the economy did indeed grow more than it would have without the [2009 Obama] stimulus but likely not as much as it might have with a different type of stimulus" (Carlino, 2017). Ultimately, just like President George W. Bush and President Bill Clinton before him, President Obama's actions would be lauded by his supporters and derided by his opponents, with a bipartisan majority appraisal simply not emerging.

Healthcare

In 2010, President Obama signed into law the Patient Protection and Affordable Care Act. The stated purpose of the act was to lower federal government spending on healthcare. In 2009, the federal government spent 10 percent of the federal budget on Medicare and Medicaid (Amadeo, 2010b); national per capita healthcare costs were twice as high as in other industrialized countries (Young & Schwartz, 2014). By 2020, this spending was forecast to increase to 20 percent of the federal budget (Amadeo, 2010b). Since Medicare and Medicaid spending is mandatory spending under current spending authorization laws that require Congress to allocate whatever monies are needed for the programs, the only way to reduce spending on healthcare is to reduce the cost of healthcare itself. Consequently, it was reasoned that the cost of healthcare could be reduced by reducing the number of hospital visits, especially emergency room visits, by making preventative care available to all Americans. This goal was specifically pursued by the imposition of a legal mandate requiring that all people have health insurance. Those that could not afford health insurance would receive subsidized healthcare paid for by increased taxes on businesses and affluent individuals. It was hoped that this would bring the great majority of the forty-six million people that did not have healthcare insurance into the system, an outcome that was required to make the law financially affordable (Young & Schwartz, 2014).

So what is the impact of the Patient Protection and Affordable Care Act? According to Mulligan, the law's provisions have been slow to take effect, so the law's effect on economic growth is only now (as of 2016) beginning to be fully felt (Mulligan, 2016). The result, however, because of the disincentives baked into the law, is likely to be a reduction in GDP by the end of the decade of $1.2 trillion and the loss of 800,000 jobs as employers are disincentivized from hiring full-time employees and small businesses are discouraged from growing employment (Mulligan, 2016). This, however, is only one view.

According to Kimberly Amadeo, the Patient Protection and Affordable Care Act was anticipated to add $940 billion to the federal budget by 2020. However, citing the Congressional Budget Office, she claims that the budget deficit will actually reduce by $143 billion during this period because of decreased reimbursements to hospitals and higher taxes on businesses and individuals (Amadeo, 2010b). In other words, the law is more than fully paid for by increased taxes and lower reimbursements.

It is not possible to say who is correct. But what if both views prevail? In this instance we would see a situation where more people have healthcare (there is evidence that this actually occured, even if some were underinsured) and the overall expense to the government is reduced (Collins, Bhupal, & Doty, 2019). This is clearly a positive outcome, but it comes at a hidden cost of $1.2 trillion in foregone economic growth and 800,000 fewer jobs. The salient point is that no matter who is correct the economic freedom of Americans is reduced in order to provide healthcare to those who need it but cannot afford it, and to those who do not need it (yet) and do not want it. Where one stands on the issue probably depends on how they would make the tradeoff between economic freedom and social justice.

Interestingly, there is a view that the government did not go far enough with the Affordable Care Act. According to Kevin Young and Michael Schwartz, 77 percent of all Americans believed that the government should be responsible for meeting each individual's basic healthcare needs (Young & Schwartz, 2014). Nevertheless, Young and Schwartz believe that public opinion was only "marginal to the policy making process itself" (Young and Schwartz 2014). Healthcare and pharma companies, however, proved to be integral to the policy process as they engaged with the administration to shape the law. The ultimate result, according to Young and Schwartz, was "a familiar form of corporate welfare: a big injection of public subsidies to expand the overall size of the U.S. healthcare market" (Young & Schwartz, 2014). Consequently, in the final analysis it appears that a Faustian bargain was made between the Obama administration and big healthcare and pharma to create a new social entitlement. Liberals did not get all that they wanted, but big business found a way to cash in.

Financial Reform

The Great Recession began in December 2007, lasted through 2009, and is generally regarded as the worst economic downturn experienced by the United States since the Great Depression of the 1930s. Many point to the housing market and the subprime lending crisis as having caused the Great Recession.

Prior to 2007 home prices in the United States had been appreciating for several years. Investors looking for good returns and low risk were eager to invest in mortgages because of their perceived low risk; and, banks and other financial institutions were motivated to fulfill this demand by packaging mortgages into custom investment vehicles and selling them. As the demand to invest in mortgages increased unabated, more mortgages were needed. Consequently, incentives were created for lenders to offer mortgage loans to more home buyers, even those buyers who would normally not qualify. The risk of lending to poorly qualified buyers was simply overlooked because the loan would be secured by an asset that, at least in recent history, had appreciated reliably.

This was the genesis of the subprime crisis. Unqualified mortgagors who fell on hard times or otherwise could not afford to meet their mortgage obligations defaulted. This problem, combined with a cyclical downturn in the housing market, was severe enough to tip the balance in the housing market in favor of supply over demand, which caused home prices to fall. The repercussions of this phenomenon were felt by lenders, as the housing-related securities they held to satisfy reserve (and margin) requirements dropped in value. A system-wide financial panic was triggered when Lehman Brothers collapsed. Congress attributed the entire crisis to the avarice of Wall Street and legislated to preclude the crisis from ever reoccurring. The result was the Dodd-Frank Wall Street Reform and Consumer Protection Act.

In 2010, President Obama signed into law the Dodd-Frank legislation, which spawned four hundred new rule makings in the financial sector. It represented the most significant change in regulation of the financial sector since the 1930s (Michael & Furth, 2017). According to the Heritage Foundation, the effects of the act were to increase lending costs and, therefore, reduce national income—by as much as 1.38 percent annually by 2026 (Michael & Furth, 2017). This finding is directly contradicted by the Brookings Institution, which states that "[t]here is some evidence, however, that the improved stability from increased capital requirements has not had a significant negative impact on the economy" (Baily, Klein, & Schardin, 2017). Moreover, "There is no settled economic consensus on the point at which increasing capital requirements will be outweighed by the economic costs of doing so" (Baily, Klein, & Schardin, 2017). Nevertheless, despite a disparity of views on the impact and equities of the law, Congress, in a very rare act of bipartisanship, rolled back key provisions of the law in 2018 when President Donald J. Trump signed the Economic Growth, Regulatory Relief, and Consumer Protection Act.

The Economic Growth, Regulatory Relief, and Consumer Protection Act sought to remedy provisions of Dodd-Frank that were viewed as "an overcorrection, resulting in unduly burdensome regulation" (Perkins et al., 2018). Specifically, the law "modifies Dodd-Frank provisions, such as the Volcker Rule . . . the qualified mortgage criteria under the Ability-to-Repay Rule, and enhanced regulation for large banks; provides smaller banks with an "off ramp" from Basel III capital requirements . . . and makes other changes to the regulatory system" (Perkins et al., 2018). The significance of the changes made to Dodd-Frank and the fact that the changes were made as the result of a bipartisan agreement in Congress suggests that the original law was indeed a heavy-handed use of government power at the expense of the private sector.

Deficit

President Obama increased the national debt by approximately $9 trillion, an increase of 86 percent, and the largest increase measured in absolute dollars of any U.S. president (Bryan, 2017). Notwithstanding, all presidents inherit different economies, under different domestic and international circumstances and conditions; all presidents inherit a financial trajectory that impacts the policy choices available to them. So this number cannot be evaluated as good or bad simply at face value. The policy choices that President Obama made that impacted the growth of the economy and the level of national debt are more revealing. Beyond the stimulus, healthcare, financial, and climate (*infra*) reforms, the other significant choice he made was in the form of the Budget Control Act of 2011.

In 2010, Republicans retook control of the House of Representatives from the Democrats. As a result, upon entering into the majority in 2011, the Republicans insisted that President Obama negotiate a reduction in spending in exchange for an increase in the national debt ceiling. Specifically, the Republicans had three demands: "tax increases must not be considered as part of any deficit reduction plan; any increase in the debt ceiling must be accompanied by a plan to slash fiscal outlays; and these spending cuts must offset the increase in the debt limit" (Constitutional Law, 2012). Importantly, under this plan President Obama would have to come back to Congress, probably in 2012 during the reelection campaign, and ask for another debt ceiling increase thus raising the specter of a partisan battle with congressional Republicans in the fall as voters were preparing to go to the polls. President Obama rejected the Republican plan and ultimately a compromise would be put forward by Speaker of the House John Boehner and Senate Majority Leader Harry Reid. This plan in effect delegated authority to President Obama to raise the debt ceiling (Constitutional Law, 2012).

Deficit reduction had long been a rallying cry for Republicans and now that they were in the majority in the House, and having a

Democrat president as a foil, they could insist on federal budget deficit reductions. But the Budget Control Act as it was passed into law was a mixed victory for both Republicans and for Democrats. This is because it limited spending on causes dear to each side in the partisan debate. Discretionary social programs would be underfunded from the point of view of Democrats and, likewise, defense programs would be underfunded from the point of view of Republicans.

The Budget Control Act of 2011, *et seq.*, imposed spending caps and a spending reduction process. Despite Congress making adjustments to the caps and spending reductions, "[t]otal discretionary spending . . . under the BCA was 13.7 percent lower on a nominal basis and 18.6 percent lower on a real basis in FY2015 than it was in FY2011" (Driessen & Labonte, 2015). Moreover, "The annual federal budget deficit decreased from $1.1 trillion (6.8 percent of Gross Domestic Product) in FY2012 to $665 billion (3.5 percent of GDP) in FY2017" (McGarry, 2018). This deficit reduction came as a result of the application of a blunt instrument in the name of the Budget Control Act. Pain was felt on both sides of the political aisle. Since neither Republicans nor Democrats were happy with the result, perhaps the most significant win, certainly from a political perspective, was the avoidance of a partisan battle on the debt ceiling in an election year. In the end, it is hard to see how kicking this can down the road benefited the economic well-being of Americans.

The Budget Control Act succeeded in bringing the budget deficit down, but apparently the political cost was too great for lawmakers. President Trump signed the Bipartisan Budget Act of 2018, which allowed defense and nondefense discretionary spending to rise above the limits imposed by the Budget Control Act of 2011. In the end, the Budget Control Act of 2011 did more or less what it was designed to do, but it also probably slowed the economic recovery from the Great Recession as the Keynesian stimulus was reduced; and, it probably slowed the growth of the economy in the longer term.

Environment

Perhaps in no other policy area was President Obama more aggressive in taking unilateral executive action than in the area of environmental policy. "The use of executive power by a president to get his wishes, particularly in a second term, is extremely common" (Shapiro, 2015). But even so, President Obama was particularly aggressive, no doubt because he was frustrated by what he perceived as intransigence from a Republican-controlled Congress. Consequently, President Obama used his "pen and phone" to issue regulations to his liking, and more than any other president he used executive power granted him by the Antiquities Act of 1906 (Nelson, 2016), and the Clean Air Act of 1963, *et seq.*, to issue regulations. Ultimately, however, President Obama's use of executive power made his policies subject to rescission by his successor, so their effect in some instances may be short-lived. Indeed, President Trump since taking office has acted against the Steam Protection Rule, the Methane Flaring Rule, the Clean Power Plan, and the Waters of the United States Rule (Letzter, 2017). President Trump has also eliminated federal blocks on the Keystone XL and Dakota Access Pipelines (Letzter, 2017).

Arguably, the biggest piece of President Obama's environmental legacy is the Clean Power Plan (Loris, 2017). The Carbon Pollution Emission Guidelines for Existing Stationary Sources: Electric Utility Generating Units, or the Clean Power Plan, was promulgated by the Obama administration in 2015. The stated aim of the plan was to lower carbon dioxide emissions. It intended to do this by reducing the use of fossil fuels (coal and oil) in the production of energy. Under the plan, states were given specific goals that could be met by transition to more expensive, albeit renewable, forms of energy. The net impact of the regulation was to increase the cost of energy consumption. Because low income households spend significantly more of their disposable income on energy, the clean power "tax" would be borne disproportionately by them. The Manhattan Institute estimated that the effect of the Clean Power Plan would be a 166 percent increase in the federal taxes of households in the bottom quintile of income (and on average a "total income loss of more than $7,000 . . . per person" in the United States) (Cass, 2016). Ultimately, the complete impact of the clean power tax is properly understood as higher prices paid by all Americans on almost all goods and services purchased as companies pass on their higher cost of energy (Loris, 2015).

President Obama's use of executive authority to promulgate what the Congress refused to legislate was offensive to some. But even more offensive was the conclusion reached by some about the anticipated benefits of the Clean Power Plan. According to Heritage, the Obama Administration's climate regulations would "avert a meager –0.018 degree Celsius (C) of warming by the year 2100" (Loris, 2015). Going farther, the Heritage Foundation concluded that if 100 percent of CO_2 emissions were reduced, global warming would not be impacted. This is primarily because of a few factors. First, there is evidence to suggest that the environment is increasingly insensitive to increases in CO_2 emissions, thus increased reductions are ineffective (Loris, 2015). Second, to achieve significant enough reductions to be meaningful, it would be necessary "to force damaging cuts from rapidly developing countries, such as India and China, and even that might not be enough" (Loris, 2015). Finally, even though CO_2 contributes 81 percent of all greenhouse gas emissions, other greenhouse gasses such as methane, nitrous oxide, and fluorinated gases contribute much more significantly to global warming (Environmental Protection Agency, NDa). For example, methane has 28 to 36 times the Global Warming Potential of CO_2, nitrous oxide 265 to 298 times the Global Warming Potential of CO_2, and fluorinated gases have a Global Warming Potential as high as tens of thousands of times greater than CO_2 (Environmental Protection Agency, NDb). The perceived economic cost and ineffectiveness of the Clean Power Plan regulations are what led Heritage to conclude that the overall policy was bad.

Not all, however, denounce the Clean Power Plan's rule making in relation to global warming. Marissa Weiss and Kathy Lambert, writing in the *Harvard Gazette*, suggest that hundreds of lives will be saved each year by Clean Power regulations, as well as a better quality of life for everyone (Weiss & Lambert, 2015). This, however, is a different argument. Heritage's argument is that the Clean Power rules will not solve global warming, thus an environmental apocalypse will not be averted because temperatures will continue to rise. Weiss and Lambert are not addressing that issue at all.

The Environmental Protection Agency seems to follow Weiss and Lambert closely when it argues for the health benefits to Americans of the Clean Power regulations; indeed, it spends more time speculating about the benefits to health, investment, and innovation, than it does making the case that the rules will remediate global warming itself (Environmental Protection Agency, NDc). Interestingly, the Environmental Protection Agency also makes the case that the production of greenhouse gases is bad in and of itself, without creating a nexus between the remedy they pursue in their rule making and the problem they are trying to solve. So in this sense, is the purpose of the Clean Power Plan to improve the quality of life of Americans or to solve Global Warming?

It is no doubt true that the Clean Power Plan will improve the quality of life of Americans by reducing pollutants in the air. Who does not want clean air? The Clean Power Plan will also no doubt spur innovation in clean energy and create jobs accordingly. But there is also a cost. In the final analysis it seems that the Obama administration wielded the enormous power of the executive branch to pursue objectives that the Congress would not support and which they could not, or at least did not, effectively link to the root cause of the problem giving rise to the purported purpose of the rule making itself.

Conclusion

Government can impose economic inefficiency on businesses and individuals by passing laws or creating regulations that are onerous. When this occurs, the economic freedom of Americans is decreased. The involvement of the federal government in the regulation of the economy can be looked at objectively. It is straightforward to look at the number of rules created by the Obama administration. From looking at the rule-making activity of the Obama administration, it is clear that that administration, significantly more than the administration of George W. Bush, and indeed more than any prior administration, used executive powers to make federal regulations, especially in the areas of healthcare, finance, and the environment. Each year it was in office, the Obama administration published more economically significant rules than each of the previous three administrations did for the corresponding year of their tenure (see George Washington University, 2018). This fact is corroborative of the conclusion pointed out above that the Obama administration decreased the economic freedom of Americans. But is this a bad thing, and should it characterize the economic legacy of Barack Obama?

It should go without saying that not all laws or regulations are bad. Nevertheless, all laws and regulations, whether good or bad, have compliance costs; and, generally it is a very imprecise science to estimate qualitatively, much less quantitatively, either the costs or the benefits of a particular law or rule—especially when you cannot agree on the policy objective that is the subject of the evaluation (see discussion of global warming above). Certainly it is difficult to reach agreement across political or philosophical boundaries on any particular estimate, because people assess good and bad very differently. So estimates of the impact of laws or rules are not necessarily the Holy Grail when it comes to evaluating the policy that gives rise to them.

This raises a profound question about economic freedom. Who is to say that economic freedom is the correct measure of economic policy or performance? Why not social justice? Social justice entails the "fair" relations between an individual and society. Consequently, the notion of social justice raises important questions. What is a "fair" distribution of wealth? What is "fair" access to opportunity? What is a "fair" distribution of the burdens that result from a prosperous, affluent society? Who actually deserves credit for building "that"? If one evaluates economic performance through the prism of economic freedom, the score reported by the Heritage Foundation completely characterizes President Obama's economic legacy. However, if one evaluates economic performance through the prism of social justice, might the answer be different?

For Obama, social justice issues were a priority that at times trumped economic considerations or were often seen as intertwined with economic policy. Timothy Stewart-Winter labeled Obama the "gay rights president," since during his tenure gay marriage became a reality and other steps were taken to achieve sexual and gender equality (Stewart-Winter, 2018). Nevertheless, some social justice issues fell short of his initial goals. For example, the Deferred Action for Childhood Arrivals (DACA) program is still in place, but on life support in the face of efforts by the Trump administration to end the program. Approximately twenty million more Americans have health insurance. But as noted recently by Bloomberg, in the first six months of 2018 only eight million were covered by the ACA-related health care exchanges while the vast majoroity are covered by Medicade expansion, 90 percent of which is paid for by the federal government.

In short, President Obama's economic legacy when viewed through the prism of social justice does fare better than it does if viewed through the prism of economic freedom, yet this assessment should be tempered by looking at overal equality. According to World Bank Open Data, the Gini Coefficient for the United States increased each year of President Obama's presidency, suggesting that income inequality in the United States was increasing (World Bank, 2018b). President Obama inherited a poverty rate of 13.2 percent and left his successor a poverty rate of 12.7 percent, a modest improvement but not enough to negate an absolute increase in the number of people living in poverty in the United States (Statista, 2018). Finally, home ownership decreased from 67.5 percent to 63.7 percent during President Obama's tenure (Federal Reserve Bank, 2018). There are other metrics that can be reported that might characterize President Obama's legacy differently, but they do not change the answers to the questions that we started with.

What role did partisan politics play in the economic performance of the United States during the Obama Presidency? Arguably, a large role. The Republican Congress forced a bad deal that resulted in the budget control act of 2011. This law accomplished its objectives in that it lowered the annual federal budget deficit, but it also probably hampered the economic recovery. Once the Democrats lost their sixty vote filibuster-proof majority in the Senate, partisan politics also played a significant role because it made impossible any meaningful legislation consistent with President Obama's stated priorities. This frustrated President Obama and led to his frequent refrain, "I have a pen and a phone." The end result was that the Obama administration resorted to executive rule making to "legislate" in important areas such as finance, healthcare, and especially the environment (but also immigration). It is hard to find any significant legislative accomplishment by President Obama once the Democrats lost complete control of the government. Partisan political bickering by both parties lies at the root of this fact. Zelzer (2018) captures the partisan reality of the times when he noted that "[t]he President could take Speaker of the House John Boehner out to play as much golf and drink as much bourbon as their hearts desired, but it wouldn't make one iota of difference."

In leading the United States economy out of recession, was President Obama an innovator, or did he adhere to economic orthodoxy? President Obama was arguably not the most liberal (progressive) president. According to FiveThirtyEight, that designation belongs to President Jimmy Carter (Silver, 2011). President Obama's ideology, according to FiveThirtyEight, was mostly in line with the center of his party (Silver, 2011). One can make of this what they will, but it does point to the conclusion that President Obama was not an innovator, unless it can be said that the policies of the Democratic party were innovative and there is simply no evidence of this. In each of the major policy areas briefly examined above, President Obama's objectives were also the long-standing objectives of the Democratic Party and he adhered to Democratic orthodoxy in his pursuit of them. While Democrats and Republicans generally want the same end results from policy, each party subscribes to a different orthodoxy in pursuit of them. Democrats generally favor more government participation in, and regulation of, the economy than Republicans. President Obama's policies favored more, not less, government involvement in the economy. His two signature legislative accomplishments and his rule-making behavior made this clear.

In the final analysis, Robert Samuelson may be right. President Obama's greatest achievement occurred during his first year as president when he stopped the United States, and probably the world, from slipping into another Great Depression. He deserves great credit for this.

References

Amadeo, K. (2010a). The balance. https://www.thebalance.com/what-was-obamas-stimulus-package-3305625.

Amadeo, K. (2010b). The balance. https://www.thebalance.com/2010-patient-protection-affordable-care-act-3306063.

Baily, N. B., Klein, A., & Schardin, J. (2017, January). The impact of the Dodd-Frank Act on financial stability and economic growth. *The Russell Sage Foundation Journal of the Social Science.*

Bryan, B. (2017, January 20). Here's how much debt the US government added under President Obama, *Business Insider.* https://www.businessinsider.com/national-debt-deficit-added-under-president-barack-obama-2017-1.

Carlino, G. (2017). Did the fiscal stimulus work? Billions were spent to recover from the great recession. How can we know whether taxpayers got a decent bang for the buck. *Economic Insights.* Federal Reserve Bank of Philadelphia Research Department. First Quarter.

Cass, O. (2016). Who pays the bill for the Obama climate agenda? Manhattan Institute: Issues. https://www.manhattan-institute.org/sites/default/files/IB-OC-0416.pdf.

Collins, S., Bhupal, H., & Doty, M. (2019). Health insurance coverage eight years after the ACA. The Commonwealth Fund. https://www.commonwealthfund.org/publications/issue-briefs/2019/feb/health-insurance-coverage-eight-years-after-aca.

Constitutional Law—Separation of Powers—Congress Delegates Power to Raise the Debt Ceiling.—Budget Control Act of 2011, Pub. L. No. 112-25, 125 Stat. 240 (to be codified in scattered sections of the U.S. Code). (2012). *Harvard Law Review, 125*(3), 867–874. http://www.jstor.org/stable/41349895.

Driessen, G. A., & Labonte, M. (2015, December 29). The Budget Control Act of 2011 as Amended: Budgetary Effects, Congressional Research Service. https://fas.org/sgp/crs/misc/R42506.pdf.

Environmental Protection Agency. (No Date (ND)a). Greenhouse gas emissions. https://www.epa.gov/ghgemissions/overview-greenhouse-gases.

Environmental Protection Agency. (No Date NDb). Understanding global warming potentials. https://www.epa.gov/ghgemissions/understanding-global-warming-potentials.

Environmental Protection Agency. (No Date NDc). Fact sheet: Clean power plan benefits: Why we need a cleaner, more efficient power sector. https://archive.epa.gov/epa/cleanpowerplan/fact-sheet-clean-power-plan-benefits.html.

Federal Reserve Bank. (2018, October). Home ownership rate for the United States. https://fred.stlouisfed.org/series/RHORUSQ156N#0.

Galston, W. (2017, July 10). Obama's uncertain legacy. Brookings Institute. https://www.brookings.edu/opinions/obamas-uncertain-legacy.

George Washington University. Regulatory Studies Center. (2018). Economically significant rules. https://regulatorystudies.columbian.gwu.edu/economically-significant-rules.

Heritage Foundation. (2018). Index of economic freedom. https://www.heritage.org/index/visualize.

IGM Forum. (2012, February 15). Economic stimulus. http://www.igmchicago.org/surveys/economic-stimulus.

Letzter, R. (2017, February 25). Here's where 5 key Obama environmental policies stand under Trump. *Business Insider.* https://www.businessinsider.com/obama-trump-environment-policies-2017-2.

Loris, N. (2015, July 7). The many problems of the EPA's clean power plan and climate regulations: A primer. Heritage Foundation, Report: Environment. https://www.heritage.org/environment/report/the-many-problems-the-epas-clean-power-plan-and-climate-regulations-primer.

Loris, N. (2017, October 10). Obama's climate plan was a failure on all accounts. Heritage Foundation. https://www.heritage.org/environment/commentary/obamas-climate-plan-was-failure-all-accounts.

McGarry, B. W. (2018, July 13). The defense budget and the Budget Control Act: Frequently asked questions. Congressional Research Service. https://fas.org/sgp/crs/natsec/R44039.pdf.

Michael, N., & Furth, S. (2017). The macroeconomic impact of Dodd Frank—and of its repeal. Heritage Foundation. https://www.heritage.org/markets-and-finance-/report/the-macroeconomic-impact-dodd-frank-and-its-repeal.

Miller, T., & Kim, A. B. (2014). Index of economic freedom, chapter 5: Defining economic freedom. https://thf_media.s3.amazonaws.com/index/pdf/2010/Index2010_Chapter5.pdf.

Mulligan, C. (2016). Has Obamacare been good for the economy? Manhattan Institute. https://www.manhattan-institute.org/download/9022/article.pdf.

National Bureau of Economic Research. (2018). https://www.nber.org/cycles/cyclesmain.html.

Nelson, A. (2016, October 10). 15 things Obama has done for the environment. MNN. https://www.mnn.com/earth-matters/wilderness-resources/stories/things-obama-has-done-environment.

Perkins, D. W., Getter, D. E., Labonte, M., Shorter, G., Su, E., & Weiss, N. E. (2018). Economic growth, regulatory relief, and Consumer Protection Act (P.L. 115–174) and Selected policy issues. https://fas.org/sgp/crs/misc/R45073.pdf.

Rauchway, E. (2018). Neither a depression or new deal: Bailout, stimulus, and the economy. In Zelzer, J. (Ed.), *The presidency of Barack Obama: A first historical assessment.* Princeton University Press.

Samuelson, R. J. (2017, January 15). What Obama deserves credit for—and doesn't. *Washington Post.* https://www.washingtonpost.com/opinions/what-obama-

deserves-credit-for--and-doesnt/2017/01/15/c097f910-d9ae-11e6-9a36-1d29 6534b31e_story.html.
Shapiro, S. (2015, June 10). Obama's use of regulation to make environmental policy: Not unusual, and not illegal. *The Conversation*. https://the conversation.com/obamas-use-of-regulation-to-make-environmental-policy-not-unusual-and-not-illegal-42875.
Silver, Nate. (2011, April 29). How liberal is President Obama? FiveThirtyEight. https://fivethirtyeight.com/features/how-liberal-is-president-obama/.
Statista. (2018). Poverty rate in the United States from 1990 to 2017. https://www.statista.com/statistics/200463/us-poverty-rate-since-1990/.
Stewart-Winter, T. (2018). The gay rights president. In Zelzer, J. (Ed.), 2018. *The presidency of Barack Obama: A first historical assessment*. Princeton University Press.
Weiss, M., & Lambwert, K. (2015). Benefits of Clean Power are clear. *Harvard Gazette*. https://news.harvard.edu/gazette/story/2015/05/benefits-of-clean-power-plan-are-clear/.
World Bank. (2018a). GDP constant 2010. https://data.worldbank.org/indicator/NY.GDP.MKTP.KD?end=2017&locations=US&start=2007.
World Bank. (2018b). GINI index (World Bank Estimate). https://data.worldbank.org/indicator/SI.POV.GINI?end=2016&locations=US&start=2000.
Worstall, T. (2013, September 20). The reason that shovel ready stimulus didn't work is that there wasn't any stimulus, *Forbes*. https://www.forbes.com/sites/timworstall/2013/11/01/the-reason-that-shovel-ready-stimulus-didnt-work-is-that-there-wasnt-any-stimulus/#254ef346dc5e.
Young, K., & Schwartz, M. (2014). Healthy, wealthy, and wise: How corporate power shaped the Affordable Care Act. *New Labor Forum*, 23(2), 30–40.
Zelzer, J., ed. (2018). *The presidency of Barack Obama: A first historical assessment*. Princeton University Press.

7

The Affordable Care Act

Obama and the ACA—Innovation by Tradition

MAX J. SKIDMORE

Introduction

The Affordable Care Act, in one sense, was a striking innovation. It had been literally a century since progressive-minded presidents had begun calling for some program that would move the country in the direction of universal health coverage. Yet—with the notable exception of Lyndon Johnson's Medicare, enormously important but limited largely to the elderly—there had not previously been any success whatever in securing such a program. President Obama's ACA broke with one hundred years of talk, effort, but no action. That alone made it highly innovative.

On the other hand, Obama's countless efforts at compromise, the inclusion of multiple revisions aimed at securing support from Republicans (all ultimately failing), the elimination of a public option (again, in an effort to placate Republicans and also, astonishingly, a former Democratic vice presidential nominee who had turned into a major legislative obstruction, Senator Joe Lieberman), and a determination to maintain the broad outlines of America's health care delivery system (private providers, private insurance, maintaining the role of Big Pharma, and protecting profits along the way) produced a complicated program. Although the ACA presented many difficulties, it did result in providing coverage to millions of people who previously had gone without, and was likely the best program that could have been enacted at the time, in view of the existing dynamics of America's political system. Despite unleashing a torrent of outrageous falsehood from its opponents who portrayed it as everything it was not, the operative principle of "Obamacare" was simply making private insurance more widely available than it had been, requiring insurance coverage, and extending Medicaid to large numbers of others who could not afford insurance. Thus, it was the most conservative program possible that could have moved the country in the direction of universal health coverage. Literally, it would not have been possible to have crafted a more conservative program that did so. In that sense, it was completely traditional.

The furor that it aroused was not only starkly partisan, it was so irrational as to be outrageous. In a more reasonable time it would have been unthinkable. All major legislation requires periodic adjustments to accommodate changing conditions, but the Republican position was to unite around calls for repeal, and in the meantime to adopt measures designed to make the program as unsuccessful as possible. Extreme rhetoric became ordinary. Ben Carson, a presidential aspirant and subsequent member of the Trump administration, in 2013, had—absurdly—called "Obamacare" the worst thing since slavery, saying even that the ACA actually *was* slavery in a way because it "made people subservient to government" (see Sullivan, 2013). As the *New York Daily News* noted, "Ben Carson Has a History of Clueless Comments About Slavery . . ." (Greene, 2017).

Rather than being laughed out of politics, however, his preposterous statement had no negative effect whatsoever. Such comments from countless important figures became commonplace as the age of Trump descended upon the country. Carson, as of mid 2019, remains a member of the Trump cabinet.

A Century of Attempts

On December 6, 2011, President Obama appeared in Osawatomie, Kansas, to give a speech on the economy (Obama, 2011). The venue was highly symbolic. A century earlier, Osawatomie was the location of a powerful, and startling, speech by former president Theodore Roosevelt, in which he outlined the need for a powerful and expanded national government to protect the people and ensure their welfare.

In a biting editorial, *The New York Times* said of Obama's speech that it "came as a relief," because for months "Republican candidates" had offered "a cascade of bad ideas." Despite being "an awfully long time in coming," Obama had delivered "the most potent blow . . . against the economic theory at the core of every Republican presidential candidacy and dear to the party's leaders in Congress. The notion that the market will take care of all problems if taxes are kept low and regulations are minimized." Such slogans may "look great on a bumper sticker," but, said Obama—and, one should add, correctly and in fact obviously to anyone who looks objectively—it does not work, nor has it ever worked (see Skidmore, 2017). Again, never had it worked, "not before the Great Depression, not in the 80s, and not in the last decade." Obama called for the rich to pay higher taxes, for tighter regulation of financial institutions, and for the United States to adopt education "as a national mission." The *Times* acknowledged that it was rare to hear a president "be so explicit about the national income gap," but scoffed at the charge that thinking about it or expressing concern is "un-American," as Newt Gingrich had blurted out cynically. The *Times* noted that Obama had spoken in the same town where "Theodore Roosevelt issued his call for a square deal in 1910, In demanding 'a new nationalism,' Roosevelt supported strong government oversight of business, a 'graduated income tax on big fortunes,' an inheritance tax and [quoting Lincoln] the primacy of labor over capital. For that," said the *Times*, TR "was called a socialist and worse, as Mr. Obama observed, having endured the same." Obama raised these issues, among others, to counter Republican presidential candidate Mitt Romney's "argument that business, unfettered, will easily restore American jobs and prosperity. Teddy Roosevelt knew better 101 years ago," reflected the *Times* perceptively, "and it was gratifying to hear his fire reflected by President Obama" (Obama in Osawatomie, 2011).

Much had happened in the century between the speeches of a former president and the then current one. At the same time, at least until Obama's ACA in 2010, far too little had happened regarding universal health coverage in the United States—alone, it should be pointed out—among all industrial countries. Even the ACA, welcome and as badly needed as it was, did not pretend to achieve universal coverage. A look at the efforts and the failures during that century will help to understand the ultimate passage of the Affordable Care Act, which Republican repetition, in an effort to discredit the program, indelibly had branded the dreaded "Obamacare."

The Roots of the Healthcare Debate

Although broad programs of social legislation, including health coverage, extend in Europe back to the 1880s in Germany, the first notable calls in the United States came from a former president, Theodore Roosevelt, early in the twentieth century. On August 31, 1910, at a commemoration of John Brown, he had journeyed to a small town in Kansas to present a rousing address. Standing on a kitchen table in the middle of a field, Roosevelt outlined his "New Nationalism" (see LaForte, 1966).

Biographies of TR are legion, and many, especially more recent ones beginning in the middle of the last century until now, are excellent. Among the best is Kathleen Dalton's superb *Theodore Roosevelt: A Strenuous Life* (Dalton, 2002). Astonishingly, in spite of the sparse population of the area, TR attracted an audience of some thirty thousand. Perhaps the speech's content, and the reaction it generated, were more astonishing still. Dalton calls it "the most important speech of his political career." She said that he pointed "toward reforms that would revive democracy and provide more protection for the victims of laissez-faire industrial capitalism—workers, widows, children, the poor, and the aged."

The Osawatomie address laid the foundation for the platform of the "Bull Moose Progressives"—of the Progressive Party's failed but valiant 1912 effort to regain the presidency for Theodore Roosevelt, after his Republican Party denied him its nomination in favor of the incumbent President William Howard Taft. The Progressive platform promised "the protection of home life against the hazards of sickness, irregular employment and old age through the adoption of a system of social insurance adapted to American use." Moreover, recognizing the national importance of the health of the population, it called for: "the union of all the existing agencies of the Federal Government dealing with the public health into a single national health service without discrimination against or for any one set of therapeutic methods, school of medicine, or school of healing with such additional powers as may be necessary to enable it to perform efficiently such duties in the protection of the public from preventable diseases as may be properly undertaken by the Federal authorities, including the executing of existing laws regarding pure food, quarantine and cognate subjects, the promotion of vital statistics and the extension of the registration area of such statistics, and co-operation with the health activities of the various States and cities of the Nation" (Progressive Platform, 1912).

Roosevelt's Bull Moose candidacy split the Republican Party, permitting the minority Democrats to emerge victorious with their nominee, New Jersey governor Woodrow Wilson. Reformers initially were dismayed at TR's defeat, but Wilson went on to become another progressive president, with whom they discovered they could work. That did not, however, move the country toward universal health care, nor, it should be added, did it move the country toward better race policies; in fact, from the Civil War until the complete reversal of policy beginning haltingly with Franklin D. Roosevelt's New Deal of the 1930s, the Democrats had been worse than the Republicans in their policies toward America's black citizens. Wilson's own racism led his administration to take the country backward in that respect. The turnaround of the Democrats, especially since LBJ, has been startling, and dramatic. Racist policies now are far more likely to come from the Republican Party, and rejected by Democrats. The most obvious case in point is the numerous voter suppression efforts, all springing from Republicans eager to seize or maintain power. These, in fact, are the most notorious denial of the vote to qualified citizens since those of the post–Civil War South. It is difficult to resist concluding that the Republican attack upon the extension of health care to large numbers of those previously left out is related to its treatment of the poor in general, and of racial minorities in particular.

During the Wilson era there was activity among private groups in support of social insurance in general, and health benefits in particular, including a short-lived consideration of government health benefits from within the American Medical Association. It began in 1915, when the AMA formed a "Social Insurance Committee" that included three physicians—Alexander Lambert, I. M. Rubinow, and S. S. Goldwater—who had been active in a different group that had advocated social insurance, the American Association for Labor Legislation. "The period of cooperation," though, "was brief. By 1918, not only had serious opposition developed within the American Medical Association, but many insurance companies and pharmaceutical houses had also begun to work against" any government program (Skidmore, 1970, p. 42; see also Anderson, 1951). This is astonishing in retrospect, in view of the AMA's subsequent frenzied opposition to any government involvement in the provision of health benefits.

In the 1930s, during consideration of the Social Security Act, President Franklin D. Roosevelt would have preferred to have health insurance included, but bowed to pressure from the AMA, which took no official position on Social Security, but had threatened to oppose the entire program if it contained provisions for health care (Skidmore, 1970, pp. 65–67; see also Witte, 1962, p. 173). FDR prudently concluded that achieving passage of Social Security without health benefits was better than nothing, since AMA opposition almost assuredly would have killed the bill, thus depriving the population of what was to become its best and most successful social insurance program, Social Security.

FDR did set forth a remarkable proposal, however, for an "Economic Bill of Rights." In his 1944 State of the Union message he set forth a program as radical as—and in more detail than—the one his distant cousin Theodore had called for in 1910 and in the 1912 Bull Moose campaign. FDR called not only for "adequate medical care and the opportunity to achieve and enjoy good health" as a right, but added a full range of other rights, such as decent housing, a good education, a "useful and remunerative job," and the like. The text of his address of January 11, 1944 may be found in many locations, including http://www.fdrlibrary.marist.edu/archives/address_text.html. It is worth mentioning that Cass Sunstein has brilliantly set forth, and analyzed, the argument in *The Second Bill of Rights: FDR's Unfinished Revolution and Why We Need it More than Ever* (2004).

FDR repeated calls for the Second Bill of Rights in his next State of the Union message in 1945, but died soon afterward. His successor, Harry Truman, faced opposition from Congress after the Republicans took over following the 1946 elections, becoming, as he characterized it in his successful reelection campaign of 1948, "The Do Nothing, Good for Nothing, Republican 80th Congress." Truman was unable to expand the New Deal, and certainly could not achieve FDR's Economic Bill of Rights—failing, for example, in his efforts to secure national health insurance—but he did manage to protect the New Deal from being rolled back by the Republican majorities in Congress. His Republican successor, Dwight Eisenhower, made no moves in the direction of national health care, but he did encourage hospital construction, and did sign into law the very important program of disability benefits through Social Security. Although this was not health care, it was related, at least in spirit. Eisenhower, also, under the rubric of "Modern Republicanism," refused attempts to roll back the New Deal, and accepted its accomplishments as settled parts of the "American Way of Life."

His Democratic successor, John F. Kennedy, made health care for the aged, "Medicare," a prime goal. He had neither the time in office, nor the legislative skills that he likely would have needed, to secure passage of the legislation. His strong efforts, though, did help pave the way to ultimate victory. He certainly succeeded in arousing the absolute fury of the American Medical Association, and in poking bears from the far right to fervent opposition, not the least of whom was former actor Ronald Reagan, who was at the heart of a surreptitious campaign by the AMA to encourage a flood of letters urging members of Congress to reject Medicare proposals. Reagan thundered that passing Medicare would lead—not only ultimately, but immediately(!)—to totalitarian dictatorship (see Skidmore, 1970, 2000; Skidmore, 1989; Skidmore, 2008, Appendix A). Its passage, more than a half-century ago, did no such thing, and in fact, enhanced freedom.

When Lyndon Johnson succeeded to the presidency, Medicare's chances of passage increased dramatically. LBJ, the greatest legislative genius certainly in the history of American politics, skillfully manipulated the Southern committee chairmen in Congress and in 1964 followed up on the enormous efforts by civil rights demonstrators, and managed to secure one of the greatest pieces of legislation in the history of the United States, the Civil Rights Act. The following year, he added to that huge accomplishment by wrenching two more monumental achievements from Congress, the Voting Rights Act, and Medicare. Although the relevance of Medicare to the Civil Rights and Voting Rights Acts may not seem immediately apparent, it also played a key role in the attack on racial segregation.

LBJ was not only a legislative genius, but his genius also encompassed an uncanny ability to make government work as it should. One of the best treatments of the era, however concise, may be found in *The Heart of Power*, by David Blumenthal and James A. Morone. In their section on Johnson's Great Society, they of course dealt with Medicare, including not only its passage, but also its implementation (Blumenthal & Morone, 2010, pp. 185–205).

Regarding implementation, they cite "three major challenges" that LBJ faced: "segregation, recalcitrant doctors and the sheer scope of the task." Although hardly mentioned if at all in the pitched battle for passage, "the White House overrode a cautious Justice Department legal interpretation and opened a new front in the Medicare campaign." The Johnson administration "committed itself to a social reform—desegregating hospitals." To LBJ, Medicare was far more than a program to pay bills for health care, "he saw it as an instrument for social change." In order to participate in Medicare—as they would have to do to survive—hospitals would have to provide "proof that they did not segregate." Thus, one may well consider Medicare to be another great civil rights measure. By any measure, "Medicare's implementation proved an extraordinary engine of social change—in one year American hospitals underwent a racial transformation that has had few parallels in any sector" (Blumenthal & Morone, 2010, pp. 197–198). The challenge of segregation was confronted and met.

Recalcitrant doctors also appeared to threaten the program. Johnson held firm, manipulated politicians and medical leaders, "made the rules for paying both doctors and hospitals extremely generous," and otherwise "managed to win over the physicians, whose cooperation was crucial to Medicare" (Blumenthal & Morone, 2010, pp. 198–201). That challenge, too, was overcome handily. The sheer scope of the task may have seemed at the time to have been the most formidable challenge of all. Nevertheless, because of thorough and careful planning, there were no bed shortages, no significant provider reluctance to participate, no confusion regarding records, no major troubles whatsoever. "Medicare launched with ease" (ibid., pp. 201–202). LBJ's administration deftly had met all challenges.

In the years following Medicare, neither the fears of opponents nor the hopes of advocates materialized. LBJ was gone. The Vietnam War had absorbed much of the reform impulse, and there was little national energy to be directed toward making Medicare a program for all. Despite proposals from President Richard Nixon, and some suggestions from others, despite a vigorous push from President Bill Clinton toward universal health coverage, and despite some options added, such as Part C, Medicare Advantage (designed primarily by conservatives as a foot in the door to privatization of the whole program) the only significant and true expansion of Medicare until the administration of Barack Obama came from an unlikely source: the administration of George W. Bush who as a rule had displayed hostility toward government programs.

Bush succeeded in adding to Medicare an enormous and expensive new benefit, Part D, voluntary coverage for prescription drugs. Prescription benefits have been a great advance, regardless of notable flaws. As I have written elsewhere (Skidmore, 2018a):

> Part D has its problems, but has turned out to work quite well. Violating all the strictures of economic fundamentalism, the administration of President George W. Bush shoved the program through Congress over the objections of Democrats, who argued that the program provided no financing mechanism. One should note that the program's major supporters were "conservatives;" Republicans who presumably were devoted to

economic fundamentalism, but who sacrificed such principles in order to gain political advantage. The Bush administration created a program without considerations of cost—and that program works.

True, Part D prohibits Medicare officials from negotiating drug prices with manufacturers, and thus adds to the absurdly high costs of American medicine. It also is true that this results in an enormous subsidy to Big Pharma. These are flaws. They could be remedied easily—and certainly should be.

The key point is the good that Part D does. It provides a huge new benefit to the American people, an important benefit that helps them survive the unspeakably high costs of American medicine. It also, to repeat, was created with no thought of, or attention to, the expense.

An additional key point is that in this instance the Bush administration ignored the admonitions from economists, who tend almost always to put dollar considerations ahead of the potential good that a given program can accomplish. Blumenthal and Morone argue the same point in their approach to implementing social programs, that one needs to "hush the economists" (Blumenthal & Morone, 2010, pp. 413–415). Lest the conventional wisdom cause opponents to insist that such an approach is irresponsible and unworkable, remember that this has always been the policy of the American government with regard to military expenditures, at least since World War II. Of course, there are frequent attempts to reduce government expenditures. They have declined since the Cold War as a percentage of GDP, although much of that results from rapid GDP growth. President Eisenhower was, perhaps uniquely, successful in reducing military costs. Nevertheless, rare (and ignored) would be a budget hawk who would demand that the budget set forth a given amount for the military, with the Pentagon having to work within rigid limits; rather, the Pentagon more or less gets what it wants (as do lobbyists), and budgetary considerations will be manipulated later—witness the acceptance of "cost overruns" when projects exceed amounts allocated.

Rather than end this section with praise for George W. Bush, he of the reckless foreign policy, let us note the superb competence of Lyndon Johnson in rolling out the entirety of the untried and vast Medicare structure without a flaw in implementation. Compare that to the cumbersome and awkward implementation of Part D that was a far less complicated program, but one that took years to make work right. Competence matters.

The Obama Administration

The Obama administration, too, hit the ground stumbling with the Affordable Care Act. The government's computer systems were inadequate, and caused great turmoil at the beginning. To the Obama administration's credit, however—despite the ritual sacrificing of a very capable, if culpable, secretary of Health and Human Services, Kathleen Sebelius—officials not only acknowledged the problem, but worked vigorously, and quickly, to rectify the troubles it caused. If LBJ represented the best at making government work and the second Bush the worst (at least until Trump), Obama fell in between, and much closer to LBJ than to Bush. Consider, for example, a cartoon in the Johnson County supplement of the *Kansas City Star* on August 8, 2018. Watching television, the viewer hears, ". . . the horrific incompetence of the Department of Health and Human Services . . . hundreds of families still separated . . . ," and thinks, "I remember when HHS incompetence was being a little late on launching a health insurance website" (Unell, 2018, "Opinion, 11JO").

All of which brings us to that Obama administration, and to its extraordinary accomplishment, after a century of dithering: passage of the Affordable Care Act. There, in that administration, we find two years of absolutely stunning achievement. Subsequently, after Republicans obtained congressional majorities, there were six more years mostly of rearguard action, and whether one supports a given course or not, that action generally was characterized by sound and sober policy.

The furor generated by Republicans who determined that their foremost duty—rather than to protect, improve, and strengthen the United States, which formerly had been presumed to be the obligation of all national office holders—was to prevent President Obama from achieving a second term as president, has obscured just how much he accomplished immediately upon taking office. Franklin Roosevelt had such startling achievements in his first hundred days that it has become a benchmark of sorts; actually, it is an irrational benchmark, because few presidents are able to do anything significant that quickly. Despite his empty boasts—to be sure, in common with most others—Donald Trump had little or nothing to show for that period (see Skidmore, 2018b).

Obama, however, well before the first hundred days—in fact, in the *very first month in office*—signed into law three highly significant measures. On January 29, the Lilly Ledbetter Fair Pay Act countered the harsh, if not irrational, conclusion of the Supreme Court (*Lilly Ledbetter v. Goodyear Tire and Rubber Co.*) that in order to be victorious when suing for pay discrimination women had to file suit shortly after the discrimination took place *even if they were not yet aware of having been subject to discrimination!* On February 4, the Children's Health Insurance Reauthorization Act expanded health insurance coverage for children that twice had been vetoed under Obama's predecessor, President George W. Bush. On February 17, The American Recovery and Reinvestment Act became the massive stimulus program designed to combat the economic crisis that had begun the year before Obama's election.

The legislative achievements continued throughout Obama's first two years, until he lost Democratic majorities in both houses of Congress for the remaining six years of his administration. They culminated in four pieces of landmark legislation in the outgoing lame-duck Congress while Democrats still retained control. One, the "Don't Ask Don't Tell Repeal Act of 2010," repealed the military's exclusion of gays. The second was the "9/11 First Responders' Health Bill" that Republicans had previously blocked. Third was the required two-thirds approval by the Senate of the New Start Treaty, despite the opposition of many Republicans, including Senate Majority Leader Mitch McConnell. This led to the reduction of nuclear stockpiles both in the United States and Russia, and provided mutual inspections. Fourth, was passage of the Food Safety and Mobilization Act.

Months before, however, on March 23, 2010, had come the Obama administration's crowning achievement, the Patient Protection and Affordable Care Act. In broad outline, the program requires employers to offer insurance, offering incentives and subsidies where necessary. It required Americans to have coverage, until Republicans succeeded in repealing the mandate to do so. Various incentives and subsidies were made available, also, to citizens who would have difficulty paying.

The ACA affected the manner in which insurers market their product. It established Health Care Exchanges, in which those who are uninsured, or the self-employed, can have access to a marketplace in which to compare policies. Small businesses can participate as purchasers also. States were to establish their own exchanges, but for those who did not, a federal exchange would be available to purchasers.

Costs have risen, to be sure. It is impossible to be precise as to the effects of the program on costs, especially since opponents have succeeded in keeping it from functioning as designed. Moreover, regardless of various measures through the years designed to control costs, lobbying on behalf of special interests has caused them to rise steadily, both before and after the ACA became law. It always will be questionable whether costs can be adequately controlled when profit is the motive that drives the system.

The new program, the Affordable Care Act, because of unanimous Republican repetition, quickly became the dreaded "Obamacare." It was the source of furious, and continuous, protest, virtually all misrepresenting the program, that led to public confusion and misunderstanding. Also reflecting the great Republican skill at framing issues, the phrase that now is commonly used to frame the issue is "government medicine," or "government health care." The freedom extolled, though, at base is the ability to remain free from health care. Although the Court did uphold the constitutionality of the ACA, it also ruled that states were free to ignore some of its mandates, affecting the program's results and complicating evaluation even more. Making the extremely complex program even more difficult for the public to understand fully, the legislation was designed to take effect gradually. A selective presentation of provisions and implementation dates follows.

In 2010, the year of passage, among other things, it required insurers to provide justification for unusual rate increases, with grants to states to conduct reviews. It provided funding for public health and prevention programs, gave a $250 rebate to recipients of Medicare Part D who reached the "doughnut hole" in their prescription coverage to help with costs, and would increase the subsidies annually until the coverage gap had closed completely. It provided tax credits to small employers who had difficulty in providing health insurance to employees, and it began protecting adult children who could remain on their parents' policies until the age of twenty-six. It also banned lifetime caps on coverage and placed restrictions on annual amounts covered; by 2014, annual limits were to be completely eliminated. It forbade policy cancellation, except for fraud or nonpayment of premiums, required coverage for immunizations and certain preventive services without extra charge.

In 2011, the ACA implemented requirements for what insurers quaintly call their "medical loss ratio"—that is, the amount they have to pay in benefits. For group plans, companies had to return 85 percent of their income in benefits; for more expensive individual plans, they had to return 80 perccent. Few plans previously returned so much to their customers. This was a major cost control policy, and was one of many dozens of controls. For 2011, the ACA also barred deductibles for colorectal cancer screening.

In 2012, the ACA began to reduce subsidies to Medicare Advantage plans; these were far more expensive to the government than standard Medicare. It also imposed fees on pharmaceutical manufacturers, and provided bonuses to high-quality plans. Subsidies for brand-name prescription drugs began in 2013 as a move toward closing the coverage gap in Medicare Part D. The ACA began to encourage preventive services under Medicaid, increasing matching payments to states with no patient cost sharing. It also raised Medicaid primary care payments up to the level Medicare provided, raised Medicare taxes on high earners, and imposed taxes on the sale of medical devices.

In 2014, the ACA was to expand Medicaid coverage to all with incomes less than 133 percent of poverty level who were under age sixty-five and ineligible for Medicare. It began to require citizens and other legal residents to have health coverage, and began to provide penalties for those who did not comply. It created a required list of basic services, guaranteed availability of insurance, and protected issuance and renewals with fees that stayed steady for a given area, except for variations permitted for age, costs in the geographic area, tobacco usage, and family circumstances.

In 2015, it increased federal matching for CHIP, the Childrens' Health Insurance Program. In 2016, it permitted states to form compacts, and allowed insurers to sell policies in any participating state. In 2018, it was to impose tax on more expensive, so-called Cadillac plans. For a complete list of the provisions from passages until full implementation, see the excellent summary of the timeline that Jacobs and Skocpol provide (2010).

This was complicated, to be sure, but it hardly justified the hysterical protests by opponents that it "seized control of American medicine." Regardless, the opposition was fierce, fighting all the way to the Supreme Court. The Court upheld the law's constitutionality, but undercut its requirement that states expand Medicaid. The decision also gave conservatives a stealth victory against the modern state as it shattered a major justification for national legislation since the New Deal, by questioning the rationale of tying legislation to its effect on interstate commerce. The Republican-led Congress, similarly, progressively weakened the ACA, and ultimately, in 2017, repealed the requirement that citizens purchase health coverage.

Regardless of the dire economic effects in states that refused to expand Medicaid under the ACA and thus left billions of dollars to go elsewhere, and regardless of the greater numbers of their citizens who were denied health care as a result, there were significant Republican elements, often succeeding, that blocked such expansion. The health and economic effects of such denial have been clearly documented. "A large body of research . . . shows that the Medicaid expansion results in gains in coverage, improvements in access and financial security, and economic benefits for states and providers" (Rudowitz & Antonisse, 2018).

Conclusion

The story of the attack on the ACA is in microcosm a story of the Republican Party since the 1980s, and its efforts to undo the New Deal and the basis of the modern welfare state. It also reveals in stark form the modern Republican efforts not only to repeal programs they oppose, which falls within the realm of traditional American political practice, but even to seek to make existing programs fail, which does not.

It is fascinating to hear the sitting president, his attorney general, and his supporters assert loudly that refugees and others who enter the United States without documentation are "lawbreakers," and "criminals" who need to be punished, cast out, have their children torn from them, and condemned. It is fascinating, because these very same politicians work diligently to encourage disrespect for an existing law of the land, the ACA, and take every measure available to them to make that law fail. They also fail to speak up when the "law and order president" pardons those who have broken laws they do not like, even to the extent of conducting armed rebellion against U.S. authorities. Their respect for "the law," obviously, vanishes if a given law offends their political ideology, or that of their political leaders, however erratic.

It is impossible to do more than speculate about the future of the ACA. The Democratic takeover of the House following the elections of 2018 ensured that the program will not be repealed prior to 2021. If they are victorious in the 2020 elections, and take over the presidency in 2021, there is strong likelihood that full universal health coverage will follow—especially if they hold the House and take the Senate. Proposals from several of their candidates suggest that it might take the form of an expanded Medicare for all with elimination of co-pays and deductibles, and the addition of benefits for visual, hearing, and dental care.

References

Anderson, O. W. (1951). Compulsory medical care insurance, 1910–1950. *The Annals*. American Academy of Political and Social Science, 273, 106–113.

Blumenthal, D., & Morone, J. A. (2010). *The heart of power: Health and politics in the oval office*. University of California Press.

Dalton, K. (2002). *Theodore Roosevelt: A strenuous life*. Alfred A. Knopf.

Greene, L. (2017, March 8). Ben Carson has a history of clueless comments about slavery before being sworn in as HUD secretary. *New York Daily News*. http://www.nydailynews.com/news/politics/ben-carson-history-offensive-comments-slavery-article-1.2992489.

Jacobs, L. R., & Skocpol, T. (2010). *Health care reform and American politics what every American needs to know*. Oxford University Press.

LaForte, R. S. (1966). Theodore Roosevelt's Osawatomie speech. *Kansas History: A Journal of the Central Plains*, 32(2), 187–200.

Obama, B. 2011. Remarks by the President on the economy in Osawatomie, Kansas. Press Release, Office of the Press Secretary, The White House. https://obamawhitehouse.archives.gov/the-press-office/2011/12/06/remarks-presidet-economy-osawatomie-kansas.

Obama in Osawatomie. (2011, December 6). Editorial. *New York Times*. https://www.nytimes.com/2011/12/07/opinion/president-obama-in-osawatomie.html.

Progressive Party Platform of 1912. *The Presidency Project*. http://www.presidency.ucsb.edu/ws/index.php?pid=29617.

Rudowitz, R., & Antonisse, L. (2018, May 16. Implications of the ACA Medicaid expansion: A look at the data and evidence. *Kaiser Family Foundation*. https://www.kff.org/medicaid/issue-brief/implications-of-the-aca-medicaid-expansion-a-look-at-the-data-and-evidence/view/footnotes/.

Skidmore, M. J. (2018a, forthcoming). Considering structural and ideological barriers to anti-poverty programs in the United States: An uninhibited, and unconventional, analysis. *Poverty and Public Policy*, 10(4).

Skidmore, M. J. (2018b). The early days of the Trump presidency: Policy rhetoric, vision, and reality. In J. Dixon & M. J. Skidmore (Eds.), *Donald J. Trump's presidency: International perspectives*. Westphalia Press.

Skidmore, M. J. (2017). *Unworkable conservatism*. Westphalia Press.

Skidmore, M. J. (2008). *Securing America's future: A bold plan to preserve and expand Social Security.* Rowman and Littlefield.

Skidmore, M. J. (2000). *Medicare and the American rhetoric of reconciliation.* Questia Media.

Skidmore, M. J. (1989, Fall). "Operation Coffeecup": A hidden episode in American political history. *Journal of American Culture, 12*(3).

Sullivan, S. (2013, October 11). Ben Carson: Obamacare worst thing since slavery. *Washington Post.* https://www.washingtonpost.com/news/post-politics/wp/2013/10/11/ben-carson-obamacare-worst-thing-since-slavery/?utm_term=.7f099b04f839.

Sunstein, C. (2004). *The second Bill of Rights: FDR's unfinished revolution and why we need it more than ever.* Perseus.

Unell, B. (2018, August 8). AREA CODES. Cartoon, Opinion, Johnson County Supplement. *Kansas City Star,* 11JO.

Witte, E. (1962). *The development of the Social Security Act.* University of Wisconsin Press.

8

Obama and the Supreme Court

SEAN J. SAVAGE

Introduction

Americans are generally familiar with the Supreme Court's power to interpret and check a president's powers through its power of judicial review. They are also aware of a president's power to influence current and future judicial decisions through his or her judicial appointments. Fewer Americans, however, recognize the interdependence and affinity between these two institutions. According to political scientist Robert Scigliano (1971), "Judicial and executive power thus appear to be similar in nature and closer to each other than either is to legislative power" (p. 4). Like other presidents, Barack Obama experienced and sought to influence these different aspects of the relationship between the presidency and the Supreme Court.

Barack Obama's presidential relationship with the Supreme Court did not begin propitiously. On the day after Obama's inauguration in 2009, it was increasingly uncertain if Chief Justice John Roberts had properly and constitutionally administered the presidential oath of office to Obama. When Roberts administered the oath at Obama's inaugural ceremony on January 20, 2009, he declined to use a written text and relied on his memory. Unfortunately, he and Obama used some different words. Greg Craig, the While House legal counsel, was concerned that if Roberts did not administer the oath of office a second time with the exact words specified by law then the constitutionality of Obama's authority as president would be frequently challenged, especially regarding his initial executive orders. Consequently, Obama invited Roberts to the White House to re-administer the oath on January 21, 2009 (Toobin, 2012).

During Obama's first term as president, both he and Roberts publicly criticized the Senate for its excessive delays and obstructionism in filling vacancies on the federal courts with Obama's nominees (Carp, Stidham, & Manning, 2011; Wolf, 2012). For Roberts, this issue was personalized by the fact that, as of January 2013, his previous position on the U.S. Court of Appeals for the District of Columbia was still vacant and had been since he became chief justice on September 29, 2005 (D. G. Savage, 2013). In his 2012 annual report on the federal judiciary, Roberts stated, "I urge the executive and legislative branches to act diligently in nominating and confirming highly qualified candidates to fill those vacancies" (Wolf, 2012). In 2013, Senate majority leader Harry Reid secured a rules change, commonly known as the "nuclear option," so that filibusters no longer applied to nominations to executive and lower court positions.

The Lilly Ledbetter Fair Pay Act of 2009 was the first bill that Obama signed into law. He signed it eight days after Roberts re-administered the oath of office to him (S. J. Savage, 2012). For Obama, the liberal policy changes that he sought during his first two years as president should have been accomplished by influencing public opinion and the legislative processes of a Democrat-controlled Congress rather than trying to influence court decisions through his solicitor general and judicial appointments (Toobin, 2012). Polls, voting behavior, and the results of the 2006 and 2008 federal elections seemed to indicate that public opinion and policy preferences had moved to the left, especially concerning such issues as health care reform, environmental protection, consumer protection, banking regulations, and campaign finance and lobbying reforms.

Replacing Souter

Two days after Obama's April 29, 2009, press conference signifying his first one hundred days as president, Associate Justice David Souter informed Obama that he would soon resign from the Supreme Court. Appointed to the Supreme Court by President George H. W. Bush in 1990, Souter was a moderate Republican who increasingly voted with the liberal minority of justices, especially on abortion rights and First Amendment cases. Voting with the dissenting liberal minority in *Bush v. Gore*, Souter was especially disturbed by the conservative majority's decision in favor of George W. Bush concerning the disputed 2000 presidential election (Toobin, 2008).

Souter's announced decision to resign so soon after the end of Obama's first hundred days as president was an abrupt reminder of the power of the Supreme Court to determine the constitutionality of a president's policies. Of course, it was highly unlikely that Obama would eventually engage in a dramatic, prolonged struggle with the Supreme Court as Franklin D. Roosevelt did during the 1930s (Shesol, 2010). Nevertheless, Souter's retirement provided Obama with the opportunity to nominate a replacement who would be more consistently and predictably liberal than Souter and could also diversify the membership of the Supreme Court (Carp, Stidham, & Manning, 2011). Latinos, the fastest growing demographic group in the United States, who were second only to African Americans in their electoral support for Obama in 2008, still lacked representation on the Supreme Court (Dunn, 2012). The number of women on the Supreme Court had declined from two to one since George W. Bush had replaced Sandra Day O'Connor, a pro-choice moderate, with Samuel Alito, an anti–abortion rights conservative.

Determined to nominate a woman to replace Souter, Obama narrowed his search to three women: Janet Napolitano, Diane Wood, and Sonia Sotomayor. Napolitano was Obama's secretary of homeland security and had previously been governor of Arizona. Unlike Wood and Sotomayor, Napolitano had never served as a judge. As with Bill Clinton's serious consideration of Mario Cuomo as a nominee to the Supreme Court, Obama was briefly attracted to the idea of nominating a former governor with no judicial experience who could become known as "the people's justice" (Toobin, 2008).

But there were complications with nominating Napolitano. She had been serving as secretary of homeland security for only a few months, and her appointment to the Supreme Court would mean that Obama would need to find and nominate another woman to her cabinet position in order to preserve the gender and ethnic diversity of his cabinet. Also, Republican senators might use Napolitano's confirmation hearings as an opportunity to criticize Obama's homeland security policies, especially regarding border security with Mexico, and to publicize any controversies from her record as governor of Arizona.

Unlike Napolitano and Sotomayor, Obama had known Diane Wood well and long before he became president. Both had taught law at the University of Chicago. After briefly working as an attorney in the Department of Justice under Attorney General Janet Reno, Wood was appointed a federal circuit court judge in 1995. In her opinions and speeches, Wood had distinguished herself as an outspoken, unapologetic liberal activist who fervently adhered to a belief in and practice of a flexible, evolving "living Constitution," as championed by the late Supreme Court justices William Brennan and Thurgood Marshall (Toobin, 2012).

Obama and some of his advisors became concerned that Wood's well-known, extensive focus on abortion rights might provoke pro-life Republicans in the Senate and pro-life interest groups to aggressively oppose her confirmation at a time when Obama wanted to develop and sustain a cooperative relationship with Congress in order to revive and reform the economy (Elman, 2011). Furthermore, Wood, like, Napolitano, is white. If Obama's first Supreme Court nominee was a white woman, the nomination would not be a "first" historically. White male Republican senators would presumably be more likely to oppose confirming a white liberal female nominee than a minority liberal female nominee.

Obama, therefore, concluded that Sonia Sotomayor was the best choice to be his first nominee to the Supreme Court (Kantor, 2012). He would make history by nominating the first Latina to the Supreme Court. Her biography included a hardscrabble childhood in the South Bronx that could have a "Horatio Alger," populist appeal to the media and the public. With degrees from Princeton University and Yale Law School, Sotomayor had a pro-choice, liberal jurisprudence similar to that of Diane Wood, but she also had experience as a tough, crime-fighting assistant prosecutor. She had received bipartisan support in her appointments as a federal district court judge and a federal circuit court judge. With recommendations from both of New York's senators, Daniel Patrick Moynihan, a Democrat, and Al D'Amato, a Republican, George H. W. Bush had nominated Sotomayor to a federal district court judgeship in 1991. Bill Clinton nominated her to a federal circuit court judgeship in 1997. Despite Republican control of the Senate, Sotomayor's nomination was confirmed by a wide margin in 1998 (Felix, 2010). Partially because of some of her more conservative opinions on economic issues, an article in ABA *Journal* referred to Sotomayor as a centrist (Adams, 2009).

There were, however, some possible political liabilities in Sotomayor's nomination. In addition to her consistent judicial support for affirmative action policies, she had repeatedly and publicly stated that affirmative action had enabled her to be admitted to Princeton and Yale because of her ethnic status. More controversially, Sotomayor had stated in a 2001 lecture that a "wise Latina" like herself could make better decisions than a white male judge because of her life experiences as a Latina (Bendavid, 2009).

Unfortunately for Obama and Sotomayor, her Senate confirmation hearings began shortly after the Supreme Court decided a controversial case involving diversity and affirmative action policies. In *Ricci v. DeStefano*, a group of mostly white firefighters claimed that Title VII of the Civil Rights Act of 1964 was violated when the city of New Haven, Connecticut, invalidated the test results of a civil service exam for promotions because none of the African American firefighters who took the exam had scored well enough to be promoted. First in a three-judge panel and later *en banc*, Sotomayor joined other members of the Second Circuit Court of Appeals in ruling in favor of the City of New Haven and against Frank Ricci and the other firefighters claiming reverse discrimination (Vicini, 2009).

Sotomayor's confirmation hearings before the Senate Judiciary Committee began on July 13, 2009, and the Supreme Court announced its decision in *Ricci v. DeStefano* on June 29, 2009. In a 5–4 decision, the Supreme Court ruled in favor of Ricci and against the City of New Haven, thereby reversing the decision of the Second Circuit Court of Appeals and disagreeing with Sotomayor. After the public learned about the Supreme Court's decision in *Ricci v. DeStefano* and Sotomayor's earlier ruling against the white firefighters, a CNN poll revealed that public support for Sotomayor's appointment to the Supreme Court had declined sharply, with only 47 percent of the respondents supporting her appointment (Steinhauser, 2009).

Emboldened by the Supreme Court's decision in *Ricci vs. DeStefano* and such poll numbers, some Republicans on the Senate Judiciary Committee, especially Senator Jeff Sessions of Alabama, were especially aggressive in challenging various statements by Sotomayor that were similar to the "wise Latina" remark. In them, she seemed to suggest that a judge's empathy is more important than his or her ability and willingness to objectively and impartially apply the facts of a case to the law. Sotomayor calmly and confidently answered the most difficult questions posed to her by Sessions and other Republican senators. She dismissed her "wise Latina" remark as a rhetorical flourish given in a speech and suggested that the senators focus on her words used in court opinions instead of speeches. She also identified Benjamin Cardozo, a moderate Republican appointed by President Herbert Hoover, as a former associate justice whom she admired (Baker & Lewis, 2009).

On July 28, 2009, the Senate Judiciary Committee recommended her confirmation by a vote of thirteen to six, with all of the Democrats and one Republican voting for her. Her confirmation by the full Senate was very similar in party line voting. The Senate confirmed her nomination by a vote of sixty-eight to thirty-one on August 6, 2009. All of the Democrats and nine Republicans voted for her confirmation. Obama commissioned her on that same day, and Sotomayor was sworn in as an associate justice of the Supreme Court by Chief Justice John Roberts on August 8, 2009 (C. Savage, 2009).

The Court and Domestic Policy

Regardless of whether Barack Obama became a one- or two-term president, his administration's domestic policy legacy seemed to depend on how productive he and a Democrat-controlled Congress were during his first two years as president. While the 2009–10 sessions of Congress failed to pass significant legislation on climate change and immigration reform, they produced the American Recovery and Reinvestment Act of 2009, the Patient Protection and Affordable Care Act of 2010, also known as the ACA or Obamacare, and the Wall Street Reform and Consumer Protection Act of 2010, also known as Dodd-Frank. Even with large Democratic majorities in both houses of Congress, Obama occasionally struggled to secure enough Democratic votes to assure passage of a major bill, especially in the House of Representatives. For example, shortly before the House voted on the Obamacare bill, Obama needed to assure a group of pro-life Democrats led by Representative Bart Stupak of Michigan that the implementation of Obamacare would not require church-affiliated, nonprofit organizations as employers, especially Catholic institutions, to include abortion, sterilization, and contraceptive coverage in their health insurance policies for their employees (Wolffe, 2010).

Like Franklin D. Roosevelt, Barack Obama assumed that the domestic policy mandate that he received from his electoral coalition was to emphasize the use of legislation and executive orders to make the American economy more prosperous, secure, and just for moderate- and low-income Americans (S. J. Savage, 2012). Nevertheless, Obama could not ignore the expectations of key voting blocs and interest groups within his coalition, namely, single women, civil libertarians, gay rights activists, and minorities, to reverse or assuage the conservative policy positions of the Bush administration on social issues and achieve such liberal policy goals as greater access to abortion services and contraceptives, the end of the "don't ask, don't tell" policy on homosexuals in the military, and federal recognition of the legalization of same-sex marriage by a growing number of states. These liberal policy goals on social issues were more likely to be advanced or threatened by federal court decisions than by acts of Congress and executive orders (Kesler, 2012).

The importance of Obama's ability and willingness to develop and apply a strategy on judicial selection and the use of the solicitor general was especially evident regarding the "don't ask, don't tell" policy. In December 2010, Congress passed, and Obama signed into law a bill that repealed the policy. However, due to the wording and requirements of this act of Congress, the "don't ask, don't tell" policy's repeal was not fully implemented until September 20, 2011 (Matland & Walker, 2011).

Consequently, there was a contentious question within the Obama administration about whether Obama should have his solicitor general participate in the appeals of federal court decisions regarding the "don't ask, don't tell" policy to the Supreme Court during his first two years as president. Obama agreed with most of his staff and advisors to refrain from a judicial strategy and concentrate on ending "don't ask, don't tell" through passage of an act of Congress and its executive implementation. However, Elena Kagan, Obama's first solicitor general, privately disagreed with Obama on this strategy. She believed that Obama should direct her to argue for the end of the "don't ask, don't tell" policy before the Supreme Court (Toobin, 2012).

A Successor for John Paul Stevens

Less than two weeks before his ninetieth birthday, John Paul Stevens announced on April 9, 2010, that he was retiring from the Supreme Court. Like David Souter, Stevens had been appointed to the Supreme Court by a Republican president, but increasingly expressed liberal positions similar to those of his Democratic colleagues. In his dissenting opinion in *Bush v. Gore*, Stevens was especially eloquent and combative in his criticism of his Republican colleagues in favor of George W. Bush in the disputed outcome of the 2000 presidential election (Toobin, 2008).

It was hardly surprising that Obama nominated Elena Kagan for the Supreme Court on May 10, 2010. In 2009, Kagan had been one of the candidates whom Obama considered for Souter's seat on the Supreme Court. Furthermore, Obama had apparently appointed Kagan as solicitor general in order to enhance her credentials for a future vacancy on the Supreme Court, especially because she had no experience as a judge and limited courtroom experience as an attorney. Before entering the Obama administration, Kagan had usually been an academic, highlighted by her service as dean of Harvard Law School (Maveety, 2011).

A Democrat-controlled Senate confirmed Elena Kagan's appointment to the Supreme Court by a vote of 63–37 on August 5, 2010. Kagan received five fewer Senate votes in her favor than Sotomayor (Pika & Maltese, 2013). More Republican senators opposed Kagan than Sotomayor due to several factors. Kagan lacked Sotomayor's history-making ethnicity and extensive experience as a federal judge. Congress and Obama had recently enacted Obamacare, and Republicans assumed that Kagan would definitely vote in favor of its constitutionality in future cases, especially because she refused to publicly commit herself to recusal during her confirmation hearings (Gerstein, 2010). In January 2010, the Democrats lost their filibuster-proof "supermajority" of sixty seats in the Senate following the special election of Scott Brown, a Republican, to a Senate seat from Massachusetts. Despite his relatively liberal positions on abortion rights and gay rights, Brown voted against Kagan's confirmation (U.S. Senate, 2013).

Friction with the Court

Regardless of whether or not Obama could achieve a liberal majority on the Supreme Court, it was evident during his first term that the Supreme Court held the power to either protect or impede his policy direction for the nation. One of Obama's earliest, strongest, and most consistent political beliefs was that the voting power and policy influence of African Americans, Latinos, and low-income Americans should be increased and protected through effective campaign finance reform laws and executive implementation and judicial interpretation of the Voting Rights Act of 1965 favoring such voting groups against restrictive state voting laws and legislative redistricting (Remnick, 2010). Shortly after Sonia Sotomayor became an associate justice in 2009, Elena Kagan, then Obama's solicitor general, argued before the Supreme Court in favor of the FEC and the relevant regulations of the Bipartisan Campaign Reform Act (BCRA) of 2002 in the case of *Citizens United v. Federal Election Commission*. On January 2, 2010, the Supreme Court ruled in favor of Citizens United, thereby allowing unlimited independent spending on political communications by corporations, labor unions, and associations according to the freedom of speech (Pika & Maltese, 2013).

Barack Obama's disagreement with this decision was obvious to television viewers of the president's State of the Union address on January 27, 2010. The chief justice of the Supreme Court and five associate justices attended this address. As Obama directly faced the Supreme Court justices sitting in front of him, he said, "With all due deference to separation of powers, last week, the Supreme Court reversed a century of law that I believe will open the floodgates for special interests, including foreign corporations, to spend without limit in our elections. I don't think American elections should be bankrolled by America's most powerful interests, or worse, by foreign entities. They should be decided by the American people" (Woolley & Peters, 2018, 87433).

After Obama publicly scolded the Supreme Court, millions of television viewers saw Associate Justice Samuel Alito vigorously shake his head and mouth the words "not true" (Dunn, 2012, p. 92). On March 9, 2010, Chief Justice John Roberts delivered a lecture at the law school of the University of Alabama. In response to a question from the audience, Roberts said that he found the president's public criticism of the Supreme Court for its decision in *Citizens United* "very troubling." He said that anybody, "including the president, is free to criticize the Supreme Court." However, the chief justice also stated that Obama violated the "decorum" of a State of the Union address (Barnes & Kornblut, 2010).

Obama was also concerned about how the Supreme Court would interpret and apply the Voting Rights Act of 1965. In its 2009 decision in *Northwest Austin Municipal Utility District No. 1 v. Holder*, the Supreme Court decided 8–1 in favor of the Obama administration by declining to rule on the constitutionality of Section 5 of the Voting Rights Act of 1965. Section 5's provisions include a requirement that state and local governments secure pre-clearance from the U.S. Department of Justice before making changes in voting laws and legislative districts. Such changes might be perceived as discriminatory toward African Americans and Latinos in the South and Southwest. With Roberts writing the majority opinion, the Supreme Court declined to rule on the constitutionality of Section 5 based on the judicial restraint concept of constitutional avoidance, thereby deferring to Congress and the U.S. Department of Justice. However, the court also ruled that legislative districts that are defined as "political subdivisions," such as this municipal utility district, could seek exemptions under Section 4(a) of the Voting Rights Act of 1965 (Liptak, 2009).

A more contentious voting rights issue for Obama, minorities, and Democrats in general was the increase in the number of state laws requiring government-issued photographic identification, such as valid drivers' licenses, for voting. In 2008, the Supreme Court upheld Indiana's voter ID law by finding that this state law did not violate the Fourteenth Amendment in *Crawford v. Marion County Election Board*. In particular, the majority opinion, written by John Paul Stevens, ruled that voter ID laws were constitutional uses of state legislative powers to prevent voter fraud and did not excessively burden residents who needed to obtain government-issued photo IDs in order to vote (Greenhouse, 2008).

Encouraged by the *Crawford* precedent and increased Republican control of governorships and state legislative seats as a result of the 2010 midterm elections, Republicans enacted similar voter ID laws in other states. Obama and other Democrats perceived voter ID laws as being especially burdensome and detrimental to the voting rights of African Americans, Latinos, young adults, and low-income Americans, all of whom tend to vote mostly Democratic. Thus, Attorney General Eric Holder was busy challenging these laws in federal courts. By the time of the 2012 general elections, the Obama administration had achieved mixed results on voter ID laws. In October 2012 a federal district court ruled to uphold South Carolina's voter ID law, while a state judge ruled that Pennsylvania could not require a valid photo ID for voting in the 2012 elections (Gregg, 2012).

A few days after the 2012 presidential election, the Supreme Court announced that it had accepted an appeal of a federal circuit court decision, *Shelby County v. Holder*, and would rule on the constitutionality of Section 5 of the Voting Rights Act of 1965 in 2013 (Liptak, 2012). On June 25, 2013, the Supreme Court ruled in *Shelby County* that Section 4(b) of this law is unconstitutional. Without Section 4(b) of this law, no jurisdiction is subject to the preclearance requirement of Section 5 unless Congress passes a new, updated coverage formula. Obama publicly criticized the *Shelby County* decision. It had the effect of encouraging states to enact more restrictive policies on voter registration and identification and pro-Republican redistricting.

Obama's critics and opponents on immigration reform, especially Republican state and local officials in states and counties that border Mexico, accused his administration of being negligent and ineffective in enforcing current immigration laws and ensuring border security. On April 23, 2010, Governor Jan Brewer of Arizona, a Republican, signed into law the Support Our Law Enforcement and Safe Neighborhoods Act, commonly known as SB1070. This Arizona state law authorized state and local police to enforce federal immigration laws and made it a misdemeanor for an illegal immigrant to not carry registration documents required by the federal government. State and local police would also have the discretion to detain any person suspected of being in the United States illegally (Archibold, 2010).

On the same day that Brewer signed SB1070 into law, Obama delivered a speech at a naturalization ceremony for members of the military. After praising the federal law that facilitated citizenship for immigrants who served in the military, Obama criticized state laws and bills directed against illegal immigrants. He denounced the "irresponsibility by others" that includes "the recent efforts in Arizona, which threatened to undermine basic notions of fairness that we cherish as Americans, as well as the trust between police and their communities that is so crucial to keeping us safe" (Woolley & Peters, 2018, 87792).

The Obama administration challenged SB1070 in federal district and circuit courts as an unconstitutional violation of the federal government's authority to make and enforce immigration laws. In 2011, the U.S. Court of Appeals for the Ninth Circuit ruled in favor of the Obama administration's position and against the Arizona law. Arizona appealed this decision to the Supreme Court.

On June 25, 2012, the Supreme Court struck down most provisions of the Arizona law. The majority opinion, written by Anthony Kennedy and joined by John Roberts, ruled that SB1070 violated the Constitution by usurping the enumerated powers of Congress and that states cannot make and enforce their own immigration rules. The only major provision of SB1070 upheld by the Supreme Court was the "show me your papers" provision requiring suspected illegal immigrants to show their registration documents to state and local police (Cohen, 2012). Obama and other opponents of the Arizona law were concerned that the Supreme Court's decision in favor of the "show me your papers" provision would increase the racial profiling of Latinos by state and local police in Arizona. In a statement responding to the Supreme Court's decision in *Arizona v. United States*, Obama said, "Going forward, we must ensure that Arizona law enforcement officials do not enforce this law in a manner that undermines the civil rights of Americans" (Woolley & Peters, 2018, 101053).

The Courts and Obamacare

However, during the late spring and early summer of 2012, Americans were more concerned about how the Supreme Court would rule regarding the Patient Protection and Affordable Care Act of 2010, also known as

Obamacare. This was an election year, and Republicans promised to either repeal or significantly change Obamacare. The media, politicians, and the general public assumed that the first major case challenging Obamacare and accepted by the Supreme Court would focus on the constitutional question of whether Obamacare's individual mandate provision violated the commerce clause (Toobin, 2012).

As a judge serving on the United States Court of Appeals for the District of Columbia Circuit, Roberts had written a dissenting opinion in the case of *Rancho Viejo, LLC v. Norton* in 2003. While his colleagues ruled to uphold a specific implementation of the Endangered Species Act as constitutional under the commerce clause, Roberts disagreed and contended that the decision was inconsistent with the *Lopez* and *Morrison* precedents. In particular, he argued that the commerce clause should not be interpreted so broadly that it gives Congress the authority to regulate and protect the California toad, an animal whose habitat is limited to one state (Gertz, 2005).

It seemed likely, therefore, that Roberts would interpret the individual mandate of Obamacare as unconstitutional according to the commerce clause. Opponents of the individual mandate generally hoped and assumed that Roberts would lead a 5–4 majority in ruling against the individual mandate. If any of the Republican justices joined the four Democratic justices in upholding the individual mandate, it was most likely to be Anthony Kennedy. Ever since Sandra Day O'Connor had retired from the Supreme Court, Kennedy had distinguished himself as the Republican justice most likely to be a swing vote in close decisions. For example, Kennedy had voted with the majority in the *Lopez* decision in striking down the Gun Free School Zones Safety Act of 1990 as a violation of the commerce clause. But he also voted with the majority in *Gonzales v. Raich* in upholding the Controlled Substances Act of 1970 as a constitutional use of Congress's power to regulate interstate commerce (Toobin, 2008).

With the 2012 presidential election intensifying partisan conflicts over Obamacare, Obama did something unusual and controversial regarding a president's relationship with the Supreme Court. More than two months before the Supreme Court announced its decision in *National Federation of Independent Business v. Sebelius*, Obama publicly lectured the Supreme Court on its responsibility in this case. During a question-and-answer period following a speech delivered to the Associated Press on April 3, 2012, Obama stated, "I expect the Supreme Court actually to recognize that and abide by well-established precedence out there. And so the burden is on those who would overturn a law like this" (Woolley & Peters, 2018, 100450).

On June 28, 2012, the Supreme Court announced its decision in *National Federation of Independent Business v. Sebelius*. By a 5–4 vote, with the majority opinion written by Chief Justice John Roberts, it upheld the Patient Protection and Affordable Care Act's individual mandate. Roberts, however, was careful to emphasize that the majority opinion was upholding the individual mandate according to Congress's power to tax by interpreting the fine for not complying with the individual mandate as a tax. Consequently, Roberts was not ruling on the individual mandate's constitutionality according to the commerce clause or the necessary and proper clause of Article 1. The chief justice wrote that "the Commerce Clause does not support the individual mandate" (SCOTUS, 2013). However, he concluded, "The Affordable Care Act's mandate that certain individuals pay a financial penalty for not obtaining health insurance may reasonably be characterized as a tax. Because the Constitution permits such a tax, it is not our role to forbid it, or to pass upon its wisdom or fairness" (SCOTUS, 2013). On another constitutional issue regarding Obamacare, seven justices, including Roberts and Elena Kagan, struck down a provision that empowered the federal government to deny all federal Medicaid funds to states that refused to participate in Obamacare's expansion of Medicaid coverage.

Roberts's vote in favor of the individual mandate should not have been very surprising. His majority opinion regarding this provision of Obamacare was based on Congress's power to tax and not on its power to regulate interstate commerce. There was no evidence that Roberts had radically changed his generally conservative interpretation of the commerce clause. Indeed, his majority opinion in *National Federation of Independent Business v. Sebelius* suggested that several provisions of Obamacare may be challenged in the future concerning this law's constitutionality according to the commerce clause. Also, Roberts's conservative jurisprudence was partially based on judicial restraint. By contrast, Antonin Scalia's judicial behavior seemed to be increasingly influenced by his desire to use judicial activism to achieve conservative policy goals. According to journalist Jeffrey Toobin (2012), "Roberts had dual goals for his time as chief justice—to push his own ideological agenda but also to preserve the court's place as a respected final arbiter of the nation's disputes. Scalia's vision of the justices as gladiators against the president unnerved Roberts" (p. 286).

Shortly after the Supreme Court announced its decision in *National Federation of Independent Business v. Sebelius*, Obama commended the Court for its decision. In contrast to the cautious, nuanced wording of Roberts's opinion upholding the individual mandate according to Congress's power to tax, the content and tone of Obama's remarks conveyed the impression that the Supreme Court's decision was a broad, confident affirmation of the Patient Protection and Affordable Care Act's constitutionality in general. Obama said that the Supreme Court "reaffirmed a fundamental principle that here in America, the wealthiest nation on Earth, no illness or accident should lead to any family's financial ruin." The president concluded, "The highest court in the land has now spoken. . . . With today's announcement, it's time for us to move forward, to implement and, where necessary, to improve on this law" (Woolley & Peters, 2018, 101087). However, in its 2014 decision in *Burwell v. Hobby Lobby*, the Court ruled that the Obamacare law cannot require "closely held" for-profit corporations as employers to provide their employees with contraceptive coverage that violates the religious beliefs of the employers.

Same-Sex Marriage

During his 2012 presidential campaign, Obama publicly announced his support of same-sex marriage. Earlier, he had urged Congress to repeal the Defense of Marriage Act of 1996 (DOMA) and directed the U.S. Department of Justice to decline to support DOMA in federal courts. In his 2013 inaugural address, Obama boldly asserted that homosexuals must become entirely equal under the law. He stated, "Our journey is not complete until our gay brothers and sisters are treated like anyone else under the law—for if we are truly equal, then surely the love we commit to one another must be equal as well" (Woolley & Peters, 2018, 102827). On December 7, 2012, the Supreme Court announced that it had accepted the case of *United States v. Windsor* concerning Section 3 of the Defense of Marriage Act of 1996. Section 3 defined only heterosexual marriage as being a legal marriage regarding the applicability of marriage for approximately one thousand federal laws and programs (Nagourney, 2012).

During Obama's second term, the Supreme Court ruled in favor of marriage equality for same-sex couples in *United States v. Windsor* in 2013 and *Obergefell v. Hodges* in 2015. In *Windsor*, the Supreme Court struck down Section 3 of the Defense of Marriage Act of 1996 as a violation of the Fifth Amendment. In *Obergefell*, it required states to issue marriage licenses to same-sex couples and to recognize the validity of same-sex couples' marriage licenses from other states according to the Fourteenth Amendment. On June 26, 2015, the same day that the Supreme Court announced its decision in *Obergefell*, Obama commended the Supreme Court for ruling "that the Constitution guarantees marriage equality" (Woolley & Peters, 2018, 110386).

Conclusion

On March 16, 2016, approximately one month after the death of associate justice Antonin Scalia, Obama announced his nomination of Merrick B. Garland to the Supreme Court. Obama expressed his confidence that the Republican-controlled Senate would confirm Garland's nomination because of Garland's distinguished record as chief judge of the D.C. circuit court (Woolley & Peters, 2018, 115077). Senate Majority Leader Mitch McConnell, however, stated that the Senate would wait until the next president nominated his or her candidate to this vacant seat. In a campaign speech delivered on October 24, 2016, in La Jolla, California, Obama warned his audience that continued Republican control of the Senate meant that Republicans would continue to "block the appointment of perhaps the most qualified jurist ever to be nominated to the Supreme Court, Merrick Garland" (Woolley & Peters, 2018, 119537). In 2017, the GOP-controlled Senate applied Harry Reid's "nuclear option" to Supreme Court nominations. Orchestrated by Senate majority leader Mitch McConnell, this rules change enabled President Donald Trump to replace Scalia with Neil Gorsuch by a simple majority vote in the Senate.

Major Supreme Court decisions during Obama's presidency either fulfilled or frustrated the achievement of liberal policy goals sought by Obama. His two appointments to the Supreme Court increased its gender and ethnic diversity while reducing its conservatism. However, the Senate's refusal to conduct hearings and vote on Obama's nomination of Merrick B. Garland prevented Obama from becoming the first president since Ronald Reagan to appoint more than two Supreme Court justices. In short, Barack Obama's relationship with the Supreme Court was similar to that of most presidents, both fulfilling and frustrating.

References

Adams, E. A. (2009, April 30). Who will replace Justice Souter? *ABA Journal*. http://www.abajournal.com/news/article/who will_replace_justice_souter/html.

Archibold, R. C. (2010, April 23). Arizona enacts stringent law on immigration. *The New York Times*. http://www.nytimes.com/2010/04/24/us/politics/24immig.html.

Baker, P., & Lewis, N. A. (2009, July 14). Republicans press judge about bias. *The New York Times*. http://www.nytimes.com/2009/07/15/us/politics/15confirm.html.

Barnes, R., & Kornblut, A. E. (2010, March 11). It's Obama vs. the Supreme Court, round 2, over campaign finance ruling. *The Washington Post*. http://www.washingtonpost.com/wp-dyn/content/article/2010/03/09/AR2010030903040.html.

Bendavid, N. (2009, June 4). Sotomayor's talk made no waves in '01. *The Wall Street Journal*. http://www.online.wsj/article/SB24404932521081845.html.

Brattebo, D. M., & Watson, R. P. (2012). Making history. In R. P. Watson, J. Covarrubias, T. Lansford, & D. M. Brattebo (Eds.), *The Obama presidency: A preliminary assessment* (pp. 401–418). State University of New York Press.

Bravin, J., & Radnofsky, L. (2012, June 29). Court backs Obama on health law. *The Wall Street Journal*. http://www.wsj.com/article/SB10001424052702304898704577480371370927862/html.

Bronner, E. (2013, January 26). A flood of suits fights coverage of birth control. *The New York Times*. http://www.nytimes.com/2013/01/27/health/religious-groups-employers-battle-contraception-mandate.html?scp=3&sq=religious+liberty&st=nyt/html.

Carp, R. A., Stidham, R., & Manning, K. L. (2011). *Judicial process in America*. CQ Press.

Cohen, A. (2012, June 25). Razing Arizona: Supreme Court sides with feds on immigration. *The Atlantic*. http://www.theatlantic.com/national/archive/2012/06/razing-arizona-supreme-court-sides-with-feds-on-immigration/258932/.html.

Dunn, J. (2012). The spirit is partially willing: The legal realism and half-hearted minimalism of President Obama. In C. McNamara & M. M. Marlowe (Eds.), *The Obama presidency in the constitutional order* (pp. 91–109). Rowman & Littlefield.

Elman, E. (2011). Defining the scope of extortion liability after *Scheidler v. NOW*. *New York University Journal of Legislation and Public Policy*, 14, pp. 213–243.

Felix, A. (2010). *Sonia Sotomayor: The American dream*. Berkley.

Gerstein, J. (2010, July 13). GOP presses Kagan on health reform recusal. *Politico*. http://www.politico.com/blogs/joshgerstein/0710/GOP-presses-Kagan-on-health-reform-recusal.html.

Gertz, E. (2005, July 23). John G. Roberts' enviro record not so green, but also not provoking a lot of protest. *Grist.* http://www.grist.org/article/gertz-roberts/.html.

Greenhouse, L. (2008, April 29). In a 6-to-3 vote, justices uphold a voter ID law. *The New York Times.* http://www.nytimes.com/2008/04/29/washington/29scotus.html?scp=10&sq=Crawford+v.+Marion&st=nyt./html.

Greenhouse, L. (2012, May 30). The fire next term. *The New York Times.* http://opinionator.blogs.nytimes.com/2012/05/30/the-fire-next-term/.html.

Gregg, C. (2012, October 2). Judge rules photo ID won't be required for Pennsylvania voters this year. CBS. http://philadelphia.cbslocal/2012/10/02/judge-rules-photo-id-wont-be-required-for-penna-voters-this-year/html.

Kantor, J. (2012). *The Obamas: A mission, a marriage.* Allen Lake.

Kesler, C. R. (2012). *I am the change: Barack Obama and the crisis of liberalism.* Harper Collins.

Liptak, A. (2009, June 22). Justices retain oversight by U.S. on voting. *The New York Times.* http://www.nytimes.com/2009/06/23/us/23scotus.html.

Liptak, A. (2012, November 10). Justices to revisit voting act in view of a changing South. *The New York Times.* http://www.nytimes.com/2012/11/10/us/supreme-court-to-revisit-voting-act-in-view-of-a-changing-south/html.

Matland, R. E., & Walker, A. L. (2011). Obama and social policy: Acclamation or alienation among women, minorities, and gays. In S. E. Schier (Ed.), *Transforming America: Barack Obama in the White House* (pp. 189–210). Rowman & Littlefield.

Maveety, N. (2011). A transformative politics of judicial selection?: President Obama and the federal judiciary. In S. Schier, Ed., *Transforming America: Barack Obama in the White House* (pp. 163–185). Rowman & Littlefield.

Nagourney, A. (2012, December 8). Worry tempers joy over gay marriage's moment in court. *The New York Times.* http://www.nytimes.com/2012/12/09/us/gay-activists-weigh-possibilities-of-marriage-ruling/.html.

Pika, J. A., & Maltese, J. A. (2013). *The politics of the presidency.* CQ Press.

Remnick, D. (2010). *The bridge: The life and rise of Barack Obama.* Knopf.

Rosen, J. (2009, May 1). The stealth justice. *The New York Times.* http://www.nytimes.com/2009/05/02/opinion/02rosen.html.

Savage, C. (2009, August 8). Sotomayor sworn in as Supreme Court justice. *The New York Times.* http://www.nytimes.com/2009/08/09/us/politics/09sotomayor/.html.

Savage, D. G. (2010, July 6). Nation's future hinges on Obama-Roberts duel. *The Wenatchee World.* http://www.wenatcheeworld.com/news/2010/jul/06/nations-future-hinges-on-obama-roberts-duel/.html.

Savage, D. G. (2013, January 5). Obama struggles to nominate, confirm federal judges. *Los Angeles Times.* http://articles.latimes.com/print/2013/jan/05/nation/la-na-obama-judges-20130106/.html.

Savage, S. J. (2012). The first hundred days. In R. P. Watson, J. Covarrubias, T. Lansford, & D. M. Brattebo (Eds.), *The Obama presidency: A preliminary assessment* (pp. 85–98). State University of New York Press.
Scigliano, R. (1971). *The Supreme Court and the presidency*. Free Press.
SCOTUS (Supreme Court of the United States). (2012). *National Federation of Independent Business v. Sebelius*. http://www.supremecourt.gov/opinions/11pdf/11-393c3a2.pdf.
Serrano, R. A. (2005, August 4). Roberts donated help to gay rights case. *Los Angeles Times*. http://articles.latimes.com/2005/aug/04/nation/na-roberts4/.html.
Shesol, J. (2010). *Supreme power: Franklin Roosevelt vs. the Supreme Court*. W. W. Norton.
Steinhauser, P. (2009, July 10). CNN poll: Do Americans want Sotomayor? *CNN*. http://www.cnn.com/2009/07/10/cnn-poll-do-americans-want-sotomayor-confirmed/.html.
Toobin, J. (2008). *The nine: Inside the secret world of the Supreme Court*. Anchor Books.
Toobin, J. (2012). *The oath: The Obama White House and the Supreme Court*. Doubleday.
U.S. Election Atlas. (2012, Novermber 9). 2012 senatorial general election results. *U.S. Election Atlas*. http://www.uselectionatlas.org/RESULTS/national.php?year=2012&f=1&off=3&elect=0.html.
U.S. Senate. (2010, August 5). U.S. Senate roll call votes 111th congress-2nd session. *Senate*. http://www.senate.gov/legislative/LIS/roll_call_vote_cfm.cfm/?congress=111&session=2&vote=00229.html.
Vicini, J. (2009, June 29). Ruling could affect promotion policies across U.S. *Reuters*. http://www.reuters.com/article/2009/06/29/usa-race-court-idUSN2936044120090629/html.
Wolf, R. (2012, December 31). Roberts urges Obama, Congress to fill federal courts. *USA Today*. http://www.usatoday.com/story/news/politics/2012/12/31/supreme-court-roberts-annual-report-federal-judiciary-budget-vacancies/1801375/html.
Wolffe, R. (2010). *Revival: The struggle for survival inside the Obama White House*. Crown.
Woolley, J. T., & Peters, G. (2018).*The American presidency project* (online). Santa Barbara, CA. http://presidency.ucsb.edu/ws/?pid=.html.
Yalof, D. A. (2012). Obama and the law: Judicial restraint at the crossroads. In B. Rockman, A. Rudalevige, & C. Campbell (Eds.), *The Obama presidency: Appraisals and prospects* (pp. 223–243). CQ Press.

9

Obama and Congress

SEAN D. FOREMAN

From Senator to President

Barack Obama was elected president in 2008 fueled by great hope and optimism. Obama, a first-term U.S. senator from Illinois, also helped his party grow its U.S. House of Representatives and Senate majorities that they won in 2006 near the end of President George W. Bush's second term. Democrats had 257 members in the House and 59 in the Senate after the 2008 election. The expectations were high for legislative action and public policy change to start the Obama era.

While Obama was a U.S. senator, he only served in Washington for two years and did not develop deep personal or political connections. What he lacked in familiar relations he made up for in party unity and numbers. Democrats united behind an Obama administration with his vice presidential selection of thirty-eight-year Senate veteran Joe Biden and cabinet picks including former senator Hillary Clinton as Secretary of State. Obama's first Chief of Staff was Rahm Emanuel (D-IL), who resigned his House seat from a Chicago-area district to serve. President Obama enjoyed a Democratic majority in the 111th Congress, with House Speaker Nancy Pelosi (D-CA) and Senate Majority Leader Harry Reid (D-NV) as his party's experienced legislative leaders.

But the chances for success in Congress were short-lived. Smooth relations with the Democratic majority 111th Congress were in stark contrast with those of the last six years of the Obama administration and a Republican-led Congress. The Democratic Senate majority grew to a high of sixty in 2009 before ultimately falling to a minority of forty-six during Obama's last term. House Democratic representation steadily dropped from 257 to 188 members (see Table 9.1).

Obama's congressional majority was used to pass several significant pieces of legislation in the first half of his first term. The signature domestic achievement of Obama working with Congress was the Patient Protection and Affordable Care Act (ACA), which came to be known as Obamacare. Efforts to pass this law would consume the first-year energy of the Obama presidency while laying the groundwork for its passage in March 2010 on largely partisan grounds. The backlash to this bill led to years of efforts by Republicans to "repeal and replace" Obamacare, either in full or incrementally.

Other early legislative accomplishments included several economic stimulus programs that were passed to stabilize the economy, and financial regulations with the Dodd-Frank Wall Street Reform and Consumer Protection Act. The Dodd-Frank law was passed in response to the economic crisis of 2007–10 and presented the greatest transformation of the financial regulatory system since the Great Depression of the 1930s. Even though the Obama administration could claim credit for saving the U.S. economy from collapse, with the growing national debt and rising national deficits, and an increase in government regulations, a countermovement arose to the financial policies pursued by Obama and congressional Democrats in the 111th Congress.

Obama's working relations with Congress and members of Congress diminished during his presidency. So did the number of Democrats he had in Congress to work with him on his policy agenda. When it came

Table 9.1. Congress Party Control and Members per Party during the Obama Presidency

Congress (years)	House of Representatives	U.S. Senate*
112th Congress (2010–11)	Republican (242–193)	Democrat (51–47–2)
113th Congress (2012–13)	Republican (234–201)	Democrat (53–45–2)
114th Congress (2004–15)	Republican (247–188)	Republican (54–44–2)

Numbers are based on November election results.
*There were two Independents in each Senate session. The Independents caucused with Democrats.

to Obama and Congress, the most important innovations in policy came in the first part of the first term and were largely driven by necessity and aided by a Democratic majority. By the second half of the second term, and with a Republican Congress, Obama was largely left to use executive orders to influence policy in any meaningful way.

Partisanship

Obama was often criticized by members of Congress, Democrats included, for not fostering closer relations with chamber leaders and those needed for key votes (Graham, 2013). Obama had served just two years in the Senate and selected Biden, with his strong connection to the chamber. But there was a chorus of Democratic voices in both the House and the Senate that felt that Obama was aloof, did little to cultivate relations, and was more willing to work with Republican leaders than with rank and file Democrats to pass budget bills (Condon Jr., 2006).

Obama inherited a hyperpartisan political environment in Washington, D.C. The 111th Congress, in session during the first two years of the Obama administration, was the most polarized in U.S. history, using DW-NOMINATE scores of congressional ideology based on voting behavior. Party polarization increased in the following three elections and with each subsequent Congress that Obama faced (Poole, 2016; Reynolds, 2016). The structural impediment imposed by a Congress with polar opposite parties makes it inherently difficult to find compromise. Add to that the divisive rhetoric on talk radio and on emerging social media, and real or contrived controversy about Obama as the first African American president or with the birth certificate issue, for example, and the political atmosphere was dense.

After the 2010 midterm election it became increasingly difficult for the Obama administration to work with Congress. When John Boehner (R-OH) became Speaker of the House, he said that he and Republicans would not "compromise" on their principles but would work to find "common ground" with Democrats. "And so finding common ground, I think, makes more sense," Boehner said on *60 Minutes* (Benen, 2010). They tried to strike deals but were ultimately unsuccessful. Obama, for his part, stated at an open cabinet meeting in January 2014 that he would use his "pen" and his "phone" to influence policies through executive orders and with persuasion from outside groups if Congress were unwilling to work with him (Epstein, 2014).

Stabilizing the Economy and Passing the Affordable Care Act

Barack Obama entered the presidency at a time of severe economic crisis. The economy had been in recession for about a year during the midst of the 2008 campaign. When Lehman Brothers collapsed on September 17, 2008, and Obama's opponent, Arizona Senator John McCain, said he would temporarily suspend his campaign, Obama's polling lead began to solidify as voters decided to switch party leadership in the White House.

The Democratic Congress did pass with President Bush a $700 million bank bailout called the Troubled Asset Relief Program (TARP) in October 2008. The next month Obama was elected president and in meetings with Bush the president-elect pushed for financial assistance to the auto industry. Congress could not agree on a bailout for auto manufacturers due to regional political differences. The Bush administration used its authority to bail out GM and Chrysler with $17.4 billion in loans to be repaid to the government and a restructuring of the companies through managed bankruptcies. The reversal was viewed as a policy victory for the new administration. "President-elect Barack Obama and Democrats had long advocated that course, and Bush had resisted it" (Contorno, 2015). This allowed Obama to later claim credit for saving the domestic automobile market.

The administration had to deal with a pending economic depression and a banking and housing collapse when it assumed office. Immediately, Obama and Democratic Party leaders pushed a $787 billion economic stimulus package called the American Recovery and Reinvestment Act (ARRA) of 2009. It was the largest domestic spending bill since FDR's New Deal and passed mainly along party lines, 244–188 in the House, with all but eleven Democrats voting for it and only one Republican supporting it. In the Senate the final vote was 61–36 with all Democrats in favor joined by three Republicans. The bill called for funding many "shovel-ready" infrastructure projects across the country as well as some subsidies and tax relief.

Critics contended that with the ARRA not enough jobs were created, that the economic recovery was historically slow, and money was wasted on nonproductive loans to some companies with ties to the administration, all while adding nearly $1 trillion to the national debt (Superville, 2014; Hendrickson, 2016). In June 2011, Obama joked at an economic summit in North Carolina that "shovel-ready was not as shovel-ready as we expected" (Ryan, 2011).

Another program designed to stimulate the economy and to benefit consumers was the Car Allowance Rebate System (CARS), commonly called the "Cash for Clunkers" policy. The program was launched in the summer of 2009 to incentivize people to trade in an older vehicle for a more fuel-efficient one. The projected outcomes were to help the environment by taking older cars off the road while increasing sales of new cars. But a report released by Brookings Institution later concluded that the program was a failed public policy. "While the program did accomplish both of its goals of stimulating the automobile market and decreasing carbon emissions, there are more cost-effective policy proposals to achieve these objectives," the study's authors concluded (Robillard, 2013). The $2.85 billion program cost about $1.4 million for every job it created compared to one job created for $95,000 of additional spending on unemployment benefits, according to the Brookings report.

However, the National Automobile Dealers Association found the program to be effective. They claimed that the report missed the benefits of an additional $900 million in state and local tax revenues generated by the program. They also had data to show that additional new car sales beyond the incentive policy were boosted by the program. Another knock on the program by the Brookings study was that it "mainly benefited wealthier and more educated Americans and provided less of a fiscal boost than programs that typically target the poor" (Robillard, 2013). Ultimately, Cash for Clunkers may have been an innovative policy initiative with laudable goals, but it demonstrates the difficulty in using government-run financial incentive programs to encourage particular economic outcomes.

Affordable Care Act, or Obamacare

The hallmark domestic policy achievement of the Obama administration was the ACA, so much so that it became popularly nicknamed—for better or worse—as Obamacare. Obama declared, "Health care reform cannot wait, it must not wait, and it will not wait another year," in his February 2009 inaugural address to Congress. If Barack Obama and like-minded Democrats could have had exactly what he wanted in a health care bill he would have likely gone much further to provide greater coverage or government-financed options to more people. But it was the politics of the possible that drove the ACA over the finish line (Stolberg, Zeleny, & Hulse, 2010).

Health care reform was on top of Obama's agenda. Obama held town halls, gave a joint address to Congress on September 9, 2009, and traveled the country making the case for it. But the administration deferred to Congress in presenting the legislation, not taking an active role in shaping it, perhaps having learned this lesson from the experience of the Clinton administration's failed attempt at health care reform in 1993–94. Democrats under Speaker Pelosi proposed a plan in July 2009 and passed their version in November with 219 Democrats and one Republican in support and 39 Democrats and 176 Republicans against it.

The Senate was working on their own plan when on August 24, 2009, Sen. Ted Kennedy (D-MA) died. A Democrat was temporarily appointed to his seat and a Senate plan passed on December 24 with sixty votes in favor and thirty-nine Republicans against. But in January 2010 Scott Brown, a Republican, won the Senate special election in Massachusetts while campaigning against the health care law. Lacking a sixtieth vote to end a filibuster and pass the controversial health care bill. Senate leaders used the rules to their advantage and voted as part of a budget resolution bill to get the Obamacare bill approved under a reconciliation procedure that only required fifty-one votes for approval. The Senate version passed the House by a 219–212 vote, with all Republicans and thirty-four Democrats voting against the plan. Credit for the law went to Speaker Pelosi for getting every last vote to get it passed and Majority Leader Reid's tactics to get it through the Senate (Stolberg, Zeleny, & Hulse 2010). It also, in part, led to Pelosi losing the speakership with the rise of the opposition to the ACA, which aided in the Republicans winning sixty-three seats and the House majority in the 2010 midterms.

2010 Midterm "Shellacking"

The first midterm election of a president's time in office generally brings negative results for his party. In the case of Barack Obama, the 2010 election fit the pattern. The sixty-three House seats won by Republicans meant that Democrats took a "shellacking," according to Obama, in an election that was a referendum on Obama and on Obamacare. It was also a reflection of a slow economy, he said, as well as a reflection of voters' frustration over the partisan politics in Washington.

In the wake of these election results, the 2010 lame duck session was particularly active with more major legislation passed in December than there had been from the March passage of the ACA through the elections. During that time Democrats and Obama passed extensions to both the Bush-era tax cuts and to unemployment benefits, a bill to benefit 9/11 first responders, ratified a nuclear arms treaty with Russia, and repealed the so-called "don't ask, don't tell" policy prohibiting homosexuals from openly serving in the U.S. military. In retrospect, this period of bipartisan policy achievements represented the calm before the storm, as major budget battles between Obama and congressional Republicans would dominate the next six years.

The 112th Congress presented the president with a Republican House majority and a Democratic Senate majority. The Senate could be a tempering force to the more conservative House as long as Democrats retained the majority. Senate Minority Leader Mitch McConnell (R-KY) in an October 29, 2010, interview said the most important thing for his party was to make Obama a one-term president, so that Republicans could capture all of the branches of government. This comment was often taken out of context and used as a quote to show that there was no chance that Republicans would work with Obama, but in the same interview, McConnell also said that if Obama flipped his position on something that it would be possible to make a deal (Farley, 2010).

One area where it appeared that compromise might be possible was on immigration reform. Major issues separated the parties concerning border security, reforming legal immigration procedures, and how to handle the millions of people who are in the United States without proper documentation. Support for a comprehensive approach to immigration reform emerged around an effort in the Senate. When a so-called Gang of Eight emerged with four Democrats and four Republicans sponsoring a bill there was support among moderates in both parties to advance this plan; it was not supported by House Republican leadership. There were reports of enough support to get it passed in the House, but when House Majority Leader Eric Cantor (R-VA) lost his primary, in part because of his willingness to work with Obama on immigration, support evaporated and Boehner never scheduled a vote. Obama instead used executive orders to provide temporary legal relief for some undocumented aliens through the Deferred Action for Childhood Arrivals (DACA) and Deferred Action for Parents of Americans and Lawful Permanent

Residents (DAPA) in November 2014, after the midterm election where Republicans won the Senate majority.

The Elusive Budget "Grand Bargain"

President Obama and Speaker Boehner also failed to reach a comprehensive economic deal. Obama and Boehner were put in the tough position of being expected to work together while their party rank and file members were at bitter war with each other. Media commentators often invoked the example of President Ronald Reagan and Speaker Tip O'Neill (D-MA) and their famous ability to work out bipartisan deals in the 1980s. Initially, Obama and Boehner tried this approach sharing some private time about four and a half months into Boehner's speakership with a round of golf. They played a foursome with Vice President Biden and Ohio Governor John Kasich at the par-72 East Course at Joint Base Andrews with limited press access. President Obama was sometimes criticized for spending too much time on the golf course. But in this case it might have been useful. White House spokesman Jay Carney said, "It may move you a little bit closer toward the kind of compromise that we need to get the things done that the American people expect to get done. If it takes a few hours out on the golf course to help that process, I think it's a worthwhile thing to do" (AP News, 2011).

The relationship between the two party leaders was doomed by the circumstances out of which it was forged. Boehner became Speaker because Republicans won the House majority in the 2010 elections buoyed by the performance of conservative candidates. The fifty-plus House members who claimed a Tea Party affiliation, many of them elected for the first time, fueled the Republican midterm win. Boehner, a member of Newt Gingrich's group of GOP leaders from the 1994 takeover, aligned with the moderate wing of the party. But both the centrist Republicans and the more conservative, Tea Party–aligned members were needed in order to pass House bills. Either that, or Boehner would need to reach across the aisle to work with House Democrats and Obama in order to advance any substantive legislation—or to even pass the budget and raise the debt ceiling. They did eke out bipartisan budget agreements but never achieved the elusive "grand bargain" in budget negotiations to which both Obama and Boehner aspired.

In March 2011, two major fiscal deadlines approached. First, spending bills needed to be passed after a short-term agreement was reached on federal spending with temporary measures. Second, the national debt limit was approaching. Rather than work to produce smaller, short-term compromises, President Obama and Republican House leaders wanted to strike what was dubbed a "grand bargain," a larger agreement to settle both matters as part of a larger compromise. Short-term deals were often passed to push the problem down the road.

The "grand bargain" essentially called for Obama and Democrats to agree to severe cuts in federal spending primarily to social welfare programs, in exchange for which Republicans would agree to raise taxes, two areas that were generally off limits for each party. If Obama and Boehner could convince their parties that compromise was possible and that each side needed to give something in order to get to the grand goal, then it would be worthwhile public policy.

On a Sunday in July 2011, President Obama and aides met with Boehner and Cantor in the White House as part of ongoing secret negotiations. When they emerged, they thought they had secured a deal. But within days it crumbled. Boehner was not going to be able to secure the votes, and Obama got "nervous about how to defend" the deal to his party base. "Against the vehement advice of many Democrats, including some of his own advisers, Obama was pursuing a compromise with his ideological opponents, a 'grand bargain' that would move into unmarked territory, beyond partisan divides, pushing both parties to places they did not want to go" (Wallsten et al., 2012). Grand ambitions for a bargain with Republicans who were hesitant to work with him ultimately led to failures in Obama's first term to deliver on promises.

Ultimately, no grand bargain was struck. The Tea Party wing of the Republican Party and pressure from the conservative party activist base succeeded in stopping a deal and in toppling Boehner. When Boehner decided to retire in 2015, designs for a grand bargain were defeated. The Boehner example of leadership was one not to be followed by his successors. The reward for trying to work with President Obama to forge bipartisan deals was to anger conservatives and alienate his party base (Thrush & Wheaton, 2015). Furthermore, when Cantor, a point person in working with the president especially on budgetary issues, was defeated by a more conservative candidate in a Republican primary in 2014, in part for his more moderate stance on immigration and perceived willingness to work with the president, it was another sign for Republican lawmakers that there was little advantage in working with Obama (Baker, 2014).

From the time it was passed, Republicans plotted and endeavored to "repeal and replace" Obamacare. First, Republicans won the House in 2010 buoyed by the Tea Party movement. The U.S. Supreme Court upheld the act's legality by a 5–4 decision in June 2012, with Chief Justice John Roberts, who was appointed by George W. Bush, as the swing vote to uphold the law and write the decision, further angering conservatives. Then Obama won reelection in November 2012 and the ACA law was seemingly securely in place. The next place where opponents could seek to stop it would be by blocking the funding for implementing the health care law.

Government Shutdown of 2013

Republicans repeatedly tried to get Obamacare overturned either legislatively or through the courts. When those efforts failed the focus shifted to the finances of health care. The 2010 midterm win fueled by Tea Party candidates gave Republicans a sort of mandate from their base to act aggressively in combating government spending. However, Democrats retained majority control of the Senate through the 2014 elections, which led to odd bipartisan coalitions both in support and in opposition to spending bills and debt ceiling votes.

House Republicans were able to get Obama and Democrats to agree to lower levels of discretionary spending on social programs in exchange for defense spending cuts through the Budget Control Act of 2011. The cuts which would automatically occur if no grand deal had been accomplished were known as sequestration of funds.

Multiple times, legislative and executive leaders found themselves on the brink of a "fiscal cliff" where budget and debt ceiling deadlines would reach hard deadlines requiring legislative action on continuing resolutions or the federal government would lose the ability to pay its bills. Combine this with continued attempts by Republicans to repeal Obamacare, and it led to a showdown. In late September 2013, it became clear that a budget bill would not pass by the October 1 start of the fiscal year. Conservative House Republicans demanded that Obamacare funding be delayed by a year. Ted Cruz (R-TX) led efforts in the Senate with delay tactics that blocked a budget vote. On October 2, President Obama linked the current budget bill and government shutdown to the upcoming public debt vote, which needed to be approved by October 17. The federal government shut down from October 1 to 17, meaning that around eight hundred thousand government personnel nonessential to national security did not report to work or get paid during that time.

It was the third-longest government shutdown and the longest since 1995–96. Boehner worked a deal with Obama to reopen the government, but to the chagrin of conservatives that would ultimately cost Boehner the speakership.

The second midterm election in 2014 resulted in Republicans gaining majority control of the Senate. With the opposition party in control of both houses of Congress, the hyperpartisan political environment, and the highly contentious issues that were at the forefront of the agenda there were few significant legislative accomplishments in Obama's second term.

Supreme Dreams and Dashed Hopes

On the judiciary, Obama had two Supreme Court justices confirmed: Sonia Sotomayor by a 68–31 vote and Elena Kagan, who had served as his Solicitor General, by 63–37. Obama made a significant number of appointments to the district and circuit courts, more than George W. Bush but fewer than Ronald Reagan and Bill Clinton (see Table 9.2). Along with two women on the high court, Obama appointed diverse judges

Table 9.2. Federal Judicial Appointments by Past Four Two-term Presidents

President (Party)	Years	Supreme Court	Courts of Appeals	District Courts	Other Federal Courts	Total Judicial Appointments
Ronald Reagan (Republican)	1981–1989	3	78	290	31	402
Bill Clinton (Democrat)	1993–2001	2	62	305	18	387
George W. Bush (Republican)	2001–2009	2	61	261	16	340
Barack Obama (Democrat)	2009–2017	2	49	268	17	334

Source: Judicial Appointments by President. United States Courts. http://www.uscourts.gov/judges-judgeships/authorized-judgeships/judgeship-appointments-president.

in terms of gender, race, and sexual orientation to other courts. But his overall progress in filling vacancies was stymied by Senate Republicans who stalled the process of confirming his nominees.

The frustration of Senate Democrats with the tactics of Republicans and their refusal to confirm any nominees to the D.C. Circuit in November 2013 led them to invoke the so-called nuclear option to abolish the filibuster requirement of sixty votes for all judges below the Supreme Court. This allowed for an increase in confirmation of Obama-nominated judges. (Grunwald, 2016). After Republicans won the majority with the 2014 elections and a vacancy on the Supreme Court opened in Obama's waning time in office, Senate Republicans were able to stall the nomination to fill it until after the 2016 presidential election.

The 115th Congress was largely a stalemate, as evidenced best by the Senate's refusal to hold hearings on President Obama's nominee for the U.S. Supreme Court, Judge Merrick B. Garland. In February 2016, Justice Antonin Scalia died leaving a vacancy on the Court nine months before a presidential election. Scalia was a conservative stalwart and Republicans vowed that his seat needed to be replaced by a justice of a similar ideological mold. Immediately, conservative talk radio activists and the party leadership circled the wagons and the Garland nomination was opposed. Few Republican Senators agreed to meet with Garland, the chief judge on the U.S. Court of Appeals for the D.C. Circuit. McConnell and Judiciary Committee chair Charles Grassley (R-IA) ensured that Garland did not get a single hearing in the Senate and there were no procedures to advance the nomination. The eleven Republicans on the Senate Judiciary Committee released a letter sharing their intention to withhold consent from the nominee until after January 20, 2017. The Republican Senate leadership was able to stall and to gin up support in its party base for the idea that a Republican president should appoint Scalia's replacement. When Donald Trump became the presumptive GOP nominee in May 2016, to ensure party support and satisfy base voters he released a list of potential Supreme Court picks. This further emboldened Senate Republicans to keep the seat open until after the November election.

Obama knew his nominee faced long odds saying, "To suggest that someone as qualified and respected as Merrick Garland does not even deserve a hearing, let alone an up-or-down vote, to join an institution as important as the Supreme Court, when two-thirds of Americans believe otherwise—that would be unprecedented" (Shear et al., 2016). But the fight was not about Garland and his qualifications. It was about Obama and his legacy, or the attempt to limit it. McConnell relished his role in denying President Obama this Supreme Court appointment saying, "One of my proudest moments was when I looked Barack Obama in the eye and I said, 'Mr. President, you will not fill the Supreme Court vacancy'" (Roarty, 2016).

McConnell and other Republicans attempted to bolster their case by citing historical precedent. They pointed to the comments of Vice President Biden when he was a senator and chair of the Judiciary Committee. In the aftermath of the 1991 Clarence Thomas nomination process, which was particularly contentious, Biden had urged President George H. W. Bush to withhold any nominees during the "political season" leading to the 1992 election. No vacancies or nominations occurred in 1992, but McConnell and other Republicans often referred to the "Biden rule" as a justification for blocking the Garland nomination.

Foreign Policy

The Obama administration can claim some noteworthy foreign policy victories but also committed some significant blunders. Obama oversaw the withdrawal of U.S. troops fighting in both Afghanistan and Iraq during his presidency and claimed credit for ending those wars. He ordered the killing of Libyan strongman Muammar Gaddafi and terrorist leaders Anwar al-Awlaki and Osama bin Laden. The administration brokered a nuclear agreement with Iran, an Asian-Pacific trade partnership, and a global climate deal, and normalized relations with Cuba.

However, a "reset" of Russian relations fell flat, and the Obama administration essentially allowed Russia to annex Crimea and to invade eastern Ukraine uncontested (Haddad & Polyakova, 2018). North Korea tested multiple rockets and attempted to develop a nuclear weapons program. ISIS emerged and spread through Iraq and Syria while Obama stretched statutory authority to use force and order drone strikes. And President Obama failed to follow up on a threat issued to the Syrian leader Bashar al-Assad, who had used deadly weapons against his own citizens, avoiding greater conflict but displaying global weakness.

Obama ran in 2008 largely on the idea that he was originally opposed to the 2003 Iraq War when, as a state senator, he made a speech in opposition to U.S. intervention. By contrast, 2008 primary opponents

Hillary Clinton and Joe Biden had voted in favor of the 2001 Authorization to Use Military Force (AUMF) in Afghanistan. This AUMF permits the president to "use all necessary and appropriate force against those nations, organizations, or persons he determines planned, authorized, committed, or aided the terrorist attacks that occurred on September 11 2001 or harbored such organizations or persons, in order to prevent any future acts of international terrorism against the United States by such nations, organizations or persons." The Obama administration used the AMUF, and a joint resolution of Congress from October 2002 expanding it to Iraq, to legally justify airstrikes against the Islamic State in Iraq and Syria (ISIS). This was criticized as an unconstitutional expansion of presidential powers into war powers territory that constitutionally belongs to Congress, but it was not openly challenged or stopped by legislative actions or judicial decisions (Ackerman, 2014). Obama sought a new AMUF during his second term but Congress did not actively advance the matter.

Efforts to attack terrorism at its source by increasing air strikes intensified under Obama. Simultaneously, the Obama administration needed to deal with Syrian president Assad, who was aggressively cracking down on dissidents while amassing an "arsenal of chemical weapons" (Chollet, 2016). When asked in August 2012 what might lead him to use military force against the Assad regime, Obama said that "a red line for us" to act would, essentially, be crossed if Assad utilized chemical weapons (Rhodes, 2018). Assad did—twice—against both the rebel opposition and innocent citizens, and when his acts were confirmed Obama faced a stark choice. On August 31, 2013, Obama announced that the United States should take military action against Syrian sites in response but that he would seek congressional approval for the strikes. He was pressured by Republicans in Congress who warned that the administration lacked the legal authority for military action. Congressional leaders "nearly all expressed some degree of support for strikes but demanded that Obama seek authorization," while simultaneously not pushing to get Republican votes and then blaming Obama for inaction (Rhodes, 2018). The president also faced different messages from his advisors regarding the efficacy of using force, and struggled as well with his own inclination against it. When the idea was presented to the public, it provoked strong opposition in polls. Ultimately, as the idea of an affirmative vote in Congress to approve military action in Syria by the Obama administration seemed doomed, a diplomatic breakthrough occurred. Russia offered to facilitate a deal to have Syria give up all of its nuclear weapons in exchange for the witholding of a U.S. military response, seemingly in response to a flip comment by Secretary of State John Kerry (Chollet, 2016).

On May 1, 2011, U.S. Special Forces, on the orders of President Obama under a Title 50 operation, entered a compound in Pakistan where Osama bin Laden, the leader of the terror group al Qaeda, was suspected of staying. A team of Navy SEALS found and killed bin Laden. Obama ordered the strike after receiving reliable CIA intelligence, holding five National Security Council meetings, and notifying the Gang of Eight congressional leaders (the Speaker, House Minority Leader, Senate Majority and Minority Leaders, and the chairs and ranking members of the intelligence committees in each chamber), as statutorily required (Rollins, 2011). A week later, members of House and Senate intelligence and military committees were permitted to view photos of bin Laden's body as proof of his death, but the pictures were not released to the public. The administration claimed it would be a risk to national security and a rallying cry to opponents to publicly release them. The death of bin Laden was a major foreign policy victory for the Obama administration and for American security. Obama and Biden also used it as an accomplishment to tout on the 2012 campaign trail, with the quip, "bin Laden is dead and General Motors is alive."

The Paris Climate Agreement and the Iran Nuclear Deal were crowning multilateral agreements for the administration. The Iran deal was highly controversial because of nuclear politics mixed with complex policies toward Iran, Israel, and Syria. Basically, it called for Iran to submit to inspections and agree to not pursue development of nuclear weapons in exchange for easing sanctions and facilitating commerce. Obama claimed credit for the Iran deal and stopping the regime's attempt to develop weapon capabilities. But critics noted that the deal was flawed and that he was able to implement it only by bypassing Congress. Sen. Tom Cotton (R-AR) who cast the lone no vote, argued that any nuclear arms agreement should follow the constitutional treaty process. But Obama avoided that by claiming waiver authorities from previous Iran sanctions bills that allowed the chief executive that power.

However, Congress passed the Iran Nuclear Agreement Review Act (INARA) of 2015 to give themselves the right to review any agreement the Obama administration made through the P5+1 negotiations. It passed the Senate 98–1 and House 400–25, and while Obama threatened to veto it, he did not as the votes were there to override his veto. This allowed members of Congress to view the agreement and provide some public transparency about the deal. Ultimately, despite bipartisan opposition that fought to filibuster procedural votes and various amendments, opponents were unable to stop the administration from making the deal.

Obama clashed with Congress again in 2016 when they passed a controversial bill called the Justice Against Sponsors of Terrorism Act (JUSTA). It was the only bill passed to override a veto from President Obama. That law provides family members of victims of terrorist acts the ability to sue governments that may have helped to sponsor those actions. In this case, the law was focused on Saudi Arabia and the belief among many Americans and many members of Congress that the Saudi government had aided and funded the hijackers (fifteen of the nineteen hijackers were Saudi citizens). The Obama administration was concerned that this law could lead to similar efforts against U.S. citizens and interests in other countries.

Leadership and Legacy

The impact of rising partisanship on the Obama administration's policies in Congress was evident. With the opposition party in control of both houses of Congress, the hyperpartisan political environment, and the highly contentious issues at the forefront, there were few substantive accomplishments through the regular legislative process in the 115th Congress. Obama's second term, starting with the government shutdown in 2013 and ending with the stalled nomination of Merrick Garland to the Supreme Court, demonstrates strained relations.

There were attempts at policy innovation even while the Obama administration dealt with significant challenges. The Great Recession that the administration inherited called for emergency stimulus programs. Then, after the partisan passage of the ACA in 2010, given the poison political environment and divided party control of Congress from 2011–15, it was difficult to cultivate legislative accomplishments.

An example of policy innovation would be the CARS program. The economic outcomes of this program faced mixed evaluations. Attempts at comprehensive immigration reform and a grand budget bargain were creative but ultimately unsuccessful. On foreign policy, Obama faced a situation where he ran for office by opposing the war in Iraq and called for a more multilateral U.S. global engagement. But Obama was forced to go it alone in the war on terror with limited support in Congress. Despite calls for a new AUMF to clarify the legal situation in Iraq and

Syria, nothing new was passed in Congress. As a result, Obama retrenched and resorted to advancing his interests through executive powers.

Ultimately, Obama's overall legislative accomplishments are lengthy, as for any two-term president, but far short of expectations in terms of major goals achieved. The impact of rising partisanship greatly hindered the Obama administration's policies. Getting the ACA passed used most of the political capital in the first two years of Obama's presidency. With the loss of the House in 2010 and later the Senate in 2014 it was a challenging relationship for Obama with congressional leaders. Attempts at immigration reform, sensible gun policies, or a cancer "moonshot" program suffered as a result.

Overall, Obama's relations with Congress were weak. Some attribute it to a lack of effort or willingness, or both, to reach out to members of Congress and build relationships. It was not a model like Lyndon Johnson, Ronald Reagan, or Bill Clinton. Obama was criticized by members of both parties for not showing interest in "schmoozing" or investing in relationships and trying to work to build networks of trust that could translate into policy action. "Critics of President Obama charge that he did not make effective use of informal contacts to persuade members of Congress to support his programs. Obama showed less interest in socializing with members of Congress than some of his predecessors, and his office of legislative liaison did not enjoy especially close ties to the legislative leaders and the rank-and-file members" (Davidson et al., 2018, p. 305). Obama claimed "close friendships" with two Republican Senators including Tom Coburn (R-OK) (Condon Jr., 2016). But Coburn stated, "My friend the president isn't a great people person in terms of reaching out. . . . And I think that's probably one of his biggest failings, is not investing enough in the relationships in the Congress" (Everett & French, 2014).

Obama "was only the third person in American history elected directly from the Senate to the presidency," after Warren G. Harding and John F. Kennedy. "Though his Senate career was only a brief four years, there were high hopes that his knowledge of Congress and the close personal relationships formed in those years would pay off in smooth executive-legislative deadlines that could dent the gridlock of recent administrations" (Condon Jr., 2016).

But Obama, similar to "Harding and Kennedy, neither of whom were Senate heavyweights, instead viewing Capitol Hill as a way station to the White House," did not build many strong relationships with Senate colleagues. And, by Obama's second term, there was enough turnover in the upper chamber that there were few remaining Senators with whom Obama had close ties. By the time of his final State of the Union Address before Congress, only forty-five Senators had served with Obama, and just 185 of the 435 House members had served when Obama was a Senator through 2008 (Condon Jr., 2016).

Entering Obama's second term, the chances for legislative success appeared bleak. The ultimate lack of results confirmed this perception. In early 2013 there was a major effort to pass gun control legislation. In the wake of Sandy Hook, Obama appointed VP Biden to head a task force on gun laws in search of consensus ground. Despite public opinion in support of some action such as universal background checks, Obama and the Democrats were unable to forge a bipartisan bill with Republicans.

Similarly, immigration policy was supposed to be Obama's signature domestic legislative agenda item for a second term. But there was a sense among advisors that it was better for Obama to not be directly involved in negotiations and instead to leave to it to legislators. President Obama's "willingness to steer clear of what is clearly the biggest political objective of his second term" was troubling to observers (Kirchgaessner, 2013). Legislative efforts to advance immigration policy ultimately failed and Obama resorted to executive actions to accomplish some limited policy goals on the issue.

This led to two critiques of President Obama: "[E]ither he's a weak leader, unable to bring Congress together to pass even a basic series of appropriations bills, let alone a sweeping immigration package, or he's a wannabe emperor, someone who acts on his own with no regard for the separation of powers or consultation with Congress," (Milligan, 2015). Either way, there was a realization that the political landscape had changed drastically from the days of presidents Johnson and Reagan, who could use congressional relationships to register legislative accomplishments. But it was not solely these prior presidents' political skills that had generated policy outcomes. There were greater chances then for bipartisan voting blocs to emerge. During Obama's presidency, changes in regional party alliances, along with a more polarized public discourse, left little room in which to be able to forge winning legislative coalitions.

References

Akerman, S. (2014, September 10). Obama's legal rationale for Isis strikes: Shoot first, ask Congress later. *The Guardian.* https://www.theguardian.com/world/2014/sep/11/obama-isis-syria-air-strikes-legal-argument.

AP News. (2011, June 19). Obama and Boehner team up to win gold match against Biden and Kasich. *Golf.com*. https://www.golf.com/ap-news/obama-and-boehner-team-win-golf-match-against-biden-and-kasich.

Baker, P. (2014, June 12). Obama's odds with Congress: Bad to worse. *New York Times*. https://www.nytimes.com/2014/06/13/us/obamas-odds-with-congress-bad-to-worse.html.

Benen, S. (2010, December 13). Boehner on compromise: "I reject the word." *Washington Monthly*. https://washingtonmonthly.com/2010/12/13/boehner-on-compromise-i-reject-the-word/.

Chollet, D. (2016, July 19). Obama's red line, revisited. *Politico Magazine*. https://www.politico.com/magazine/story/2016/07/obama-syria-foreign-policy-red-line-revisited-214059.

Condon, G., Jr. (2016, January 14). Why Obama has so few friends on the Hill. *The Atlantic*. https://www.theatlantic.com/politics/archive/2016/01/why-obama-has-so-few-friends-on-the-hill/459084/.

Contorno, S. (2015, January 22). Obama says automakers have paid back all the loans it got from his admin "and more." *Politifact*. https://www.politifact.com/truth-o-meter/statements/2015/jan/22/barack-obama/obama-says-auto makers-have-paid-back-all-loans-it-/.

DeBonis, M., & Mufson, S. (2015, May 12). Senate Democrats vote to block Obama on trade. *Washington Post*. https://www.washingtonpost.com/politics/democrats-threaten-to-stall-trade-legislation-in-the-senate/2015/05/12/08f71d66-f8c0-11e4-9ef4-1bb7ce3b3fb7_story.html?noredirect=on&utm_term=.32e3e256d7f5.

Epstein, J. (2014, January 14). Obama points to 2014's pen-and-phone strategy. *Politico*. http://www.politico.com/story/2014/01/obama-state-of-the-union-2014-strategy-102151.html.

Everett, B., & French, L. (2014, July 9). Tom Coburn leaves brasher peers in wake. *Politico*. https://www.politico.com/story/2014/07/tom-coburn-politics-108686_Page2.html#continue.

Glastris, P., Cooper, R., & Hu, S. (2012, March). Obama's top 50 accomplishments. *Washington Monthly*. https://washingtonmonthly.com/magazine/marchapril-2012/obamas-top-50-accomplishments/.

Graham, D. A. (2013, February 4). Congressional Democrats are angry at Obama . . . again. *The Atlantic*. https://www.theatlantic.com/politics/archive/2013/02/congressional-democrats-are-angry-at-obama-again/272844/.

Grunwald, M. (2016, August 8). Did Obama win the judicial wars? *Politico*. https://www.politico.com/story/2016/08/obama-courts-judicial-legacy-226741.

Farley, R. (2010, October 30). President Barack Obama claims Mitch McConnell says his main goal is for GOP to regain the White House. *Politifact*. https://www.politifact.com/truth-o-meter/statements/2010/oct/30/barack-obama/president-barack-obama-claims-mitch-mcconnell-says/.

Haddad, B., & Polyakova, A. (2018, March 5). Don't rehabilitate Obama on Russia. *Brookings*. https://www.brookings.edu/blog/order-from-chaos/2018/03/05/dont-rehabilitate-obama-on-russia/.

Kirchgaessner, S. (2013, June 3). Global insight: Obama's frosty relationship with Congress bodes ill. *Financial Times*. https://www.ft.com/content/51f49574-c9fc-11e2-af47-00144feab7de.

Milligan, S. (2015, January 26). On his own. *Us News*. https://www.usnews.com/opinion/blogs/susan-milligan/2015/01/26/why-obama-and-congress-cant-get-along.

Poole, K. (2016, October 20). House and Senate means 1879–2016 (as of October 2016). *Vote view blog*. https://voteviewblog.com/2016/10/20/house-and-senate-means-1879-2016-as-of-october-2016/.

Reynolds, M. (2016, December 30). President Obama's legislative legacy and what it means for the next administration. *Brookings*. https://www.brookings.edu/blog/fixgov/2016/12/30/president-obamas-legislative-legacy-and-what-it-means-for-the-next-administration/.

Rhoades, B. (2018, June 3). Inside the White House during the Syrian "red line" crisis. *The Atlantic*. https://www.theatlantic.com/international/archive/2018/06/inside-the-white-house-during-the-syrian-red-line-crisis/561887/.

Roarty, A. (2016, August 6). Tea party–aligned Kentucky gov may end 95-year Democratic reign. *Rollcall*. http://www.rollcall.com/news/politics/34561-2.

Rollins, J. (2011, May 5). Osama Bin Laden's death: Implications and considerations. *Congressional Research Service*. https://fas.org/sgp/crs/terror/R41809.pdf.

Robillard, K. (2013, October 30). Brookings: Cash for clunkers failed. *Politico*. https://www.politico.com/story/2013/10/brookings-cash-for-clunkers-program-barack-obama-administration-cars-stimulus-099134.

Shear, M., Davis Hirschfeld, J., & Harris, G. (2016, March 16). Obama chooses Merrick Garland for Supreme Court. *New York Times*. https://www.nytimes.com/2016/03/17/us/politics/obama-supreme-court-nominee.html?_r=0.

Stolberg, S. G., Zeleny J., & Hulse, C. (2010, March 20). Health vote caps a journey back from the brink. *New York Times*. https://www.nytimes.com/2010/03/21/health/policy/21reconstruct.html?mtrref=www.google.com.

Thrush, G., & Wheaton, S. (2015, September 25). Boehner and Obama: Caught in a bad bromance. *Politico*. https://www.politico.com/story/2015/09/obama-boehner-bromance-214094.

Wallsten, P., Montgomery, L., & Wilson, S. (2012, March 17). Obama's evolution: Behind the failed "grand bargain" on the debt. *Washington Post*. https://www.washingtonpost.com/politics/obamas-evolution-behind-the-failed-grand-bargain-on-the-debt/2012/03/15/gIQAHyyfJS_story.html?utm_term=.65279ad26af5.

10

The Obama Administration's Approach to Disaster Response and Recovery

DAVID HARMS HOLT AND
CASEY MAUGH FUNDERBURK

Comforter-in-Chief

The president of the United States serves many roles beyond being head of government, and those roles have expanded and over time. The American presidency's evolution includes a historic transformation toward personal, direct contact with the American people. Noted presidential scholar Theodore Lowi (1986) argued that the presidential evolution requires public relations experts seeking messaging to "somehow find a way to control events" (p. 178). Modern-day presidents play a variety of roles as they interact with the citizens of the nation. At times they must demonstrate compassion and sensitivity and offer support in times of chaos. At other times they must demonstrate strength, resolve, or anger. Language, optics, and political style rely on successful communication of the message. Keith V. Erickson (2000) asserts that "[p]residents enact a variety of fictive personae (personal and public) in order to heighten their authority and to avoid imposed characterizations" (Erickson, 2000, p. 142). Meyrowitz (1985) when writing about Ronald Reagan's role as the Great Communicator, suggests that "Americans today accept that the President himself must be a skilled actor and that he must *perform* the role of President rather than simply *be* President" (Meyrowitz, 1985, p. 303). Meyrowitz goes on to argue:

> Today's presidents and presidential hopefuls are judged by the same standards, those of "good television": are they lively and humorous; do they look friendly and alert; are their facial expressions pleasant to watch; can they offer off-the-cuff remarks without much thinking, pausing or stumbling over words; and do they shape their words and expressions to the requirements of the camera and microphone rather than those of the crowd? (p. 304)

Presidents recognize the value of capitalizing on a rhetorical exigence, or the ability to connect the appropriate response with the occasion and audience. Robert Hariman's (1995) work *Political Style* suggests that "to the extent that politics is an art, matters of style must be crucial to its practice" (p. 3). Hariman further argues, "Values can only be taken seriously once performed successfully" (p. 10). The embedded relationship between performance and the underlying message holds especially true for presidential rhetoric. The president's performative style must complement the message. A mismatch of delivery and message results in failed communication.

Barack Obama played many presidential roles during his eight-year presidency. Comforter-in-Chief emerged as a role he would often be called upon to play, as natural and anthropogenic disasters, mass shootings and domestic terrorism occurred frequently during the Obama presidency. Not surprisingly, the role of Comforter-in-Chief, enacted when the nation grieves after a disaster, can help calm and soothe a grieving public. Presidents such as Ronald Reagan and Bill Clinton expertly communicated the Comforter-in-Chief role. Likewise, Barack Obama effectively presented as Comforter-in-Chief throughout his presidency. This chapter provides a historical overview of the events that required Obama to communicate as Comforter-in-Chief, setting the stage for an analysis of the themes that emerged from his speeches to grieving audiences after tragedy. Obama's speeches saw him break from his typical responses by the end of his presidency. Mass shootings became too painful to pretend that comfort was the only answer, emerging in a rhetoric of culpability. Between 2009 and 2016, Obama assumed the role of Comforter-in-Chief many times, slowly refining his response to racial tensions, tragedies, violent acts, and environmental and natural disasters. By the end of his presidency, formal responses to events became routine, even predictable. Obama had the lesson of his predecessor George W. Bush's slow response to Hurricane

Katrina to show him what to avoid as well as the brilliant speeches of Ronald Reagan to show him what to emulate. In the Challenger disaster speech, presented from the White House, Reagan canceled the State of the Union address to speak about the tragedy (Moyer, 2016), delivering one of the consistently heralded top speeches of the century. Edmiston (2016) notes of Obama, "There was, however, a template for these sorts of things—an unofficial guideline laid out in the speeches of his predecessors on how to be presidential in times of tragedy."

Obama's responses relied on a set of repeated themes. This essay first accounts for the series of tragedies and disasters that occurred during Obama's two-term presidency. Next, we define and rhetorically analyze the themes used to construct the Comforter-in-Chief role. Finally, we conclude by discussing the routine nature of Obama's responses after eight years of tragedy.

Tragedies Compelling Response

President Obama's earliest response to a domestic issue came after the April 2009 influenza outbreak (Table 10.1 on page 208–209). H1N1, commonly known as "Swine Flu," became a world pandemic. From April 2009 to 2010, Swine Flu eventually hospitalized more than 274,000 people in the United States and killed more than twelve thousand (Shrestha et al., 2010). The Obama administration declared a public health emergency on April 26 to allow for twelve million doses of flu-fighting medications to ship from federal stockpiles (AP, 2009). Popular opinion conflated annual flu with the potential of Swine Flu, even further inflating fears of the virus. In response, Obama declared a national emergency on October 23 and issued statements to ease concerns (AP, 2009).

On July 16, 2009, Henry Louis Gates Junior's neighbor called police to investigate Gates, whom he believed to be a suspicious person attempting to break into Gates's home. Gates's subsequent arrest for disorderly conduct (later dropped) ignited a national conversation about racial tensions. President Obama and Vice President Joe Biden invited Gates and the arresting officer, Cambridge, Mass., Police Sergeant Joseph Crowley, to the White House to drink beers and to discuss the incident (Plinkington, 2009). Though not acting as Comforter-in-Chief, Obama demonstrated early signs of compassion and sensitivity around a delicate issue, a sign of the role he might play in the future tragedies.

Table 10.1. Obama's Responses to Domestic Tragedies

Selected Event	Classification	Event Date	Obama Response Date	Obama Speech or Visit
Beer Summit	Police/Race Relations	16 July 2009	22 July	24 July
H1N1 Outbreak	Health Concern	April 2009 (start)	24 October	
Fort Hood Shooting	Gun Violence	5 November 2009	5 November	10 November
Upper Big Branch Explosion	Industrial Accident	5 April 2010	15 April	25 April
Deepwater Horizon	Industrial Accident	20 April 2010	15 June	
Giffords Shooting	Gun Violence	8 January 2011	12 January	12 January
Joplin Tornado	Natural Disaster	22 May 2011	22 May	29 May
Martin Shooting	Gun Violence	26 February 2012	23 March	
Waldo Canyon Fire	Wildfire	26 June 2012		30 June
Aurora Colorado Shooting	Gun Violence	20 July 2012	20 July	23 July
Sikh Temple Shooting	Gun Violence	5 August 2012	5 August	
Hurricane Sandy	Natural Disaster	29–30 October 2012	28 October	31 October
Sandy Hook Shooting	Gun Violence	14 December 2012	14 December	
Moore Tornado	Natural Disaster	20 May 2013	22 May	26 May
Boston Marathon Bombing	Gun Violence and Bombing	15 April 2013	16 April	18 April
Navy Yard Shooting	Gun Violence	16 September 2013	16 September	23 September
Fort Hood Shooting	Gun Violence	2 April 2014	2 April	9 April
Brown Shooting	Police/Race Relations	9 August 2014	12 August	
Jewish Community Center	Gun Violence	13 April 2014	14 April	
Arkansas Tornadoes	Natural Disaster	27 April 2014		7 May

Emanuel AME Church	Gun Violence	18 June 2015	18 June	26 June
Chattanooga Recruiting Center	Gun Violence	16 July 2015	16 July	21 July
Umpqua Community College	Gun Violence	1 October 2015	1 October	9 October
Island Regional Center	Gun Violence	2 December 2015	2 December	6 December
Kalamazoo Shootings	Gun Violence	20 February 2016	22 February	
Pulse Nightclub	Gun Violence	12 June 2016	12 June	16 June
Dallas Police Shooting	Police/Race Relations	8 July 2016	8 July	12 July
Baton Rouge Police Shooting	Police/Race Relations	17 July 2016	17 July	
Louisiana Floods	Natural Disaster	12 August 2016	23 August	23 August

Obama's first response to a disaster occurred after an industrial accident on April 5, 2010, at Massey Energy's Upper Big Branch Coal Mine in Raleigh County, near Montcoal, West Virginia. The worst mining disaster since 1984, the explosion killed twenty-nine of the thirty-one workers in the mine (AP, 2010A). An investigation of Massey Energy found the company to be negligent and guilty of flagrant safety violations (NRC, 2012). Specifcally, investigators found that old and broken equipment sparked a fire to coal dust and methane gas, resulting in a flare up. An aged water suppression system allowed the explosion to expand (NRC, 2012). On April 25, Obama delivered a eulogy and pledged to honor the victims by improving safety in mines. He voiced his empathy for lost family and loved ones (White House, 2012). Eventually, the event led to a criminal investigation and conviction of Don Blankenship, the CEO of Upper Big Branch.

Obama's first environmental disaster response came after the April 20, 2010, Deepwater Horizon explosion. The ultra-deep-water rig broke records for depth of drilling at more than 35,000 feet beneath water that was 4,100 feet deep. On April 20, the drilling platform suffered an uncontrolled blowout that killed eleven and eventually sank the drilling rig on April 22. The company made several failed attempts to stop the blowout on the ocean floor, but the leak continued for almost five months (capped on September 19). The oil spill leaked an estimated 4.9 million barrels of crude oil at a rate of about 53,000 barrels a day (AP, 2010B). The oil slick spread over 3,850 square miles and killed more than 4,500 animals (AP, 2010B). The Deepwater Horizon disaster stayed in the news cycle throughout the entire summer, with live feeds of oil gushing from the ocean floor. Critics deemed the disaster Obama's "Katrina Moment" for the slow speed of his administration's response, which initially insisted on relying upon those connected to the rig to plug the leak. The Obama administration continued to emphasize the importance of making things right, eventually placing a temporary moratorium on deep water drilling to prevent future catastrophes. Obama called the event a "horrific disaster" and vowed to hold those responsible accountable (AP, 2010C).

In early 2011, an act of gun violence against a U.S. Representative from Arizona, Gabrielle Giffords, commanded national attention. On January 8, Giffords, a newly reelected Democrat, was holding a constituents' meeting in a parking lot outside of a Safeway supermarket when twenty-two-year-old Jared Lee Loughner opened fire and shot

Giffords and eighteen others; six later died (CNN, 2017A). Democrats across the country seized the moment to address gun violence, a theme that ran throughout the course of the Obama administration, repeatedly challenging Obama to find adequate responses to gun violence. Obama called the shooting an "unspeakable act" and added, "We can do better" (*Washington Post*, 2011).

Texas governor Rick Perry issued complaints about the Obama administration not declaring a disaster area for the Texas wildfires of late April 2011, at which time Obama became publicly involved in wildfire mitigation (Stewart, 2011). Though the Obama administration had issued more than individual county disaster declarations, Governor Perry's admonition resulted in a state of emergency for all of Texas (FEMA, 2011A). By June 27, 2011, when the Arizona wildfires emerged, Obama quickly responded with a promise for aid (FEMA, 2011B).

While Governor Perry demanded federal funds for wildfires, Joplin, Missouri, endured a devastating Enhanced-Fujita Scale (EF-5) tornado on May 22, 2011. The tornado, which lasted thirty-eight minutes, created a swath of damage one mile wide and 22.1 miles long (Wheatley, 2013) and destroyed more than seven thousand houses and killed 158, with over 1,000 people injured. It was the deadliest tornado since 1947 (Wheatley, 2013). In the aftermath, Obama toured the damage on May 29 and gave an emotive speech about the solidarity of the population, and promised that the federal government would be there well after the cameras left (Sulzberger, 2011).

Gun violence returned to national attention on February 26, 2012, when George Zimmerman shot and killed seventeen-year-old African AmericanTrayvon Martin, in Sanford, Florida. Zimmerman placed a call to 911 services from his van to report a suspicious person (CNN, 2018A). Though instructed to stay in his van, he exited the vehicle and shot Martin, claiming self-defense. Under Florida's "stand your ground" law, Zimmerman was not charged. On March 13, 2012, the Sanford Police Department recommended charging Zimmerman with manslaughter; however, on July 13 a jury found him "not guilty" on all charges (CNN, 2018A). Obama called on the nation to do some "soul searching" over the growing controversy and the national conversation, pointing to race as a factor in the shooting (Obama, 2013B).

Obama addressed issues in Colorado twice in the summer of 2012. First, he toured the damage caused by the Colorado fires on June 29, 2012, and second, he responded to a mass shooting in an Aurora movie theater. On July 20, 2012, James Eagan Holmes discharged tear gas and multiple firearms, killing twelve people and injuring seventy (*New York Times*, 2017; CNN, 2018B). Responding to a shocked and confused public, both Obama and Mitt Romney suspended all campaign advertising in Colorado. Obama ordered flags to be flown at half staff and addressed the nation immediately after the tragedy where he reminded listeners that "we are all united as one American family" (Obama, 2012A).

Just before the 2012 presidential election, Hurricane Sandy made landfall near Brigantine, New Jersey, where it impacted twenty-four states and caused more than $65 billion in damage. The Obama administration and FEMA pre-positioned the National Guard and declared nine federal states of emergency for the East Coast on October 28. Meanwhile, Mitt Romney, Obama's Republican opponent, opposed Obama's position of deploying a federal response, arguing the states should provide support (Cohen, 2012). Days before the election, on October 31, Obama toured damaged New Jersey sites with the Republican governor of New Jersey, Chris Christie. Ultimately, Obama demonstrated that government response had improved drastically since Hurricane Katrina in 2005, and according to an ABC News poll, 78 percent of the respondents deemed Obama's response either "good" or "excellent" (Wyler, 2012).

The shock of gun violence returned to the national conversation just after Obama's reelection, on December 14, 2012, when Adam Lanza shot his mother and then proceeded to the Sandy Hook Elementary school in Newtown, Connecticut, where he killed twenty children and six adults before taking his own life. Most of Lanza's victims were six or seven years old. Immediately following news of the shooting, a tearful Obama spoke from the White House briefing room, followed several days later by his participation at a vigil on December 16 in Newtown (NPR, 2012). The Sandy Hook Massacre reignited a national conversation around gun control. Many in Congress called for banning assault weapons, but the legislation failed (Cooper, 2018).

The shootings at a political gathering, a movie theater, and an elementary school held a nation in fear, and in each case Obama's response set out to ease fears, calm tensions, and unite a grieving public. However, on April 15, 2013, Dzhokhar and Tamerlan Tsarnaev, legal immigrants from Kyrgyzstan, set off two pressure cooker bombs twelve seconds apart near the finish line at the 117th running of the Boston Marathon. At approximately 2:49 p.m., the explosions killed three people and wounded

260 others, as recorded on security and Marathon onlookers' cameras (Morrison & O'Leary, 2015). More than one thousand law enforcement personnel, with coordination by the FBI, used the recorded footage to identify the two suspects. In the aftermath of the Marathon bombings, the brothers proceeded on a killing and stealing rampage lasting four days, until their capture. Tamerlan died in a hospital, and in his testimony Dzhokhar claimed that the attack was intended to serve as retaliation for U.S. forces invading Muslim countries (Morrison & O'Leary, 2015). Dzhokhar Tzarnaev was sentenced to death on May 15, 2015. The Obama administration called the bombing an act of terror and praised the law enforcement response. On November 16, 2015, while speaking at a G20 meeting in Turkey, Obama characterized the attack as "two brothers and a crock pot" (Levenson, 2015).

In Spring 2013, Obama responded to tornado devastation in Moore, Oklahoma, and then, in 2014, Mayflower, Arkansas. Both storms caused death and massive destruction in areas all too familiar with tornadic activity. Obama spoke about community resilience and community spirit, reassuring audiences on the federal response (Obama, 2013A; AP, 2014).

On August 9, 2014, at 11:51 a.m., responding to a call reporting a robbery by two individuals at the Ferguson Market convenience store, Ferguson police dispatched officer Darren Dean Wilson, to confront Michael Brown, a teenager, about what appeared from video footage to be Brown stealing a box of cigarillos (Brown, 2014). An altercation ensued, which resulted in Michael Brown's death by gunshot. Amid conflicting accounts of the interactions leading to Brown's shooting and growing mistrust of the Ferguson Police Department, riots broke out following a candlelight vigil in Ferguson. While more than a dozen businesses were vandalized and thirty people arrested, protests and riots continued with hundreds marching. Michael Brown's parents held a conference to ask for the violence to stop (Brown, 2014). National attention focused on Ferguson for days, eventually leading to intervention by the National Guard on August 18. On August 12, Obama released a statement calling the death of Brown heartbreaking and noting that his death had prompted strong passions. Obama called on the demonstrators to let the Department of Justice do its job, and urged Brown's mourners to act in ways that would heal, not wound (Larotonda & Good, 2015). The Ferguson event marked the first physical protest by the group "Black Lives Matter," which had formed after the Trayvon Martin shooting in 2012.

Homegrown Terrorism

With the news media outlets covering mounting racial tensions, costly natural disasters, and recurrent mass shootings, homegrown terrorism gained national attention once again on December 2, 2015, when the largest mass shooting since Sandy Hook occurred in San Bernardino, California. Syed Rizwan Farook and Tashfeen Malik killed fourteen people and injured twenty-two at the Inland Regional Center's Christmas party (Ortiz, 2015) in what was later deemed an act of homegrown terrorism. Farook, who held permanent legal residency in Pakistan as well as natural-born U.S. citizenship, attended a holiday party at the center, his place of employment, that morning but left after a dispute with colleagues (Ortiz, 2015). He returned a short time later with Malik, both of them wearing ski masks and tactical gear, and killed two people outside the building before entering and firing into the crowd. Ultimately, both Farook and Malik died after a shootout with police. Motives in the case appeared to be inspired by Islamic terrorism propagated by ISIS, as inferred from the techniques used to construct their pipe bombs, as well as Facebook postings. Obama again called for "common sense" gun safety laws and background checks (Obama, 2015).

Just six months later, on June 12, 2016, another homegrown terrorist attack occurred when Omar Mateen entered the Pulse Nightclub in Orlando, Florida, killing forty-nine people and injuring fifty-three (Lotan et al., 2017). Mateen opened fire around 2:02 a.m. and during the event called 911 several times to pledge allegiance to ISIS and tell the operator that he wanted America to stop bombing his country. Born in the United States, the twenty-year-old Mateen's parents were Afghani. Deemed a terrorist attack, the Pulse Nightclub shooting was the most lethal since 9/11. In the aftermath, Obama pledged support for the investigation into the attack and called the event an "act of hate" and an "act of terror" (White House, 2016). He and Vice President Joe Biden visited the Pulse nightclub to lay a wreath and speak at a memorial service on June 16.

In addition to the increasing concerns over terrorist attacks, a twenty-five-year-old veteran, Micah Xavier Johnson, opened fire on a group of police officers in Dallas, Texas, killing five and injuring nine on July 7, 2016 (Selk et al., 2016). Just before 9 p.m., Johnson parked his SUV and took cover at street level and fired upon police officers who were monitoring a peaceful protest against police officer shootings.

Johnson killed three officers and injured three others before fleeing to a new location where he engaged another officer, killing him. After an estimated seven hundred rounds had been exchanged between Johnson and the police, Johnson holed up in a computer server room and refused to speak to non-Black officers. A robot armed with C-4 explosive entered Johnson's space; Johnson attempted to disable the robot, which detonated and killed him (Selk et al., 2016). Obama responded from Warsaw, Poland, while at a NATO meeting, once again condemning gun violence and mourning, this time alongside the Dallas Police Department (Moore, 2016). Just ten days later, Gavin Eugene Long shot six officers, killing three, in Baton Rouge, Louisiana, during a protest inspired by a police shooting. Obama again condemned the violence, and stated that these attacks on public servants were an attack on the rule of law and must stop (Obama, 2016B).

While the nation mourned the loss of innocent lives and feared the next attack, a natural disaster impacted Louisiana. The floods in Louisiana began on August 12, 2016, after multiple parishes received more than inches of rain over several days. The highest recording came from Watson, Louisiana, just west of Baton Rouge, at 31.39 inches of rain. *The Washington Post* called the storm the "no name storm" (Brown et al., 2016). By August 15, ten rivers had flooded, eight of them registering record levels. In the end, approximately 146,000 homes were damaged, thirteen people died, and damages were estimated between $10 and $15 billion. On August 23, Obama and a bipartisan group toured the area, pointing out that no first responder or victim cares about political parties when they are helping each other (Hersher, 2016).

Obama's Rhetorical Response

The Comforter-in-Chief role, as previously noted, is one that all presidents find themselves playing whenever tragedy befalls the nation or world. Some presidents rise to the occasion beautifully and others find themselves challenged by or avoid the role. While language choice and optics during the memorial occasion matter deeply, tone also plays a significant role in its efficacy. The analysis that follows relies on textual analysis around themes that regularly emerged in Obama's memorializing addresses following tragic events. Extracted from the contextual information in the preceding section, we analyzed five representative events spanning the Obama presidency. These five speeches cover the various types of tragedy outlined above and span Obama's two terms as president, providing a set of speeches that are consistent in nature and tone with similar addresses throughout his presidency. Furthermore, these speeches represent some of the most widely publicized tragedies that occurred during the Obama presidency, allowing the authors to draw from a range of reporting news organizations and reactions to the speeches. Those tragedies are: Upper Big Branch Mine Explosion (2010), the Joplin Tornado (2011), the Sandy Hook School shooting (2011), Hurricane Sandy (2012), and the Orlando shooting at the Pulse nightclub (2016). In these cases, speeches delivered at memorial services, as well as press briefings and updates, comprise the corpus of the texts analyzed for each tragic event.

Discourse analysis of President Obama's rhetorical responses to tragedy revealed that Obama's performance of the Comforter-in-Chief role relied on seven themes to effectively communicate with his intended audience. The emergent themes are: comfort, invocation of scripture, humanizing stories, president as parent, the family, bipartisanship, and the notion that people are good.

Comfort

Reinforcing the Comforter-in-Chief persona, the term *comfort* emerged as a major component in President Obama's speeches after tragedy. The concept of comfort serves as a reminder of the appropriate first response to tragedy. Comfort, often used at the beginning of an address, situates the term as a natural, appropriate response to major tragedy, which aligns with the purpose of Obama's addresses. In initial responses to tragedy, comfort precedes calls for change, retaliation, or resolution. Inclusive pronouns such as *we, our,* and *us* situate the president as a representative of the nation, sent to comfort the audience. Inclusive pronoun use combined with the term *comfort* reinforces the Comforter-in-Chief role. At the Sandy Hook prayer vigil on December 16, 2012, Obama commented, "And you must know that whatever measure of comfort we can provide, we will provide; whatever portion of sadness that we can share with you to ease this heavy load, we will gladly bear it. Newtown—you are not alone" (Mechaber, 2012). Reminding the audience that a nation grieves alongside the community impacted by the tragedy, Obama carefully wove the notion of comfort into the inclusive language.

As much as comfort itself emerged in the rhetorical responses to tragedy, the concept of the limitations of comfort likewise emerged. Obama infused a sense of his recognition that while he spoke to bring comfort, it was likely that none exists in the midst of tragedy. Astute self-awareness hallmarks the responses given. In the same Sandy Hook address, Obama articulated the insufficiency of the attempt: "We chase after some earthly goal, whether it's wealth or power or fame, or just simple comfort, we will, in some fashion, fall short of what we had hoped" (Mechaber, 2012). He remarked to the grieving community at Sandy Hook, "I am very mindful that mere words cannot match the depths of your sorrow, nor can they heal your wounded hearts. I can only hope it helps for you to know that you're not alone in your grief" (Mechaber, 2012). After the Upper Big Branch mine explosion, the president admitted the failure of efforts to provide comfort after mass tragedy: "Nothing we say can fill the hole they leave in your hearts, or the absence that they leave in your lives" (Lee, 2010). Eulogies regularly call attention to the emptiness of words and the failure of language to adequately capture feelings, and Obama repeatedly attempted to use language to comfortwhile admitting the limitation of language to truly provide relief.

Invocation of Scripture

One marker of the Comforter-in-Chief role relies on the concept of comfort to connect the tragic moment shared by the grieving public to a path forward out of their sorrow. Obama's command of the concept of comfort, both in terms of its healing power and its limitations, provided a powerful platform from which he could invoke specific themes meant to further certify his role as Comforter-in-Chief. In particular, Obama inserted scriptural references into the vast majority of his speeches surrounding tragedy.

In a predominately Christian nation, biblical references are expected in post-tragedy presidential remarks. Not surprisingly, Obama utilized both direct quotations from Christian doctrine as well as indirect references to scripture. Additionally, he invoked spiritual hymns to comfort his audiences, reinforcing the idea that a higher power is in control. During the Joplin, Missouri, memorial service for the victims of a 2011 tornado, Obama invoked scripture directly, stating, "You have lived the words of Scripture: We are troubled on every side, yet not distressed; we are perplexed, but not in despair; Persecuted, but not forsaken; cast down, but not destroyed" (Obama, 2011B). As he memorialized the miners killed at Big Branch, he noted, "There's a psalm that comes to mind today—a psalm that comes to mind, a psalm we often turn to in times of heartache. 'Even though I walk through the valley of the shadow of death, I will fear no evil, for You are with me; your rod and your staff, they comfort me'" (Lee, 2010). At the memorial for the victims of the Pulse nightclub shooting in Orlando, Obama ended his lengthy address with:

> May God bless all who we lost here in Orlando. May He comfort their families. May He heal the wounded. May He bring some solace to those whose hearts have been broken. May He give us resolve to do what's necessary to reduce the hatred of this world, curb the violence. And may He watch over this country that we call home. (Obama, 2016A)

When a president speaks at a memorial service, he stands alongside spiritual leaders and government officials and often his speech takes on the tone of a eulogy. Obama's Sandy Hook prayer vigil address served as a eulogy for the nation; rather than remembering individuals, the speech eulogized the tragedy. To capture the appropriate tone, Obama opened the service with scripture, stating, "Scripture tells us: 'do not lose heart. Though outwardly we are wasting away . . . inwardly we are being renewed day by day . . . we have a building from God, an eternal house in heaven, not built by human hands'" (Mechaber, 2012). While the Sandy Hook memorial speech served to directly address those in attendance, Obama's message was designed to comfort and heal the nation.

At memorial services, scripture occupies an appropriate space for a grieving audience; however, presidential briefings can often carry a different tone. Typically, briefings are a president's first effort to respond to an event prior to attending in person. Briefings serve to assure the American public that the president is aware of important events. When a president chooses to brief the nation, it is a conscious choice, reserved for only the most important events. The Sandy Hook tragedy called for a presidential briefing; a quick and direct response to the nation after a major tragic event. The Sandy Hook briefing uniquely served as a moment for Obama to situate himself as Comforter-in-Chief. The briefing employed spiritual references, which presidents rarely do during a briefing. Obama closed the briefing by noting, "May God bless the memory of the victims and, in the words of Scripture, heal the brokenhearted and bind up their wounds" (Slack, 2012). The Sandy Hook tragedy centered on the deaths of ten young children, which created a special exigence for the briefing, allowing the president to break from the traditional response. Certainly, tragedies with loss of life require presidents to comfort the community and the nation simultaneously, which is why the addresses must remain localized to the audience at hand and generalized to the nation at large. This delicate balance, in many ways, determines the success of the address and reinforces the role of Comforter-in-Chief when the occasion requires it.

Personalizing the Narrative

Presidential addresses often employ personal stories or anecdotes to reinforce their connection with the event. Narratives personalize the speech by creating a real, human connection to the tragedy, putting a face and name on the suffering. For Obama, by humanizing his messages he showed his local audience that he held a personal connection with the community. As Comforter-in-Chief, Obama carefully crafted stories about local victims as well as local heroes, reinforcing a close, personal relationship to the tragedy. When speaking in the aftermath of Hurricane Sandy, most of Obama's address covered a message of hope and perseverance, but to end his address he told a story of a couple who lost their two sons. Obama reflected, "I had the opportunity to give some hugs and communicate thoughts and prayers to the Moore family. They lost two young sons during the course of this tragedy" (Obama, 2012B). Obama noted that the Moore family attended the speech to thank Lieutenant Kevin Gallagher, of the New York Police Department, who helped them through their loss. Obama held up the lieutenant as an example of heroism, going above and beyond the call of duty. Embedding the narrative of loss with the spirit of heroism allowed Obama to further appeal to his audience and personalize the tragedy.

For a national audience, a personal narrative serves to connect the tragedy in one community to the reality that tragedy can happen in any community. In the memorial in Joplin, Obama told two stories of men who selflessly saved others and tragically lost their own lives. After recounting their heroism, Obama connected the heroic acts to a prevailing message of love:

> What we do know is that in a split-second moment where there's little time for internal reflection or debate, the actions

of these individuals were driven by love—love for a family member, love for a friend, or just love for a fellow human being. (Obama, 2011B)

By connecting personal narratives to an overarching theme, Obama connected the personal to the universal. The rhetorical strategy to broaden the conversation past the local audience further connects a nation to the president. For the role of Comforter-in-Chief to be communicated locally and translate nationally, Obama had to carefully place humanizing narratives within the address.

The President as Parent

As the perceived caretakers of the nation, the president is expected to resolve crisis and support both individuals and the nation during trying times. The role of caretaker strongly relies on presidential rhetoric that frames the president as both a human and a parental figure. Reinforcing the Comforter-in-Chief persona, President Obama encouraged audiences to see him as a parent in several instances. In the presidential briefing immediately following Sandy Hook, Obama squarely placed himself in a parental role, stating, "We've endured too many of these tragedies in the past few years. And each time I learn the news I react not as a president, but as anybody else would—as a parent. And that was especially true today. I know there's not a parent in America who doesn't feel the same overwhelming grief that I do" (Slack, 2012). Connecting to the nation through the shared relationship of parent allows Obama to position himself as a common man, connected through tragedy. Placing himself in the role of parent humanizes the president, narrowing the gap between the people and the president. Obama further reinforced the parental narrative during the Sandy Hook memorial service when he said, "This evening, Michelle and I will do what I know every parent in America will do, which is hug our children a little tighter and we'll tell them that we love them, and we'll remind each other how deeply we love one another" (Mechaber, 2012). Again, a humanizing narrative with which parents across the nation can identify. The more strongly the characterization of self pulls the president into a relatable role, in this case that of parent, the more likely the audience will be to identify Obama as Comforter-in-Chief.

While the Sandy Hook examples overtly communicate the everyday, very human qualities of the president, more subtle examples exist in speeches around tragedy. During his Hurricane Sandy response, Obama noted, "And obviously, I expressed to them—as a father, as a parent—my heartbreak over what they went through" (Obama, 2012B). First, Obama led the sentence with, "and obviously," to communicate the natural response he has to the victims of the hurricane. By including such an overt expression, the president does not leave to chance any belief that comforting families might not be second nature to him. Comforting families remained a clear and present strategy in Obama's rhetorical approach to tragedy. In addition to his insistence on identifying himself in the familiar role of parent or father, he employed familial terminology regularly to create unity and community for his audiences.

Unity and Community

After tragedy strikes a community, coming together helps to heal and reconcile the wounds. As Comforter-in-Chief, Obama spent time rhetorically constructing a narrative of family. The narrative reinforced the picture of Obama as the great unifier through tragedy. By reminding audiences that the nation shares in their grief, and suggesting that we are all brothers and sisters, an American ideology framed with a message of community and unification was emphasized.

During Sandy Hook, Obama underlined his message of solidarity, stating, "Whatever portion of sadness that we can share with you to ease this heavy load, we will gladly bear it. Newtown—you are not alone" (Mechaber, 2012). The address highlighted a shared responsibility for the tragedy and a shared burden of grief. In Joplin, after the tornado, the theme of shared responsibility continued as Obama said, "You've demonstrated a simple truth that amid heartbreak and tragedy, no one is a stranger. Everybody is a brother. Everybody is a sister. We can all love one another" (Obama, 2011B). Unifying the community by identifying everyone as either a sister or brother invites them to share the burden of unification after a tragedy.

Finally, Obama connected tragedy to a shared national identity in his speech following the Pulse nightclub shooting. He stated, "These families could be our families. In fact, they are our family—they're part of the American family" (Obama, 2016A). Obama took local and individual relationships and expanded them to encompass the nation, reinforcing the relationship all community members have in common with one another. All three of these examples show the rhetorical style of Comforter-in-Chief, where the president removed himself from the discourse to emphasize the community and its shared responsibility for healing after tragedy.

Bipartisanship

Though on its surface, talk of government action may seem antithetical to comforting a nation, as government action can be perceived as cold or even calculated, Obama used bipartisan policy building as a foundation for hopeful next steps. Playing the role of Comforter-in-Chief, the president remains a president, with influence over the political will needed to change policy or support federal declarations of disaster. By intentionally weaving a clear bipartisan message into his addresses, Obama reinforced his role as Comforter-in-Chief. During Hurricane Sandy, Obama inserted familiar Democrat and Republican names into the conversation to demonstrate bipartisan cooperation in recovery efforts, proclaiming:

> So, what I've committed to doing is to work with the outstanding congressional delegation led by your Senators Chuck Schumer and Kirsten Gillibrand, also working with Governor Christie and the Jersey delegation to try to come up with a game plan for how we're going to be able to resource the rebuilding process. But it's going to require everybody focused on getting the job done. We're going to have to put some of the turf battles aside. We're going to have to make sure that everybody is focused on doing the job as opposed to worrying about who is getting the credit. (Obama 2012B)

Obama took his remarks farther than simply dropping names; he pointed out the challenges of partisan politics in recovery efforts and pledged to overcome them. It is important to note that Obama used "we" and "our" for most of the address, yet when shifted to politics, he used "I" language to connote the strength of the office of the president. His language shift was consistent.

During the Pulse nightclub aftermath, Obama spent a great deal of time discussing political will and topics such as gun violence and homegrown terrorism. In the Pulse address he stated, "Now, if we're honest with ourselves, if, in fact, we want to show the best of our humanity, then we're all going to have to work together at every level of government, across political lines, to do more to stop killers who want to terrorize us" (Obama, 2016A). President Obama's language of bipartisan coming together placed the audience in a position of agreement. Bipartisanship emerged as a marker of ensuring the president had the best interests of the nation at heart, further reinforcing the comforting role.

The Notion that People Are Good

The final rhetorical theme found while analyzing these five tragic moments during Obama's tenure as president relates to the concept of good and evil. Despite evil in the world, people are good and reasonable people try to do the right thing. By reinforcing the concept that violent or tragic acts are not the norm, this reaffirms that those in the listening audience are not to blame for force majeure, anthropogenic disasters, or deranged acts of violence. This rhetorical turn, likewise, reinforces the "everyman" narrative common in presidential addresses. For example, at the Sandy Hook prayer vigil, Obama stated, "They lost their lives in a school that could have been any school; in a quiet town full of good and decent people that could be any town in America" (Slack, 2012). He reinforced that people are basically good and reminded the audience that this tragedy resonated so loudly because it could have been anywhere. This way of relating to his audience places the president on common ground with them, presenting the situation as translatable and relatable.

Sometimes, the Comforter-in-Chief role is exemplified best through a reminder that while tragedy occurs, people themselves are basically good. In Joplin after the tornado, Obama delivered remarks playing on the theme of nature as evil and cruel, he framed the message around the basic instinct in us all to do good. He commented, "In a world that can be cruel and selfish, it's this knowledge—the knowledge that we are inclined to love one another, that we're inclined to do good, to be good—that causes us to take heart" (Obama, 2011B). President Obama magnified the nature of humankind as pure at heart.

Conclusions

The theme of Comforter-in-Chief replayed throughout the Obama presidency as he consoled, allayed fears, and supported broken families. As the years wore on, Obama's rhetorical response to tragedy became expected, in part because only so much can be said to bring comfort after tragedy when you speak day after day, week after week, about preventable situations. Edmiston (2016) argues that, "As the shootings continued, his speeches became almost formulaic. He spoke of the victims' acts of bravery, how they kissed a spouse before they left for work; he quoted scripture; and ended with call for perseverance." Additionally, Obama became more frustrated with Congress's inaction. During his Pulse nightclub address, in the final year of his presidency, he devoted sentence after sentence to Congress's lack of response to the need for stronger gun control policy. This departure from his standard memorializing speech included, "I hope that senators who voted 'no' on background checks after Newtown have a change of heart. And then I hope the House does the right thing and helps end the plague of violence that these weapons of war inflict on so many young lives" (Obama, 2016A). He went on to assign blame to congressional inaction, stating, "And if we don't act, we will keep seeing more massacres like this—because we'll be choosing to allow them to happen. We will have said, we don't care enough to do something about it" (Obama, 2016A). Indeed, Obama's infusion of blame and frustration increased as the number of memorial speeches grew. The Pulse nightclub shooting came after years of tragic mass shootings and was by far the deadliest. Remaining resolute in responding to the call to comfort the nation remains a central role for the president; however, the nature of Obama's approach shifted as he inflected blame, something Edmiston (2016) refers to as the "presidential hector." In hectoring audiences for their moral failing and Congress for their inaction, Obama's declared resolve was strengthened and his critique of Congress became more direct.

  The roles a president performs are often defined by the events that occur during his tenure. Obama was slow to address the nation early in his presidency. He opted to make broad policy announcements with H1N1 or Deepwater Horizon. He did address the Big Branch Mine explosion, but that might have been politically motivated to shame the coal industry. However, the shooting of Congresswoman Giffords and eighteen others at a political gathering called for a Comforter-in-Chief, and Obama responded. Trayvon Martin's death and Michael Brown's death with its subsequent riots forced Obama to respond to a nation facing racial turmoil. Natural disasters (Hurricane Sandy, tornadoes, floods, wildfires), mass shootings (Aurora movie theater, Sandy Hook elementary school, and Pulse nightclub), homegrown terrorism (San Bernardino and Boston Marathon bombings), and shootings of police officers (Dallas and Baton Rouge) forced Obama to be the Comforter-in-Chief again and again. The thematic elements highlighted in this article became the hallmarks not only of a Comforter-in-Chief, but of a president tired of his own approach brought on by a repeating need to memorialize tragedy. While President Obama played Comforter-in-Chief expertly throughout his two-term presidency, ultimately the weight of repeated tragedy began to reveal a man frustrated by being called to play comforter so very often.

References

Associated Press. (2009). Obama declares swine flu national emergency. *NBC News*. http://www.nbcnews.com/id/33459423/ns/health-cold_and_flu/t/obama-declares-swine-flu-national-emergency/#.W42gRLhG2WU.

Associated Press. (2010A). 25 dead in West Virginia mine blast, Worst since 1984. *WBUR News*. http://www.wbur.org/news/2010/04/06/mine-explosion.

Associated Press. (2010B). BP oil spill: Disaster by numbers. *The Independent*. https://www.independent.co.uk/environment/bp-oil-spill-disaster-by-numbers-2078396.html.

Associated Press. (2010C). Full text of President Obama's BP oil spill speech. *Reuters*. https://www.reuters.com/article/us-oil-spill-obama-text-idUSTRE65F02C20100616.

Associated Press. (2014). President Obama tours tornado-ravaged Arkansas, pledges support. *NBC News*. https://www.nbcnews.com/storyline/deadly-tornado-outbreak/president-obama-tours-tornado-ravaged-arkansas-pledges-support-n99681.

Brown, E. (2014, August 14). Timeline: Michael Brown shooting in Ferguson, MO. *USA Today*. https://www.usatoday.com/story/news/nation/2014/08/14/michael-brown-ferguson-missouri-timeline/14051827/.

Brown, E., Cusick, A., & Berman, M. (2016, August 17). Louisiana flooding is the country's "worst natural disaster" since hurricane Sandy, Red Cross says. *Washington Post*. https://www.washingtonpost.com/news/post-nation/wp/2016/08/17/louisiana-flood-victims-face-long-road-back-to-normal-i-lost-everything/?utm_term=.9eb577debf14.

CNN. (2017A). Arizona Safeway shooting fast facts. *CNN*. https://www.cnn.com/2013/06/10/us/arizona-safeway-shootings-fast-facts/index.html.

CNN. (2017B). Hurricane Sandy fast facts. *CNN*. https://www.cnn.com/2013/07/13/world/americas/hurricane-sandy-fast-facts/index.html.

CNN. (2018A). Trayvon Martin shooting fast facts. *CNN.* https://www.cnn.com/2013/06/05/us/trayvon-martin-shooting-fast-facts/index.html.

CNN. (2018B). Colorado theater shooting fast facts. *CNN.* https://www.cnn.com/2013/07/19/us/colorado-theater-shooting-fast-facts/index.html.

Cohen, T. (2012, October 30). Hurricane Sandy highlights how Obama and Romney respond to disasters. *CNN.* http://www.cnn.com/2012/10/30/politics/disaster-role-government/index.html.

Cooper, M. (2017, October 2). Congress has basically done nothing on gun control since Sandy Hook shooting. *Newsweek.*

Edmiston, J. (2016, July 15). Obama turns away from his role as comforter-in-chief after endless speeches on tragedies. *National Post.* https://nationalpost.com/news/world/obama-turns-away-from-his-role-as-Comforter-in-Chief-after-endless-speeches-on-tragedies.

Erickson, K. V. (2000). Presidential rhetoric's visual turn: Performance fragments and the politics of illusionism. *Communication Monographs, 67*(2): 138–157.

FEMA. (2011A, September 9). Texas-wildfires: FEMA-4029-DR. Federal Emergency Management Agency.

FEMA. (2011B, June, 2). Arizona wallow fire (FM-2915). Federal Emergency Management Agency.

Hariman, R. (1995). *Political style: The artistry of power.* University of Chicago Press.

Hersher, R. (2016, August 23). President Obama tours flood destruction in Louisiana. *NPR.* https://www.npr.org/sections/thetwo-way/2016/08/23/491046184/president-obama-to-tour-flood-destruction-in-louisiana.

Larotonda, M., & Good, C. (2015). Obama says "We may never know what happened" in Ferguson but defends DOJ. *ABC News.* https://abcnews.go.com/Politics/obama-happened-ferguson-defends-doj/story?id=29441456.

Lee. J. (2010, April 25). To the families of Upper Big Branch Mine: "Our hearts ache alongside you." https://obamawhitehouse.archives.gov/blog/2010/04/25/families-big-branch-mine-our-hearts-ache-alongside-you.

Levenson, E. (2015, November 16). Obama describes Boston Marathon bombing as "two brothers and a crock pot." *Boston.com.* https://www.boston.com/news/national-news/2015/11/16/obama-describes-boston-marathon-bombings-as-two-brothers-and-a-crock-pot.

Lotan, G. T., Minshew, C., Lafferty, M., & Gibson, A. (2017). Orlando nightclub shooting timeline: Four hours of terror unfold. *Orlando Sentinel.* http://www.orlandosentinel.com/news/pulse-orlando-nightclub-shooting/os-orlando-pulse-nightclub-shooting-timeline-htmlstory.html.

Lowi, T. (1986). *The personal presidency: Power invested, power unfilled.* Cornell University Press.

Mechaber, E. (2012, December 16). President Obama at prayer vigil for Connecticut shooting victims: "Newtown, you are not alone." https://obamawhitehouse.archives.gov/blog/2012/12/16/president-obama-prayer-vigil-connecticut-shooting-victims-newtown-you-are-not-alone.

Meyrowitz, J. (1985). *No sense of place: The impact of electronic media on social behavior.* Oxford University Press.

Moore, J. (2016). Transcript of Barack Obama's speech on Dallas shootings. *Newsweek.* https://www.newsweek.com/transcript-barack-obamas-speech-dallas-shootings-478825.

Morrison, S., & O'Leary, E. (2015, January 5). Timeline of Boston Marathon bombing events. *Boston.com.* https://www.boston.com/news/local-news/2015/01/05/timeline-of-boston-marathon-bombing-events.

Moyer, J. W. (2016, January 28). Exactly the right words, exactly the right way: Reagan's amazing Challenger disaster speech. *Washington Post.* https://www.washingtonpost.com/news/morning-mix/wp/2016/01/28/how-ronald-reagan-explained-the-challenger-disaster-to-the-world-its-all-part-of-taking-a-chance/?noredirect=on&utm_term=.2d23fd2478f2.

NPR. (2012, December 16). Transcript: President Obama at Sandy Hook prayer vigil. *NPR.* https://www.npr.org/2012/12/16/167412995/transcript-president-obama-at-sandy-hook-prayer-vigil.

New York Times. (2017). Mass shootings in the U.S. *New York Times.* https://www.nytimes.com/interactive/2016/us/mass-shootings-timeline.html.

Obama, B. (2011A, May 29). Remarks by the president after touring tornado damage in Joplin, Missouri. https://obamawhitehouse.archives.gov/the-press-office/2011/05/29/remarks-president-after-touring-tornado-damage-joplin-missouri.

Obama, B. (2011B, May 29). Remarks by the president at a memorial service in Joplin, Missouri. https://obamawhitehouse.archives.gov/the-press-office/2011/05/29/remarks-president-memorial-service-joplin-missouri.

Obama, B. (2012A, July 20). Remarks by the president on the shootings in Aurora, Colorado. https://obamawhitehouse.archives.gov/the-press-office/2012/07/20/remarks-president-shootings-aurora-colorado.

Obama, B. (2012B, November 15). Remarks by the president after surveying damage from hurricane Sandy. https://obamawhitehouse.archives.gov/the-press-office/2012/11/15/remarks-president-after-surveying-damage-hurricane-sandy.

Obama, B. (2013A, May 26). Remarks by the president after touring the tornado damage in Oklahoma. https://obamawhitehouse.archives.gov/the-press-office/2013/05/26/remarks-president-after-touring-tornado-damage-oklahoma.

Obama, B. (2013B, July 19). Remarks by the president on Trayvon Martin. https://obamawhitehouse.archives.gov/the-press-office/2013/07/19/remarks-president-trayvon-martin.

Obama, B. (2015, December 3). Statement by the president on the shooting in San Bernardino, California. https://obamawhitehouse.archives.gov/the-press-office/2015/12/03/statement-president-shooting-san-bernardino-california.

Obama. B. (2016A, June 16). Remarks by the president in a statement to the press. https://obamawhitehouse.archives.gov/the-press-office/2016/06/16/remarks-president-statement-press.

Obama, B. (2016B, July 17). Statement by the president on the shootings in Baton Rouge, Louisiana. https://obamawhitehouse.archives.gov/the-press-office/2016/07/17/statement-president-shootings-baton-rouge-louisiana.

Ortiz, E. (2015). San Bernardino shooting: Timeline of how the rampage unfolded. *NBC News.* https://www.nbcnews.com/storyline/san-bernardino-shooting/san-bernardino-shooting-timeline-how-rampage-unfolded-n473501.

Plinkington, E. (2009, July 30). Barack Obama meets professor and the policeman—Over a beer. *The Guardian.* https://www.theguardian.com/world/2009/jul/31/barack-obama-beer-summit.

Richardson, V. (2016). Obama's refusal to interrupt vacation amid Louisiana flooding stirs anger. *Washington Times.* https://www.washingtontimes.com/news/2016/aug/18/obamas-golf-vacation-amid-louisiana-flooding-stirs/.

Selk, A., Wise, H., & Shine, C. (2016). Eight hours of terror: How a peaceful protest turned into the Dallas police's deadliest day. *Dallas News.* http://interactives.dallasnews.com/2016/dallas-police-ambush-timeline/.

Shrestha, S. S., Swerdlow, D. L., Borse, R. H., Prabhu, V. S., Finelli, L., Atkins, C. Y., & Meltzer, M. I. (2011, January 1). Estimating the burden of 2009 pandemic influenza A (H1N1) in the United States (April 2009–April 2010). *Clinical Infectious Diseases, 52,* Issue suppl_1, S75–S82. https://doi.org/10.1093/cid/ciq012.

Slack, M. (2012, December 14). President Obama speaks on the shooting in Connecticut. https://obamawhitehouse.archives.gov/blog/2012/12/14/president-obama-speaks-shooting-connecticut.

Stewart, R. (2011, April 29). CNN Politics. http://politicalticker.blogs.cnn.com/2011/04/29/perry-laments-lack-of-federal-aid-for-wildfires/.

Sulzberger, A. G. (2011, May 30). Visiting Joplin, Obama offers message of comfort. *New York Times.* https://www.nytimes.com/2011/05/30/us/30joplin.html.

U.S. Nuclear Regulatory Commission. (2012). *Safety Culture Communicator,* NRC Case Study 4. https://www.nrc.gov/docs/ML1206/ML12069A003.pdf.

Washington Post. (2011, January 13). Obama's Tucson speech transcript: Full text. *Washington Post*. http://www.washingtonpost.com/wp-dyn/content/article/2011/01/13/AR2011011301532.html.

White House. (2010, April 25). Obamawhitehouse.gov. https://obamawhitehouse.archives.gov/the-press-office/remarks-president-and-vice-president-memorial-service-upper-big-branch-miners.

White House. (2016, June 12). President Obama on the tragic shooting in Orlando. https://obamawhitehouse.archives.gov/blog/2016/06/12/president-obama-tragic-shooting-orlando.

Wheatley, K. (2013, May 22). The May 22, 2011, Joplin, Missouri EF5 tornado. *Tornado History*, May 2013. https://www.ustornadoes.com/2013/05/22/joplin-missouri-ef5-tornado-may-22-2011/.

Wyler, G. (2012). WAPO/ABC POLL: Obama gets a hurricane Sandy bump, Pulls back into a tie with Mitt Romney. *Business Insider*. https://www.businessinsider.com/obama-hurricane-sandy-bump-wapo-poll-2012-10.

III

Foreign and Security Policy

11

Obama and the Wars in Afghanistan and Iraq

ROBERT J. PAULY JR.

Introduction

In 2008, Senator Barack H. Obama built the national security and foreign policy planks of his presidential campaign on pledges to bring U.S military forces home from their principal engagements in the Greater Middle East, in Afghanistan and Iraq. Further, Obama emphatically accused the Bush administration of employing tactics in the global struggle against Islamist extremist terrorist organizations that belied American values, including, most significantly, the "torture" and indefinite detention of suspected enemy combatants from groups such as Al Qaeda at Guantanamo Bay. These themes, which Obama emphasized consistently and repeatedly throughout his Democratic primary campaign and then his subsequent victorious presidential race against Arizona Senator John McCain, also proved central to his administration's national security and foreign policies from 2009–2017. Unfortunately, Obama's determination to stick as closely to his original strategy and policy scripts as possible prevented adjustments that might have mitigated the costs the United States incurred in both turbulent countries on his watch.

The purpose of this chapter is to identify and explain the Obama administration's strategies and policies toward Afghanistan and Iraq in an appropriately interconnected fashion. It does so by addressing seven research questions and presenting and assessing the extent of the validity of seven corresponding central arguments. The research questions are as follows. First, what pledges did Obama make regarding U.S. strategy and policy toward Afghanistan and Iraq during the 2008 American presidential campaign and how did those promises play out in practice in the White House? Second, what strategies and policies did the Obama administration develop and implement toward Afghanistan and how and why did such policies evolve from 2009–17? Third, what strategies and policies did the Obama administration develop and implement toward Iraq and how and why did such policies evolve from 2009–2017? Fourth, in what ways were the Obama administration's strategies and policies toward Afghanistan and Iraq connected? Fifth, what were the most significant strengths and weaknesses of the Obama administration's strategies and policies toward Afghanistan? Sixth, what were the most significant strengths and weaknesses of the Obama administration's strategies and policies toward Iraq? Seventh, what insights should scholars, policymakers, and practitioners draw from the Obama administration's strategies and policies toward Afghanistan and Iraq?

The main arguments are as follows. First, central to Obama's 2008 election campaign were pledges to withdraw American military forces from their most significant existing engagements in the Greater Middle East, those in Afghanistan and in Iraq. Second, Obama emphasized shifting the U.S. strategic focus in the Greater Middle East from Iraq to Afghanistan, in terms of both policy pronouncements and apportionment of resources in the struggle against Islamist extremist terrorist organizations, especially Al Qaeda and the Taliban. Third, Obama focused quickly on his promise to bring U.S. forces home from Iraq, drawing down the American military presence expeditiously, with full withdrawal completed in December 2011. That move, in turn, allowed for a shift in focus to counterinsurgency and counterterrorism efforts in Afghanistan in the struggle with Al Qaeda and the Taliban.

Fourth, the most important connections between the Obama administration's strategies and policies toward Afghanistan and Iraq were fourfold: (1) both were central to targeting Islamist extremist terrorist groups, albeit for different reasons, as the shift in focus and troop strength in favor of Afghanistan bolstered efforts against Al Qaeda and the Taliban, but also contributed to an environment conducive to the genesis and expansion of the Islamic State across much of both Iraq and Syria from 2012–16; (2) the intrastate violence prevalent in each case was driven by a combination of domestic insurgencies and related internal and transnational terrorist groups; (3) violent Islamist extremist groups in Afghanistan and Iraq posed threats to U.S. (and allied) domestic government forces within both states but also, more broadly, to government and civilian targets in the West; and (4) in neither case were the domestic security forces capable of managing threats posed by those actors absent significant American military training and operational support.

Fifth, with respect to the Obama administration's strategies and policies toward Afghanistan, the strengths were threefold and the weaknesses were twofold. The strengths: (1) strategically, shifting the emphasis from Iraq to Afghanistan proved beneficial to the interconnected struggles against Al Qaeda and the Taliban; (2) ultimately, that shift in focus to counterterrorism in Afghanistan helped with the planning and conduct of the May 2011 Navy SEAL Team operation in Abbottabad, Pakistan, that eliminated Al Qaeda leader Osama bin Laden; and (3) rather than withdraw all American forces from Afghanistan at the end of 2014, as the Obama administration did in Iraq in 2011, the president made a prudent decision to leave a 9,800-strong follow-on force to support the continuing struggle against the Taliban and remnants of Al Qaeda. And the weaknesses: (1) the Obama administration reduced the U.S. force presence too rapidly in the aftermath of the killing of Bin Laden; and (2) the administration placed too great an emphasis on the use of drone strikes relative to other tactics in the struggle against Al Qaeda and the Taliban, both in Afghanistan, neighboring Pakistan, and elsewhere in the Greater Middle East.

Sixth, the most significant strengths and weaknesses of the Obama administration's strategies and policies toward Iraq were as follows. The strengths were twofold: (1) Obama kept his most significant campaign promises—the withdrawal of all American forces from Iraq by the end of 2011; and (2) the Obama administration's shift in military emphasis from Iraq to Afghanistan from 2009–11 was a sensible short-term approach, one that helped produce the elimination of Bin Laden. And the weaknesses were threefold: (1) the emphasis on bringing U.S. servicemen and women home from Iraq contributed to insufficient consideration of negotiating a status of forces agreement with Baghdad to allow for a follow-on American military presence to help mitigate a deterioration in the security environment; (2) the abrupt U.S. military force withdrawal reduced the extent of American leverage over the Shi'a majority government of Prime Minister Nouri al-Maliki to prevent him from excluding the Sunni minority from political power in Iraq to the extent that he did; and (3) the Obama administration did not place nearly enough emphasis on countering Islamist extremist groups in Iraq, particularly after Bin Laden's death.

Seventh, policymakers and practitioners should draw the following insights from the Obama administration's interconnected strategies and policies toward Afghanistan and Iraq: (1) reluctance to adjust strategic objectives and the policies designed to achieve such ends is typically an imprudent course of action, as demonstrated by the hasty withdrawal from Iraq in 2011; (2) withdrawing all of one's forces from a state under reconstruction rather than leaving a follow-on force is likely to result in a need for further intervention in the future; (3) there are typically nuanced, if not clear, distinctions between counterinsurgency and counterterrorism operations, ones that can undermine the extent to which they are complementary and/or mutually reinforcing; and (4) the conduct of counterterrorism operations always comes with political costs for leaders to manage.

The chapter addresses the aforementioned questions and assesses the arguments that ensued through the presentation of the following seven related sections. The first section presents a synopsis of Obama's 2008 presidential campaign pledges and his administration's subsequent strategies and policies toward Afghanistan and Iraq from 2009–17. The second section identifies and explains the Obama administration's strategies and policies toward Afghanistan from 2009–17. The third section identifies and explains the Obama administration's strategies and policies toward Iraq from 2009–17. The fourth section identifies and explains the most significant strengths and weaknesses of the Obama administration's strategies and policies toward Afghanistan. The fifth section identifies and explains the most significant strengths and weaknesses of the Obama administration's strategies and policies toward Iraq. The sixth section assesses the parallels, distinctions, and connections between the Obama administration's strategies and policies toward Afghanistan and Iraq, respectively, and the consequences for U.S. interests and those of its allies. And the seventh section presents conclusions on the Obama administration's strategies and policies toward Afghanistan and Iraq, and suggests the most significant insights scholars, policymakers, and practitioners should draw from both, and then offers strategy and policy recommendations moving forward.

Connecting Obama's Strategies and Policies on Afghanistan and Iraq: An Overview

When then-senator Obama decided to run for president, he had a clear foreign policy agenda in mind, one driven by the costs of U.S. commitments to related counterterrorism, counterinsurgency, and nation- and state-building efforts in Afghanistan and Iraq since the winter of 2001–02 and spring of 2003, respectively. (For overviews of U.S.-led interventions in Afghanistan and Iraq, please see Dougherty & Pauly, 2017, pp. 112–130 and 149–171; Covarrubias, Lansford, & Pauly, 2004; and Pauly, 2005).

In his speech accepting the Democratic Party presidential nomination in August 2008, Obama stressed,

> You don't defeat a terrorist network that operates in 80 countries by occupying Iraq. . . . As commander in chief, I will never hesitate to defend this nation, but I will only send our troops into harm's way with a clear mission and a sacred commitment to give them the equipment they need in battle and the care and benefits they deserve when they come home. I will end this war in Iraq responsibly, and finish the fight against al-Qaida and the Taliban in Afghanistan. (Obama, 2008)

The president remained consistent regarding that theme in his January 2009 inaugural address, suggesting, "Recall that earlier generations faced down fascism and communism not just with missiles and tanks, but with sturdy alliances and enduring convictions. . . . We are the keepers of this legacy" (Obama, 2009a). In practice, the Obama administration set about shifting its emphasis from nation- and state-building operations in Iraq to counterterrorism and counterinsurgency efforts targeting both Al Qaeda and the Taliban in Afghanistan expeditiously in 2009, with the hunt for Bin Laden identified as the principal operational point of emphasis.

In terms of strategic focus and policy planning, Obama articulated that approach in the May 2010 National Security Strategy (NSS) of the United States, pledging that "[e]ven as we end one war in Iraq, our military has been called upon to renew our focus in Afghanistan as part of an effort to disrupt, dismantle and defeat al-Qa'ida and its affiliates" (White House, 2010, p. 3). However, he also gave a proverbial nod to the importance of winding down America's wars across the Middle East and the deployments sustaining them, stressing that "our strength and influence abroad begins with the steps we take at home" (White House, 2010, p. 3).

Over the course of the year after the release of the May 2010 National Security Strategy, the United States stuck closely to the strategy specified therein to focus on the struggle against Al Qaeda, emphasizing the South Asian theatre of operations over Iraq. That approach paid off with the successful raid that eliminated Bin Laden in May 2011. However, it also led the Obama administration to overestimate the positive effects of Bin Laden's death.

A month after the successful operation in Abbottabad, the Obama administration released its first National Strategy for Counterterrorism (White House, 2011), which included assessments of progress in the struggles against Islamist extremist terrorism broadly but also in the cases of Afghanistan and Iraq in particular and also charted the U.S. path forward. On balance, the document struck a triumphant tone with respect to the Al Qaeda core group in Afghanistan and Pakistan, although that optimism was tempered with an acknowledgment of the increasing relative power and influence of affiliated groups such as Al Qaeda in the Arabian Peninsula (AQAP) and Al Qaeda in the Islamic Maghreb (AQIM) (White House, 2011).

By February 2015, when the administration issued its final National Security Strategy, circumstances in Afghanistan and Iraq alike reflected strains of continuity as well as change in the fight against violent Islamist extremism, which grew directly out of circumstances on the ground in both places. With its founder dead, Al Qaeda and, more significantly, its affiliates from North Africa and the Sahel to the Arabian Peninsula and the Levant remained significant (and growing) threats. Worse, the Taliban maintained, if not increased, its power and influence in Afghanistan and the Islamic State, which arose from the proverbial ashes of Al Qaeda in Iraq (AQI) and controlled a self-proclaimed "Caliphate" extending across a wide swath of territory in Iraq and Syria at that juncture. Yet, the document focused on a broad range of traditional and nontraditional security threats rather than emphasize Islamist extremist terrorism in particular. With respect to the daunting challenges associated with the latter, it acknowledged the importance of working to "degrade and defeat" the Islamic State (White House, 2015).

Explanation of Obama's Strategies and Policies toward Afghanistan, 2009–17

During the 2008 presidential campaign, Obama pledged that his emphasis in the struggle against Islamist extremism would be on Afghanistan. Consequently, his administration's overarching strategy and accompanying policies toward Afghanistan in 2009 focused on reinvigorating the hunt for Bin Laden in the contexts of U.S. counterterrorism operations in Afghanistan and Pakistan. Perhaps more importantly, especially from the perspectives of those in the Muslim majority regions of the world, he elaborated a bit more on that theme in a June 2009 address in Cairo, Egypt, stressing, "We do not want to keep our troops in Afghanistan. . . . It is agonizing for America to lose our young men and women. It is costly and politically difficult to continue this conflict. We would gladly bring every single one of our troops home if we could be confident that there were not violent extremists in Afghanistan and now Pakistan determined to kill as many Americans as they possibly can. But that is not yet the case. . . . And despite the costs involved, America's commitment will not weaken" (Obama, 2009b).

The first step toward intensifying the U.S.-led counterterrorism and counterinsurgency campaigns in Afghanistan was drawing down American force levels in Iraq. As those levels fell in Iraq, they rose in Afghanistan. From January 2009 to May 2011, for example, the U.S. military presence in Iraq dropped from 144,000 to 88,000, while increasing from 33,000 to 100,000 in Afghanistan (Livingston & O'Hanlon Afghanistan Index; Livingston & O'Hanlon Iraq Index; WHOPS, May 2010). That approach proved beneficial, primarily in terms of expanding counterterrorism efforts against Al Qaeda in both the Afghan theatre and in neighboring Pakistan but also with respect to the counterinsurgency campaign against the Taliban.

Strategically, the force increases allowed for the conduct of more counterterrorism operations on the ground, which Washington supplemented by marked increases in the use of drone strikes on high-level targets in the leadership of both al Qaeda and the Taliban, as well as Al Qaeda affiliates across the Greater Middle East (Zenko, 2017). Those shifts reflected the broader aims and tactics articulated in the May 2010 U.S. National Security Strategy, which emphasized, "We will always seek to delegitimize the use of terrorism and to isolate those who carry it out. Yet this is not a global war against a tactic—terrorism or a religion—Islam. We are at war with a specific network, al-Qa'ida, and its terrorist affiliates who support efforts to attack the United States, our allies, and partners" (White House, 2010).

The most strategically significant short-term outcome of the Obama administration's strategic shift was the May 2011 SEAL raid on Bin Laden's compound in Abbottabad, which was situated just miles from an elite Pakistani military academy. That operation proceeded relatively smoothly, resulting in the death of Bin Laden in a firefight inside the compound without any American casualties, although one U.S. helicopter suffered a hard landing and had to be destroyed on the ground.

In the subsequent June 2011 U.S. National Strategy for Counterterrorism, building on the recent success against Al Qaeda's core leadership structure, Obama noted, "To put it simply: We are bringing targeted force to bear on al-Qa'ida at a time when its ideology is also under extreme pressure. Nevertheless, we remain keenly vigilant to the threat al-Qa'ida, its affiliates, and adherents pose to the United States" (White House 2011, 1).

Regrettably, despite its pledges in that strategic document, the Obama administration misperceived the extent to which Bin Laden's death allowed for a marked reduction in emphasis on (and force levels in) Afghanistan. By December 2011, the U.S. force presence in Afghanistan had dropped to 91,000. It stood at 68,000 in December 2012, 47,000 in December 2013 and 9,800 in December 2014 (Livingston & O'Hanlon Afghanistan Index). Those precipitous drops complicated the struggle against Islamist extremist terrorist groups from that point forward, as acknowledged in the February 2015 U.S. National Security Strategy, which emphasized, "In Afghanistan, we have ended our combat mission and transitioned to a dramatically smaller force focused on the goal of a sovereign and stable partner in Afghanistan that is not a safe haven for international terrorists" (White House, 2015, p. 9).

Explanation of Obama's Strategies and Policies toward Iraq, 2009–17

In Iraq, above all, Obama made sure to keep his promise as central as any emphasized during the campaign: withdraw all American forces as expeditiously as possible. His reasons were many, beginning with a belief that U.S. intervention there was unjustified, on the basis of either international law or the threats Saddam's Iraq had posed to the security interests of the United States and its allies in 2003.

The first step toward fulfillment of the promised U.S. withdrawal from Iraq was to set and then follow through on implementation of a clear timetable, one that identified and continually emphasized the removal of all forces (combat and noncombat alike) by the end of December 2011. Further, minimal attention was given to negotiating approval of a follow-on force of any extent after that date. In the May 2010 U.S. National Security Strategy, for instance, Obama emphasized that "we are transitioning to full Iraqi sovereignty and responsibility—a process that includes the removal of our troops, the strengthening of our civilian capacity, and a long-term partnership to the Iraqi Government and people" (White House, 2010, p. 4).

Further, the June 2011 U.S. National Strategy for Counterterrorism acknowledged the need to retain a focus on AQI but failed to explain in sufficient depth how best to do so without a significant American military footprint in Iraq. The document stressed, "Iraq's security and political situation is improving after years of instability that enabled groups such as al-Qa'ida in Iraq (AQI) to spread chaos and sectarian conflict. AQI continues to be the main focus of U.S. CT [counterterrorism] efforts in Iraq, as it poses a threat not only to stability but to our military forces. In addition, AQI continues to plot attacks against U.S. interests in the region and beyond" (White House, 2011, pp. 13–14) Above all, the Obama administration's perspective on the prospects for post–U.S. withdrawal security and stability in Iraq articulated in that strategic document proved an overly optimistic case of wishful thinking.

Ultimately, the departure of all U.S. military forces (those who had served there previously in combat and noncombat roles alike) contributed to an environment conducive to the rise of the Islamic State from the proverbial ashes of AQI. A rise that was accelerated by the political instability and insecurity that grew out of the Arab Spring of 2010–11, most notably so in places such as neighboring Syria in the Levant and Libya in North Africa. In the former case, U.S. acquiescence in European leadership of a NATO air campaign in support of rebel forces led to the end of the regime of Col. Muammar Qadafi in Libya but also left that country wholly unstable and insecure from late 2011 through the end of Obama's final term in January 2017. Obama proved equally unable to effectively manage the chaos in Syria from 2011–14, with those shortcomings punctuated by his failure to follow through on a pledge to intervene militarily if President Bashar al-Assad's regime used chemical weapons against its own people when Damascus did just that in the summer of 2013.

Given the extent of the threats the Islamic State posed to the interests of the United States and its allies within (but also outside of) the Greater Middle East by the spring of 2014 (and, more importantly, how rapidly such threats arose), Obama changed course and began deploying U.S. troops, primarily Special Forces, back to Iraq, albeit in numbers no higher than the low thousands rather than tens of thousands or more. The purposes for sending those forces to both Iraq (and, eventually, Syria as well) were twofold: first, conduct Special Forces raids targeting Islamic State forces, especially those in leadership positions; second, train and support allies to participate effectively in the fight against the Islamic State, whether Iraqi government counterterrorism forces or Syrian Defense Forces and Kurdish militias in Syria.

The Obama administration's final National Security Strategy, released in February 2015, acknowledged the significance of the evolving challenges presented by the Islamic State, which Washington branded the Islamic State in Iraq and the Levant (ISIL), noting, "We have undertaken a comprehensive effort to degrade and ultimately defeat ISIL. We will continue to support Iraq as it seeks to free itself from sectarian conflict and the scourge of extremists. Our support is tied to the government's willingness to govern effectively and inclusively and to ensure ISIL cannot sustain a safe haven on Iraqi territory" (White House, 2015, p. 10).

Strengths and Weaknesses of Obama's Strategies and Policies toward Afghanistan

As with any set of strategies and policies, those the Obama administration developed and implemented in Afghanistan from 2009–17 had both strengths and weaknesses. Those strengths and weaknesses are identified and explained below.

The most significant strengths of the Obama administration's approach to managing the challenges of related counterterrorism and counterinsurgency and broader nation- and state-building efforts in Afghanistan were threefold. First, strategically, shifting the American military and policy emphases from Iraq to Afghanistan was a prudent decision that proved beneficial to the related struggles against Al Qaeda and the Taliban, albeit only over the short term. Above all, it made sense to focus more on the fight against Al Qaeda and its Taliban allies in 2009, given the lack of progress in mitigating the threats posed by the former and its affiliates. That was especially true for most Americans, who had grown impatient as the costs mounted increased in Iraq, while Al Qaeda's capabilities did not appear to decline significantly.

Second, Obama's shift in focus to counterterrorism efforts in Afghanistan assisted in the effective planning and implementation of the successful SEAL operation in Abbottabad. The additional forces moved to Afghanistan, concurrent with the drawdown in Iraq, helped to increase the pressure on Al Qaeda and the Taliban alike. Over time, that increased pressure proved effective.

Third, rather than withdraw all American forces from Afghanistan at the end of 2014, as the Obama administration had done in Iraq in 2011, the president made the sensible decision to leave a 9,800-strong follow-on force to support the ongoing struggle against the Taliban and remnants of Al Qaeda. While insufficient to produce any progress in the struggle against the Taliban insurgency, it did allow for the requisite training to help enhance the capabilities of the Afghan security forces, a benefit not afforded to the Iraqi government following the full U.S. military withdrawal at the end of 2011.

The most significant weaknesses of the Obama administration's approach to managing the challenges of related counterterrorism and counterinsurgency and broader nation- and state-building efforts in Afghanistan were twofold. First, the administration reduced the U.S. force presence too rapidly amid what proved to be an imprudent wave of triumphalism in the aftermath of the elimination of Bin Laden in the successful SEAL operation of May 2011. Obama's rhetoric following the successful raid on Bin Laden's compound in Abbottabad reflected his impression that the United States had Al Qaeda and Islamist extremist terrorist groups on the defensive. Ultimately, the Obama administration's assessment of progress in the struggle against Al Qaeda and its affiliates proved grossly inaccurate. Second, Obama placed too great an emphasis on the use of drone strikes relative to other tactics in the struggle against Al Qaeda and the Taliban, both in Afghanistan and in neighboring Pakistan. Rather than attempt to use a range of tools to mitigate the threats posed by violent Islamist extremist organizations, the president focused on drone strikes against the leadership circles of such groups and their affiliates instead of using the capture and interrogation tactics his immediate predecessor had employed for intelligence-gathering purposes. Given the widespread domestic and international criticism of the Bush administration's use of enhanced interrogation techniques against detained enemy combatants, and Obama's repudiation of that approach while campaigning in 2008, his rejection of such techniques was understandable. However, Obama need not have largely abandoned human intelligence gathering efforts to the extent he did.

Strengths and Weaknesses of Obama's Strategies and Policies toward Iraq

As was the case regarding the Obama administration's strategies and policies toward Afghanistan, those Washington developed and implemented in Iraq from 2009–17 also had both strengths and weaknesses. Those strengths and weaknesses are identified and explained below.

The most significant strengths of the Obama administration's approach to managing the challenges of related counterterrorism and counterinsurgency and broader nation- and state-building efforts in Iraq were twofold. First, Obama kept his promise to bring American forces home from Iraq by December 2011. Given the dearth of public support for the maintenance of the requisite deployments to support U.S.-led nation- and state-building efforts in Iraq with markedly greater costs than benefits, Obama's decision to draw down the occupation expeditiously made sense, especially since the drawdown there allowed for a more direct focus on the fight against Al Qaeda in Afghanistan. Second, the U.S. shift in military emphasis from Iraq to Afghanistan from 2009–11 was a sensible decision that helped produce the elimination of Bin Laden. It also helped provide for the requisite training of the Afghan security forces that expected to eventually take over a greater share of the responsibility for their state's defense.

The most significant weaknesses of the Obama administration's approach to managing the challenges of related counterterrorism and counterinsurgency and broader nation- and state-building efforts in Iraq were threefold.

First, Obama's emphasis on bringing U.S. servicemen and women home from Iraq contributed to insufficient consideration of negotiating a status of forces agreement to allow for the requisite follow-on presence to help mitigate a deterioration in the security environment. Instead, the United States ignored worries over a renewal of interconnected Islamist extremist terrorism and sectarian conflict in Iraq in favor of the struggle against Al Qaeda and the Taliban in Afghanistan. One can defend the shift in emphasis to Al Qaeda and the hunt for Bin Laden in particular. It is much more difficult to defend the Obama administration's neglect of the fight against Al Qaeda and (in the notable case of the Islamic State) its rivals once Bin Laden was dead. Second, the abrupt U.S. military force withdrawal reduced the amount of American leverage over the Shi'a majority government of Prime Minister Nouri al-Maliki to prevent him from marginalizing the Sunni in Iraq to the extent he did. Nor was the timing at all fortuitous, as it coincided broadly with the 2010–11 Arab Spring, which helped to cast much of the Middle East into political instability and intrastate conflict and the dire accompanying circumstances for the population at worst. By 2013–14, Iraq and Syria were both experiencing the latter. Third, Obama did not place nearly enough emphasis on (or allow loose enough rules of engagement in countering) Islamist extremist groups in Iraq, particularly after the elimination of Bin Laden. The administration's rapid drawdown and continual emphasis on the December 2011 final withdrawal date and failure to leave a follow-on force in place rendered it much easier than necessary for the Islamic State to emerge.

Obama's Strategies and Policies toward Afghanistan and Iraq: Parallels and Distinctions

As is typically the case with any administration's strategies and policies toward different countries in a given region of the world, there both parallels and distinctions between the Obama administration's approaches to them cases of Afghanistan and Iraq from 2009–17. Identifying the connections and the principal factors driving such connections, in turn, provides a useful analytical foundation for the closing observations and policy recommendations articulated in the concluding section of the chapter.

The strategic and policy parallels central to that foundation are threefold. First, above all, the Obama administration's strategies and policies toward Afghanistan and Iraq reflected the president's determination to reduce markedly the American force presence in the Greater Middle East. Maintaining U.S. military commitments in either Afghanistan or Iraq at the levels the Bush administration had would preclude that outcome. Ultimately, the administration took the requisite actions to ensure that force reduction outcome.

Second, in terms of American security interests in particular, both Afghanistan and Iraq presented daunting and, more often than not, interconnected counterterrorism and counterinsurgency challenges that were difficult to manage effectively. Given his emphasis on bolstering resources dedicated to the fight against Al Qaeda and the Taliban, it was natural to shift resources opened up by the drawdown in Iraq to Afghanistan. Once there, those resources were devoted primarily to the counterterrorism campaign against Al Qaeda, while Washington's NATO allies bore much of the counterinsurgency burden.

Third, Afghanistan and Iraq were both cases with, at best, limited chances for significant short- or longer-term improvements in economic prosperity, political stability, and the requisite maintenance of security to ensure the former two. Each produced economic and physical costs without the matching political and security benefits to justify carrying on with the existing commitments in either of those places.

The strategic and policy distinctions central to that foundation are fourfold. First, while the American public had soured on maintenance of Washington's military commitments at existing levels in the Greater Middle East long before the commencement of Obama's presidency, in relative terms it was always easier to justify the U.S. presence in Afghanistan, given the role of the Taliban in protecting Al Qaeda while that terrorist group planned the 9/11 attacks. Further, the failure to find evidence of any significant continuing WMD developmental programs in Iraq or credible connections to Al Qaeda demonstrated that the most pronounced direct security threats were in Afghanistan.

Second, the American military force level in Iraq when Obama took office dwarfed the one in Afghanistan at that juncture. Those deployment levels alone, coupled with the aforementioned logic of switching strategic emphasis to Afghanistan, meant an expeditious drawdown in Iraq was essential for Obama to keep his promises to bring most, if not all, American servicemen and women home from the Middle East while concurrently providing more resources for the struggle against Al Qaeda. Once Bin Laden was neutralized, the case to draw down in Afghanistan was also be easier to make.

Third, the Obama administration grossly underestimated the extent to which the lack of a follow-on force in Iraq would afford the remnants of AQI to take advantage of the Arab Spring to reemerge in the form of the Islamic State in both Iraq and neighboring Syria. Nor did the administration anticipate how rapidly the Islamic State would spread much farther afield across the Greater Middle East generally and in places such as Afghanistan and Libya specifically and, worse, to Muslim communities in the West.

Fourth, as the consequences of the rapid force drawdown to zero became increasingly apparent from 2012–14 in Iraq, the Obama administration made a prudent choice to leave a follow-on force in Afghanistan. The strategic logic was that the U.S. troops remaining, along with a complementary NATO commitment, could continue training Afghan security forces for (and supporting them in) counterterrorism and counterinsurgency efforts against Taliban, remnants of Al Qaeda, and an emerging Islamic State threat from 2014–16. Although that approach proved relatively effective in the short term, it did little to mitigate the rising strength or long-term resolve exhibited by the Taliban in particular.

Conclusions

This chapter was designed to explain and assess the utility of the Obama administration's strategies and policies toward Afghanistan and Iraq by focusing on six central issue areas. First, it identified the linkages between Obama's 2008 presidential campaign pledges and his administration's subsequent strategies and policies toward Afghanistan and Iraq from 2009–17. Second, it identified and explained the Obama administration's strategies and policies toward Afghanistan from 2009–17. Third, it analyzed the Obama administration's strategies and policies toward Iraq from 2009–17. Fourth, it summarized and explored the most significant strengths and weaknesses of the Obama administration's strategies and policies toward Afghanistan. Fifth, it identified and explained the most significant strengths and weaknesses of the Obama administration's strategies and policies toward Iraq. And, sixth, it assessed the parallels, distinctions, and connections between the Obama administration's strategies and policies toward Afghanistan and Iraq, respectively, and the consequences for U.S. interests and those of America's allies.

With respect to the first issue area, it is important to recognize that the Obama administration's overarching strategy toward the Greater Middle East was a complicated and challenging one designed to create a perception of American humility growing out of marked military force reductions while maintaining a focus on the struggle against Al Qaeda and its Islamist extremist affiliates. That approach was also quite consistent with his emphasis throughout his political career on avoiding the brand of strong and direct American leadership that had led to U.S. military intervention in Iraq in particular and the marked costs that course of action entailed. As pertains to the second issue area, Obama was relatively consistent in his approach to Afghanistan during over his two terms, generally emphasizing the often (but not always) interconnected counterterrorism and counterinsurgency campaigns against Al Qaeda and the Taliban. Those connections, however, waned soon after the elimination of Bin Laden in May 2011.

Regarding the third issue area, the Obama administration followed precisely the approach toward Iraq forecast by Obama himself throughout the 2008 presidential campaign. However, he did so only until it became openly evident that the full U.S. military withdrawal carried with it an increased Iraqi vulnerability in the years that followed. Most significantly, that vacuum served as an opportunity for Islamist extremists, which the Islamic State in particular took full advantage of, especially during Obama's second term.

As to the fourth issue area, the Obama administration's strategy and policy approaches to Afghanistan had both important strengths and weaknesses that carried with them both benefits and costs. On balance, the benefits and costs of the Obama administration's approach toward Afghanistan and, for that matter, Central and South Asia more broadly, were roughly equivalent. Consider the most important benefit—the elimination of Bin Laden—which was a victory for the United States and a setback for Al Qaeda, but one from which that terrorist group could (and did) recover. The most significant costs came with the decision to rapidly draw down the American presence in Afghanistan in 2014, which the Taliban used to its advantage in the insurgency it is still engaged in today.

With respect to the fifth issue area, the Obama administration's strategy and policy approaches to Iraq had both important strengths and weaknesses, with accompanying costs and benefits. Ultimately, the decision to withdraw fully from Iraq at the end of 2011 was beneficial in limiting further damage from a conflict that had already cost more than $1 trillion and, more importantly, the lives of nearly 4,500 American servicemen and women (Watson Institute). However, the failure to leave a follow-on force reduced the extent of any such benefits, as subsequent redeployments were needed for the fight against the Islamic State.

Last, with respect to the sixth issue area, four especially useful insights can be drawn from the parallels, distinctions, and connections between the Obama administration's strategies and policies toward Afghanistan and Iraq, respectively, and consequences for U.S. interests and those of America's allies.

First, a withdrawal of forces from any country under occupation is best approached without revealing definitive timelines that only afford adversaries, whether primarily insurgent or transnational terrorist groups, advance notice of windows of opportunity to mount future offensive campaigns. The Obama administration's maintenance of a preset December 2010 full withdrawal date without the provision of a follow-on force left Iraq vulnerable to an Islamic State takeover of territory across the north and west of the country. To its credit, the administration avoided a similar error in Afghanistan by arranging for a 9,800-strong follow-on after the U.S. withdrawal in December 2014. Present and future U.S. leaders and policymakers would be prudent to do the same.

Second, the intrastate conflicts of the post–Cold War era, with the cases of Afghanistan and Iraq representing the most notable examples, illustrate the interconnected challenges posed by the concurrent management of counterterrorism and counterinsurgency operations in a given country. In both Afghanistan and Iraq, the United States had to adapt to changing circumstances that affected the conduct of counterterrorism and counterinsurgency operations with subtly, if not always significantly, different objectives. The Taliban and Al Qaeda, for example, shared an Islamist extremist ideology but had different political objectives, with the former intent to undermine the Afghan government via an insurgency and the latter focusing on broader Greater Middle Eastern and global ambitions. The volatile mix of insurgency, terrorism, and sectarianism, with both domestic and international participants involved, produced an equally complex picture.

Third, insurgent movements and terrorist groups are at best manageable rather than removable challenges, much as a "war" on terrorism can never really be won. While victories can be achieved in individual "battles" such as the operation that eliminated Bin Laden, they are typically transitory ones. The cases of Afghanistan and Iraq in the 2000s and 2010s only reinforce insights drawn from past struggles with terrorist organizations situated in regions and countries across the world. At best, one can mitigate the threats that terrorist groups present but the motivating ideologies always remain and eventually drive others to renew a given cause.

Fourth, ultimately, domestic political factors always play a significant, if not always decisive, role in determining the length of stay of U.S. military forces after intervention abroad, as well as the size of that presence, its mission, and costs deemed acceptable to continue pursuit of its objectives. Obama's principal objectives in Afghanistan and Iraq alike and the relationship between the two, at least in terms of the basics (shift in focus from the latter to the former to facilitate near-full withdrawal from both), date to his 2008 presidential campaign. Further, generally speaking, those decisions reflected public opinion in the United States, as the citizenry grew progressively more dissatisfied with massive military deployments in Afghanistan and Iraq that produced markedly more costs than benefits and had negative effects on perceptions of America abroad.

References

Covarrubias, J., Lansford, T., & Pauly, R. J. Jr., eds. (2016). *The new Islamic State: Ideology, religion, and violent extremism in the 21st century*. Routledge.

Dougherty, K., & Pauly, R. J. Jr. (2017). *American nation-building: Case studies from Reconstruction to Afghanistan*. McFarland.

Livingston, I. S., & O'Hanlon, M. (2002–present). Afghanistan index. Brookings Institution. https://www.brookings.edu/afghanistan-index/.

Livingston, I. S., & O'Hanlon, M. (2002–present). Iraq Index. Brookings Institution. https://www.brookings.edu/iraq-index/.

Obama, B. (2008, August 28). Democratic Convention nomination acceptance address. National Public Radio. https://www.npr.org/templates/story/story.php?storyId=94087570.

Obama, B. (2009a, January 21). Inauguration address. White House Office of the Press Secretary. https://obamawhitehouse.archives.gov/blog/2009/01/21/president-barack-obamas-inaugural-address.

Obama, B. (2009b, June 4). Remarks by the president on a new beginning. White House Office of the Press Secretary. https://obamawhitehouse.archives.gov/the-press-office/remarks-president-cairo-university-6-04-09.

Pauly, R. J. Jr. (2005). *U.S. foreign policy and the Persian Gulf: Safeguarding American interests through selective multilateralism*. Ashgate.

Pauly, R. J. Jr. (2004). *Strategic preemption: U.S. foreign policy and the Persian Gulf*. Ashgate.

Watson Institute Costs of War Project. Brown University (2001–present). https://watson.brown.edu/costsofwar/.

White House. (2010, May). National security strategy of the United States. http://nssarchive.us/NSSR/2010.pdf.

White House. (2011, February). National strategy for counterterrorism. https://obamawhitehouse.archives.gov/sites/default/files/counterterrorism_strategy.pdf.

White House. (2015, February). National security strategy of the United States. https://obamawhitehouse.archives.gov/sites/default/files/docs/2015_national_security_strategy_2.pdf.

White House Office of the Press Secretary (WHOPS). (2010, May). Facts and figures on drawdown in Iraq. White House.

Zenko, M. (2017, January). Obama's final drone strike data. Council on Foreign Relations. https://www.cfr.org/blog/obamas-final-drone-strike-data.

12

The Arab Spring and the Middle East

WAYNE F. LESPERANCE JR. AND
JOHN M. CALLAHAN

Introduction

In the run-up to the 2008 election, a tremendous amount of attention was paid to the next president's foreign policy goals in the world. Then-senator Barack Obama distinguished himself from Democratic primary opponents by riding an increasingly popular opposition to the war in Iraq and Afghanistan. Indeed, during the summer of 2008, candidate Obama took the unprecedented step of visiting Afghanistan, Iraq, and Israel before extending his tour to Europe (MacAskill, 2008). From a political perspective, this whirlwind tour of the region was a necessary response to criticisms that Obama lacked sufficient foreign policy experience. However, from a policy perspective, the regional tour set the stage for subsequent visits and meetings with Arab, Turkish, and Israeli leadership. Arguably, President Obama's inaugural address was informed by the growing relationship with his counterparts throughout the Middle East, Southwest Asia, and North Africa. More specifically he sought to engage them in that inaugural speech with his promise of, "a new way forward, based on mutual interest and mutual respect" (Neuman, 2009).

Early on in his presidency, Barack Obama returned to the region to deliver a speech, later entitled "A New Beginning," at Cairo University on June 4, 2009. The speech, billed as fulfilling a campaign promise to deliver a major address from a Muslim capital, came on the heels of a series of outreach meetings and visits to regional heads of state. The speech itself focused on a number of issues including the Middle East peace process, nuclear weapons, democracy, human rights, and economic development. Arguably, the importance of the speech was more attributed to the location in which it took place, Cairo, Egypt, than to its substance. Still, as this chapter will show, several important themes for the Obama presidency were foretold in the Cairo address.

In the pages that follow, the chapter will focus on a number of the larger foreign policy issues President Obama faced in his time at the White House. Of course, looming large in this presidency is the Arab Spring. Syria is also an important player in the Obama presidency and is divided into two parts—the "red line" declaration by the president and the fight against the Islamic State in Syria. This chapter also considers the development of the Joint Comprehensive Plan of Action agreement between the P5 plus EU and Iran concerning Iranian nuclear weapons.

The Arab Spring

Prelude: Doctrines, Pivots, and Wikileaks

During his election campaign in 2008, then-candidate Obama expressed what would become known as the "Obama Doctrine." The doctrine had three tenets. The first was that the U.S. would focus on and take the lead on humanitarian actions; the second was that any military actions must be in response to a specific challenge to U.S. national security, and the third was that U.S. forces would not invade an Islamic country to overthrow an established government, even in the case of dictatorships (Klein, 2013, p. 213).

One of the first challenges for the administration came from Iran. Fueled by social media and a desire for reform, Iran suffered from political upheaval from 2009–10 which had the potential to overthrow the Ahmedinejad regime. While initially professing support for the goals of the protesters, the administration generally took a wait-and-see approach, refusing to commit to physical or political support for the protests (Lizza, 2011). The criticism the administration received for its stance may have helped to set the stage for its reactions to the events that followed across the region.

On November 17, 2011, the president, on a trip to Australia, announced his proposed "Pivot" to Asia, and a renewed focus on that region, implicitly at the expense of Europe and the Middle East. Within weeks of that speech, events in the Arab world would make both the Obama Doctrine and the Pivot dead letters. But first, an international espionage scandal would play its part in shaping events. The first major shock in the Middle East/North Africa region took place on November 28, 2010, with the WikiLeaks scandal. Among the leaked documents were comments on two regional actors, Tunisia and Libya. The disparaging nature of the commentary poisoned U.S.-Libyan relations, which had generally been good since the end of the Cold War. Unvarnished U.S. opinions were taken as an insult by the United States to the Libyan leader and his family, with the U.S. ambassador being withdrawn shortly before the outbreak of the Arab Spring (Chorin, 2012, p. 171). U.S.-Tunisian relations suffered similarly and with equally bad timing.

The term *Arab Spring* or *Spring, 2011*, refers to a series of populist, often Islamist uprisings, which overturned the established political order across the Middle East and definitively ended the Obama administration's stated desire to change its fundamental focus to Asia (Lieberthal, 2011). Starting with an incident in Tunisia, the Arab Spring rapidly engulfed Egypt and spread to points east and west. While revolts were crushed in the Gulf state of Bahrain, they flared in Syria. As of 2018, the revolts are in effect still going on in Libya, Syria, and Yemen.

With popular dissent already fanned by the WikiLeaks scandal, the Arab Spring began in Tunisia on December 2010, with the protest suicide of Mohamed Bouazizi, a street merchant who claimed abuse at the hands of a female law enforcement official. Fanned by social and traditional media, the protests, dubbed the "Jasmine Revolution," forced Tunisian President Zine El Abidine Ben Ali to flee the country by mid-January 2011. Ben Ali had long been supported by the United States and its European allies. The Obama administration chose to remain neutral in Tunisia almost to the last minute. As late as two days before Ben Ali's flight, the White House claimed to not be taking sides, although rhetoric did switch to supporting the revolutionaries soon thereafter (Hamid, 2015). From that time on, the administration vacillated between support for and against revolutionary movements across the region.

Egypt was next to experience unrest as a result of what Obama was rapidly coming to see as a democratically inspired Arab uprising. Reacting to police brutality in the country, widespread protests began on January 25, 2011. Having made its fundamental choice in Tunisia, the Obama administration supported the Egyptian protestors. On January 28, the

NSC principals' committee discussed the growing crisis, with Secretary of State Hillary Clinton and Secretary of Defense Robert Gates, along with National Security Advisor Thomas Donilon, and Vice President Joseph Biden urging that the U.S response be measured and cautious. (Clinton, 2014, p. 339). That day, Obama called for Hosni Mubarak, the president of Egypt, to step down, while dispatching Department of State Africa expert and former ambassador to Egypt Frank Wisner to discuss reform with both the Egyptian government and protest leaders. Three days later, Obama decided that enough was enough, and on February 1 he announced to the world that the transition to a new government "must begin now." By February 11, Mubarak left office, replaced by a Muslim Brotherhood government, which held power until its ouster in a military coup on July 3, 2013. Ironically, the dictatorial nature of the Islamist administration of Mohamed Morsi, which fell in 2013, led then-secretary of state John Kerry to state that the military-led coup was "restoring democracy" to the country ("Egypt Army," 2013).

As the situation in Egypt was flaming out with the withdrawal of Mubarak, similar challenges in Libya were flaring up. But in Libya there was no significant attempt to negotiate, and intervention became inevitable. The move toward armed intervention was facilitated by the conservative Arab League and Gulf Cooperation Council, which saw the populist Arab Spring as a mortal threat to its ultraconservative, mainly monarchist members. The result was a NATO and U.S.–led armed intervention, code named "Operation Odyssey Dawn," to enforce a no-fly zone and later to provide direct combat air support to Libyan rebels. The offensive, which began in March and April 2011, included approximately one hundred cruise missile attacks and 1,900 aircraft and support aircraft sorties. With this level of support, which added 24,000 sorties between April and October, the rebel movement ultimately expanded its operations westward and overthrew Muammar Gaddafi. In the end, Gaddafi was brutally murdered during his capture, and a largely Islamist and anti-Western coalition has taken over the country.

The Libyan intervention took place as a result of the influence a few central players in the administration. United Nations Ambassador Susan Rice and National Security Council staffer Samantha Power, although relatively junior in the administration, had unique ties to the president and easy access and strong influence with him. Most critically, Secretary of State Hillary Clinton came to support the idea of intervention and together they won the National Security Council votes on intervention.

With Egypt, and its vital stabilizing role in the Middle East, under siege, thirty years of diplomacy, and the security of U.S. ally Israel seemed to be at risk (Prashad, 2012). Furthermore, significant oil contracts between the United States and Libya were at risk given the unrest there, and this was exacerbated by the significant role Libya played in supplying petroleum to America's European allies (Prashad, 2012). Thus, the three pillars of Washington's traditional Middle East policy; oil, stability, and the protection of Israel, all seemed to be in danger in Egypt and even more so in Libya. On February 4, 2011, Iran added to the turmoil in the region when Ayatollah Ali Khamenei pronounced an "Islamic Awakening" across the region (Prashad, 2012).

On February 14, 2011, the Arab Spring directly threatened the Persian Gulf and its conservative leadership, with protests breaking out in Bahrain and later in Yemen. With oil and key U.S. partners in the Persian Gulf, as well as its own military 5th Fleet Headquarters at risk in Bahrain, the Obama administration tacitly supported a swift and brutal crackdown on dissent led by the Saudi military, even while publicly criticizing regime efforts to suppress dissent and demanding political reforms (that were never implemented) ("The Obama Administration," 2016). In summary, the events unfolding on the Arabian Peninsula served to strengthen Arab resolve regarding events further west, in Libya (Gates, 2014).

Beginning on February 15, a series of crackdowns by the Libyan government spiraled into a pattern of ever-increasing protest and repression. In contrast to the Egyptian army, which maintained a separate stance from the government, the Libyan armed forces, which were largely foreign, had no reservations about suppressing its citizens when ordered to by Gaddaffi (Clinton, 2014).

Meanwhile, efforts began in the international community to punish Libya for its actions. On February 17, the U.N. Human Rights Council, at the urging of Washington, removed Libya from its membership (Lizza, 2011). President Obama addressed the situation again six days later, acknowledging and pledging U.S. support to the democratic aspirations of the Libyan protesters, but falling short of promising intervention ("Obama on," n.d.). On February 28, France unilaterally began humanitarian support missions. On the same day the French acted, the United States stepped up the rhetoric, with Secretary Clinton calling, for the first time, for Gaddafi to leave office (Lizza, 2011). By mid-March, the French began to push for armed intervention, particularly before Libyan government forces could reach Benghazi. It was widely expected that a massacre would take place in what was essentially the capital of the resistance movement.

In her memoirs, Secretary Clinton noted that, in spite of discussion of a no-fly zone, by March 9 there was still no consensus on intervention, although discussions had become more frequent and heated. On the first, a heated exchange took place in the Senate between pro-no-fly zone Senator John McCain on one hand and Defense Secretary Gates and Chairman of the Joint Chiefs Admiral Michael Mullen on the other (Gates, 2011). In this exchange, Gates and Mullen were joined by Marine General James Mattis, leader of U.S. Central Command (Gates, 2014).

On March 10, Clinton testified to Congress that international authorization was a prerequisite for U.S. action. That authorization quickly came, however, with an Arab League request for humanitarian intervention to the United Nations. Although its own request did not mention military action, on March 12 the Arab League, now supported by the Gulf Cooperation Council, threw its support behind a United Kingdom request to the United Nations Security Council for a no-fly zone over Libya (Prashad, 2012). Within the administration, debate continued, with Susan Rice and NSC staffers Powers and Ben Rhodes supporting intervention, citing the nascent UN Responsibility to Protect (R2P) Doctrine as justification for action (Prashad, 2012). They were supported by Senator John McCain, who remained critical of the administration's inaction. Gates and Clinton, who held the key votes, remained against intervention, but Clinton gradually shifted her position to the pro-intervention camp, grasping on to the doctrine of Responsibility to Protect (R2P) as justification (Gates, 2014). Over a three-day period, Clinton convinced Obama to act, with Washington supporting the passage of UN Security Council Resolution (UNSCR) 1973 within weeks (Gates, 2014). On March 17, the final decision to act was taken by the Obama after consultation with the NSC principals and their key deputies (Gates, 2014).

Having decided to act, the administration insisted that it do so under NATO auspices in terms of command and control (Daalder & Stavridis, 2012). Obama called this "Leading from behind," and it entailed coordinating the efforts of fourteen NATO member states and four partner countries, including the United Arab Emirates (Clinton, 2014). Every member of NATO, at that time twenty-eight nations, voted for the military intervention in Libya. Of these, half provided material support, with the lion's share of the command and control being provided by the United States (Gates, 2014). Military operations were scheduled to begin on March 21 (U.S. Operation Odyssey Dawn), but the French commenced air strikes nearly two days early, which threw planning efforts into disarray (Gates, 2014). From this point on, military tactical and operational requirements took over the calculus of planning for the intervention. Air strikes require preliminary attacks to eliminate radar and surface to air missiles, for example, and the preparatory strikes to achieve this end were an escalation that was actually not in line with the intent of UNSCR 1973.

At first the intervention in Libya was deemed a success in terms of cost for gain, but in hindsight Obama eventually called the intervention one of his biggest mistakes (Obama said that he did not regret the act of intervention, but rather the lack of follow-up and management after the fall of Gaddafi) (Friedman, 2014). Through the summer of 2011, under increasing airstrikes, and with improvements and streamlining of leadership among the Libyan rebels, Gaddafi's forces faced a series of defeats. On October 20, having fled Tripoli, Gaddafi was captured and executed in a combined NATO and rebel attack on his fleeing military convoy, and shortly thereafter the Islamist Libyan National Transitional Council declared victory in the Libyan Civil War.

The Libya intervention had significant consequences for U.S. foreign policy, particularly after the death of U.S. Ambassador Stephens and three other Americans in an Islamist attack on the American consulate in Benghazi on September 11, 2012, and the takeover of Libya by an Islamist government generally affiliated with the Islamic State in Iran and Syria (ISIL). Libya soured the United States against further humanitarian interventions (including the R2P concept), and this would have unfortunate repercussions for the other growing crisis in the Middle East and worldwide. The two most notable manifestations of the new reluctance to intervene were seen in the Syrian Civil War and that in Eastern Ukraine in Spring 2014.

Syria, Civil War, and the Decision Not to Intervene Through 2014

What is now called the Syrian Civil War was an outgrowth of the Arab Spring, and has become its deadliest and longest-lasting manifestation.

Unrest began to manifest itself in Syria just as the United States was making its decision to intervene in Libya, and while it remained mired in the world economic crisis and the political battle, which led to the sequestration crisis of Spring 2013 and severe cuts in the defense budget. However, Syria was a very different case than other notable Arab Spring events. Led by U.S. ambassador to Syria Robert Ford, Arabists in the State Department predicted that the Assad regime would respond positively to the Arab Spring, but this is the opposite of what actually happened (Gates, 2014).

Although Syria is not a major oil producer, it differed from the North African victims of the Arab Spring in that it had strong historical ties to Russia and Iran, both powerful regional actors whose presence would help to deter Obama from intervention in the country. There was also a critical difference in technology in Syria. Whereas social media was a key enabler in tech-savvy Tunisia and Egypt, and traditional telephone technology enabled tech-backward Libya, the Syrian government aggressively and successfully suppressed social media platforms such as Facebook and Twitter, crippling the efforts of protestors to coordinate their activities, and of outside players to influence events in the country. A key example of the difference is the so-called Syrian Electronic Army. The regime-backed group, which had become expert at diluting and disputing the messaging of rebel groups, was bold enough to hack President Obama's reelection campaign website during the summer of 2012.

The opening round of protests in Syria took place in March 2011, and the regime's release of political prisoners, rather than appeasing the protesters, added fuel to the movement (Panetta, 2014, p. 410). Washington's response to the outbreak of rebellion was primarily rhetorical, developing into a call for regime change and culminating in an imposition of sanctions on the government of Syrian dictator Bashir al Assad by April (Panetta, 2014, p. 410). As spring moved into summer, the administration continued to call for Assad to relinquish power (Panetta, 2014, p. 410). Syria, of course, did not involve oil, but it did involve Russia and Iran, making intervention a difficult issue to justify and frame, particularly in concert with the demonstrated capability of the regime to resist efforts by social media–augmented rebels to discredit the regime, a factor which had been central to the other revolutions (Lindgren, 2013).

Syria was noteworthy by the lack of unity in its various protest and rebel groups compared to the other manifestations of the Arab

Spring. For Libya, it was Gaddaffi's western Libyan forces attempting to dominate eastern groups centered in Benghazi. Egypt saw a blend of socialists, Islamists, capitalists, and reactionary conservatives combining their efforts to overthrow Mubarak (Auroagh, 2012). In Syria, the makeup of the rebels was far more decentralized and prone to internal conflict, including pro-Iranian, Shiite, and Al Qaeda–supported elements. The regime, already ruling from a minority, was used to surviving by playing off the groups mentioned above against one another, and, through the undiluted strength of the Ba'ath political party, was far more capable of continued dominance.

In July 2012, Damascus announced that it would use its stockpile of chemical weapons to defend itself from aggression. On August 20, Obama responded by stating that use of chemical weapons would be a "Red Line" that would change the calculus of his decision making on intervention ("Timeline of," 2013). In spite of further rhetorical warnings of this nature, Damascus used chemical weapons near Aleppo in March 2013 and again, most infamously, on August 21, 2013, in an attack on Ghouta that killed 1,500 Syrians. In response, there were widespread calls for intervention, specifically a call for airstrikes by Senator McCain (Panetta, 2014). While the Obama administration had increased support for the Free Syrian Army in June, it was incredibly difficult to determine who among the numerous Syrian rebel groups were actually aligned with U.S. interests. The rise of the Islamic State made it even more difficult to tell who was who among the Islamist groups in Syria, resulting in U.S. aid going to groups that were actually in league with Al-Qaeda (Clinton, 2014). Ultimately, there was little international support for a Syria coalition, while key players who had remained neutral in Libya, such as Russia, openly opposing intervention. America's most important Western partner, the UK, declined to participate after a parliamentary vote against Prime Minister David Cameron's suggestion of support ("Syria Crisis," 2013). The factor that, more than a year later, drove the United States to intervene in Syria was the emergence of the fundamentalist Islamic State, and the threat that group posed to oil markets and overall stability in the Middle East. As was the case in Libya, that later intervention would receive the support of the Gulf Cooperation Council, which saw a dire threat to its monarchical governments from ISIL, which wanted to overthrow them all in favor of an Islamic Caliphate.

An end note to the administration's Middle East involvement, separate from the issue of the rise of, and fight against, ISIL, is the

Yemen operation, which is still ongoing. On March 25, 2015, the White House announced that it would be providing logistical and intelligence support to members of the Gulf Cooperation Council as it conducted military operations in Yemen. The purpose of the operation was twofold, although both justifications were provided by Saudi Arabia. The first was to reinforce the rule of Saudi-backed Abed Rabbo Mansour Hadi, and second was to defend the territory of Saudi Arabia from attacks by the Iranian-backed Houthi rebels. Obama backed up the offer of military support by reaffirming the U.S. commitment to its relationships with both Saudi Arabia and the GCC. Below the surface, the administration was looking for support for its then-nascent nuclear deal with Iran, and tacitly linked its support for the Saudi and GCC operation to their support for that deal (Zenko, 2017). As of 2019, the Yemen operation is still underway and has cost the lives of more than thirteen thousand people, mainly civilians caught in the crossfire.

Iran

The Islamic Republic of Iran has factored prominently in U.S. foreign policy since the 1979 Islamic revolution in Iran. With the end of a client-state relationship with the United States, presidents from Reagan to Obama were confronted with a Persian Gulf state acting against American interest in the region and beyond. Specifically, presidents representing both Republicans and Democrats raised Iran's support for Islamic extremism, promotion of instability in neighboring states, hostility toward Israel, and clandestine nuclear weapons program as ongoing matters or concern. It was this latter issue, concern over Iran's nuclear ambitions, which led to the Joint Comprehensive Plan of Action (JCPOA) concluded in Vienna on July 14, 2015.

A number of events led to the start of the JCPOA talks in November 2013. Concern by the international community that Iran had clandestinely developed nuclear weapons are well documented and established. The United States' ability to convince allies, however, to implement significant sanctions on Iran met with mixed results. As a result, despite American disapproval, Tehran managed to escape the full impact of Washington's containment policy through trade with European partners whose concerns did not manifest in a more punitive approach to Iran. This difference of approach between the United States and its allies began to change with the election in 2005 of Mahmoud Ahmadinejad to the presidency of the Islamic Republic.

Ahmadinejad was a hard-liner in the regime, with strong ties to the clerics and the Revolutionary Guard in Iran. He was critical of the prior president's attempts to negotiate with the West to ease sanctions in return for the cessation of uranium enrichment, going so far as accusing of treason the Iranian negotiators involved in efforts to trade uranium enrichment for an end to sanctions ("Country Profiles," 2018). Subsequently, under his leadership, the Paris Agreement and other international efforts to restrict uranium enrichment and other proliferation activities faltered, with talks largely ending. The Iranian president determined that the proposals being offered Iran were, "heavy on demands, light on incentives, did not incorporate Iran's proposals, and violated the Paris Agreement" (Lyons, 2015). In early 2006, Iran resumed its uranium enrichment at the Natanz research facility.

What followed was a series of events that brought key states together to apply pressure on Iran to resume negotiations. The United States, then led by President George W. Bush, publicly considered a military option. Other members of the permanent five (P5) of the United Nations Security Council coalesced around resolutions to apply greater diplomatic and economic pressure on Iran to bring the government back to the table. In all, six resolutions were passed in the UN between 2006 and 2010 demanding a cessation of Iran's enrichment activities and encouraging Iran to comply with its Non-Proliferation of Nuclear Weapons Treaty (NPT) and International Atomic Energy Agency (IAEA) obligations.

President Obama inherited a growing crisis in the form of Iranian noncompliance. In the face of the efforts by a coalescing international community to force adherence to international norms around nonproliferation, Iran remained steadfast in its violative activities. Concerns grew as intelligence indicated the development of new production facilities and a general fear that as Iran approached the nuclear threshold, states such as Israel would be increasingly likely to employ force to delay Iranian efforts.

By Obama's second term, a nuclear deal with Iran had become a major objective of his administration and a cornerstone of his foreign policy legacy (Ghitis, 2015). In March 2013, President Obama authorized a series of secret bilateral talks with Iranian officials in Oman. Later that year in June, Hassan Rouhani succeeded Ahmadinejad as president of Iran. Rouhani was viewed as more pragmatic than his predecessor and open to resuming negotiations over Iran's nuclear programs (Davenport, 2018). Immediately following his inauguration, in August 2013, Rouhani called for a resumption of talks between Iran and the P5+1 members regarding Iran's nuclear programs. A month later, presidents Rouhani and Obama spoke via telephone and Secretary of State John Kerry met with his counterpart, Iranian foreign minister Mohammad Javad Zarif (Davenport, 2018). The presidential telephone call and the meeting between Kerry and Zarif were the first high-level contacts between the United States and Iran since the 1979 Iranian revolution. These meetings represented the start of the process that ultimately led to the adoption of the Joint Plan of Action (JPOA) in November 2013. The JPOA served as a temporary agreement freezing Iranian nuclear activities and easing economic sanctions while a more permanent arrangement was pursued (Gearan & Warrick, 2013). Signatories included Iran and the P5+1 (The five permanent members of the Security Council plus Germany) countries.

The signatories to the JPOA continued to meet for nearly two years following the agreement. In April 2015, the P5+1 arrived at another milestone in the nuclear negotiations with Iran when they concluded a framework for the final arrangement. This framework agreement was signed in July 2015 by the P5+1 states, and a corollary Roadmap Agreement was concluded between Iran and the IAEA (Gordan & Sanger, 2015). The final agreement was called The Joint Comprehensive Plan of Action (JCPOA) and was signed on July 15, 2015.

The terms of the JCPOA agreement as they related to Iran were as follows: (1) the elimination of medium-enriched uranium; (2) 98 percent reduction of low-enriched uranium; (3) a reduction of two-thirds of existing gas centrifuges; and (4) commitment by Iran for fifteen years to limit uranium enrichment up to 3.67 percent, a non–weapons grade level (Perkovich et al., 2015). Other restrictions included limiting all enrichment activities to a single facility for ten years. Iran also agreed it would not build new heavy water facilities for fifteen years.

All parties agreed that compliance would be maintained through a monitoring system carried out by the IAEA. A comprehensive list of facilities was determined and agreed upon by the signatories. Each of these declared facilities became subject to inspection by the IAEA. In exchange for this agreement and compliance with the provisions, Iran was slated to receive significant sanction relief from its fellow signatories, the United Nations, and the European Union. The sanctions relief alone translated into approximately $40 billion per year for Tehran ("Iran

Nuclear," 2018). Per the deal, Iran gained access to more than $100 billion in assets, some of which had been frozen since the 1979 revolution.

A number of measures were included to provide signatories with recourse should Iran be found to be violating the terms of the agreement. First, parties to the JCPOA included a "snapback" provision, which created the option to automatically reinstitute sanctions in the event breaches of the agreement were found to have taken place. Second, the United States agreed to the JCPOA subject to regular certification by the president of the United States that Iran remained in compliance (it was this certification that President Trump threatened to withhold in 2018 that raised questions about the future of the JCPOA).

The JCPOA was met with widespread approval across the globe. More than ninety countries endorsed the agreement in addition to numerous international organizations (Lew, 2015). The agreement had its share of critics as well, however. Israeli prime minister Netanyahu described the JCPOA as a "capitulation" to Iran (Lew, 2015). Saudi Arabia was highly critical of the deal, while many other U.S. allies in the region held the "view that Iran [was] running circles around the United States and outplayed Obama" (Ghitis, 2015). Critics within the United States expressed concerns about verification and suggested that the agreement was imperfect. Indeed, the JCPOA was the subject of numerous discussions during the 2016 presidential election cycle. New questions about the future of the agreement emerged during the Trump administration and prompted renewed sanctions on Iran, leading that country to retaliate by relaunching its uranium enrichment program in violation of the JCPOA in 2019. Subsequently, tensions rapidly escalated between the two countries (Wong, 2019; Van Sant, 2019).

Conclusion

Since the end of World War II, the Middle East, North Africa, and Southwest Asia have factored prominently on the agenda of every American president. From the campaign trail to his inaugural address, President Barack Obama offered a new approach to the region. His speech in Cairo just after taking office made good on a campaign promise to deliver a major address from a Muslim capital.

Still, as this chapter has demonstrated, the challenges of the region to this American president were manifold and unexpected. The Arab

Spring quickly turned to an Arab Winter and the emergence of the Islamic State in Iraq and Syria was unexpected, underestimated, and was met with policy responses inadequate to the challenge. Little progress was made on the Arab-Israeli challenges, with Palestinians continuing to suffer from poor leadership and support in their own country, the region, and the international community.

The JCPOA represents a bright spot, arguably, in Obama's work in the region. Despite its critics, it has led to a period of unprecedented diplomacy between Washington and Iran. What's more, by all accounts, Iran has remained in compliance with the agreement. Certainly, as a first step in thwarting Iranian nuclear ambitions diplomatically, the agreement and President Obama deserve credit. At the end of the day, no postwar president has ended a presidency unaffected by the Middle East. President Obama is no different. His "new beginning" might have never reached its zenith, but with the challenges he experienced, some contributions were made.

References

Auroagh, M. (2012). Social media, mediation, and the Arab revolutions. *Triple-C*, 10(2), 518–536.

Chorin, E. (2012). *Exit Gaddafi: The hidden history of the Libyan revolution*. Saqi Books.

Country Profiles: Iran. (2018). *Nuclear threat initiative*. https://www.nti.org/learn/countries/iran/nuclear/.

Clinton, H. (2014). *Hard choices*. Simon and Schuster.

Daalder, I., & Stavridis, J. (2012, March 31). NATO's victory in Libya. *Foreign Affairs*. https://www.foreignaffairs.com/articles/libya/2012-02-02/natos-victory-libya.

Davenport, K. (2018, December 14). Timeline of nuclear diplomacy with Iran. *Arms Control Association*. https://www.armscontrol.org/factsheet/Timeline-of-Nuclear-Diplomacy-With-Iran.

Egypt army "restoring democracy," says John Kerry. (2013, August 1). *The BBC*. https://www.bbc.com/news/world-middle-east-23543744.

Friedman, T. (2014, August 8). Obama on the world: President Obama talks about Iraq, Putin, and Israel. *The New York Times*. http://www.nytimes.com/2014/08/09/opinion/president-obama-thomas-l-friedman-iraq-and-world-affairs.html.

Gates, R. M. (2011, March 31). Statement on Libya by Robert Gates. House Armed Services Committee, March 2011. http://www.voltairenet.org/article169227.html.

Gates, R. M. (2014). *Duty, Memoirs of a secretary at war*. Alfred A. Knopf.

Gearan, A., & Warrick, J. (2013, November 23). World powers reach nuclear deal with Iran to freeze its nuclear program. *The Washington Post*. https://www.washingtonpost.com/world/national-security/kerry-in-geneva-raising-hopes-for-historic-nuclear-deal-with-iran/2013/11/23/53e7bfe6-5430-11e3-9fe0-fd2ca728e67c_story.html?utm_term=.a5d57bcc9f58.

Ghitis, F. (2015, April 2). Is Obama too desparate for an Iran deal? *CNN*. https://www.cnn.com/2015/04/02/opinions/ghitis-iran-obama-deal/index.html.

Gordon, M., & Sanger, D. (2015, July 14). Deal reached on Iran nuclear program; Limits on fuel would lessen with time. *The New York Times*. https://www.nytimes.com/2015/07/15/world/middleeast/iran-nuclear-deal-is-reached-after-long-negotiations.html.

Hamid, S. (2015, October 9). Islamism, the Arab Spring, and the failure of America's do-nothing policy in the Middle East. *The Atlantic*. https://www.theatlantic.com/author/shadi-hamid/.

Iran nuclear deal: Key details. (2018, May 8). *BBC News*. https://www.bbc.com/news/world-middle-east-33521655.

Klein, E. (2013). *The amateur: Barack Obama in the White House*. Regnery.

Lew, J. (2015, August 13). The high price of rejecting the Iran deal. *New York Times*. https://www.nytimes.com/2015/08/14/opinion/the-high-price-of-rejecting-the-iran-deal.html.

Lieberthal, K. (2011, December 21). The American pivot to Asia. *Foreign Policy*. https://foreignpolicy.com/2011/12/21/the-american-pivot-to-asia/.

Lindgren, S. (2013). The potential and limitations of Twitter activism: Mapping the 2011 Libyan uprising. *Triple C, 11*(1), 207–220.

Lizza, R. (2011, May 2). The consequentialist: How the Arab Spring remade Barack Obama's foreign policy. *The New Yorker*. https://www.newyorker.com/magazine/2011/05/02/the-consequentialist.

Lyons, K. (2015, July 14). Iran nuclear talks: A timeline. *The Guardian*. https://www.theguardian.com/world/2015/apr/02/iran-nuclear-talks-timeline.

MacAskill, E. (2008, July 18). US elections: Obama embarks on crucial international tour. *The Guardian*. https://www.theguardian.com/world/2008/jul/18/barackobama.uselections2008.

Neuman, J. (2009, January 21). Obama's Muslim outreach. *Los Angeles Times Blogs*. https://latimesblogs.latimes.com/washington/2009/01/obamas-muslim-m.html.

Obama on rebellion in Libya. (2013). *The History Channel*. http://www.history.com/topics/joe-biden/speeches/obama-on-rebellion-in-libya.

Panetta, L. (2014). *Worthy fights*. York: Penguin.

Perkovich, G, Hibbs, M., Acton, J., & Dalton, T. (2015, August 8). Parsing the Iran deal. *Carnegie Endowment for International Peace*. http://carnegieendowment.org/2015/08/06/parsing-iran-deal/iec5.

Prashad, V. (2012). *Arab spring, Libyan winter.* AK Press.

Syria crisis: Cameron loses Commons vote on Syria action. (2013, August 30). *BBC.* http://www.bbc.com/news/uk-politics-23892783.

The Obama administration rewards oppression in Bahrain. (2016, October 26). *The Washington Post.* https://www.washingtonpost.com/opinions/global-opinions/the-obama-administration-rewards-repression-in-bahrain/2016/10/26/b21c4e58-9ae9-11e6-9980-50913d68eacb_story.html?utm_term=.18430a113f87.

Timeline of U.S. Syrian crisis. (2013, August 31). *Reuters.* http://www.reuters.com/article/2013/08/31/us-syria-crisis-timeline-idUSBRE97U0D820130831.

Van Sant, S. (2019, July 10). President Trump warns of new sanctions on Iran after breaches of nuclear deal. *NPR.* https://www.npr.org/2019/07/10/740481969/president-trump-warns-of-new-sanctions-on-iran-after-breaches-of-nuclear-deal.

Wong, E. (2019, June 24). Trump imposes new sanctions on Iran, adding to tensions. *New York Times.* https://www.nytimes.com/2019/06/24/us/politics/iran-sanctions.html.

Zenko, M. (2017, March 27). Happy anniversary to America's shameful travesty of a war in Yemen. *Foreign Policy.* https://foreignpolicy.com/2017/03/27/happy-anniversary-to-americas-shameful-travesty-of-a-war-in-yemen/.

13

Obama's Leadership in Addressing Climate Change

WAYNE LAW, ALANNA LECHER, JONATHAN SMITH, AND APRIL WATSON

Introduction

President Barack Obama's first inaugural speech, delivered in January 2009, challenged the nation with the task of rebuilding the economy, an economy which at that point had fallen into the "Great Recession" of 2008. In the midst of doing so, he brought to light what many consider the hallmark of his two terms as the president of the United States: his stance on human-driven climate change. Obama did not directly criticize former president George W. Bush's "hostility to climate policy and . . . its misuse and abuse of climate science" (Dunlap & McCright, 2008, p. 7) but rather stressed the importance of science, as well as the need to use scientific discoveries to utilize alternative energy sources and, by extension, stimulate new job growth and increase innovation in alternative fuels (Phillips, 2009). Scholars in the months leading up to the 2008 elections recognized Obama's marked climate agenda. Dunlap and McCright (2008), for example, offered the League of Conservation Voters (LCV) scorecard as evidence of the then-candidate's stances on environmental issues. This score ranged from a low of 0 to a high of 100, with points being added for all pro-environmental votes. While Senator John McCain had an environmental agenda that promised more action than his Republican predecessors, his LCV score was a 26. Obama's was an 86 (7).

Climate Change and U.S. Politics

Overshadowing the 2008 election was the troubled history of climate science and the denial of climate science by an increasingly more vocal right wing. While historically both sides of the political aisle in the United States were in favor of protecting the environment, a chasm between the two parties emerged as the country entered the 1980s (Dunlap & McCright, 2010). Possibly fueling this divide was the growing concern over environmentalism, which came with and after other social movements such as feminism and civil rights. These movements were challenges to the dominant powers of the time and represented a conflict in the pursuit of "free market" enterprises (p. 243).

What was unique in the 1990s and early 2000s was the denial of science. How did much of the country come to reject evidence provided by scientists? While the 1970s and the early to mid-1980s witnessed increased taxes, trickledown economics, cutbacks, and limitations on spending, as had been the legacy of post–World War II America, the late 1980s saw the fall of the Berlin Wall and the end of the Soviet Union, perhaps signaling some the end of that austerity. Whereas market capitalism had typified the period before, a New Right might be said to characterize the 1980s and beyond (Antonio & Brulle, 2011). They heavily favored economic autonomy with unfettered consumer choice, and strident reductions in regulations and taxation. In particular, and led by Ronald Reagan, they opposed government action aimed at "social capitalism" or a capitalist system built on reducing inequality with moderate welfare provisions (Antonio & Brulle, 2011). As environmental policies typified "big-government style regulations" that restrict the free market, such policies were in conflict with Republican goals of deregulation. Indeed, conservatives now framed these regulations as no less than a "planetary menace" (p. 196) and cited recessions prompted by too much government interference as evidence of their role in market suppression.

Coupled with this was a direct challenge to environmental science, which was just growing as a field in the 1970s. Environmentalists of the time might have been leery of scientists initially (for having created, for example, nuclear weapons and radioactive contamination); however, it became clear that scientists would be the allies of environmentalists. Credibility was needed by environmentalists at the time after the publication of *The Population Bomb* by Paul Ehrlich in 1968. Widely read at the time, *The Population Bomb* inaccurately predicted global famine in the 1970s and 1980s caused by overpopulation. While the integration of science into the environmental movement created a solid platform on which politicians who wanted to address environmental issues could stand, the alarmist nature of the *The Population Bomb*, which caused undue panic in some readers, undermined future environmental policies as many learned to distrust environmentalist predictions from the publication. Continuing on with the integration of science into environmentalism, the newer field of environmental science explored the interaction between humans and their environment, and as such, scientists began to highlight concerns over air and water pollution, contamination as a byproduct of industrial processes, and global warming. This was important to environmentalists, but seen as a direct confrontation by industrialists and the Republican Party, as regulations meant to limit pollution would indirectly limit economic growth (McCright & Dunlap, 2010).

By the 1990s, the United States had entered the "Republican Revolution" (McCright & Dunlap, 2011, p. 158) with Republicans gaining control of Congress. Some congressional Republicans argued against the existence of human-induced climate change, ultimately polarizing American opinion on the topic. From the most extreme wing of the party came attacks on the science behind global warming, which was framed as "junk science" as well as "scientifically uncertain." While the U.S. economy took a dip in the early 1990s, by the end of the Clinton administration the country had once again entered a boom period. Clinton agreed to environmental regulations; however, George W. Bush dismantled many of those policies and refused to sign the Kyoto Protocol, which was intended to reduce greenhouse gas emissions. Throughout the 2000s, declines in the economy as well as deregulation of environmental protections took their toll, with many Americans dismissing climate change as a priority. The 2001 attacks on the United States during George W. Bush's first term as president prompted increased spending on defense including a "war on terror" that included military offensives in Afghanistan, where Osama bin Laden was reported as hiding, and later Iraq. The Bush administration also crafted the Bankruptcy Abuse Prevention and Consumer Protection Act, which made it more difficult for individuals to expunge debt. By 2008, the United States suffered a financial crisis that eventually became known as the Great Recession and which pushed unemployment above 9 percent, with housing prices falling 31 percent (Amadeo, 2018a). These issues pushed climate change concerns out of the minds of the American public. In surveys conducted between 2007–09 by the Pew Research Center, for instance, overall belief in climate science declined significantly, regardless of political affiliation. Of note is the low percentage of both Americans and Chinese who believed that climate change was a serious problem, as these two countries are among the top carbon emitters in the world (Antonio & Brulle, 2011). McCright and Dunlap (2011) found that the chasm between liberals/Democrats and conservatives/Republicans had widened in the early 2000s, possibly in response to both the economic crises and the debate over climate change responsibility. While liberals were more likely to accept climate change as a current threat, and that there was an anthropogenic origin to global warming, conservatives were likely to deny this was the case, despite increased evidence (pp. 178–180). It was this challenge, then, that incoming president Obama faced in 2008.

U.S. Energy Dependence on Nonrenewable Sources

Since the 1950s three nonrenewable energy sources—coal, natural gas, and petroleum—have accounted for nearly 90 percent of U.S. energy consumption (Energy Information Administration, 2018). Nuclear power, a fourth source of nonrenewable energy, was also used starting in the 1960s. As energy demands have continued to increase over the last seventy years, the use of renewable sources just reached 10 percent in 2016 (Energy Information Administration, 2018). Reliance on fossil fuels presents two major problems: (1) fossil fuels are a finite source; and (2) burning fossil fuels emits carbon dioxide and other air pollutants such as methane, nitrous oxide, and mercury, which pose serious health risks.

Fossil fuels are formed from the remains of dead animals and plants that have been buried by layers of rock and compressed inside the earth over millions of years. Different types of fossil fuels form based on what combination of organic matter was present, how long it was buried, and the pressure conditions as time passed. Fossil fuels are extracted from deep below the earth's surface using drills or mines. Once extracted, fossil fuels are then burned in power plants to produce electricity or refined to be used as fuel for heating or transportation. The combustion of fossil fuel has accounted for 77 percent of CO_2 emissions, and is the largest contributor of U.S. greenhouse gases (Environmental Protection Agency, 2018). In addition to the production of greenhouse gases and the consequences that it can bring, air pollutants, such as methane, nitrous oxide, and mercury, released during the burning of fossil fuels, are leading to increased health effects such as lung damage (Brunekreef & Holgate, 2002), low birth weight among children (Ritz & Yu, 1999), and asthma (Peterson & Saxon, 1996).

The Recovery Act

President Obama recognized the risks that reliance on fossil fuels presented to the environment, public health, and the economy. He saw the importance of investing in clean energy alternatives such as wind and solar power, as well as electric vehicles. In February 2009, shortly after taking office, Obama signed into law the American Recovery and Reinvestment Act of 2009 (ARRA), nicknamed the Recovery Act. The primary objective of the ARRA was to save existing jobs and create new ones. However, it was also the single largest investment in clean energy ever, as more than one-eighth of the total ARRA spending was for clean energy investments. More than $90 billion was directed to strategic clean energy investments and tax incentives that were meant to promote job creation and deployment of low carbon technologies, while approximately $150 billion was leveraged to be used in private and nonfederal investments for clean energy. Evidence of the impact of the ARRA was evaluated in 2016 and showed remarkable success. The Council of Economic Advisors (CEA) (2014) estimated that from 2009 to 2012, ARRA clean energy–related programs supported approximately 720,000 jobs (full-time jobs over one year). By 2015, clean energy–related programs were estimated to support roughly 900,000 job years (Executive Office of the President of the United States, 2016). Aside from increased employment, ARRA funding also helped to significantly boost the solar and wind generation industries. One way it did this was to provide significant funds to the Department of Energy's Loan Program, aimed at offering loans to ARRA projects, which commercial lenders are often unwilling or unable to take a risk on. This led to the creation of several solar photovoltaic generator facilities that are larger than 100MW and supported one of the world's largest onshore wind farms, which pioneered the use of a 3MW turbine for its electrical generation, leading to overall cost reductions (The White House, 2016a). By 2015, solar electricity generation had increased over thirty times compared to 2008 levels, while wind generation had increased by over three times (Executive Office of the President of the United States, 2016). ARRA investments also helped decrease the technology costs of renewable energy generation. By reducing the price of solar systems by 50 percent, renewable energy technology became more competitive against fossil fuel generation. The Executive Office of the President of the United States (2016) also reports the successes of the ARRA in terms of boosting infrastructure through improved residential energy efficiency in more than one million homes, increasing the capacity to train students in solar and other clean energy careers, increasing energy storage, and laying the groundwork for cleaner and more energy-efficient transportation systems.

Despite these successes, notable failures such as the Solyndra bankruptcy debacle crippled Obama's political momentum and diminished his credibility with Republicans. Solyndra was a solar photovoltaic start-up company emerging in the mid-2000s that had applied for a federal loan in 2006 (Flood, 2013). As part of the ARRA and the Department of Energy's Loan Programs, the review process was expedited and the company was provided $535 million in funding on March 20, 2009 (Flood, 2013). Just two years later, Solyndra was forced to lock its doors and file for bankruptcy, not only losing the $535 million investment from the federal government, but also putting more than one thousand employees out of work (Flood, 2013). This was viewed as a harbinger for future disasters by the Republicans. The incident fueled conservatives' distrust of social capitalism, and weakened Obama's ability to claim ARRA job creation and renewable energy industry development as an unfettered success. When the loan was restructured in March 2011, conservatives became increasingly skeptical and wary of government funding provided to renewable energy industries, and when news surfaced that the DOE had rushed the loan without consulting the Treasury, and that the timing of the loan announcement might have occurred early so that Joe Biden could proclaim a successful endeavor, the Republicans became apoplectic (Flood, 2013). In the hearings that followed the bankruptcy, Republicans painted a picture of a corrupt or inept government that could no longer be trusted to handle these investments wisely (Wald, 2011). What was not explained was that the reasons for Solyndra's collapse were multifaceted, mostly dealing with increased cost of production and cheap alternatives produced by China, and not necessarily because of any mismanagement of funds provided by the federal government (Flood, 2013; Noguchi, 2011). However, the lack of due diligence on the part of the DOE became apparent during the course of those hearings (Flood, 2013). In the following days, Senate Minority Leader Mitch McConnell indicated that there would be increased resistance to any jobs programs proposed by the president (Madison, 2011). Solyndra became a partisan talking point, and any efforts to continue government funding of the renewable energy industry fell on the increasingly deaf ears of a now GOP-controlled Congress.

Continued Efforts for Clean Energy

Throughout his administration, President Obama continued to move the U.S. economy toward American-made clean energy sources. In June 2013, he put forward a Climate Action Plan that targeted reductions in carbon pollution through the modernization of power plants and cleaner forms of American-made energy. Among the executive actions delineated in the Climate Action Plan were specific directions to the Department of the Interior to permit projects on renewable sources (wind and solar) on public lands that would provide power for more than six million homes, as well as deploy renewables on military instillations (Executive Office of the President, 2013).

In August 2015, President Obama demonstrated his commitment to clean power even further by announcing the Clean Power Plan. This plan set forth, for the first time ever, set limits on carbon pollution from U.S. power plants. The Clean Power Plan also established a Clean Energy Incentive Program. This program created incentives for projects that planned construction with electricity generated from renewables and prioritized early investment in energy efficiency projects within low-income communities. At the end of that month, President Obama announced even more executive actions and private sector commitments to promote the use of simple and low-cost technologies to help households save on energy bills. Programs included property-assessed clean energy financing for single-family homes, solar power housing to more than forty military bases across the United States, and the creation of an interagency task force to promote a clean energy future for all Americans (White House, 2015).

By 2016, Obama's plans were proving to be effective. Solar electricity generation had increased thirtyfold and solar jobs were growing twelve times faster than the rest of the economy. Cross-government partnerships were announced through the "Clean Energy Savings For All" initiative, which set a goal to increase access to solar energy and promote efficiency across the United States, particularly in low- and moderate-income communities (The White House, 2016b). Obama also understood the impact of the transportation sector on greenhouse gas emissions. He announced the 21st Century Clean Transportation Plan. This plan, funded by a new fee paid by oil companies, set out to increase investments in clean transportation infrastructure. In order to reduce traffic and provide other ways for families to get to work and school, the plan was set to expand transit systems in cities, suburbs, and rural areas, and reward state and local government for innovations that led to cleaner and more resilient transportation systems (White House, 2016c). Executive actions were also made to provide financing to improve the electric vehicle charging infrastructure for the nation, and partnered with the private sector to scale up electric vehicles (White House, 2016d).

Obama championed the idea that clean energy was the key to slowing climate change, protecting public health, and building a stronger economy. As the president (2017) stated in his Policy Forum in *Science*, "We have long known, on the basis of a massive scientific record, that the urgency of acting to mitigate climate change is real and cannot be ignored." He also demonstrated that a reduction in carbon emissions can be consistent with a thriving economy. In contrast to previous periods where carbon emissions reductions led to a decrease in economic growth, Obama's efforts culminated in the start of an era where cleaner energy use resulted in greater than 10 percent of economic growth, from 2008 to present day. In the *Cabinet Exit Memo*, U.S. Department of Energy Secretary Ernest Moniz (2017) revealed that in the eight years of the Obama administration, wind power had increased three times (from 25 gigawatts to 75 gigawatts) and solar by 2,500 percent (from 1.2 gigawatts to 31 gigawatts). The Obama administration set out on a mission to dramatically grow clean energy jobs and advance the major scientific and technological discoveries in the nation. It is a direct result of Obama's commitment to clean energy that America began transitioning to a clean-energy economy. Obama (2017) was even optimistic that, despite the energy policies of the Trump administration, the momentum of clean energy created during his administration is irreversible and it is the best way to address the challenges that face the planet, public health, and the economy.

Reduction of Federal Government Carbon Emissions

One method of assessing how an organization affects climate change is through analysis of its carbon footprint. The commonly accepted definition of a carbon footprint is "a measure of the exclusive total amount of carbon dioxide emissions that is directly and indirectly caused by an activity or is accumulated over the life stages of a product" (Wiedmann & Minx, 2008, pp. 1–11). Carbon dioxide emissions occur as a result of electricity usage, when fossil or biomass fuels are used to generate electricity and heat for an institution, and when members of that institution travel via some method powered by fossil fuel combustion (e.g., gasoline-based car or airplane). Products purchased by an institution are also included in the institution's carbon footprint, as the carbon emissions that accumulate over the life cycle of the product is included in the institution's carbon footprint. For example, when a wooden desk is built, fossil fuels are burned to run the equipment that logs the timber, transport the timber to the mill, generate electricity that runs the mill and the factory that manufactures a desk from a log, transports the desk to the institution, and disposes of the desk when the institution no longer requires its use. If the desk is disposed of in a landfill where it decomposes, producing carbon gases, or is burned in an incinerator, those carbon emissions are also included in the product's carbon footprint. All of the carbon emissions produced during the lifecycle of the product the institution purchased are included in the organization's carbon footprint as well. Therefore, the carbon footprint provides a comprehensive assessment of an institution's carbon emissions and informs how an organization contributes to climate change.

Obama sought throughout his presidency to reduce the carbon footprint of the federal government, specifically among the federal agencies that fell under the command of the executive branch. As explained in one executive order, "Federal leadership in energy, environmental water, fleet, buildings, and acquisition management will continue to drive national greenhouse gas reductions and support preparations for the impacts of climate change" (Obama, 2015a, p. 1). The executive orders that provided the framework through which the carbon footprint was reduced spanned a wide range of the daily functions of the federal government, and the orders became more refined and comprehensive over time. An early executive order on November 9, 2011, reduced the travel provisions of federal agency employees, required agencies to critically evaluate the need for an electronic device before purchasing it, reduced printing and the purchase of promotional items, and encouraged federal agencies to increase the fuel efficiencies of vehicles (Obama, 2011). All of these provisions resulted in an immediate reduction of the carbon footprint of the federal government.

As his administration progressed, the executive orders that addressed the carbon footprint of the federal government evolved as well. Changes to federal agency policies and practices became cohesive in how targets were set for the entire federal government as exampled in executive order 13693, *Planning for Federal Sustainability in the Next Decade*: "Through a combination of more efficient Federal operations such as those outlined in this Executive Order, we have the opportunity to reduce agency direct greenhouse gas emissions by at least 40 percent over the next decade while at the same time fostering innovation, reducing spending, and strengthening the communities in which our Federal facilities operate" (Obama, 2015a, p. 1). This later executive order not only included guidelines to reduce printing or consumption of goods, limit travel, and increase fuel efficiency; it also attempted to optimize office space and increase the efficiency of federal buildings by providing incremental goals for energy use reduction. Furthermore, included in the order were specific fuel efficiency targets for agency fleets that became more stringent over the course of years. Executive Order 13693 included new provisions as well, such as creating and implementing educational programs for employees of federal agencies to learn about their agency's carbon footprint and how changes in their behavior would positively or negatively contribute to the agency's carbon footprint. Additionally, the order created the position of the Federal Chief Sustainability Officer whose purpose was to provide oversight on these sustainability initiatives in concert with the Chairman of Environmental Quality and the Director of the Office of Environment and Management. These three positions would assist federal agencies in developing sustainability goals, devising plans of action to achieve those goals, and keeping the agencies accountable to those goals. Therefore, Executive Order 13693 provided a comprehensive plan for reducing the federal government's carbon footprint across a wide variety of avenues while also creating the support system needed by agencies to do so.

Executive Order 13693 not only influenced the magnitude of the federal government's carbon footprint; it impacted federal spending as well. Many of the sustainability measures implemented through the order also resulted in a reduction in federal spending, such as increasing the efficiency of buildings that reduced electrical costs or reductions in printing that required less paper and ink to be purchased. As these sustainability measures reduced federal spending, they appealed to a wide range of politicians, which gave the ideas persistence within the federal government. When the presidency transitioned from the Obama administration to the Trump administration many executive orders relating to environmental issues were revoked altogether. Although executive order 13693 was revoked, it was replaced by a similar executive order by President Donald Trump, Executive Order 13834 *Efficient Federal Operations*. This newer executive order maintained many of the general ideas of the order it replaced with respect to how agencies should "increas[e] efficiency, optimiz[e] performance, eliminat[e] unnecessary use of resources, and protec[t] the environment" (Obama, 2018, p. 1).

Additionally, Executive Order 13834 continued the roles of the Federal Chief Sustainability Officer, Chairman of Environmental Quality, and the Director of the Office of Environment and Management in increasing sustainability and reducing the federal government carbon footprint. The main difference between the executive orders released by presidents Obama and Trump was in that the latter executive order lacked the specificity of energy reduction goals, instead referring to statutory requirements. Thus, the movement toward practices that reduce the federal government's carbon footprint that was initiated by Obama's executive orders continued through the next administration.

Paris Agreement

In January 2015, Obama began his year with these words: "And that's why I will not let this Congress endanger the health of our children by turning back the clock on our efforts. I am determined to make sure that American leadership drives international action" (Obama, January 20, 2015). By the end of 2015, leaders from 196 countries, including the United States, signed the Paris Agreement. The path to the agreement, however, was not a smooth one, and the agreement was hailed as one of the most important of Obama's presidency (Chait, 2015). In order to understand the outcomes of the Paris Agreement, it is necessary to examine the political winds amid which the Obama administration operated. Historically, both sides of the congressional aisle embraced environmental protection, including such actions as Franklin Delano

Roosevelt's Soil Conservation Service, or Richard Nixon's signing of the National Environmental Policy Act in the 1970s. However, by the 1980s, Reagan's view of environmental regulations as a strain on the economy prompted the conservative pushback on environmental initiatives (Dunlap & McCright, 2008). An increasing divergence between the two major political parties made addressing climate change even more challenging throughout the 1980s and to the present.

However, successful climate actions were enacted during the 1980s. The Montreal Protocol was a global conference on the reduction of ozone-depleting materials such as chlorofluorocarbons. The Protocol was considered one of the most successful worldwide environmental initiatives. As a result of the conference, 197 countries pledged to reduce use of the ozone-harming substances (Environmental Protection Agency, 2018). The achievements of the Montreal Protocol inspired global environmentalists to push for more sweeping reforms, especially in the realm of global warming, which was an emerging environmental concern. One of the key features of the Montreal Protocol was its hard targets for change. Countries agreed to set deadlines for the phaseout of ozone-harming substances, with poorer countries allowed more time for this phaseout. This agreement worked well, so much so that the representatives of the member countries formed the Intergovernmental Panel on Climate Change (IPCC) in 1989 (United Nations Framework Convention on Climate Change 2018). From there, the IPCC scheduled regular conferences in preparation for crafting a legally binding document similar to Montreal Protocol, to set carbon emission targets for countries. In 1997, the parties held a final meeting in Kyoto, Japan.

The resultant Kyoto Protocol was widely regarded as a "fiasco" from the beginning (Plumer, 2015). Although President Bill Clinton agreed to the Kyoto Protocol in 1997, in 2001 President George W. Bush withdrew from the agreement. Other major countries that failed to meet their emission reduction goals withdrew as well, without penalty. In addition, developing countries actually increased carbon output during this time, which quickly outweighed cuts that were made by larger developed countries (Plumer, 2015). One of the hard learned lessons from the Kyoto Protocol was the need for action by developing countries in addition to larger countries. Mandating emissions targets was one of the failures of the Kyoto Protocol; by mandating emissions targets, countries felt less inclined to join the agreement.

Meanwhile, throughout his two terms, Obama tackled the issue of global warming in a manner unequaled by any previous president. Following Kyoto, it became apparent that large industrial countries such as China would need to fully participate in the agreement, with developed countries like the United States leading the way. However, up to the point of Obama's presidency, no U.S. president had a clear and concise climate agenda. Indeed, according to presidential scholar Douglas Brinkley, Obama "[came] to Paris with a moral authority that no other president has had on the issue of climate change" (Davenport, 2015).

Obama entered his second term as president with a strong mandate to set emission reduction targets, among other climate-related actions. In his January 2015 State of the Union address, Obama made it clear that he intended to tackle the thorny issue of climate change, with or without Congressional approval. He highlighted the scientific evidence of climate change, as well as the growing concern that climate change represented a threat to both national security and economic growth. Obama stated: "The Pentagon says that climate change poses immediate risks to our national security. We should act like it" (Obama, January 20, 2015).

These dual frames of climate change as influencers of national security and economic growth were important, as the Obama administration attempted to address the needs and concerns of the conservatives in Congress. Frames are "interpretative storylines that set a specific train of thought (Nisbet, 2009, p. 15)." As mentioned elsewhere in this chapter, climate change policies often conflicted with the priorities of economic growth on the Right; thus, it was incumbent on the Obama administration to reframe the issue of global warming in a way that was accessible to conservatives. Following the Kyoto Protocol, many conservatives attacked the prevailing research explaining climate change, with even more vocal charges against the validity of the science behind the warnings of human-driven global warming (Dunlap & McCright, 2008). One of the strongest rallying points on the political Right was the negative economic impacts the United States had taken (and might continue to take) in order to tackle climate-related issues. Obama often attempted to cast climate-related initiatives within the framework of economically positive action, as well as appeals to national security, in order to make his reforms on climate more closely aligned with the goals of conservatives. Indeed, environmentalists such as Nordhaus and Schellenger urged climate activists to utilize this so-called economic development frame in order to reconfigure economic constraints (environmental regulations) as opportunities for economic growth (renewable energy resources, for example) (Nisbet, 2009).

Leading up to the Paris meeting, the Obama administration faced considerable pushback in Congress when positing climate-related goals for enactment, to which they responded by pursuing executive actions aimed at reaching those goals by going around the opposing Congress. This began even in Obama's first term as president, with Executive Order 13514, which focused on increasing sustainability actions within the federal government, with an aim to both reduce energy demands and to "create a clean energy economy" (Obama, 2009, p. 1). In the second term of his presidency, Obama reinforced his position regarding the necessity of governmental actions for climate change mitigation by issuing Executive Order 13653 in November 2013. This executive order made plain the Obama administration's growing concern with the defense of natural resources as an issue of national security. Again, he tasked the federal government with pursuing and supporting investments that encouraged sustainability as well as providing incentives to the investments. In addition, he packaged those words with the urgency of protecting public health, particularly among the most vulnerable populations (Obama, 2013). By August 2015, Obama tackled emissions reductions head-on by imposing even stronger versions of EPA regulations instituted in 2013 and 2014. States were allowed autonomy over emissions reductions; however, each state had a target to meet. These emission reduction goals met with immediate resistance from Republicans and corporations alike, utilizing phrases such as "war on coal" or "cap-and-tax," referring to the cap-and-trade systems the 2013 EPA rules encouraged. In this type of plan, states capped energy usage and emissions and corporations had to "buy" credits in order to pollute (Davenport & Harris, 2015). Once again, the administration framed these rules with financial incentives to participate, such as advance credits in the cap-and-trade system, but without much success in inspiring agreement from conservatives (Davenport & Harris, 2015).

Enter the Paris Agreement. While past agreements, such as the Kyoto Protocol, had required signatories to sign a legally binding emissions reduction target (European Council, 2018), the Paris Climate Agreement aimed for middle of the road reductions, particularly from large countries such as the United States and China. These conservative emission reduction goals might have stemmed from the need to get larger countries to join the Agreement. Conferences held between 1997 (the time of the Kyoto Protocol) and 2015 guided world leaders in the construction of the new Climate Agreement. Because of the failings of Kyoto, the Paris Agreement was structured to allow individual countries to set their own emissions reduction targets. At the time of the Paris Agreement, governments settled on national climate action plans that were viewed as a starting point to limit climate change (European Commission, 2018). The targets of the agreement were aimed at limiting temperature increase to 1.5°C globally, with a long-term goal to hold the increase at less than 2°C for the current century.

In a statement following the Paris Agreement, Obama praised the participants of the accord while taking to task those who expressed doubt over economics:

> Now, skeptics said these actions would kill jobs. Instead, we've seen the longest streak of private-sector job creation in our history. We've driven our economic output to all-time highs while driving our carbon pollution down to its lowest level in nearly two decades. And then, with our historic joint announcement with China last year, we showed it was possible to bridge the old divides between developed and developing nations that had stymied global progress for so long. (Obama, 2015)

Here, Obama raised the rallying points he had utilized in his 2009 inauguration speech, that as a nation the United States would improve the economy while increasing environmentally friendly innovations, as well as imposing restrictions that would reduce carbon emissions.

A large part of the Obama administration's negotiations over the Paris Agreement were devoted specifically to including large carbon emitters such as China in the deal. Obama spent a great deal of time in talks with the Chinese president Xi Jinping during the Paris conference. This was in addition to a pact struck by Obama and Xi in 2014 to reduce carbon emissions (Taylor & Branigan, 2014). Obama also jumped through hoops to include other major polluting countries such as India, Brazil, and Mexico. The language of the Paris Agreement was specifically crafted to exclude legally binding emissions targets as well as financial burdens (Goldenburg, 2015). These points were aimed at sidestepping a Republican-controlled Congress, which had already expressed hard-line resistance to climate-related regulations.

In November 2015, Republican senators took Obama to task, expressing their concerns that his actions regarding climate restrictions on carbon-producing industries would significantly harm the U.S. economy, while strengthening foreign enterprises, a critique of the economic gains made by countries like India under the Kyoto Protocol (which of course the United States did not ratify). Even as the agreement was in the midst of negotiations in Paris, many Republicans sought to challenge any limitations that might emerge as a result of U.S. agreement to the climate deal. Senators Inhofe and Barrasso drafted a letter to Obama, endorsed by thirty-five other senators, outlining their resistance to any climate deals that would benefit developing nations at the expense of American enterprises (Davenport, 2015). Obama published a scholarly article opposing this idea, reflecting on growth in the economy as a byproduct of growth in the renewable energy sector. As a part of this work, Obama urged that, while subsequent administrations might not follow his plan, "it would undermine our economic interests to walk away" from the Paris Agreement (Obama, 2017, p. 129). While the Obama administration attempted to frame climate change issues as an economic concern, as well as offering renewable energy innovations as a driver of economic growth, the reality was that the changes proposed by the Paris Agreement meant huge spending on renewable energy and efficiency (Clémençon, 2016), and as a result (among other reasons) it was rejected by many conservatives.

While conservatives challenged Obama for potentially devastating the economy with his environmental restrictions, not to mention his perceived attacks on a "free market"–based economy, many others felt that Obama played more of a middle of the road approach. Particularly in light of the Paris Agreement, he sacrificed much in order to achieve the deal, including structuring the agreement in such as way that he did not have to ratify it through Congress. In the process, smaller island nations were dismayed that their nations' needs were ignored in favor of more generalized targets and pledges in the Paris Agreement (Goldenburg, 2015). Some scholars have also criticized the climate deal as not stringent enough in terms of emissions cuts, or a "tragedy of the commons"–type scenario in which many groups might capitalize on products like fossil fuels without paying a penalty (Nordaus, 2015). As Clémençon (2016) pointed out, targeting major carbon emitters such as coal plants or the agriculture industry might have been a far stronger stand than the pledges of the Paris Agreement.

One of the main concerns of scholars examining the agreement was the 2016 election. Immediately following the Paris climate talks, Republican candidates for president, including Donald Trump, promised to immediately abandon and/or dismantle Obama-led environmental regulations. Alternately, Democratic candidates campaigned on either continuing in Obama's efforts to reduce carbon emissions, or maintaining the status quo. Trump won the 2016 election. On June 1, 2017, he announced the United States would stop cooperating with the Paris Agreement.

Conclusion

Is his approach to climate change part of Obama's legacy? Certainly this was among his top achievements. Pundits speculated that "climate change will become the heart and soul of [Obama's] presidency" (Davenport, 2015), should his agenda withstand new legislation and policies that conflict with his environmental initiatives. Some Republicans criticized his administration as economically devastating in its performance, with more efforts directed at helping developing countries than at the United States. Yet, even while tackling environmental issues, Obama was also the biggest job creator in U.S. history, with job growth increasing and unemployment declining under his administration (Lewis, 2017). This was due in no small part to the Recovery Act and development of renewable energies through Department of Energy lending. If Obama wanted to frame his climate change actions as positive for economic gains, there was evidence (at least indirectly) to support him.

Obama also pushed for carbon reduction regulations in 2014 and enacted the Clean Power Plan in 2015, both aimed at addressing global warming, and his administration enacted stricter fuel efficiency standards that would reduce oil consumption by twelve billion barrels between 2012 and 2025 (Amadeo, 2018b). Additionally, through the use of several executive orders, Obama's administration formed plans to reduce the carbon footprint of the federal government and increase energy efficiency in all government operations. This made so much common sense even across political divides that Donald Trump continued these actions toward an efficient government despite his political disagreement with Obama on nearly every other issue.

If commitment to ideals and lingering influence reflect legacy, then Obama managed that goal. Even as Trump withdrew from the Paris Climate Agreement, Obama praised those nations that remained in the compact. Indeed, the Climate Action Tracker, an independent scientific analysis dedicated to tracking climate action, found that the United States actually continued to reduce its carbon output, rather than increase it, after Obama's term in office ended (Climate Action Tracker, 2018). While the Trump administration has denounced much about climate change, there has thus far been no governmental consensus on exactly *what* to do. Instead, it has been left to individual states and corporations to set those goals, which thus far have continued on the Obama-era trajectory, with renewable energy "the dominant driver of U.S. energy" (Mooney, 2018). State-level cuts to emissions have also been enacted, partially in response to Trump's pledge to pull out of the Paris Agreement (Mooney 2018). Perhaps the legacy of climate action will continue as projected under Obama; as of now it is difficult to say for certain. Or perhaps, the United States will be witness to, as Obama put it, "the irreversible momentum of clean energy" (2017). If one agrees with climate science, then direct action is required, and there is no room for delay. Environmentalists can hope that momentum is indeed irreversible.

References

Amadeo, K. (2018a, May 9). Bush administration economic policies: How George Bush affected the economy. *The Balance*. https://www.thebalance.com/bush-administration-economic-policies-3305556.

Amadeo, K. (2018b, August 13). What has Obama done? 13 Major Accomplishments. *The Balance*. https://www.thebalance.com/what-has-obama-done-11-major-accomplishments-3306158.

Antonio, R. J., & Brulle, R. J. (2011). The unbearable lightness of politics: Climate change denial and political polarization. *The Sociological Quarterly*, 52(2), 195–202.

Brunekreef, B., & Holgate, S. T. (2002). Air pollution and health. *The Lancet*, 360(9341), 1233–1242.

Chait, J. (2015, December). The Paris climate deal is President Obama's biggest accomplishment. *The New York Times*. http://nymag.com/daily/intelligencer/2015/12/climate-deal-is-obamas-biggest-accomplishment.html.

Clémençon, R. (2016). The two sides of the Paris Climate Agreement: Dismal failure or historic breakthrough? *Journal of Environment and Development, 25*(1), 3–24.

Climate Action Tracker. (2018). *Current policy projections.* https://climateactiontracker.org/countries/usa/current-policy-projections/.

Council of Economic Advisers (CEA). (2014). The economic impact of the American Recovery and Reinvestment Act five years later. https://obamawhitehouse.archives.gov/sites/default/files/docs/erp_2014_chapter_3.pdf.

Davenport, C. (2015, November 29). Obama's legacy at stake in Paris talks on climate accord. *The New York Times.* https://www.nytimes.com/2015/11/29/us/politics/obama-takes-second-term-resolve-on-climate-to-paris.html.

Davenport, C., & Harris, G. (2015, August 2). Obama to unveil tougher environmental plan with his legacy in mind. *The New York Times.* https://www.nytimes.com/2015/08/02/us/obama-to-unveil-tougher-climate-plan-with-his-legacy-in-mind.html.

Dunlap, R. E., & McCright, A. M. (2008). A widening gap: Republican and Democratic views on climate change. *Environment: Science and Policy for Sustainable Development, 50*(5), 26–35.

Dunlap, R. E., & McCright, A. M. (2010). 14 climate change denial sources, Actors and strategies. *Routledge Handbook of Climate Change and Society.* Routledge.

EIA. (2018, September 15). Monthly energy review. https://www.eia.gov/totalenergy/data/monthly.

Environmental Protection Agency. (2018). *International actions—The Montreal Protocol on substances that deplete the ozone layer.* https://www.epa.gov/ozone-layer-protection/international-actions-montreal-protocol-substances-deplete-ozone-layer.

Environmental Protection Agency. (2018). Inventory of U.S. greenhouse gas emissions and sinks 1990–2016. https://www.epa.gov/sites/production/files/20181/documents/2018_complete_report.pdf.

European Commission. (2018). Paris agreement. *International Action on Climate Change.* ec.europa.eu/clima/policies/international/negotiations/paris_en.

European Council. (2018). *International agreements on climate action.* http://www.consilium.europa.eu/en/policies/climate-change/international-agreements-climate-action/.

Executive Office of the President of the United States. (2013). The President's climate action plan. https://obamawhitehouse.archives.gov/sites/default/files/image/president27sclimateactionplan.pdf.

Executive Office of the President of the United States. (2016). A retrospective assessment of clean energy investments in the Recovery Act. https://obamawhitehouse.archives.gov/sites/default/files/page/files/20160225_cea_final_clean_energy_report.pdf.

Flood, E. (2013, Winter). Solyndra: Rhetoric and reality in a partisan age. *DttP: Documents to the People, 41*(4), 41–46. https://heinonline.org/HOL/P?h=hein.journals/dttp41&i=147.

Goldenberg, S. (2015). How US negotiators ensured landmark Paris Climate Agreement was Republican-proof. *The Guardian.*

Lewis, N. (2017, December 14). Comparing the "Trump economy' to the "Obama economy." *The Washington Post.* https://www.washingtonpost.com/news/fact-checker/wp/2017/12/14/comparing-the-trump-economy-to-the-obama-economy/?utm_term=.0d3fd6035009.

Madison, L. (2011, September 16). Republicans point to Solyndra as evidence against Obama's jobs plan. *CBS News.* https://www.cbsnews.com/news/republicans-point-to-solyndra-as-evidence-against-obamas-jobs-plan/.

McCright, A. M., & Dunlap, R. E. (2011). The politicization of climate change and polarization in the American public's views of global warming, 2001–2010. *The Sociological Quarterly, 52*(2), 155–194.

Mooney, C. (2018, June 1). Trump withdrew from the Paris climate deal a year ago. Here's what has changed. *The Washington Post.* https://www.washingtonpost.com/news/energy-environment/wp/2018/06/01/trump-withdrew-from-the-paris-climate-plan-a-year-ago-heres-what-has-changed/?utm_term=.0b1c54e41ed3.

Nisbet, M. C. (2009). Communicating climate change: Why frames matter for public engagement. *Environment: Science and Policy for Sustainable Development, 51*(2), 12–23.

Noguchi, Y. (2011, September 14). Political divide at congressional hearing on Solyndra. NPR: All Things Considered. https://www.npr.org/2011/09/14/140474848/political-divide-at-congressional-hearing-on-solyndra.

Nordhaus, W. D. (2015). A new solution: The climate club. *The New York Review of Books, 62*(10), 36–39.

Obama, B. (2018, May 17). Executive Order 13834. White House.

Obama, B. (2017). The irreversible momentum of clean energy. *Science, 355*(6321), 126–129.

Obama, B. (2015a, March 19). Executive Order 13693. White House.

Obama, B. (2015b, January 20). *Remarks by the president in State of the Union Address.* https://www. whitehousegov/the-press-office/2015/01/20/remarks-president-stateunion-address-january-20-2015.

Obama, B. (2013). Preparing the United States for the impacts of climate change. Executive Order 13653. White House.

Obama, B. (2011, November 9). Executive Order 13589. White House.

Obama, B. (2009, October 5). Federal leadership in environmental, energy, and economic performance. Executive Order 13514. White House.

Patterson, B., & Saxon, A. (1996). Global increases in allergic respiratory disease: The possible role of diesel exhaust particles. *Annals of Allergy, Asthma & Immunology, 77*(4), 263–270.

Phillips, M. (2009). President Barack Obama's inaugural address. *The White House*.
Plumer, B. (2015, December 14). Past climate treaties failed. So the Paris deal will try something radically different. https://www.vox.com/2015/12/14/10105422/paris-climate-deal-history.
Ritz, B., & Yu, F. (1999). The effect of ambient carbon monoxide on low birth weight among children born in Southern California between 1989 and 1993. *Environmental Health Perspectives, 107*(1), 17–25.
Taylor, L., & Branigan, T. (2014). U.S. and China strike deal on carbon cuts in push for global climate change pact. *The Guardian*, 12.
United Nations. (2018). *Framework convention on climate change*. http://unfccc.int/timeline/.
Wald, M. L. (2011, November 17). Panel hears defense of loan to Solyndra. *The New York Times*. https://www.nytimes.com/2011/11/18/business/energy-environment/energy-secretary-defends-solyndra-loan.html.
White House. (2015, August 24). FACT SHEET: President Obama announces new actions to bring renewable energy and energy efficiency to households across the country. https://obamawhitehouse.archives.gov/the-press-office/2015/08/24/fact-sheet-president-obama-announces-new-actions-bring-renewable-energy.
White House. (2016a, February 25). FACT SHEET: The Recovery Act made the largest single investment in clean energy in history, driving the deployment of clean energy, promoting energy efficiency, and supporting manufacturing. https://obamawhitehouse.archives.gov/the-press-office/2016/02/25/fact-sheet-recovery-act-made-largest-single-investment-clean-energy.
White House. (2016b, July 19). FACT SHEET: Obama administration announces clean energy savings for all Americans initiative. https://obamawhitehouse.archives.gov/the-press-office/2016/07/19/fact-sheet-obama-administration-announces-clean-energy-savings-all.
White House. (2016c, February 4). FACT SHEET: President Obama's 21st century clean transportation system. https://obamawhitehouse.archives.gov/the-press-office/2016/02/04/fact-sheet-president-obamas-21st-century-clean-transportation-system.
White House. (2016d, July 21). FACT SHEET: Obama administration announces federal and private sector actions to accelerate electric vehicle adoption in the United States. https://obamawhitehouse.archives.gov/the-press-office/2016/07/21/fact-sheet-obama-administration-announces-federal-and-private-sector.
Wiedman, T., & Minx, J. (2008). A definition of "carbon footprint." In C. C. Pertsova (Ed.), *Ecological economics research trends* (pp. 1–11). Nova Science Publishers.

14

China, Russia, and U.S. Primacy in World Affairs

WILLIAM KEETON

Introduction

The election of Barrack Obama as the first African American president of the United States ensures that his presidency will be historic. However, Obama's foreign policy legacy will remain a matter of intellectual debate for decades to come. Many of the president's critics fail to acknowledge his successes, while his proponents often overemphasize them. His extensive use of executive orders and executive agreements opened his legacy to undoing by future presidents. Furthermore, the president demonstrated a clear preference for domestic policy concerns during his tenure.

As with most presidents, Obama's foreign policy was shaped by both immediate and long-term concerns. The war on terror dominated U.S. security policy throughout Obama's presidency. The death of al-Qaeda leader Osama bin Laden in 2011 demonstrated decisive leadership in the face of less than perfect information and without the approval of the Pakistani government (Dueck, 2011). However, the rise of the Islamic State was met with little initial focus or understanding. Ultimately, the war on terror cost the United States more than $100 billion per year and permeated almost every other foreign policy issue during Obama's presidency (Belasco, 2009).

While the war on terror was a constant and immediate threat, the resurgence of Russia and the rise of China presented vastly different challenges for Obama and his foreign and security team. A key theme of Obama's legacy is that he made every effort to reconnect and build new positive relations with Russia and China by attempting to accommodate differences in an effort to find "shared purposes for peaceful outcomes" and "remake America" (Dueck, 2011). This reflected the president's approach to U.S. foreign policy, which downplayed notions of American exceptionalism in favor of a much more critical interpretation of the country's role in the post–World War II era. This view was based in what Carl Pedersen (2009, pp. 31–33) described as Obama's "rooted cosmopolitanism" that emphasized his "dual identity as an American citizen and a citizen of the world." His foreign policy was described by supporters as pragmatic realism which emphasized equality among regimes. Detractors asserted that Obama "seemed to believe America owed bows, apologies, and confessions to its many victims across the world and therefore had no right to put itself forward as a standard-bearer for human rights" (Feith & Cropsey, 2012).

Four key themes emerge as part of the administration's overall failure in foreign policy and were also captured by what other researchers would suggest: "the absence of a well-grounded geopolitical understanding for grand strategy; a naïve engagement approach; pervasive politicization; and overcommitting while underdelivering" (Singh, 2016, p. 19). This chapter will first provide an overview of foreign policy construction and then focus on Obama's Russian policy, primarily the "reset" initiatives. The chapter will then review the president's China policy in the context of that nation's economic and military growth, while addressing the significant issues arising in the South China Sea and Obama's attempts to pivot or rebalance the United States toward Asia.

Foreign Policy in Perspective

Foreign policy is overwhelmingly interconnected with other policy areas, ranging from economic policy to security concerns and geographic areas of focus. National interests typically overlap from one issue area to the next and from region to region. However, foreign policy is all too often viewed and assessed through a singular lens such as the framework of U.S.-Russian policy or U.S.-Chinese policy, as if these areas could be effectively isolated from each other. Instead, foreign policy must be viewed through the complex web of interests that permeate the broader goals of the United States. Furthermore, foreign policy success or failure is best judged over the long run. There are some significant points of complexity and depth in each of the Obama administration's Russia and China policies that resulted in limited success in the near term, but will likely play out in more positive outcomes in the decades to follow (Stent, 2012). It can also be argued that the major limitation of any president's foreign policy is how astonishingly short-sighted that policy tends to be relative to other nations because of the U.S. electoral system, which potentially results in a new Congress every two years, complete with new constraints and relationships. In addition, president's policies run the risk of being altered or even rescinded by the next administration.

Foreign policy is best defined as the strategies and actions taken to guide and influence government relations with the rest of the world (Lantis, 2012). Having a grand strategy aids in setting national goals and priorities, as well as deciding how these goals will be achieved and by which means, including diplomacy, economic influence, or the use of military force. An overarching question is: Who really develops U.S. foreign policy? The fact is that many institutions aid the president in crafting and implementing foreign policy. Three key institutions are the State Department, the Department of Defense and the Central Intelligence Agency (CIA) (Chirot, 2008). Regrettably, there was a trend of dysfunctionality among these institutions, particularly at the State Department, during the Obama administration. At a time when these institutions needed to be at their best, they came up woefully short in guiding President Obama. Writing in *Foreign Policy*, Joseph Cassidy claimed in 2015 that "[t]he State Department seems to lurch from disaster to distraction, responding to many crises, but preventing few. Its influence in Washington, and American diplomatic influence globally, is waning" (Cassidy, 2015). Cassidy goes on to argue that the department was handicapped by micromanagement, bureaucratic infighting, and a rigid hierarchy, comments echoed by others (see Carafano & Gonzalez, 2017; De Young, 2015). U.S. diplomacy was further harmed by infighting between the State Department and the White House over policy priorities, with the Obama administration often seeking solutions that had domestic appeal but were not in the foreign policy interests of the United States. For instance, the shift to emphasize drone strikes to counter terrorism deemphasized diplomatic efforts to persuade Pakistan to suppress the Taliban (Nasr, 2013).

The interests of the United States and its values shape the nation's foreign policy. Developing an effective foreign policy includes sufficient analysis of another nation's national security and economic interests. Washington must also communicate and evaluate international reactions to U.S. policies (Rothschild & Shafranek, 2017). For instance, following the multilateralism of the 1990s and early 2000s, there has been a growing shift as nations once again embrace nationalism, heightened sovereignty, and increased protectionism of key economic interests. U.S. policy must therefore balance its post–World War II emphasis on multilateralism with the rise of populism and the concurrent rejection of globalism by some states. Foreign policy also involves differing interpretations of the state's values and national security interests (Mouritzen, 2012). These values and security interests should promote U.S. priorities and goals, often through securing the necessary economic resources to preserve the impression of national strength and power (Smith, 2010).

Some argue that diplomacy is the centerpiece of any nation's foreign policy. This is not necessarily the case. Diplomacy is based on the hard power of the nation to bring about change and create influence (Nau, 2010). These hard power strengths are predominately economic power and military might (Vuving, 2012). The threat of force backed by military strength is an undeniable asset in the pursuit of national interests (Swistek, 2012). Diplomacy has little impact without the ability to force other actors to change policy. Influence and power are consequently inseparable (Swistek, 2012). Therefore, when two key states having near equal strength in terms of hard power are vying for influence, the stakes are higher and the challenges more complex. Diplomacy accomplishes its goals through careful analysis and consideration of the strength of other actors, combined with the willingness to use hard power to achieve goals and interests (Mouritzen, 2012). It is not surprising that foreign policy is extremely complex, endlessly changing, and divisive when two nations hold divergent positions but share similar strengths.

U.S. foreign policy is also reflective of the goals and beliefs of the president and the nation's foreign affairs and security leaders. Once in office, Obama demonstrated a deep belief that conflict was the result of a failure to cooperate and seek common solutions (Singh, 2016). The new president argued that effective policy and conflict avoidance required both sides to embrace compromise and accommodation. Set against these preconditions, Obama, ever the pragmatist, wanted to keep his campaign promises to end wars in Iraq and Afghanistan, promote peace throughout the world, and rebuild positive relations with Russia and China through a lens of "shared purpose and cooperation" (Dueck, 2011). To achieve this, the president sought to set an example for other nations to emulate, while reevaluating and reordering U.S. interests.

Russia

When Obama entered office, there were three key, interconnected parameters that defined U.S.-Russian relations. In some instances, the administration was slow to realize or accept these crucial restrictions on policy, while in other cases, events exacerbated these constraints. First, to be clear, the Cold War is not over, or, at the minimum, U.S.-Russian relations are in a "new Cold War" (Charap & Shapiro, 2016; Cohen, 2006; Hove, 2016). One argument is that the old Cold War continues because the conditions for victory were not completely achieved. There are four fundamental considerations that must be achieved before victory can be declared, and only two of the four have been satisfied. These parameters include the dismantling of the enemy state, in this case the Soviet Union (complete), the collapse of the adversary's economy (complete), regime change (not complete), and lastly the defeat of the opponent's military (not complete, especially in light of the continuing nuclear capability of the successor state) (Hove, 2016). What keeps the Cold War alive and will continue to do so is the fact that Russia and the United States maintain large stockpiles of nuclear weapons, have an adversarial relationship and a mutual distrust (Zysk, 2017). To this extent, the Cold War was less a specific conflict and more a descriptor for a long-standing adversarial relationship between two global rivals, in much the same way as France and Germany competed for hegemony in Europe through multiple wars and conflicts. The new Cold War has merely continued the international competition for power and influence between Washington and Moscow and will continue to dominate future relations (Hove, 2016).

Second, government pronouncements and grand statements do not necessarily translate into policy. Asserting a desire to "reset" relations with Russia did not create the desired outcome no matter how sincerely or passionately the president may have embraced the goal. This was especially true when the other party was not committed to this idea or new relationship (Lonsdale, 2013). Through both of Obama's terms, efforts to repair U.S.-Russian relations were met by platitudes from Russian officials, but these responses did not signal policy change. Instead,

Moscow pursued aggressive and destabilizing policies. The duplicity of Moscow's policy was often geared toward domestic audiences where Russian president Vladimir Putin was able to show his "contempt for the protocols and protagonists of Western order" through "a sly dance of mockery" (Kaylan, 2014).

Third, and related to the other two points, never underestimate Putin or believe you have an agreement or commonality of interests with him (Kuchins & Zevelev, 2012). Putin's domestic and foreign policy are deeply intertwined and based on the continuation of rivalry with the West and opposition to U.S. interests and initiatives (Boyle, 2017; Cohen, 2006; Hove, 2016). Putin is also comfortable with his duplicity on the world state. The Russian president is "not hiding his insincerity; he wants his deceit to be part of the visible theater. . . . [I]t's not enough that he's scoffing at them [Western leaders], he's tipping a wink that he wants it to be known" (Kaylan, 2014). By ignoring diplomatic norms and conventions, Putin believes he is demonstrating his strength and reinforcing the weakness, or at least perception of weakness, of his Western counterparts, including Obama.

All three of the above points were a reality check for President Obama. They help explain the president's inability to reset relations with Russia and highlight the missed opportunities that consistently arose during his tenure. When President Obama first met Russian president Dmitry Medvedev, in 2009, there was a general sense that relations might improve and that the Cold War could finally be put behind U.S. and Russian relations (Hove, 2016). However, Medvedev was not the real leader in Russia (McFaul, 2018). He only served as the face of government for Putin during the latter's tenure as prime minister (because of term limits, Putin stepped down as president in 2008 and served as prime minister until 2012, before being elected again as president). With the United States deeply entrenched in two regional conflicts (Iraq and Afghanistan) and a global financial crisis plaguing the U.S. economy, Putin wisely knew Obama had little room to maneuver on many issues. In the short term, this allowed Putin to pursue without penalty regional and geopolitical goals that the United States opposed but had little will to influence or stop(Kuchins & Zevelev, 2012). Moreover, for Putin, it created an opportunity to further secure his power base. The Obama administration naively accepted Russian aggression with the hope that by minimizing any criticism or reaction they would not upset the delicate nature of the "reset" initiative (Boyle, 2017). Ultimately, this made

Obama appear weak and uninformed, as the "reset" policy was sorely miscalculated, misunderstood, and underestimated.

Vladimir Putin

The unlikely goal of a reset in U.S.-Russian relations reflected the administration's misunderstanding of Putin. Vladimir Putin was a product of the Soviet secret service, the Komitet gosudarstvennoy bezopasnosti (KGB), and a fierce nationalist (Zygar, 2016), and epitomized the disruptive actor in geopolitics. Trained in deception at the height of the Soviet Union, Putin embraced chaos as a strategy to disrupt and weaken opponents (Kovalev, 2017). The collapse of the Soviet Union had a deep psychological impact on the future leader. Putin's values and ideology were too deeply ingrained in the past of the former Soviet Union to change. Though beyond the scope of this chapter, a deeper understanding of the culture and purpose of KGB would enlighten any reader on the lengths to which the average KGB officer would go to protect the state (see Kovalev, 2017). From an insider's perspective, Kovalev (2017, p. 205) made the following observation:

> A KGB officer is accustomed to playing to his interlocutor and lying in order to ingratiate himself and not fail in his current mission. What sort of an agent would he be otherwise? If he makes a mistake, he immediately wriggles out of it; moreover, others always prepare the ground in advance to implement his plan. But if the plan fails, then he makes every effort to deny his own role in the unsuccessful provocation. This is hardly the mark of diplomacy.

Putin in the classical Machiavellian sense is a man set on obtaining and retaining power (McFaul, 2018). Putin has always maintained a genuine dislike of the West (United States) and democracy (Kovalev, 2017). He consistently opposed U.S. interests. Putin made his views perfectly clear on the collapse of the Soviet Union when he stated unequivocally that the collapse of the Soviet Union was "the biggest geopolitical catastrophe [or disaster] of the century" (No sign of breakthrough at Russia-Ukraine gas talks, 2013). One lingering impact of the collapse of the USSR was that as many as twenty-five million ethnic Russians found themselves outside Russian territory. A consistent goal of Putin has been to regain control of areas with large numbers of ethnic Russians, a foreign policy priority that has resonated with ordinary Russians. Those actions were clear in Georgia, Chechnya, and Ukraine (Crimea and Donbass). Obviously, Putin's rhetoric about supporting democracy, maintaining human rights, and capitalism was designated to pacify Western nations, including the United States, and mislead naive media (Zygar, 2016). Meanwhile, Putin centralized power and created an increasingly authoritarian system in Russia, while sowing chaos in the global order.

Putin's rhetoric at the 2007 Munich security conference should have been a signal for U.S. officials. The Russian leader skillfully portrayed the United States as having double standards and being hypocritical in world affairs, a point easily picked up by Obama in the 2008 presidential campaign. Putin highlighted the dangers of a world with one hegemon (Kuchins & Zevelev, 2012). He cleverly cited Franklin Roosevelt's quote that "the peace of countries everywhere is in danger. Saying these words remains topical today" (Zygar, 2016). Putin's message should have been clear, that Russia, as was the case with the Soviet Union, was going to check (counterbalance) the unipolar supremacy of the United States. Russia clearly viewed this unipolar supremacy as a threat to all nations' sovereignty and their interests (Kuchins & Zevelev, 2012). Putin, additionally, tried to redirect any judgment of the legality of military action (or use of force) back to the approval of the UN, where Russia continued to yield a veto.

Putin the spy (KGB agent) understood the value of intelligence gathering and knew how to use this information (Kovalev, 2017). In Putin's world, control and order were the hallmarks of successful governance. Putin clearly blamed the United States for creating unrest in Russia and supporting demonstrations aimed at undermining the Russian state and, more specifically, undermining Putin, a fact that he would not soon forget and for the restitution of which would eventually get his payback on the United States with the eviction of NGOs and limitations on oil companies in their business dealings (McFaul, 2018). He particularly blamed the Obama administration and Secretary of State Hillary Clinton for supporting the toppling of the Ukrainian President Viktor Yanukovych in 2014 (McFaul, 2018). By this point, reset was certainly dead, at least in the mind of Putin.

Putin has played the Russian nationalist card well. He recaptured the former Soviet Union's national pride. Not unlike other dictators, Putin blamed others, in this case the West and mainly the United States, for

Russia's economic pain and humiliation during the collapse of the Soviet Union. Putin has regained lost territory and influence in the Southern Caucasus (Georgia, Armenia, and Azerbaijan), pushed back on NATO expansion, and embraced allies who were diametrically opposed to the United States, primarily Iran, North Korea, and Syria (Zygar, 2016). This was particularly true of Syria, where Russia has continued to support President Bashar al-Assad in the Syria civil war.

The case of Syria illustrates the complications Obama faced in U.S.-Russia relations, and the overlap of foreign policy from region to region. To be clear on Syria, all the options that were available to Obama administration were bad. The country's civil war threatened to further destabilize the region and create an opening for the Islamic State. Concurrently, U.S. support for the 2011 Arab Spring placed the country diametrically opposed to the existing regime in Syria. Yet the president also created additional problems, when he, for instance, declared on August 20, 2012, that any Syrian use of chemical weapons would be a "red line" that would prompt a U.S. military response. When the Assad regime used chemical weapons against rebels on August 21, 2013, Obama chose not to retaliate, prompting criticism over the president's weakness in foreign affairs. Moreover, Obama's position toward Putin only began to alter and become more decisive and firm after the downing of Malaysia Airlines flight 17 in 2014 by Ukrainian separatists using Russian military hardware. At this point, the reality of whom Obama was dealing with in Putin must have left the U.S. president feeling that he was being outmaneuvered on many geopolitical fronts.

Why did Obama miscalculate his ability to reset relations with Russia? Putin was not an unknown figure to State Department officials, including Secretary of State Hillary Clinton and the nation's foreign policy elites. Obama's predecessor George W. Bush had misjudged his relationship with Putin, especially in light of Putin's increasingly authoritarian rule during Bush's second term, along with Russia's invasion of Georgia in 2008. Did the State Department misadvise Obama or did the president and his circle of advisors choose to ignore the information in the hopes of a better relationship?

Reset and Russian Relations

It may have been an omen when Clinton went to Moscow to meet Russian foreign minister Sergey Lavrov bearing a red button that was meant to be labeled "reset" but because of a botched translation read "overload" (Zygar, 2016). Moreover, the State Department failed to even account for the possibility of a clash of cultural perspective by checking to find out whether "reset" held any significance for Russian leaders. Deputy Foreign Minister Sergei Ryabkov pointed out that "reset' was an American phrase and held little meaning in the Russian language (Stent, 2012). Nonetheless, there was considerable public support for a rapprochement. In 2010, many polls in the United States suggested that 50 percent of Americans held a favorable view of Russian relations, while some 60 percent of Russians viewed the United States in the same manner (McFaul, 2018). A revised Russia policy was especially appealing to the Obama administration since it viewed Bush's Russia policy as having been a strange mix of aggression and waffling, equally distracted by the war on terror overseas and the possibility of a domestic terrorist attack (Stent, 2012).

Obama and his foreign policy team believed the United States had to adopt either of two options. One, the United States could continue to invest in two costly wars with no clear definition of victory and ramp up an aggressive approach toward countries such as Russia or Iran; or, two, the country could try to end the wars and promote a new era of cooperative relations with adversaries (Stent, 2012). For endeavoring to embrace the second approach, Obama received the Nobel Peace Prize in 2009.

Obama's new approach in foreign policy reflected his constructivist view of geopolitical threats. The president believed that threats are not necessarily caused by real differences, but are instead constructed from insecurities which are amplified by perceptions of insecurity and manifested in who we think is our enemy or foe (Nau, 2010). Obama also sought to recast the unilateral, militaristic policies of the Bush administration. Nau (2010) points out that "George W. Bush became the poster child for unilateralism and assertive American leadership. Obama is now the rock star for a new era of multilateralism." (p. 45). Obama's approach to foreign policy was held in high regard in Europe. Polls in Europe showed 85 percent approval ratings for Obama, as compared to less than 20 percent for Bush (Nau, 2010). Tough and aggressive rhetoric by any U.S. president is a cause for worry in Europe (Kuchins & Zevelev, 2012). Obama's emphasis on cooperation and collaboration was especially well received at the beginning of his tenure among most of the major allies of the United States.

However, the reality remained that Russia continued to view the United States with the deepest suspicions. This was especially true in regard to NATO expansion in what was perceived to be Russia's backyard (Kuchins & Zevelev, 2012). NATO expansion was and will be continue to be a major sticking point for U.S-Russia relations as Moscow has continued to view the alliance as a primarily anti-Russian coalition (Cornell, 2016).

Putin faces a bigger problem than NATO expansion. The annexation of Crimea in 2014 essentially pushed Ukraine permanently away from Moscow's orbit and sent shock waves into the other former states of the Soviet Union. The annexation achieved its main goal, a domestic win for Putin that solidified the image of the president as the defender of Russians everywhere. For the United States, the maintenance of Ukrainian democracy remains a major foreign policy interest, as a symbol of Western political, economic, and social influence (McFaul, 2018). If democracy prevails in Ukraine, it will serve as the foundation for other states in their efforts to transition away from authoritarianism (McFaul, 2018). Any policy for Russia must take into account how Ukraine will factor into this equation in the future (Cornell, 2016). Nevertheless, Obama's policy was inconsistent and perceived to be as waffling as that of his predecessor toward Georgia, albeit on a much grander scale.

President Obama truly believed that if he extended the hand of friendship and understanding, a new relationship with Russia was possible. He believed that modern Russia was no longer the same threat as the Soviet Union had been during the Cold War and that the superpower struggle was, in fact, over (Boyle, 2017). Obama was committed to the idea that the United States needed to put the Cold War behind it and make every effort to promote peace and reconciliation with Russia (Lonsdale, 2013). However, the Putin regime continued to view the end of the formal Cold War as a defeat that had to be overcome (Kuchins & Zevelev, 2012). Russia's reality was to have been one of two superpowers one day and significantly marginalized the next. The collapse was quick and decisive. Russian leaders who were in power were left scrambling to save what resources they could and rebuild the nation's military. While Obama saw his election as the perfect opportunity to reset relations, Russian policy continued to emphasize the reestablishment of the nation as a superpower, and the reclamation of its sphere of influence.

In 2011, Russia's relations with the United States declined precipitously over the Western military campaign in Libya and the possibility that Washington might seek to again use force in the emerging crisis in Syria (Cornell, 2016). Russia desperately attempted to paint the Syrian crisis as being different from that of Libya in that the rebels and the Free Syrian Army were Islamic extremists and terrorists affiliated with the Islamic State (Allison, 2013). Russia was not completely wrong in this regard. The initial U.S. assessment was that Assad was within months of being swept from power. But, as time progressed and Assad held onto to power, the creation of the Syrian National Council (SNC) was perceived as a means to create dialogue and possibly find a way to allow Assad to leave without a further escalation of the war. Russia dismissed the SNC, labeling it a group of expatriate pro-Western intellectuals and former politicians that was completely under the control of the West (Allison, 2013). Russia's influence was dwindling in the region and the loss of Syria would have eliminated Moscow's last major ally (Cornell, 2016). Therefore, Russian policy was based on the maintenance of the Assad regime (Cornell, 2016).

Obama's efforts to craft a more cooperative policy with Russia were hard for many political elites in the United States to accept. This was evident in President Obama's address to the UN General Assembly where he suggested that previous administration policies were seen "as a time when many around the world had come to view America with skepticism and distrust" (Nau, 2010, p. 46), not the least of whom was Russia. President Obama's critics argued that his soft-hearted pacifist and apologetic approach was a foreign policy mistake with Russia (Rubin, 2014). They pointed out that the continuous negotiations on the New Strategic Arms Reduction Talks (New START) favored Russia more than the United States, and U.S. concessions should have been seen as a goodwill gesture by Moscow (Blank, 2010). However, the United States needed Russian cooperation to prevent Iran and North Korea from expanding or developing nuclear weapons capabilities. This was particularly true for Iran, where Russia could clearly make it more difficult for Obama (Blank, 2010). A nuclear-capable Iran was a risk too high for Obama to take (Dueck, 2011). Obama was willing to pay a high price to stop Iranian's nuclear development, and made the reduction of nuclear weapons his highest priority for the Russian "reset" policy (Lonsdale, 2013; Woolf, 2013). U.S.-Russian relations had at its core the issue of missile defense and nuclear proliferation, and Obama wanted to leave a legacy of reducing those risks with his New START initiative (Deyermond, 2013; Lonsdale, 2013).

Reset and New START

The New START treaty that was signed in April 2010 replaced the 1991 version of the accord. In 1967, the United States maintained a shocking 31,255 warheads (Kroenig, 2013). The New START treaty reduced that stockpile for both countries to 1,550 strategic warheads. However, Russia was able to maintain approximately 1,850–2,000 nonstrategic (tactical) nuclear weapons, ten times as many as the United States, although any estimations of Russia's capabilities were unofficial as no verification of Russia's true tactical nuclear capability exists (Zysk, 2017). Russia has continued to expand its tactical nuclear weapons since they are not covered by New START (Woolf, 2013). Not including tactical nuclear weapons as part of the treaty was, and continues to be, a strategic mistake. Additionally, Obama supported further cuts for the United States, and suggested that it would limit itself to one thousand nuclear warheads (Kroenig, 2013), a pledge not likely to be supported by future administrations in light of Russia's stockpile.

The New START treaty set a seven-year window in which to implement the agreement and remained in effect for ten years (Woolf, 2013). Monitoring and verification under the treaty were less aggressive, less costly, and less complex. Key provisions set out how the use of the national technical means (NTM) will gather data and monitor forces as well as other primary activities; utilizing a more cost-effective database that identifies warhead numbers, types, and locations. The database will also share information on when any of these weapons are moved, which will account for all warheads and prevent the disinformation tactic of not counting a warhead that is in transit (Woolf, 2013). This verification is supported by inspections (type I and type II) supporting more open transparency and allowing the United States and Russia to confirm information during data exchange. One of the key provisos was to ensure that no more than seven hundred ICBMs were deployed under the treaty (Woolf, 2013). It is worth pointing out that in 1991 the U.S. and Russia had more than ten thousand warheads between them, a figure significantly reduced from its peak in 1967. New START would support a further reduction of more than 80 percent when implemented (Woolf, 2013).

It is understandable that other nations would pursue a nuclear capability, particularly Iran and North Korea. Nuclear weapons provide a deterrent to both conventional and nuclear attack. Nuclear weapons also give a state a seat at the big table with other superpowers. An Iranian acquaintance once stated to the author with respect to Iran's nuclear ambition, "It is where you get respect." That was a powerful statement. True, the use of nuclear weapons seems unconscionable to many and the United States remains the only nation to have used atomic weapons in war. New START represents a move in the right direction for U.S.-Russian relations and should be seen more as a success rather than a failure in the context of those relations.

The reset might not have delivered all that was promised or expected. Perhaps Obama's true, recurring failing is in not managing expectations properly. More specifically, too many false expectations emerged during Obama's tenure. Like most presidents, he was never going to achieve all that he set out to do. It is unfortunate that Obama's peaceful and accommodating position was viewed as a sign of weakness on the part of Russia, but Putin effectively exploited the U.S. president's goals, leaving Obama looking amateurish on the geopolitical stage. The reality remains that all future conflicts with Russia will be complex and interlinked. Russia will likely continue to seek opportunities to undermine U.S. interests and Western cohesion as it did under Obama. Russia made significance advances in reasserting itself in geopolitical matters during Obama's presidency. Reducing the perception that the United States is a threat to Russia will possibly improve relations and secure the future that Obama had envisioned (Cornell, 2016). However, Putin will remain the central figure in determining U.S.-Russian relations, making future cooperation unlikely except when it is clearly in Russia's interest to do so.

China

Game over: China is the next great superpower. It is only a matter of time before it eclipses the United States. China is not the world's hegemon presently, but it has the capability and strategy in place to grow its economic and military influence throughout the world (Vuving, 2012). In the modern phase of China's long history, the empire/country faced a series of national humiliations and Beijing's post-1949 policy revolved around efforts to grow internally in order to assert itself externally, first on a regional level and then, increasingly, on an international scale (Ju, 2015). Domestically, contemporary Chinese leadership remains focused primary on maintaining and enhancing the power and influence of the Communist Party. When Obama entered office, Hu Jintao was China's president. In March 2013, he was succeeded by Xi Jinping. In general, foreign policy changed little from one president to the next, although, under Xi, the country expanded efforts to secure global influence and became more assertive on regional issues.

Tensions between a rising superpower and a hegemon in decline are inevitable. More specifically, Kroenig (2013, p. 44) explains that "[i]nternational relations theory tells us that transitions between reigning hegemons and rising challengers often produce conflict," which is also referred to as the Thucydides trap. This single fact will shape U.S.-Chinese relations well into the future. Nonetheless, throughout his presidency Obama was at pains to emphasize that he did not see U.S.-Chinese relations as a zero-sum game. He repeatedly publicly welcomed the rise of a peaceful China that accepted and behaved consistently with international norms. A sore point during Obama's tenure was China's currency manipulation (Wang, Lin, and Yang, 2012). China was repeatedly accused of violating World Trade Organization (WTO) currency rules as part of its efforts to expand its economy and gain global market shares (Allison, 2017; Wang, Lin, and Yang, 2012). However, Obama failed to seriously address the issue, despite domestic and international calls to do so, because he believed that he would be seen as antagonistic and that it could harm efforts at collaboration in other areas (Chow, 2017; Nymalm, 2013). Obama also chose to avoid addressing growing competition and tension between the United States and China over energy policy. As part of a broad effort to secure its energy supply for the immediate future, China sought to acquire long-term contracts and access to fossil fuels, especially oil, as well as energy technology. Chinese companies were often accused of reverse engineering to acquire this technology and knowledge. The continued growth of China's economy will demand a steady, and an increasing, supply of inexpensive energy.

U.S.-Chinese relations are never going to be simple and straightforward. Relations between the two countries and interests are even more complex and complicated than those between the United States and Russia. The United States remains the world's dominate power and seeks to maintain that status. China has adopted a slow but steady approach to its geopolitical goals. Meanwhile, economically, the United States and China are connected at the hip whether each side sees it or not. The simple fact is that the United States is China's largest trading partner, and China's seventh-largest trading partner in 2011 was not another nation, it was Wal-Mart (Green, 2012).

Understanding the significance of the economic relationship, President Obama made a concerted "pivot, or rebalancing" toward the Asian Pacific region as one of his foreign policy priorities, and attempted to avoid any major confrontation or serious escalation with China. The pivot also provided a means to refocus U.S. policy after the nation's reversals and gaffes in the Middle East. Consequently, Obama choose to downplay U.S.-Japanese relations and the significant strife over the South China Sea. In light of China's growing economy and increasing military capability, U.S. policy often appeared at risk of waffling on these contentious matters.

Obama likely understood that China was well on its way to becoming a global superpower, but this realization was not fully appreciated or accepted by the U.S. public and some political leaders, who sought a more aggressive approach to counter Chinese influence. Obama accepted that a Cold War–style containment policy toward China would not be effective, a point he made repeatedly in press conferences and addresses. Obama and his advisors perceived their approach to be pragmatic, but many of America's Asian allies began to question whether the strategic commitment of the United States to the region was weakening. Close allies such as Australia and the Philippines began to reevaluate their links with the United States, a shift that will likely accelerate under the unpredictable administration of Trump. Wesley (2018, n.p.) made the following observation of Australian policy:

> For the past quarter-century, Canberra's policy has been to support U.S. primacy and U.S. efforts to prevent the rise of rivals. Trump's election forces us to confront the failure of that policy and the implausibility of the restoration of the U.S.'s position of dominance. Rather, Australian policymakers must acknowledge the overwhelming reality that our future will increasingly be shaped by Beijing, not by Washington.

Relationships with key nations in Asia required close monitoring and nurturing if they were to be maintained, but this was a necessity that the Obama administration failed to embrace. The 2019 election of conservative Scott Morrison as prime minister in Australia might provide more opportunities for closer geostrategic cooperation between Washington and Canberra on issues such as immigration and trade.

China's Economic and Military Strength

Understanding Chinese history and culture is key to relations with Beijing (Cunningham-Cross & Callahan, 2011). China's culture is grounded in collectivism and nationalism, unlike the emphasis on individualism that is exercised in the United States (Allison, 2017). Moreover, 90 percent of Chinese view themselves being Han (Chinese). The cultural view in China of governance emphasizes the central role of government in all aspects of social, economic, and political policy (Sole-Farras, 2016). U.S. policy toward China has been far too parochial and is generally unaware of the changes taking place in the region amid the growing influence of Beijing. Allison (2017) took this point farther, suggesting that the United States and China share a similar trait in that each country suffers "an extreme superiority complex."

During Obama's tenure, China eclipsed Japan as the world's second-largest economy (White, 2010). While China's economic might was steadily growing, thanks to decentralization and aggressive trade policies, Obama was confronted with the turmoil of the global financial crisis and record federal deficits in the United States. Projections continuously showed China overtaking the United States as the world's largest economy in the near future. China had multiple decades of 6 to 10 percent economic growth, achieving over $9 trillion GDP in 2011, while U.S. GDP was approximately $15 trillion that year. Meanwhile, the trade balance shifted from $30 billion in China's favor in 1994 to more than $200 billion by 2005 (Seo, 2017) and $365 billion by 2015 (Chow, 2017).

China's expanding economic power has allowed the country to become more assertive both regionally and globally, and to expand its influence through programs such as the 2013 "Belt and Road Initiative" (BRI). The BRI is focused on advancing China's interests regionally and enhancing its foreign policy and diplomatic relations by integrating infrastructure projects and improving trade. Ultimately, China pledged $1 trillion in economic and development assistance to other nations in an effort to better integrate its economy with theirs, especially in developing states, and to bypass the traditional global financial giants, the International Monetary Fund (IMF) and the World Bank.

China is in the midst of an industrial revolution that very much mirrors that of the United Kingdom and the United States in the late 1700s and early 1800s. China has experienced mass migration from the countryside to urban centers which transformed hundreds of millions of farmers into factory workers. Additionally, China made an aggressive transition from state-owned enterprises to publicly and nonstate-owned companies (Vuving, 2012). In 2011, China's National People's Congress approved a new Five-Year Plan, a national development plan that set out to stimulate Chinese consumption over investment and exports and to slow down annual GDP growth to 7 percent. According to Vuving (2012), "starting from the 2020s, China will likely have a sufficient amount of high-tech wealth to substantially challenge U.S. hard power in Asia. The 2030s and 2040s will likely be the apex of an intense competition between China and the United States for primacy in Asia as well as globally" (p. 417). However, one of China's major challenges remains the need to secure long-term energy supplies. The need for stable energy sources will be a major priority for China. This priority for Beijing is one that the Obama administration might have more effectively leveraged to gain concessions in other areas, including the trade deficit between the United States and China.

In the light of the long-term, slow decline in U.S.-Chinese relations that began in the 1980s, Obama tried to use soft power to improve ties between the two states, primarily by utilizing frameworks such as the Trans-Pacific Partnership (TPP) and ASEAN. However, China was busily endeavoring to develop alternative institutions to those dominated by the United States. For instance, in 2016, China established the Asian Infrastructure Investment Bank (AIIB) with support from an additional fifty-seven members as part of the plan to support the BRI and promote infrastructure projects. China has also used trade and investment to counter U.S. soft power. The number of nations that have adopted China as their number one trading partner has increased. China meanwhile has surpassed the United States as the world's largest trading state, with just over $4 trillion in external trade.

China's growing economic prowess has allowed Beijing to dramatically increase the military strength and reach of the People's Liberation Army (PLA). In fact, much of the economic strategy pursued in China from Mao onward can be best understood in the context of national defense (Prime, 2012). Under the leadership of Xi Jinping, the Chinese Communist Party's strategic goal has emphasized the "China Dream of national rejuvenation," which is grounded in the BRI. In the same manner as Obama's TPP initiative, China intended to strengthen their regional relations through the BRI strategy and minimize or deter criticism of expansionistic policies or approaches by fostering economic development projects in cooperating countries. Many poorer countries welcome the foreign direct investment opportunity, and China has seized the initiative where the United States has often waffled and missed out (U.S. Department of Defense, 2018).

Militarily, no nation currently matches the United States in power projection. "National security is not a luxury good but a constitutional duty of the federal government and a president's highest responsibility; fully funding it should be a priority. But the Obama administration's complacency about world order abetted the Pentagon's egregious politicization" (Singh, 2016, p. 33). The United States has ten supercarriers, with the *USS Gerald R Ford* due for activation once successful sea trials are complete. The U.S. Navy also can bring into service an additional nine retired carriers. In comparison, the PLA has plans for an improved naval force of up to three hundred surface ships and submarines. The PLA launched their first aircraft carrier (the *Liaoning*) in 2012. Additionally, the PLA plans for up to approximately seventy submarines by 2020. China's air force has 4,700 aircraft making it the third most powerful force in the world and the dominant air force in the region (U.S. Department of Defense, 2018).

South China Sea

Much of China's growing military power is focused on regional strategic imperatives, such as the expansion of sovereignty over the South China Sea. Beijing has defined the region as a "core interest" for China. China has become more aggressive in the region, which has been a source of geopolitical and military disputes among several of the region's nations—primarily, China, Taiwan, Philippines, Malaysia, Vietnam, and Brunei, as well Singapore, Indonesia, and Thailand—for the past two decades. The main disputed territorial claims in the South China Sea include three archipelagos or island sets that are claimed by China: the Paracel Islands (affecting primarily Vietnam), the Spratly Islands, and the Scarborough Shoal (affecting primarily the Philippines and Brunei). In recent years ASEAN nations have become involved in efforts to promote peaceful dialogue on many of the most contentious issues, particularly regarding the scale and pace of China's dredging activities. Additionally, the United States, Japan, Australia, and India have expressed a vested interest in the South China Sea and in freedom of navigation, respect for international law, and potential resource exploration of the seabed's petroleum and natural gas (Hongfang, 2011; Simon, 2012). The South China Sea will continue to play a critical role in the bigger Indo-Pacific geopolitical world of foreign policy.

Economically, the South China Sea serves as a major commercial gateway for shipping throughout the world. Nearly one-third of all shipping passes through this area, representing almost $5 trillion in goods. More crucially, the region holds an estimated seven to ten billion barrels of oil and an additional nine hundred trillion cubic feet of natural gas (Kaplan, 2011). Two of the main U.S. allies in the region, Japan and South Korea, have major interests in the East China Sea, as well as strategic and economic imperatives in the South China Sea. Many of these nations have overlapping claims to the tiny islands (particularly the Spratly Islands) as well as the shallow shoals in the South China Sea. China has claimed twelve of the islands or shoals (Kaplan, 2011). On many of the shoals and sandbars in the Spratly Islands, China has built structures or tried to enhance its claim through reclamation and dredging projects. In doing this, China is effectively constructing small naval and surveillance bases among areas that remain contested among China, Vietnam, the Philippines Malaysia, Taiwan, and Brunei. By his second term, Obama seemed to accept that it was too late for the United States to reverse this trend without a major confrontation. The administration seemed to focus its hopes on international support for freedom of navigation and the 1982 United Nations Convention on the Law of the Sea (UNCLOS).

As part of China's claim to all areas in the South China Sea, Beijing made an official submission to the United Nations in May 2009 extending its territory to the outer limits of the continental shelf, and mapped out a specific U-shaped (or nine-dash line) to represent their claim (Simon, 2012). China has asserted that these areas were historically subject to Chinese sovereignty and, therefore, that Beijing's claims predate any others. However, this position is not supported by UNCLOS and clearly sets the stage for future conflicts to erupt, particularly as each nation has increased its naval presence in the area. UNCLOS states that islands covered under the two hundred nautical miles exclusive economic zone (EEZ) must support life to constitute an island. Many of these shallow shoals, archipelagoes, and rocky reefs, which China claims as islands, do not meet this definition according to UNCLOS (Hongfang, 2011).

Geographically, the Philippines is less than 130 nautical miles from the Spratly Islands, while China's mainland is more than eight hundred nautical miles from the territory. In 2016, the Philippines brought a case to The Hague against China under the UNCLOS and received a ruling in its favor, that China had violated the Philippines' EEZ. Nonetheless, China continued to narrowly interpret the EEZ and mistakenly views the South China Sea as an extension of their national waters. Control of the South China Sea would allow China to restrict navigation and exclude any military surveillance or movement through the area, which is the likely core of the problem, along with the economic potential of exploration (U.S. Department of Defense, 2018).

During Obama's tenure, the U.S. Navy frequently conducted freedom of navigation operations in the South China Sea. This initially demonstrated to China that the United States rejected Beijing's claims of sovereignty and that the United States would continue to promote free passage through international waters and respect for international law. Obama made several trips to Asia to reassure key allies that they could count on U.S. support and backing in the South China Sea. During a 2014 visit to the Philippines, Obama stated firmly that the United States stood with its close ally. The president specifically affirmed that the U.S. commitment to defend the Philippines was "ironclad." Obama's message was firm, clear, and consistent. During the visit, the leaders of the United States and the Philippines signed the Enhanced Defense Cooperation Agreement granting expanded access to naval ports and increasing military cooperation through joint military exercises. However, during his second term, Obama also began suspending many of the unilateral U.S. Navy exercises in the region an effort to deescalate tensions with China. He also canceled a planned 2016 trip to the Philippines over comments made by Philippines president Rodrigo Duterte.

Ultimately, Obama took a very cautious approach with his "pivot" to China in Asia. Though the president did not want to overplay his hand, he held the door open for diplomacy and increased U.S. cooperation with China, suggesting that it was not his intention to contain China's rise. Obama sought a prosperous and stable China that met its obligations with all stakeholders and conformed to international standards. The president correctly identified that the key to a successful foreign policy toward China would be determined by the relations the United States had with other Indo-Pacific partners such as Australia, India, Indonesia, and Japan. However, a policy of containment toward

China was simply a waste of time and resources, and set a course for reckless confrontation. Increasingly, world leaders make China their first stop rather than the United States once they assume office. China will continue to use its economic power to influence its strategic goals and shape its foreign policy. China's rise to superpower is somewhat a moot point, for whether it happens in the next ten years or next one hundred requires a policy that acknowledges this new reality and finds common ground and avoids conflict. There is a transitional friction unfolding in U.S.-Chinese relations, and Obama wisely made an effort to gently move the United States into a more cooperative relationship with China.

Conclusion

This chapter has attempted to highlight key points of President Obama's foreign policy strategy toward two geopolitical rivals, Russia and China. Successful foreign policy depends on many factors and the ability to balance often competing or overlapping interests and priorities. Obama came into office with the hope of fostering change and peaceful cooperation by finding "shared purpose" through increased diplomacy, all the while downplaying U.S. economic and military assertiveness. Obama wanted to appear and speak with confidence without appearing arrogant and condescending toward other nations, especially in discussions of the role of the United States in the world. Obama as peacemaker and accommodator did not achieve immediate success but the role he attempted reflected the type of leadership and foreign policy that will certainly be required in the future, when the United States does not enjoy hegemonic supremacy. As Dueck (2011, p. 20) suggested, "[F]oreign governments or transnational actors do not feel obliged to alter their basic policy preferences or to make unwanted concessions of their [policy] simply because an American president is accommodating or charismatic." This simple observation helps explain why many of Obama's foreign policies had limited success in the short run, but serve as a lesson for future presidents.

Accommodations and concessions do not automatically generate a quid pro quo response. However, deepening dialogue with rivals such as Russia and China, and minimizing or eliminating negative rhetoric should not necessarily be viewed as weakness. During Obama's presidency, the United States did not need to remind the world it was a superpower. Increasingly, U.S. presidents will face a multipolar world in which the nation is required to better balance its interests with those of other nations. Nonetheless, there will also be occasions when the United States must take a leadership role to maintain international peace and stability. Obama's legacy with Russia and China offers both examples of the success of a softer approach to foreign policy and the consequences of the failure to act.

References

Allison, R. (2013). Russia and Syria: Explaining alignment with a regime in crisis. *International Affairs*, 89(4), 795.
Allison, G. (2017). China vs. America managing the next clash of civilizations. *Foreign Affairs*, 96(5), 80–89.
Belasco, A. (2009). *Cost of Iraq, Afghanistan, and other global war on terror operations since 9/11*. Diane Publishing.
Blank, S. (2010). Beyond the reset policy: Current dilemmas of U.S.-Russia relations. *Comparative Strategy*, 29(4), 333–367.
Boyle, M. (2017). The tragedy of Obama's foreign policy. *Current History*, 116(786), 10–16.
Carafino, J. J., & Gonzalez, M. (2017, August 29). Tillerson deserves cheers for fixing State's dysfunctional diplomacy, *The Hill*. https://thehill.com/blogs/pundits-blog/the-administration/348471-tillerson-deserves-cheers-for-fixing-states.
Cassidy, J. (2015, July 20). 10 ways to fix America's ailing State Department. *Foreign Policy*. https://foreignpolicy.com/2015/07/20/state-department-kerry-obama/.
Charap, S., & Shapiro, J. (2016). US-Russian relations: The middle cannot hold. *Bulletin of the Atomic Scientists*, 72(3), 1–6.
Chirot, D. (2008). Returning to a sane foreign policy. *Society*, 45(5), 425–428.
Chow, D. C. K. (2017). Can the United States impose trade sanctions on China for currency manipulation? *Washington University Global Studies Law Review*, 16(2), 295.
Cohen, S. F. (2006). The New American Cold War. *The Nation*, 283(2), 9.
Cornell, S. E. (2016). The fallacy of "compartmentalisation": The West and Russia from Ukraine to Syria. *European View*, 15(1), 97–109.
Cunningham-Cross, L., & Callahan, W. A. (2011). Ancient Chinese power, modern Chinese thought. *The Chinese Journal of International Politics*, 4(4), 349–374.
Deyermond, R. (2013). Assessing the reset: Successes and failures in the Obama administration's Russia policy, 2009–2012. *European Security*, 22(4), 500–523.

DeYoung, K. (2015), August 4). How the Obama White House runs foreign policy. *Washington Post*. https://www.washingtonpost.com/world/national-security/how-the-obama-white-house-runs-foreign-policy/2015/08/04/2befb960-2fd7-11e5-8353-1215475949f4_story.html.

Dueck, C. (2011). The accommodator: Obama's foreign policy. *Policy Review*, 169, 13.

Feith, D. J., & Cropsey, S. (2012, October 16). How the Russian "reset" explains Obama's foreign policy. *Foreign Policy*. https://foreignpolicy.com/2012/10/16/how-the-russian-reset-explains-obamas-foreign-policy/.

Green, M. (2012). China's periphery: Implications for U.S. policy and interests. *Orbis*, 56(3), 357.

Hongfang, S. (2011). South China Sea issue in China-ASEAN relations: An alternative approach to ease the tension. *International Journal of China Studies*, 2(3), 585-III.

Hove, M. (2016). The emergence of the new Cold War: The Syrian and Ukraine conflicts. *Jadavpur Journal of International Relations*, 20(2), 135–156.

Ju, H. (2015). *China's maritime power and strategy history, national security, and geopolitics*. World Scientific Publishing Company, Singapore.

Kaplan, R. (2011). The South China Sea is the future of conflict. *Foreign Policy*, 188, 76–85.

Kaylan, M. (2014, September 4). Putin's duplicity is a kind of theater: What is his real message? *Forbes*. https://www.forbes.com/sites/melikkaylan/2014/09/04/putins-duplicity-is-a-kind-of-theater-what-is-his-real-message/#29cc9af05948.

Kovalev, A. A. (2017). *Russia's dead end: An insider's testimony from Gorbachev to Putin*. Translated by S. I. Levine. Potomac Books.

Kroenig, M. (2013). Think again: American nuclear disarmament. *Foreign Policy*, 202: 42–49.

Kuchins, A. C., & Zevelev, I. A. (2012). Russian foreign policy: Continuity in change. *The Washington Quarterly*, 35(1), 147–161.

Lantis, J. S. (2012). *US foreign policy in action: An innovative teaching text*. Wiley.

Lonsdale, D. (2013). Obama's second term: Time for a new discourse on nuclear strategy. *Comparative Strategy*, 32(5), 459–473.

McFaul, M. (2018). Russia as it is. *Foreign Affairs*, 97(4), 82–92.

Nasr, V. (2013). *The dispensable nation: American foreign policy in retreat*. Johns Hopkins University Press.

Nau, H. (2010). Obama's foreign policy. *Policy Review*, 160, 27–47.

No sign of breakthrough at Russia-Ukraine gas talks. (2013, March 4). *States News Service*. http://link.galegroup.com.ez.library.latrobe.edu.au/apps/doc/A321145006/EAIM?u=latrobe&sid=EAIM&xid=92ddab20.

Nymalm, N. (2013). The end of the "liberal theory of history"? Dissecting the US Congress' discourse on China's currency policy. *International Political Sociology, 7*(4), 388–405.

Pederson, C. (2009). *Obama's America*. Edinburgh University Press.

Prime, P. B. (2012). Sustaining China's economic growth: New leaders, new directions? *Eurasian Geography and Economics, 53*(6), 688.

Rothschild, J. E., & Shafranek, R. M. (2017). Advances and opportunities in the study of political communication, foreign policy, and public opinion. *Political Communication, 34*(4), 634–643.

Rubin, M. (2014). Why "reset" failed: Diplomacy with rogues rarely works. *World Affairs, 177*(2), 74–81.

Seo, J. (2017). Strange bedfellows and US China policy in the era of polarized politics. *Korean Journal of Defense Analysis, 29*(1), 47–69.

Simon, S. (2012). Conflict and diplomacy in the South China Sea, *Asian Survey, 52*(6), 995–1018.

Singh, R. (2016). *After Obama: Renewing American leadership, restoring global order*. Cambridge University Press.

Smith, H. (2010). Foreign policy formulation, *American Diplomacy*. https://go.gale.com/ps/anonymous?id=GALE%7CA220137224&sid=googleScholar&v=2.1&it=r&linkaccess=abs&issn=10948120&p=AONE&sw=w.

Sole-Farras, J. (2016). A discourse called China and the PRC's foreign policy and diplomacy. *Journal of Chinese Political Science, 21*(3), 281.

Stent, A. (2012). US-Russia relations in the second Obama administration. *Survival, 54*(6), 123–138.

Swistek, G. (2012). The nexus between public diplomacy and military diplomacy in foreign affairs and defense policy. *Connections: The Quarterly Journal, 11*(2), 79–86.

U.S. Department of Defense. (2018). *Annual report to Congress: Military and security developments involving the People's Republic of China*. https://media.defense.gov/2018/Aug/16/2001955282/-1/-1/1/2018-CHINA-MILITARY-POWER-REPORT.PDF.

Vuving, A. L. (2012). The future of China's rise: How China's economic growth will shift the Sino-U.S. balance of power, 2010–2040. *Asian Politics and Policy, 4*(3), 401–423.

Wang, C. H., Lin, C. H. A., & Yang, C. H. (2012). Short-run and long-run effects of exchange rate change on trade balance: Evidence from China and its trading partners. *Japan & The World Economy, 24*(4), 266–273.

Wesley, M. (2018). Will Australia defend the "rules-based order" in Asia? *The Australian*. https://www.theaustralian.com.au/news/inquirer/reimagining-australiasplace-in-a-new-world-order/news-story/804d7c5780ad0b45361922ac5e702dd5.

White, H. (2010). Power shift: Australia's future between Washington and Beijing. *Quarterly Essay, 39*: 1–74.

Woolf, A. F. (2013, December 5). *The new START treaty: Central limits and key provisions*. CRS: R41219. Congressional Research Service.

Zygar, M. (2016). *All the Kremlin's men: Inside the court of Vladimir Putin*. PublicAffairs.

Zysk, K. (2017). Nonstrategic nuclear weapons in Russia's evolving military doctrine. *Bulletin of the Atomic Scientists, 73*(5), 322–327.

IV

Conclusion

15

Barack Obama
The Post-Presidency

MICHAEL J. DEVINE

During the historic visit to the People's Republic of China in 1972, President Richard Nixon reportedly sought to engage the scholarly Chinese premier Zhou Enlai in a conversation about French history. Zhou was known to be an authority on this subject. According to various and conflicting sources, when the American leader asked the premier for his evaluation of the effect of the French Revolution of 1789 on the course of world history, Premier Zhou pondered the question briefly and then responded, "It's too early to say" (Campbell, 2011; McGregor, 2011). Whether or not Zhou's observation was recorded correctly, it is certainly true that events in history require time for proper assessment, as only with the passage of decades can individuals and their deeds be viewed with a degree of objectivity and in a proper historical context. Clearly, an appraisal of President Barack Obama's brief post-presidency at this time serves only as an initial assessment. In addition, the post-presidency of America's first African American chief executive has only begun and is likely to continue for decades in ways that will impact his legacy. Finally, any reading of President Obama's post-presidential years must consider the extraordinary and volatile transition that has transpired from Obama to the Trump administration.

President Obama departed the White House as a popular national figure. His administration had halted a dangerous slide toward a financial meltdown during its first year in office, and proceeded steadily to build a strong, growing economy throughout two terms. He had also avoided entanglements in new military involvements abroad and his commitment to the multinational Paris climate change accords and the agreement to forestall Iran's nuclear ambitions met with public approval. Meanwhile, his major efforts in health care and immigration, the Affordable Care Act and Deferred Action on Childhood Arrivals (DACA), were generally supported by a majority of Americans. He enjoyed public approval ratings of 60 percent during his final year in office. As he left the White House in January 2017, a Quinnipiac University poll showed 29 percent of Americans rating him as the greatest president since World War II (following only Ronald Reagan at 30 percent); and, about the same time, in a C-SPAN survey of nearly one hundred presidential scholars, President Obama was ranked twelfth among all America's presidents (Nelson). Furthermore, the popular vote victory of nearly three million by Democratic candidate Hillary Clinton in 2016, despite her weak and troubled campaign against Donald Trump, can be seen as something of a referendum in favor of President Obama. Perhaps his successor sensed he would have a tough act to follow.

The Assault on the Obama Legacy

In the two years since the surprising victory of Donald Trump in the 2016 presidential election, the Obama presidential legacy has undergone relentless and unprecedented attacks from the new administration. In breaking with tradition, President Trump has not restrained himself from constantly criticizing his immediate predecessor, as well as earlier administrations. Beginning on inauguration day, President Trump remained in the mode he had established throughout his divisive presidential campaign. Rightly or not, he claimed that all of President Obama's actions weakened the nation at home and abroad. Beyond his harsh campaign-style attacks, Trump has seemed determined, with the help of a compliant, if not wholly supportive, Republican Congress to overturn every Obama administration initiative on issues related to banking reform, the environment, civil rights, and federal involvement in primary and secondary education. President Obama's signature legislative achievement, the Affordable Health Care Act, or 'Obamacare,' served as a favorite target of President Trump's scorn, although efforts to repeal or replace it have failed thus far.

Ignoring the success President Obama achieved in rescuing the nation and the world from the financial meltdown of 2008 and restoring the nation's economic health by 2016, President Trump repeatedly asserted that he came to the presidency with America in economic decline and approaching ruin. President Trump has insisted that his policies brought a disastrous national economy to a level of prosperity previously unknown to Americans—and all in just several months! President Trump has maintained, against obvious evidence to the contrary, that the Obama administration was ineffective in enforcing border security, irresponsible in allowing military preparedness to languish, and foolish in negotiating unfavorable international trade agreements. Abroad, President Trump has reversed traditional United States policies on economic and environmental cooperation, distanced the United States from NATO allies, scrapped a multinational nuclear arms agreement with Iran, and attempted to establish a warm relationship with Russia's increasingly dictatorial and belligerent Vladimir Putin. He has also claimed to have resolved the nuclear threat posed by North Korea's Kim Jung Il, all while taking every opportunity to publicly decry his predecessor's alleged failure in world affairs.

Where has former president Obama been during this nasty, unprecedented, and ceaseless onslaught on his presidential record? Until the weeks prior to the November 2018 mid-term elections, he remained detached, aloof, and, for the most part, unseen. Like most former presidents of recent decades, he has enjoyed time for relaxation and travel. Obama has also worked on authoring a presidential memoir. Following an intense bidding war, both Barack and Michelle Obama signed a book deal with a huge advance from their publisher, Penguin Random House. The joint agreement for $65 million dwarfed all previous advances paid to former occupants of the White House (Ahmed, 2017). (Michelle's *Becoming* was an instant best-seller when published in 2018.) Obama also looked after the uncertain efforts to establish his legacy with a presidential library and the creation of the Obama Foundation. A notoriously devoted father, he has understandably attended to family matters. He and former first lady Michelle chose to live in Washington, D.C., rather than returning to their home in Chicago, at least while their younger daughter Sasha completes high school with her classmates at the Sidwell Friends School. Meanwhile, elder daughter Malia entered Harvard University, met a British classmate who became her boyfriend, and acquired a degree of notoriety for her fashionable looks, smoking in public, trendy outfits, and a campy music video (Thompson & Eilperin, 2017).

Given the radical break with tradition in many areas of presidential conduct demonstrated by President Trump, many have questioned Obama's restraint and his reluctance to engage in controversial political issues, challenge President Trump's heated rhetoric, or even defend the accomplishments of his administration. President Obama's serene, cool, and reserved presence remains in stark contrast to his successor's flair for the contentious, outrageous, dramatic, and flamboyant. At a press conference in Lima, Peru, where he attended a summit of the Asia-Pacific Economic Cooperation leaders, just weeks after the shocking victory of Donald Trump in 2016 Presidential election, President Obama addressed the likelihood that the president-elect would govern in the same extraordinary divisive way in which he campaigned. "People should take a wait-and-see approach in how much his policy proposals once in the White House, once he's sworn in, match up with some of the rhetoric of his campaign," President Obama calmly stated. "My simple point is that you can't assume that the language of his campaign matched up with the specifics of governing, legislation, regulators, and foreign policy" (Blow, 2018). In spite of the new president's attacks, in the months following President Trump's inauguration the former president followed tradition and maintained a low public profile, much to the consternation of his former staff members and supporters. To many, Obama appeared conflicted as to whether the 2016 election was a rejection of his vision of America or a kind of unfortunate mishap. He nearly disappeared from view and he avoided mentioning Trump by name when speaking publicly. Obama seemed to hold a belief that America was fundamentally sound and capable of correcting itself from the Trump presidency without his participation (Heer, 2018; Debenedetti, 2018).

Then, after nearly two years out of the spotlight, it appeared Obama had at last concluded that Trump's actions as president were no less divisive than his campaign slogans, personal attacks, and outbursts. Perhaps the former president, recognizing the unusual nature of the Trump presidency, had finally broken from the genteel tradition of the exclusive ex-presidents' club, which avoids direct, personal criticism of the current occupant of the Oval Office; and sitting presidents avoid attacks on their predecessors. Speaking in September 2018 at the University of Illinois in Champaign-Urbana, Obama expressed his concerns about the direction in which President Trump was leading the nation. While his views on the Trump presidency were not especially original or presented in a forceful manner, the fact that the former president had entered the arena ahead of the 2018 mid-term elections encouraged his followers. Obama's public reengagement also sparked hopes that his voice might challenge President Trump's overwhelming dominance over the nation's political discourse (Blow, 2018). The 2018 mid-term elections will halt the extent to which Obama legacy is further diminished, at least temporarily, by the allegations, policies, and directives of his successor. The Democratic election victories, retaking control of the U.S. House of Representatives and electing Democratic governors and legislatures in several key states, will place some restraints on President Trump's determined drive to build its own legacy on the ashes of the preceding administration. The 2018 mid-term elections provided a measure of vindication for Obama, and in 2020 his legacy will surely be judged further by the extent to which his public reinvolvement in a presidential campaign is viewed as significant in assisting the Democratic candidate in securing the White House.

The Presidential Center

Almost as baffling as Obama's hesitancy to respond publicly to Trump's assault on the accomplishments of his presidential administration has been the unexpected controversy in Chicago over the direction of his presidential library. Although several suitors, including the University of Hawaii in Honolulu, and Columbia University in New York City, made determined bids for his presidential library, it was a forgone conclusion that the city of Chicago would win the prize once it became official. Initially, there appeared to be enthusiastic support for housing the new facility in the former president's adopted home. Several sites were considered for the library's location on the city's South Side, where a young Barack Obama served as a community organizer, taught at the University of Chicago Law School, and launched his political career. The private Obama Foundation began raising big money for construction and there appeared to be near unanimous agreement that the presidential library of the nation's first African American president would add a significant landmark, as well as an educational and cultural attraction to the "Windy City." However, the project soon ran into unanticipated conflict and controversy. The high-handed tactics of the Obama Foundation leadership and the Chicago mayor's office alienated many local interest groups (Bowean, 2018). At this time, as residents of Chicago's historic neighborhoods that will be affected by the library (those surrounding the University of Chicago and lining Lake Michigan) await a resolution, excitement over the planned Obama Center may be fading (Rhodam, 2018).

The complex envisioned by the Obama Foundation will not be a presidential library in the traditional sense. Rather, it will be a "Presidential Center" that will house conference facilities, an auditorium, museum exhibits, a training center for active citizenship and even a sports complex. A 235-foot "museum tower" will dominate the surrounding landscape, and the only library at the Obama Center may be a branch of the Chicago Public Library. This represents a clear break from tradition, although in recent years the role of the private foundations has been allowed to eclipse the presence of the federal agency charged with responsibility for presidential records, the National Archives and Records Administration (NARA). All presidents since Franklin D. Roosevelt, who established his library on his family's estate at Hyde Park, New York, have housed presidential documents, artifacts, and the personal papers of the president, his family members, and associates. These public records and historical materials have been placed in privately funded facilities turned over to NARA's management for use by scholars and the education and enjoyment of school groups and visitors from throughout the world. What will happen to the (mostly digital) documents of the Obama presidency, along with the artifacts and personal papers, remains uncertain—although by law the public materials of the presidency must be stored and curated by NARA somewhere (United States Government Accountability Office, 2011). Exactly how this fundamental departure from the traditional presidential library model came about seems to involve "mystery and intrigue" between the powerful Obama Foundations and the leadership of the NARA. Whatever caused the departure from precedent, the situation does not bode well for the continued operation of the thirteen presidential libraries currently administered by NARA (Clark, 2018; Hufbauer, 2018). In addition, this new model, if that is what it is, creates uncertainty about what will be without a doubt a presidential library (or center) like no other—that of President Donald J. Trump.

Over the past decade, the private foundations associated with the NARA-managed presidential libraries have been allowed to overshadow the federal facilities they are intended to support. Many have erected huge edifices that dwarf the adjoining federal libraries (restricted in size by congressional action), and their enormous public relations and programming budgets often give the public the mistaken impression that private foundations actually manage the libraries. The decision by the Obama Foundation to eliminate the federal presence altogether is, perhaps, the logical outcome of the recent NARA policy empowering private foundations. However the situation in Chicago came about, it leaves undecided where the official records of the Obama presidency will be archived by NARA, and how they will be managed by professional, federal government archivists and made available to the public (Schuessler, 2019). Most of the official records of the Obama presidency are digital. Nevertheless, they will require cataloging and management. Declassification matters must be addressed and professional staff will need to handle reference inquiries and calls from those filing Freedom of Information Act (FOIA) requests. NARA officials and professional staff will remain responsible for these important missions.

There also remain questions regarding artifacts and personal papers of the president, his associates, and family members. Meanwhile, there exist loud critics who fear that the Obama Center might resemble a kind of presidential theme park, and various South Side neighborhood groups, citizen activists, and historic preservation organizations have expressed concern about the center's impact on local real estate prices and the "gentrification" of historically black neighborhoods. Civic organizations have also voiced strong opposition to the use of precious and historic Jackson Park lakefront land for the presidential center (Clark, 2018; Hufbauer, 2018). The City of Chicago, under Mayor Rahm Emanuel, President Obama's former chief of staff, has aggressively pushed the project ahead, ignoring the protests. The city failed to offer new park land to replace the eleven acres to be taken up by the Obama Center. Furthermore, in one move that outraged critics of the project, the parks department cut down dozens of one-hundred-year-old trees after promising to wait until all permits had been properly secured. This assertive drive from City Hall may soon change, as the highly unpopular mayor did not seek another term in 2019.

At present, a wide range of civic organizations are prepared to demand more engagement from the city and the Obama Foundation, all of which may lead to another delay of the groundbreaking ceremony scheduled for 2019 (Devine, 2018). It is ironic indeed that the former president, who began his public career as a community activist, is now confronted by community activists opposed to the efforts of his foundation and his erstwhile chief of staff.

So how will the post-presidency of Barack Obama be evaluated by future historians? Much will depend on whether the Trump administration is allowed to continue brutally and systematically to dismantle the achievements of America's first African American president. How the Obama Center is ultimately received, and how the record of the Obama years is archived and made accessible to researchers will also be factors. In addition, the post-presidency of President Obama is only beginning; and in the years ahead, the former president may decide to actively defend and perhaps seek to advance his own legacy. Obama is a young former president with great energy, intelligence, and a wealth of good will at home and aboard. He also possesses exceptional communication skills. (He was a best-selling author well before he became a national political figure.) How adroitly and assertively he will employ these significant assets remains to be seen. As for the post-presidency of Barack Obama and its ultimate impact on history, if asked, Zhou Enlai would likely add, "It's too early to say."

References

Ahmed, T. (2017, March 1). Barack and Michelle sign joint book deal worth $65 million: Report. *Newsweek*. https://www.newsweek.com/barack-and-michelle-obama-sign-joint-book-deal-worth-over-65-million-report-562409.

Blow, C. (2018, September 9). Obama's back! *The New York Times*. https://www.nytimes.com/2018/09/09/opinion/obamas-back.html.

Bowean, L. (2018, August 9). Obama Foundation first annual report shows spike in fundraising. *The Chicago Tribune*. https://www.chicagotribune.com/news/obamacenter/ct-met-obama-financial-report-20180809-story.html.

Campbell, W. (2011, June 14). "Too early to say": Zhou was speaking about 1968, not 1789. mediamythalert.worldpress.com.

Clark, B. (2018). In defense of presidential libraries: Why the failure to build an Obama Library is bad for democracy. *The Public Historian*, 40, 96–103.

Debenedetti, G. (2018, June 24). Where is Barack Obama? *New York Magazine*. http://nymag.com/intelligencer/2018/06/where-is-barack-obama.html.

Devine, M. (2018). Presidential libraries and their foundations: A time for reform. *The Public Historian*, 40(2), 111–115.

Heer, J. (2018, June 25). Barack Obama's very traditional retirement is controversial. *The New Republic*. https://newrepublic.com/minutes/149364/barack-obamas-traditional-retirement-controversial.

Hufbauer, B. (2018). A brief critique of public history in presidential libraries. *The Public Historian*, 40(2), 104–110.

McGregor, R. (2011, June 10). Zhou Enlai's caution lost in translation. *Financial Times*. http://archive.li/huuQI.

Mortice, Z. (2018, September 25). After Rahm, what comes next for the Obama Library? *CITYLAB*. https://www.citylab.com/design/2018/09/after-rahm-what-comes-next-obama-library/571075/.

Nelson, M. (N.D.). Barack Obama: Impact and legacy. Miller Center, University of Virginia. https://millercenter.org/president/obama/impact-and-legacy.

Obama Foundation. (2015, May 13). *Barack Obama Presidential Center announcement*. https://www.youtube.com/watch?v=FcFzEkqRIaI.

Rhodam, M. (2018, July 19). Barack Obama is beloved in Chicago, but activists are divided over his future presidential center. *Time Magazine*. http://time.com/longform/barack-obama-chicago-presidential-center/.

Schuessler, J. (2019, February 20). The Obama presidential library that isn't. *The New York Times*.

Thompson, K. & Eilperin, J. (2017, March 26). Two months out of office, Barack Obama is having a post-presidency like no other. *The Washington Post*. https://www.washingtonpost.com/lifestyle/two-months-out-of-office-barack-obama-is-having-a-post-presidency-like-no-other/2017/03/24/6b4d1c05-f4a8-462b-ad7f-664ac35d0c06_story.html?noredirect=on&utm_term=.8d987438580f.

United States Government Accountability Office, Congress. (2011). *Framework governing use of presidential library facilities and staff national archives: GAO-11-39*. National Archives.

Appendix A
Grading President Obama

Note: The editors of this book asked each contributor to provide a letter grade (ranging from "A+" to "F") for Obama's presidency. Obama was rated on nine categories as well as on his performance "within the context of the times." The contributors also offered an overall letter grade. The appendix below lists the results.

Public Persuasion: B+ (mean=3.3; mode=B+; range=A+ to C)

Crisis Leadership: B (mean=2.9; mode=A, A–, B+, B–; range=A to F)

Economic Management: B– (mean=2.6; mode: B, C; range=A to D)

Moral Authority: B+ (mean=3.4; mode=A; range=A+ to F)

International Relations: C (mean=1.9; mode=B; range=B to F)

Administrative Skills: B (mean=3.0; mode=B; range=A to C)

Relations with Congress: C– (mean=1.7; mode=C; range=B– to D–)

Vision (Agenda Setting): B+ (mean=3.2; mode=B+; range=A to C)

Pursued Equal Justice for All: B (mean=3.0; mode= B; range=A to F)

Performance within Context of Times: B– (mean=2.8; mode=B+; range= A– to F)

Overall grade: B– (mean=2.7; mode=B+; range=B+ to D+)

Key: A=4.0, A–=3.7, B+=3.3, B=3.0, B–=2.7, and so on, with F=0

Appendix B
Barack Obama Biography

Born: Honolulu, Hawaii (August 4, 1961)

Home: Chicago, Illinois

Marriage: To Michelle Robinson (October 3, 1992)

Children: Malia (b. 1998), Sasha (b. 2001)

Religion: United Church of Christ

Education: Attended Occidental College (1979–1981); BA, Political Science from Columbia University (1983); JD from Harvard Law School (1991)

Books: *Dreams from My Father: A Story of Race and Inheritance* (Times Books, 1995); *The Audacity of Hope: Thoughts on Reclaiming the American Dream* (Crown, 2006); *Of Thee I Sing: A Letter to My Daughters* (Random House, 2010)

Career: Financial Consultant in New York City (1983–85); Community Organizer in Chicago (1985–88); Lawyer with Miner, Barnhill & Galland Law Firm in Chicago (1991–95); Senior Lecturer, University of Chicago Law School (1992–95)

Political Office: Illinois State Senate (1997–2005); U.S. Senate (2005–08), member of the Health, Education, Labor and Pensions Committee; Foreign Relations Committee; Veterans Affairs Committee; and Environment and Public Works Committee

Appendix C
The Obama Administration

Cabinet

Secretary of State: Hillary Rodham Clinton (2009–13); John Kerry (2013–17)

Secretary of Treasury: Timothy F. Geithner (2009–13); Jack Lew (2013–17)

Secretary of Defense: Robert M. Gates (2009–11); Leon Panetta (2011–13); Chuck Hagel (2013–15); Ash Carter (2015–17)

Attorney General: Eric H. Holder. (2009–15); Loretta Lynch (2015–17)

Secretary of Interior: Kenneth L. Salazar (2009–13); Sally Jewell (2013–17)

Secretary of Agriculture: Thomas J. Vilsack (2009–17)

Secretary of Commerce: Gary F. Locke (2009–11); John Bryson (2011–12); Penny Pritzker (2013–17)

Secretary of Labor: Hilda L. Solis (2009–13); Tom Perez (2013–17)

Secretary of Health and Human Services: Kathleen Sebelius (2009–14); Sylvia Matthews Burwell (2014–17)

Secretary of Housing and Urban Development: Shaun L.S. Donovan (2009–14); Julian Castro (2014–17)

Secretary of Transportation: Ray LaHood (2009–13); Anthony Foxx (2013–17)

Secretary of Energy: Steven Chu (2009–13); Ernest Moniz (2013–17)

Secretary of Education: Arne Duncan (2009–16); John King (2016–17)

Secretary of Veterans Affairs: Eric K. Shinseki (2009–14); Bob McDonald (2014–17)

Secretary of Homeland Security: Janet A. Napolitano (2009–13); Jeh Johnson (2013–17)

Cabinet Level/Senior Staff/Executive Office of the President

Vice President: Joe Biden (2009–17)

Chief of Staff: Rahm Emanuel (2009–10); Bill Daley (2010–12); Jack Lew (2012–13); Denis McDonough (2013–17)

Director of National Intelligence: Dennis C. Blair (2009–10); James R. Clapper (2010–17)

National Security Advisor: James L. Jones (2009–10); Thomas E. Donilon (2010–13); Susan Rice (2013–17)

Ambassador to the United Nations: Susan Rice (2009–13); Samantha Power (2013–17)

Solicitor General: Elena Kagan (2009); Neal Katyal (2010–11); Don Verrilli (2011–16); Ian Gershengorn (2016–17)

Administrator, Environmental Protection Agency: Lisa P. Jackson (2009–13); Gina McCarthy (2013–17)

Director, Office of Management and Budget: Peter Orszag (2009–10); Jack Lew (2010–12); Sylvia Matthews Burwell (2013–14); Shaun Donovan (2014–17)

U.S. Trade Representative: Ronald Kirk (2009–13); Michael Froman (2013–17)

Chair, Council of Economic Advisors: Christina D. Romer (2009–10); Austan Goolsbee (2010–11); Alan Krueger (2011–13); Jason Furman (2013–17)

White House Counsel: Greg Craig (2009–10); Bob Bauer (2010–11); Kathryn Ruemmler (2011–14); Neil Eggleston (2014–17)

Director, National Economic Council: Lawrence H. Summers (2009–10); Gene Sperling (2011–14); Jeffrey Zients (2014–17)

Press Secretary: Robert Gibbs (2009–11); Jay Carney (2011–14); Josh Earnest (2014–17)

Senior Advisors: Valerie Jarrett (2009–17); David Axelrod (2009–11); Peter Rouse (2009–10); David Plouffe (2011–13); Daniel Pfeiffer (2013–15); Brian Deese (2015–17); Shailagh Murray (2015–17)

Select Bibliography

Journals, Periodicals, and Official Sources

Allison, G. (2017). China vs. America managing the next clash of civilizations. *Foreign Affairs, 96*(5), 80–89.

Allison, R. (2013). Russia and Syria: Explaining alignment with a regime in crisis. *International Affairs, 89*(4), 795.

Anderson, O. W. (1951). Compulsory medical care insurance, 1910–1950. *The Annals*. American Academy of Political and Social Science, 273, 106–113.

Antonio, R. J., & Brulle, R. J. (2011). The unbearable lightness of politics: Climate change denial and political polarization. *The Sociological Quarterly, 52*(2), 195–202.

Auroagh, M. (2012). Social media, mediation, and the Arab revolutions. *Triple-C, 10*(2), 518–536.

Baily, N. B., Klein, A., & Schardin, J. (2017, January). The impact of the Dodd-Frank Act on financial stability and economic growth. *The Russell Sage Foundation Journal of the Social Science*.

Baumgartner, J. C. (2017). Polls and elections: Under the radar: Public support for vice presidents. *Presidential Studies Quarterly, 47*(1), 1–12.

Blank, S. (2010). Beyond the reset policy: Current dilemmas of U.S.–Russia relations. *Comparative Strategy, 29*(4), 333–367.

Blessing, T. H. (2003). Presidents and significance: Partisanship as a source of perceived greatness. *White House Studies, 3*(1).

Boyle, M. (2017). The tragedy of Obama's foreign policy. *Current History, 116*(786), 10–16.

Burrell, B., Elder, L., & Frederick, B. (2010). From Hillary to Michelle: Public opinion and the spouses of presidential candidates. *Presidential Studies Quarterly, 41*(1), 156–176.

Charap, S., & Shapiro, J. (2016). US-Russian Relations: The middle cannot hold. *Bulletin of the Atomic Scientists, 72*(3), 1–6.

Chirot, D. (2008). Returning to a sane foreign policy. *Society, 45*(5), 425–428.

Chow, D. C. K. (2017). Can the United States impose trade sanctions on China for currency manipulation? *Washington University Global Studies Law Review, 16*(2), 295.

Clark, B. (2018). In defense of presidential libraries: Why the failure to build an Obama Library is bad for democracy. *The Public Historian, 40*, 96–103.

Clémençon, R. (2016). The two sides of the Paris Climate Agreement: Dismal failure or historic breakthrough? *Journal of Environment and Development, 25*(1), 3–24.

Cohen, J. E. (2001). "The poll": Popular views of the vice president: Vice presidential approval. *Presidential Studies Quarterly, 31*(1), 142–149.

Cornell, S. E. (2016). The fallacy of "compartmentalization": The West and Russia from Ukraine to Syria. *European View, 15*(1), 97–109.

Cunningham-Cross, L., & Callahan, W. A. (2011). Ancient Chinese power, modern Chinese thought. *The Chinese Journal of International Politics, 4*(4), 349–374.

Devine, M. (2018). Presidential libraries and their foundations: A time for reform. *The Public Historian, 40*(2), 111–115.

Deyermond, R. (2013). Assessing the reset: Successes and failures in the Obama administration's Russia policy, 2009–2012. *European Security, 22*(4), 500–523.

Dueck, C. (2011). The accommodator: Obama's foreign policy. *Policy Review 169*, 13.

Dunlap, R. E., & McCright, A. M. (2008). A widening gap: Republican and Democratic views on climate change. *Environment: Science and Policy for Sustainable Development, 50*(5), 26–35.

Felzenberg, A. (1997). There you go again: Liberal historians and the New York Times deny Ronald Reagan his due. *Policy Review* (March–April).

Goldstein, J. K. (2008). The rising power of the modern vice presidency. *Presidential Studies Quarterly, 38*, 374–389.

Hongfang, S. (2011). South China Sea issue in China-ASEAN relations: An alternative approach to ease the tension. *International Journal of China Studies, 2*(3), 585-III.

Hove, M. (2016). The emergence of the new Cold War: The Syrian and Ukraine conflicts. *Jadavpur Journal of International Relations, 20*(2), 135–156.

Hufbauer, B. (2018). A brief critique of public history in presidential libraries. *The Public Historian, 40*(2), 104–110.

Jacobson, G. C. (1996). The 1994 House elections in perspective. *Political Science Quarterly, 111*(2), 202–223.

Kaplan, R. (2011). The South China Sea is the future of conflict. *Foreign Policy, 188*, 76–85.

Kroenig, M. (2013). Think again: American nuclear disarmament. *Foreign Policy, 202*, 42–49.

Kuchins, A. C., & Zevelev, I. A. (2012). Russian foreign policy: Continuity in change. *The Washington Quarterly, 35*(1), 147–161.

Lindgren, S. (2013). The potential and limitations of Twitter activism: Mapping the 2011 Libyan uprising. *Triple C, 11*(1), 207–220.

Lonsdale, D. (2013). Obama's second term: Time for a new discourse on nuclear strategy. *Comparative Strategy, 32*(5), 459–473.

McCright, A. M., & Dunlap, R. E. (2011). The politicization of climate change and polarization in the American public's views of global warming, 2001–2010. *The Sociological Quarterly, 52*(2), 155–194.

Nisbet, M. C. (2009). Communicating climate change: Why frames matter for public engagement. *Environment: Science and Policy for Sustainable Development, 51*(2), 12–23.

Nymalm, N. (2013). The end of the "liberal theory of history"? Dissecting the US Congress' discourse on China's currency policy. *International Political Sociology, 7*(4), 388–405.

Parry-Giles, S. J., & Blair, D. M. (2002). The rise of the rhetorical first lady: Politics, gender ideology, and women's voice. *Rhetoric & Public Affairs, 5*(4), 565–600.

Paul, N., & Perreault, G. (2018). The first lady of social media: The visual rhetoric of Michelle Obama's Twitter images. *Atlantic Journal of Communication, 26*(3), 164–179.

Pious, R. M. (2003). Reflections of a presidency rater. *White House Studies, 3*(1).

Prime, P. B. (2012). Sustaining China's economic growth: New leaders, new directions? *Eurasian Geography and Economics, 53*(6), 688.

Rothschild, J. E., & Shafranek, R. M. (2017). Advances and opportunities in the study of political communication, foreign policy, and public opinion. *Political Communication, 34*(4), 634–643.

Rubin, M. (2014). Why "reset" failed: Diplomacy with rogues rarely works. *World Affairs, 177*(2), 74–81.

Schlesinger, A. M. (1962, July 29). Our presidents: A rating by 75 historians. *New York Times Magazine*, 12–13, 40–41, 43.

Schlesinger, A. M. (1948, November 1). Historians rate the U.S. presidents. *Life Magazine*, 65–66, 73–74.

Schlesinger Jr., A. M. (2003). Commentary. *White House Studies, 3*(1), 75–77.

Schlesinger Jr., A. M. (1996, December 15). The ultimate approval rating. *New York Times Magazine*, 46–47.

Seo, J. (2017). Strange bedfellows and US China policy in the era of polarized politics. *Korean Journal of Defense Analysis, 29*(1), 47–69.

Skidmore, M. J. (2018). Considering structural and ideological barriers to anti-poverty programs in the United States: An uninhibited, and unconventional, analysis. *Poverty and Public Policy, 10*(4) (forthcoming).

Skidmore, M. J. (1989). "Operation Coffeecup": A hidden episode in American political history. *Journal of American Culture, 12*(3) (Fall).

Sole-Farras, J. (2016). A discourse called China and the PRC's foreign policy and diplomacy. *Journal of Chinese Political Science, 21*(3), 281.
Stent, A. (2012). US-Russia relations in the second Obama administration. *Survival, 54*(6), 123–138.
Swistek, G. (2012). The nexus between public diplomacy and military diplomacy in foreign affairs and defense policy. *Connections: The Quarterly Journal, 11*(2), 79–86.
United States Government Accountability Office, Congress. (2011). *Framework governing use of presidential library facilities and staff national archives: GAO-11-39*. National Archives.
Vuving, A. L. (2012). The future of China's rise: How China's economic growth will shift the Sino-U.S. balance of power, 2010–2040. *Asian Politics and Policy, 4*(3), 401–423.
Watson, R. P. (2003, Fall). Ranking the first ladies: Polling elites to evaluate performance. *PRG Report* (Presidency Research Group of the American Political Science Association, now renamed the Presidents and Executive Politics section), *26*(1), 15–22.
Watson, R. P. (1999). Ranking the presidential spouses. *The Social Science Journal, 36*(1), 117–136.
Wayne, S. J. (2003). Evaluating the president: The public's perspective through the prism of pollsters. *White House Studies, 3*(1), 35–40.
Wang, C. H., Lin, C. H. A., & Yang, C. H. (2012). Short-run and long-run effects of exchange rate change on trade balance: Evidence from China and its trading partners. *Japan & The World Economy, 24*(4), 266–273.
White, H. (2010). Power shift: Australia's future between Washington and Beijing. *Quarterly Essay, 39*, 1–74.
Wiedman, T., & Minx, J. (2008). A definition of "carbon fooprint." In C. C. Pertsova (Ed.), *Ecological economics research trends* (pp. 1–11). Nova Science Publishers.
Young, K., & Schwartz, M. (2014). Healthy, wealthy, and wise: How corporate power shaped the affordable care act. *New Labor Forum, 23*(2), 30–40.
Zysk, K. (2017). Nonstrategic nuclear weapons in Russia's evolving military doctrine. *Bulletin of the Atomic Scientists, 73*(5), 322–327.

Books and Monographs

Axelrod, D. (2015). *Believer: My forty years in politics*. Penguin.
Bailey, T. (1967). *Presidential greatness*. Stanford University Press.
Baker, P. (2013). *Days of fire: Bush and Cheney in the White House*. Doubleday.
Barber, J. D. (1992). *The presidential character: Predicting performance in the White House*. 4th ed. Prentice-Hall.

Select Bibliography

Baumgartner, J. C., & Crumblin, T. F. (2015). *The American vice presidency: From the shadow to the spotlight*. Rowman & Littlefield.

Berman, L. (1986). *The new American presidency*. Little, Brown.

Blumenthal, D., & Morone, J. A. (2010). *The heart of power: Health and politics in the Oval Office*. University of California Press.

Blumenthal, S. (1980). *The permanent campaign: Inside the world of elite political operatives*. Beacon Press.

Borrelli, M. A. (2011). *The politics of the president's wife*. Texas A&M University Press.

Burns, J. M. (1984). *The power to lead: The crisis of the American presidency*. Simon & Schuster.

Burns, J. M. (1973). *Presidential government: The crucible of leadership*. 2nd ed. Houghton Mifflin.

Bush, B. (1992). *Millie's book: As dictated to Barbara Bush*. Harper Perennial.

Bush, L. (2010). *Spoken from the heart*. Scribner.

Chambers, V., ed. (2017). *The meaning of Michelle: 16 writers on the iconic first lady and how her journey inspires our own*. St. Martin's Press.

Chorin, E. (2012). *Exit Gaddafi: The hidden history of the Libyan revolution*. Saqi Books.

Clinton, H. (2014). *Hard choices*. Simon & Schuster.

Clinton, H. (2000). *An invitation to the White House: At home with history*. Simon & Schuster.

Covarrubias, J., Lansford, T., & Pauly, R. J. Jr., eds. (2016). *The new Islamic State: Ideology, religion, and violent extremism in the 21st century*. Routledge.

Cronin, T. E., & Genovese, M. A. (2009). *The paradoxes of the American presidency*. Rev. ed. Oxford University Press.

Daley, D. (2016). *Ratf**ked: Why your vote doesn't count*. Liveright.

Dalton, K. (2002). *Theodore Roosevelt: A strenuous life*. Alfred A. Knopf.

Dougherty, K., & Pauly, R. J. Jr. (2017). *American nation-building: Case studies from Reconstruction to Afghanistan*. McFarland.

Dyson, M. E. (2016). *The Black presidency: Barack Obama and the politics of race in America*. Houghton Mifflin Harcourt.

Edwards, G. C. III, & Wayne, S. J. (2009). *Presidential leadership: Politics and policy making*. 8th ed. Wadsworth.

Felix, A. (2010). *Sonia Sotomayor: The American dream*. Berkley.

Galvin, D. J. (2009). *Presidential party building: Dwight D. Eisenhower to George W. Bush*. Princeton University Press.

Gates, R. (2014). *Duty: Memoirs of a secretary at war*. Random House.

Goldstein, J. K. (2016). *The White House vice presidency: The path to significance, Mondale to Biden*. University Press of Kansas.

Gonnella-Platts, N., & Fritz, K. 2017. *A role without a rulebook: The influence and leadership of global first ladies*. George W. Bush Institute.

Greenstein, F. I. (2000). *The presidential difference: Leadership style from FDR to Clinton*. Free Press.
Greenstein, F. I. (1988). *Leadership in the modern presidency*. Harvard University Press.
Hariman, R. (1995). *Political style: The artistry of power*. The University of Chicago Press.
Heilemann, J., & Halperin, M. (2010). *Game change*. HarperCollins.
Hodgson, G. (1980). *All things to all men: The false promise of the modern American presidency*. Simon & Schuster.
Jacobs, L. R., & Skocpol, T. (2010). *Health care reform and American politics What every American needs to know*. Oxford University Press.
Jeffries, M. P. (2013). *Paint the White House black: Barack Obama and the meaning of race in America*. Stanford University Press.
Ju, H. (2015). *China's maritime power and strategy history, national security, and geopolitics*. World Scientific Publishing Company.
Katz, J. E., Barris, M., & Jain, A. (2013). *The social media president: Barack Obama and the politics of digital engagement*. Palgrave Macmillan.
Kantor, J. (2012). *The Obamas: A mission, a marriage*. Allen Lake.
Kernell, S. (2006). *Going public: New strategies of presidential leadership*. 4th ed. CQ Press.
Kesler, C. R. (2012). *I am the change: Barack Obama and the crisis of liberalism*. Harper Collins.
Klein, E. (2013). *The amateur: Barack Obama in the White House*. Regnery.
Kovalev, A. A. (2017). *Russia's dead end: An insider's testimony from Gorbachev to Putin*. Translated by S. I. Levine Potomac Books.
Light, P. C. (1984). *Vice-presidential power: Advice and influence in the White House*. Johns Hopkins University Press.
Lowi, T. (1986). *The personal presidency: Power invested, power unfilled*. Cornell University Press.
Lucidon, A. (2017). *Chasing light: Michelle Obama through the lens of a White House photographer*. Ten Speed Press/Crown.
Meyrowitz, J. (1985). *No sense of place: The impact of electronic media on social behavior*. Oxford University Press.
Milkus, S. M., & Nelson, M. (2007). *The American presidency: Origins and development, 1776–2007*. 5th ed. CQ Press.
Murray, R. K. (1994). *Greatness in the White House: Rating the presidents*. 2nd ed. Pennsylvania State University Press.
Nasr, V. (2013). *The dispensable nation: American foreign policy in retreat*. Johns Hopkins University Press.
Neal, A. (2018). *The oral presidency of Barack Obama*. Lexington Books.
Natalle, E. J., & Simon, J. M., eds. (2015). *Michelle Obama: First lady, American rhetor*. Lexington.

Neustadt, R. (1991). *Presidential power and the modern presidency: The politics of leadership from Roosevelt to Reagan*. Free Press.

Neustadt, R. (1980). *The politics of leadership from FDR to Carter*. John Wiley & Sons.

Obama, M. (2018). *Becoming*. Crown.

Obama, M. (2012). *American grown: The story of the White House kitchen garden and gardens across America*. Crown.

Panetta, L. (2014). *Worthy fights*. Penguin.

Pederson, C. (2009). *Obama's America*. Edinburgh University Press.

Pederson, W., & McLaurin, A. (1987). *The rating game in American politics*. Irvington.

Popkin, S. L. (1994). *The reasoning voter: Communication and persuasion in presidential campaigns*. 2nd ed. University of Chicago Press.

Prashad, V. (2012). *Arab spring, Libyan winter*. AK Press.

Renshon, S. A. (1975). *Psychological analysis and presidential personality: The case of Richard Nixon*. Atcom.

Rozell, M. J., & Sollenberger, M. A. (2015). *Encyclopedia of public administration and public policy*. 3rd ed. Taylor and Francis.

Schlesinger Jr., A. M. (2004). *The imperial presidency*. Reprint from 1974. Mariner Books.

Scott, K. D. (2017). *The language of strong Black womanhood: Myths, models, messages, and a new mandate for self-care*. Lexington.

Shogun, R. (1999). *The double-edged sword: How character makes and ruins presidents, from Washington to Clinton*. Westview Press.

Skidmore, M. J. (2017). *Unworkable conservatism*. Westphalia Press.

Skidmore, M. J. (2008). *Securing America's future: A bold plan to preserve and expand Social Security*. Rowman & Littlefield.

Skidmore, M. J. (2004). *After the White House: Former presidents as private citizens*. Palgrave Macmillan.

Skidmore, M. J. (2000). *Medicare and the American rhetoric of reconciliation*. University of Alabama Press (1970; republished by Questia Media).

Skowronek, S. (2011). *Presidential leadership in political time: Reprise and reappraisal*. University Press of Kansas.

Slevin, P. (2015). *Michelle Obama: A life*. Alfred A. Knopf.

Sunstein, C. (2004). *The second Bill of Rights: FDR's unfinished revolution and why we need it more than ever*. Perseus.

Toobin, J. (2012). *The oath: The Obama White House and the Supreme Court*. Doubleday.

Toobin, J. (2008). *The nine: Inside the secret world of the Supreme Court*. Anchor Books.

Warshaw, S. A. (2009). *The co-presidency of Bush and Cheney*. Stanford University Press.

Watson, R. P. (2014). *The presidents' wives: The office of the first lady in US politics*. 2nd ed. Lynne Rienner.

Watson, R. P. (2000). *The presidents' wives: Reassessing the office of first lady*. Lynne Rienner.

Watson, R. P., Covarrubias, J., Lansford, T., & Brattebo, D. M., eds. (2012). *The Obama presidency: A preliminary assessment*. State University of New York Press.

Watson, R. P., Pederson, W. D., & Williams, F. J. (2010). *Lincoln's enduring legacy*. Lexington Books.

Witcover, J. (2014). *The American vice presidency: From irrelevance to power*. Smithsonian Books.

Witcover, J. (2010). *Joe Biden: A life of trial and redemption*. William Morrow.

Witte, E. (1962). *The development of the Social Security Act*. University of Wisconsin Press.

Wolffe, R. (2010). *Revival: The struggle for survival inside the Obama White House*. Crown.

Woodward, B. (2010). *Obama's war*. Simon & Schuster.

Wright, L. A. (2016). *On behalf of the president: Presidential spouses and White House communications strategy today*. Praeger.

Yon, R. M. (2017). *Emerging from the shadows: Vice presidential influence in the modern era*. Doctoral Dissertation.

Zygar, M. (2016). *All the Kremlin's Men: Inside the court of Vladimir Putin*. PublicAffairs.

About the Editors

Tom Lansford, PhD, is professor of political science at the University of Southern Mississippi, Gulf Coast, where he also served as academic dean of the Gulf Coast Campus from 2009–14. His research interests include foreign and security policy, and the U.S. presidency. Dr. Lansford is the author, coauthor, editor, or coeditor of more than fifty books, and the author of more than one hundred scholarly essays, book chapters, encyclopedia entries, and reviews. Recent sole-authored books include *9/11 and The Wars in Afghanistan and Iraq: A Chronology and Reference Guide* (2011). His edited collections include *George W. Bush: Evaluating the President at Midterm* (2004), *Judging Bush* (2009), *The Obama Presidency: A Preliminary Assessment* (2012), and *A Transformation in American National Politics: The Presidential Election of 2012* (2015). Dr. Lansford has served as the co-editor of the journal *White House Studies* since 2010 and the editor of the *Political Handbook of the World* since 2012.

Douglas M. Brattebo, PhD, is associate professor of political science and director of the James A. Garfield Center for the Study of the Presidency at Hiram College. Among the courses Brattebo teaches are Ethics in U.S. Foreign Policy, American Government, The American Presidency and the Executive Branch, The U.S. Congress, Political Parties and Interest Groups, The Virtues, Leadership, and Legacy of Abraham Lincoln, and Engaged Citizenship. He also leads study courses to Australia, New Zealand, and the ancient forests of the U.S. Pacific Coast. Brattebo has won campuswide teaching awards at Hiram College (2016) and at the U.S. Naval Academy (2002). He is co-editor of five books, most recently the two-volume set *A Transformation in American National Politics: The Presidential Election of 2012* (2015) and *Culture, Rhetoric, and*

Voting: The Presidential Election of 2012 (2015). He has published two dozen peer-reviewed chapters including, most recently, an assessment of the demographic dilemmas facing the Republican Party, the politics surrounding the Patient Protection and Affordable Care Act, the narrow 2014 reelection victory of U.S. Senator Mark Warner (D-VA), and the upset 2016 reelection victory of U.S. Senator Ron Johnson (R-WI).

Robert P. Watson, PhD, is Distinguished Professor of American History and director of Project *Civitas* at Lynn University. He has served on the boards of numerous scholarly journals, presidential foundations, and community organizations, has been interviewed thousands of times by local, national, and international media outlets, was the political analyst for WPTV 5 (NBC) for many years, and has hosted regular community "town halls," voter registration drives, civic education programs, and training workshops for civics teachers and elected officials across south Florida. Watson has published more than forty books and two hundred scholarly articles, essays, and chapters. His recent books include *The Ghost Ship of Brooklyn* (2017), *The Nazi Titanic* (2016), *America's First Crisis* (2014), *The Presidents' Wives* (2nd edition 2014), *Affairs of State* (2012), and the forthcoming *George Washington's Final Battle* (2020). Several of his books have won awards, appeared at major literary festivals, and are in international translation. Watson has won several campuswide teaching awards at multiple universities.

Casey Maugh Funderburk, PhD, is the vice provost and an associate professor of communication studies at The University of Southern Mississippi, Gulf Coast. She has also served as director of interdisciplinary studiesand director of the speaking and writing center while at the University of Southern Mississippi. She completed her PhD at Penn State and her MA at Colorado State, specializing in communication studies and rhetoric, and has won multiple outstanding teaching awards. Maugh has published several book chapters on rhetoric and politics and has presented numerous papers on topics such as development policies and the Peace Corps, rhetorical analyses of the White House antidrug campaign, feminism, women in politics, and the Equal Rights Amendment.

About the Contributors

Paul Burton is a business executive who has lived and worked overseas in China, Eastern and Western Europe, Latin America, the Middle East and Africa. He holds a PhD in international development, a law degree, an MBA, and he is a graduate of the National Defense University. Dr. Burton is a former military officer whose interests are in development issues, especially as they relate to economic competitiveness and the use of technology in fostering economic growth.

John M. Callahan is program director for international studies, homeland security, and public policy programs at New England College. His research focuses on U.S. foreign policy, national security decision making, and European politics, although he is also an avid military historian. Dr. Callahan recently published his first book, *Explaining Wars of Choice* (2018), and recently contributed a chapter to *Explaining Wars of Choice*. He also serves as an associate editor for *The Handbook of Homeland Security* and the *Palgrave Encyclopedia of Global Security Studies*. Prior to completing his PhD in 2015, Dr. Callahan served as a public affairs officer and trainer for a variety of organizations including the U.S. State Department, the Office of the Director of National Intelligence, and the Department of Defense.

Michael J. Devine served as the director of the Harry S. Truman Library, director of the American Heritage Center at the University of Wyoming, director of the Illinois State Historical Society, assistant director of the Ohio Historical Society, and Illinois State Historian. He was a Fulbright Scholar in Argentina and Korea, the Haughton Freeman Professor of American History at Johns Hopkins University in Nanjing, China, and Public Policy Fellow with the Woodrow Wilson Center. Devine has co-edited several books and published several articles and chapters on Harry Truman, Korean politics, and other issues. He completed his PhD in U.S. diplomatic history from Ohio State University.

Michael J. Ferro resides in Tallahassee, Florida, where he provides policy and data analysis for a national education reform organization. In August 2018, he commissioned as a second lieutenant in the Florida Army National Guard, where he serves as platoon leader in the 144th Transportation Company. He holds a Master's degree in public administration and a graduate certificate in homeland security studies from Florida State University and a Bachelor's degree in history from the University of Florida.

Sean D. Foreman is an associate professor of political science in the Department of History and Political Science at Barry University in Miami Shores, Florida. He was president of the Florida Political Science Association in 2012–13 and is the chair of the education committee for the Greater Miami Chamber of Commerce. Foreman is co-editor of *the Roads to Congress 2010* (2011), where he wrote about the 2010 midterm elections and Marco Rubio's election to the U.S. Senate, and co-editor of *The Roads to Congress 2012* (2013), in which he also wrote about the Florida District 26 campaign (Rivera versus Garcia). His article "Top 10 Reasons Why Barack Obama Won the Presidency in 2008 and What It Means in the 2012 Election" was published in the *Florida Political Chronicle* in August 2012.

Raymond Frey is professor of history at Centenary University in Hackettstown, New Jersey. In 2006, he was the Gates-Ferry Foundation Distinguished Lecturer at Centenary. In 2000 and again in 2004, Dr. Frey prepared a White House briefing document on Bess Truman for First Lady Laura Bush. He also contributed chapters on the Trumans in *The Presidential Companion*, as well as *Life in the White House: A Social History of the First Family and the President's House*, and *American First Ladies*. He is also a member of the editorial board of *White House Studies*. Professor Frey is also one of the leading scholars of New Jersey history and has written two textbooks on the state—*New Jersey, A Journey of Discovery*, and *New Jersey, Our Home*. He has contributed to the *New Jersey Encyclopedia*, and regularly lectures on New Jersey history around the state.

About the Contributors

David Harms Holt is an associate professor of geography in the School of Biological, Environmental, and Earth Sciences at the University of Southern Mississippi. Dr. Holt's research interests are political geography, migration, resilience, necrogeography, environmental geography, and sustainability. He received his PhD in environmental dynamics from the University of Arkansas at Fayetteville in 2002. Dr. Holt currently teaches world regional geography, conservation of natural resources, sustainable development, and cartography at the University of Southern Mississippi. Among Dr. Holt's publications are *Religious, Cultural, and Minority Rights: Foundations of Democracy* (2016), a book chapter in *The New Islamic State: Ideology, Religion, and Violent Extremism in the 21st Century* (2016), multiple entries in *Afghanistan at War: From the 18th-Century Durrani Dynasty to the 21st Century (2017)*, and journal articles in *Dendrochronologia*, *Physical Geography*, and the *Journal of Archaeological Science*.

Jeremy Hunt is a native of Johns Creek, Georgia. He graduated from the United States Military Academy at West Point in 2015 and was commissioned as an active duty Army officer. He spent his first three years as a military intelligence lieutenant stationed at Fort Stewart, GA. During that time, he deployed to Ukraine where he served on a multinational mission to train the Ukrainian Armed Forces. Outside of his role in the Army, Jeremy volunteers as a leadership strategist for the Douglass Leadership Institute. Jeremy recently married the love of his life—Ky September—and they now reside at an Army base near Tucson, Arizona.

William Keeton is a retired United States Army lieutenant colonel. During his twenty-year career, he held several command and director positions and managed budgets of more than $500 million dollars. From 2000 to 2003, he was the U.S. exchange officer to the Australian Army teaching logistics, leadership, strategic military planning and working with the U.S. Embassy's Australian diplomatic mission. Dr. Keeton is currently a lecturer at La Trobe University in Australia in the School of Business, Department of Management. He is a graduate of the U.S. Institute of Peace, the Australian Institute of Company Directors Course, and holds a PhD in management (La Trobe University, Australia). His PhD research received the La Trobe University Nancy Millis award (medal) in 2017 for "Excellence in Research." He has taught, developed, or tutored in fifteen different management and leadership subjects during this period.

Wayne Law completed his PhD at Washington University in St. Louis where he studied evolution, ecology, and population biology. A botanist and ecologist, he has conducted research on plant conservation in Kosrae, Pohnpei, Palau, and the Federated States of Micronesia, the Eastern Himalayas, and throughout the Caribbean and Pacific. Law worked previously at the New York Botanical Garden, where he managed the Geographic Information System Laboratory, and is assistant professor of science and co-coordinator of the environmental studies program at Lynn University.

Alanna Lecher received her PhD in earth and planetary sciences from the University of California, Santa Cruz. Her work and publications focus on biogeochemistry and the impact of humans and geology on the chemical cycles of the earth. She has conducted studies all over the world, including on the California coast, Gulf of Mexico, Gulf of Aqaba in Israel, and the Arctic Ocean. Lecher is assistant professor of natural and applied sciences and co-coordinator of the environmental studies program at Lynn University.

Wayne F. Lesperance Jr. holds the rank of professor of political science and the title of vice president of academic affairs at New England College in Henniker, New Hampshire. He is also a frequent commentator in regional and national newspapers and is a regular guest on local and regional radio programs, where he is frequently quoted on public policy, the political process, and emerging trends in politics. Dr. Lesperance is associate editor of the *Political Handbook of the World 2016–2017*, a contributor to the *The New Islamic State: Ideology, Religion, and Violent Extremism in the 21st Century* (2016) and author of "American Foreign Policy and the 2016 Election," in addition to many other articles and chapters in peer-reviewed journals, textbooks, and other publications.

Elizabeth J. Natalle has a PhD in communication from Florida State University and is an associate professor of communication studies at the University of North Carolina at Greensboro. In pursuing a research agenda on women's voices, she specializes in first ladies and women's public speaking. Dr. Natalle is the co-author of *The Woman's Public Speaking Handbook*, co-editor of *Michelle Obama: First Lady, American Rhetor*, and author of *Jacqueline Kennedy and the Architecture of First Lady Diplomacy*.

Robert J. Pauly Jr. is an associate professor of international development at the University of Southern Mississippi. His research interests focus broadly on the fields of U.S. foreign policy, national security, and homeland security, with emphases on American policy toward the states of Europe and the Greater Middle East as well as the evolving relationships between states and nonstate actors in the Muslim and Western worlds. Dr. Pauly is the author and editor of seven books and more than forty-five academic articles, essays, and book chapters, including, most recently, *American Nation-Building: Cases from Reconstruction to Afghanistan* (2017) and *The New Islamic State: Ideology, Religion and Violent Extremism in the 21st Century* (2016). He is also co-editor of the peer-reviewed academic journal *White House Studies*, contributes to the Council on Foreign Relations' Academic Outreach Initiative, and analyzes U.S. foreign policy for a range of media outlets.

Sean J. Savage is a professor of political science at Saint Mary's College in Notre Dame, Indiana. He is the author of multiple articles and books, including *Roosevelt: The Party Leader, 1932–1945* (1991), *Truman and the Democratic Party* (1997), and *JFK, LBJ, and The Democratic Party* (2004). He earned an Emerging Scholar Award from the American Political Science Association for his first book, *Roosevelt: The Party Leader*. Professor Savage's third book, *JFK, LBJ and the Democratic Party*, was published in 2004 and won a Choice Award for Outstanding Academic Title of 2005. *The Senator from New England: The Rise of JFK* is his most recent book.

Max J. Skidmore is University of Missouri Curators' Professor of Political Science, and Thomas Jefferson Fellow. He teaches at the University of Missouri—Kansas City and has been Distinguished Fulbright Lecturer in India and Senior Fulbright Scholar at the University of Hong Kong. He specializes in the presidency, American political thought, and the politics of Social Security, Medicare, and health care, and is founder and president of the Caucus on Poverty, Inequality, and Public Policy of the American Political Science Association. He edits the journal *Poverty and Public Policy* and is a member of the Scholars' Strategy Network and the National Academy of Social Insurance. He is the author of more than one hundred articles and book chapters, and of approximately two dozen books, including *Securing America's Future*, *Presidential Performance*, *After the White House: Former Presidents as Private Citizens*, *Legacy to the World: A History of America's Political Ideas*, and *Hong Kong and China: Pursuing a New Destiny*. His PhD is from the University of Minnesota.

Jonathan Smith teaches courses in science, anatomy, and biochemistry, and focuses his research on biomechanics, neurology, ergonomics, public health, and environmental sustainability. He worked previously at the Life West Health Center in California and is currently assistant professor of science at Lynn University.

Joseph J. St. Marie is an associate professor of international development at the University of Southern Mississippi and program coordinator for the international development doctoral program. Dr. St. Marie received his undergraduate political science degree from Gonzaga University, his MA from the University of Idaho and PhD from Texas Tech University. Dr. St. Marie's research agenda includes work on conflict process in ethnic conflict and civil war, inflation targeting, and governance changes. He has published in various academic journals, and co-authored a book *Revolutionary Iran and the United States: Low-Intensity Conflict in the Persian Gulf* and is working on a strategy and cybersecurity.

April Watson completed her PhD in geosciences from Florida Atlantic University. Her work in the community includes using geographic information systems, remote sensing systems, and developing predictive models to study prehistoric archaeological sites, and her research examines relationships between humans and their environment, prehistoric ceramics, environmental sustainability, and mathematical modeling of human/environmental spatial relationships. She serves as secretary of the Florida Archaeological Council and assistant professor at Lynn University.

Richard M. Yon serves as an assistant professor in the Department of Social Sciences and the director of cadet development for the Combating Terrorism Center at West Point, which provides him with oversight of the Terrorism Studies Minor and the Academic Individual Advanced Development (Internship) Program for both the Combating Terrorism Center and the Department of Social Sciences. Dr. Yon teaches courses in homeland security and defense, American politics, American presidency, legislative politics, and American political development. Dr. Yon's most recent research examines the role of the vice president where he has interviewed vice presidents, chiefs of staff, cabinet secretaries, national security advisors, and other members of presidential administrations as part of this research. He holds a doctoral degree in political science from the University of Florida and two master's degrees in political science from Florida Atlantic University and the University of Florida.

Index

Afghanistan, 34–35, 111, 197–198, 234–240, 242–243, 245–249, 251, 292, 294
Affordable Care Act, 37, 81, 114, 117, 138, 160–165, 172, 194, 318
   attempts to overturn, 19, 81, 82, 177–180
   impact, 136–137
   passage, 186, 189–190
   past healthcare reforms, 154–160
   popularity, 124
Al-Assad, Bashar, 33, 197–198, 241, 258, 297, 300. See also Syria
Al-Maliki, Nouri, 34, 235, 244. See also Iraq
Al Qaeda, 33, 233–240, 242–249, 259, 289. See also Bin Laden, Osama; Terrorism
Alito, Samuel, 169, 175
American Recovery and Reinvestment Act, 38, 135, 161, 172, 188, 271–272
Arab Spring, 241, 244, 246, 252–258, 297. See also Egypt; Libya; Syria
Arizona v. United States, 177
Australia, 252, 304, 307, 309. See also Morrison, Scott

Aurora, Colorado Theater Shooting, 208, 211, 224. See also Gun Control; Mass Shootings
Authorization to Use Military Force (2001), 198. See also Iraq; Islamic State; Syria
Axelrod, David, 64, 105

Baton Rouge Police Shooting, 209, 215, 225. See also Gun Control; Mass Shootings
Belt and Road Initiative, 305–306. See also China
Ben Ali, Zine El Abidine, 253. See also Arab Spring; Tunisia
Benghazi Attack (2019), 257
Biden, Jill, 110–111
Biden, Joseph R., Jr., 25–26, 27–34, 37–41, 61, 63, 64, 185, 198, 207, 214, 272
   role in domestic policy, 37–39
   role in role in foreign policy, 34–37
   vice-presidency, 31–34
   See also "Bidenisms" ("Joe Bombs") "Bidenisms" ("Joe Bombs")
"Bidenisms" ("Joe Bombs"), 32–34
Bin Laden, Osama, 32, 36, 197, 199, 235, 237–238, 239–240, 243–245, 246, 247, 248, 269, 289

Black Lives Matter, 213. *See also* Ferguson Riots
Boehner, John, 78, 81, 140, 146, 187, 191, 192–195. *See also* Grand Bargain
Boston Marathon Bombing, 208, 212, 224. *See also* Terrorism
Brown, Michael. *See* Ferguson Riots
Budget Control Act of 2011. *See* Grand Bargain
Burwell v. Hobby Lobby, 180
Bush, Barbara, 117
Bush, George H. W., 4, 15, 16, 28, 47, 90, 93, 168, 170, 197
Bush, George W., 5, 11, 28, 30, 34, 47, 69, 93, 96, 135, 136, 144, 160, 161, 169, 172, 173, 185, 191, 194, 195, 261
    environmental policies, 267, 269, 278
    executive orders, 76
    foreign policy, 297–298
    Great Recession, 188
    Hurricane Katrina, 206
    Medicare expansion, 158–159
Bush, Laura, 108, 109, 111, 116, 124

Cameron, David, 259. *See also* United Kingdom
Cantor, Eric, 191, 193
Car Allowance Rebate System ("Cash for Clunkers"), 189
Carbon Footprint, 275–277. *See also* Climate Change
Carter, James E., 4, 7–8, 12, 15, 19, 28–29, 47, 146
Carter, Rosalynn, 108
Central Intelligence Agency (CIA), 78, 199, 291
Cheney, Richard B., 25, 26, 28–30, 31

China, 29, 113, 143, 272, 289–290, 302–310
    climate change and environmental policies, 279, 280, 281
    See also Belt and Road Initiative; Hu Jintao; Pivot to Asia; South China Sea; Xi Jinping.
CIA. *See* Central Intelligence Agency
Citizens United v. Federal Election Commission, 174, 175
Clean Energy Incentive Program, 271, 273–274. *See also* Clean Power Plan; Climate Change
Clean Power Plan, 142–143, 273, 283. *See also* Clean Energy Incentive Program, Climate Change
Climate Change, 17, 18, 19, 83, 134, 172, 267–270, 274, 275, 278–284. *See also* Clean Energy Incentive Program; Clean Power Plan; Intergovernmental Panel on Climate Change (IPCC); Paris Climate Accords
Clinton, Hillary R., 35, 49–54, 68, 198, 254, 296, 297
    appointment as secretary of state, 55–56
    Arab Spring, 255–256
    first lady, 109, 116, 117, 124
    presidential campaign (2016), 61–65, 82, 106, 107, 318
Clinton, William J., 4, 8, 10, 11–12, 15, 31, 47–56, 61–65, 66–69, 82, 90, 93, 96, 136, 158, 170, 185, 190, 195, 206
    environmental policies, 269, 278
    relationship with Obama, 56–60
Cotton, Tom, 199
Crawford v. Marion County Election Board, 176

Crimea, 197, 296, 299. See also Putin, Vladimir, Russia
Cruz, Ted, 194
Cuba, 121, 197

D'Amato, Alfonse, 170
Dallas Police Shooting, 209, 214, 215. See also Gun Control; Mass Shootings
Deepwater Horizon Oil Spill, 208, 210, 224
Defense of Marriage Act (DOMA) of 1996, 67, 180–181. See also Same Sex Marriage
Defense Policy, 28, 141, 194, 258, 269
Deferred Action for Childhood Arrivals (DACA), 76, 81, 145, 190, 199, 224, 318. See also Immigration
Deficit, U.S., 17, 18, 137, 140–141, 146
Democratic National Committee (DNC), 92, 93
Democratic Party, 17, 41, 48, 56, 57–61, 66, 67, 87, 88, 90–97, 98, 105, 146, 188
Diplomacy, 56, 121, 264, 291–292, 309, 310
Dodd-Frank Wall Street Reform and Consumer Protection Act, 139–140, 172, 186
Don't Ask, Don't Tell Policy, 37, 67, 161, 172–173, 191
Drone Strikes, 197, 235, 239, 243, 291
Duterte, Rodrigo, 309. See also Philippines

Economic Freedom, 133–135, 138, 144
Economic Stimulus Act of 2008, 134, 136

Egypt, 239, 252, 253–255, 258, 259. See also Arab Spring; Mubarak, Hosni
Eisenhower, Dwight D., 3, 4, 8, 12, 15, 156, 159
Elections, 57, 95, 156, 175, 187, 88–93
  2008 elections, 168, 267
  2010 elections, 16, 56, 88–89, 97–98, 176, 192
  2012 elections, 89, 176
  2014 elections, 16, 37, 194, 196
  2016 elections, 98
  2018 elections, 68, 164, 318, 321
  2020 elections, 40, 47, 164
Emanuel, Rahm, 185, 323
Environmental Protection Agency, 143, 280
EU, see European Union
European Union (EU), 252, 262
Executive Memoranda, 76
Executive Orders, 75–83, 275–277, 280, 283, 289

FBI. See Federal Bureau of Investigation
Federal Bureau of Investigation (FBI), 213
Ferguson Riots, 213. See also Black Lives Matter
Filibuster, 88, 146, 174, 190, 200
  nuclear option, 196
Foreign Policy, 3, 14, 17, 29, 34–37, 41, 54, 62, 121, 159, 197–200, 233, 236, 251, 257, 261, 289–293, 297, 298–303, 304, 309, 310, 320
Fossil Fuels, 142, 270–271, 272, 275, 303. See also Climate Change
France, 13, 255, 293

Gaddafi, Muammar, 254, 255, 257. See also Arab Spring; Libya

Garland, Merrick, 181, 196–197, 200
Gates, Henry Louis, Jr., 207
Gates, Robert, 34, 36, 254, 256
Gerrymandering, 88, 97–98
Government Shutdown (2013), 194–195, 200
Grand Bargain, 192–194. *See also* Boehner, John
Great Recession, 17, 57, 67, 133, 135, 136, 138, 141, 200, 267, 269
Guantanamo Bay Naval Base, 78, 233
Gulf Cooperation Council (GCC), 254, 260
Gun Control, 17, 76, 83, 202, 212, 224. *See also* Mass Shootings

Haiti, 111
Holder, Eric, 176
Hu Jintao, 303
Hurricane Sandy, 208, 212, 216, 219, 221, 222, 224
Hurwitz, Sarah, 109

IMF. *See* International Monetary Fund
Immigration, 77, 80–81, 82, 83, 93, 96, 146, 172, 176, 177, 191, 201–202, 318. *See also* Deferred Action for Childhood Arrivals (DACA)
Intergovernmental Panel on Climate Change (IPCC), 278. *See also* Climate Change
International Atomic Energy Agency (IAEA), 261–262. *See also* Iran Nuclear Deal
International Monetary Fund (IMF), 305
Iran, 8, 15, 18–19, 197, 199, 252, 258–263, 297, 298, 300, 301–302, 319. *See also* Iran Nuclear Agreement Review Act; Iran Nuclear Deal
Iran Nuclear Agreement Review Act, 199. *See also* Iran Nuclear Deal
Iran Nuclear Deal, 18, 199, 252, 260–263, 318. *See also* Iran Nuclear Agreement Review Act
Iraq, 34, 37, 197–198, 233–238, 239–249, 264, 269, 292, 294. *See also* Iraq War
Iraq War, 51, 197, 200, 251. *See also* Iraq
Islamic State of Iraq and Syria (ISIS), 95, 198, 234, 238, 241, 244–245, 246, 248, 252, 257, 259, 264, 289, 297, 300. *See also* Iraq, Syria; Terrorism
Islamic State of Iraq and the Levant (ISIL). *See* Islamic State Iraq and Syria

Japan, 121, 278, 304, 305, 315, 308, 309
Jarrett, Valerie, 108
Johnson, Andrew, 4, 5, 7
Johnson, Lyndon, 4, 5, 12, 151, 159, 201, 202
  Medicare, 157–158
  vice presidency, 29
Joint Comprehensive Plan of Action (JCPOA). *See* Iran Nuclear Deal
Joplin, Missouri Tornado, 208, 211, 216, 217, 219, 221, 223
Justice Against Sponsors of Terrorism Act, 200

Kagan, Elena, 173–174, 179
Kennedy, Anthony, 177, 178
Kennedy, John F., 2, 3, 4, 10, 12, 15, 52, 76, 77, 90, 156, 201
Kennedy, Edward "Ted," 52, 190

Index

Kennedy, Jacqueline, 112–113, 124
Kennedy, Robert, 67
Kerry, John, 109, 199, 254, 262
Kim Jung Il, 319. *See also* North Korea
Komitet gosudarstvennoy bezopasnosti (KGB), 295, 296
Kurds, 241. *See also* Syria
Kyoto Protocol, 269, 278–279, 280, 281, 282. *See also* Climate Change

Let Girls Learn Initiative, 112, 116, 121–122. *See also* Obama, Michelle
Let's Move Campaign, 112, 114, 115, 116–119, 122, 123. *See also* Obama, Michelle
Libya, 241, 246, 258–259, 300
   U.S.-led intervention and civil war, 35, 253–257, 299
   See also Arab Spring; Benghazi Attack (2019); Gaddafi, Muammar
Lilly Ledbetter Fair Pay Act, 161, 168

Malaysian Airlines Flight 17, 297. *See also* Ukraine
Mass Shootings, 206, 211, 214, 224. *See also* Aurora, Colorado Theater Shooting; Baton Rouge Police Shooting; Dallas Police Shooting; Gun Control; Pulse Nightclub Shooting; San Bernardino Shootin; Sandy Hook Shooting
McCain, John S., 92, 133, 188, 233, 256, 259, 267
McConnell, Mitch, 161, 181, 191, 196, 197, 273
Me Too Movement, 40–41, 68, 107

Medvedev, Dmitry, 294
Medicare, 13, 137, 151, 156–159, 162
Mondale, Walter F., 25, 26, 27, 28–29, 30
Morrison, Scott, 304. *See also* Australia
Moynihan, Daniel Patrick, 170
Mubarak, Hosni, 254, 259. *See also* Arab Spring; Egypt

Napolitano, Janet, 169–170
National Archives and Records Administration (NARA), 322
National Federation of Independent Business v. Sebelius, 178–180
National Security Council, 27, 35, 36, 199, 254
National Security Strategy (2010), 237, 239, 240
National Security Strategy (2015), 238, 240, 242
National Strategy for Counterterrorism (2011), 238, 240, 241
Nixon, Richard M., 4, 7–8, 11, 12, 15, 16, 51, 98, 158, 278, 317
Nobel Peace Prize, 298
North Atlantic Treaty Organization (NATO), 2, 215, 241, 245, 246, 297, 299, 319
   Libya intervention, 254–256, 257
   See also Libya
North Korea, 197, 297, 300, 301. *See also* Kim Jung Il
Northwest Austin Municipal Utility District No. 1 v. Holder, 175
Nuclear Option. *See* Filibuster

Obama, Barack, 3, 5, 7, 11, 76, 167, 185, 251–252, 289–290
   comforter-in-chief, 205–207, 215–225

Obama, Barack *(continued)*
  economic policy, 133–134, 135–141, 144–146, 188–189, 271–273, 274–284
  elections, 49–55, 60–65, 88–97, 99, 190–192
  environmental policies, 141–144
  executive orders, 75–83, 94
  foreign policy, 197–200, 236–249, 257–264, 293–305, 310–311
  healthcare reform, 160–165
  partisanship, 187–188
  post-presidency and legacy, 65–69, 200–202, 317–324
  public approval rankings, 31
  presidential assessment, 16–19
  relationship with vice president, 30–39
  same sex marriage, 30
  Supreme Court, 172–173, 174–181, 195–197
  Supreme Court nominations, 168–172, 173–174
  See also Obama Doctrine; Obama For America (2008 OFA); Obama Foundation; Organization for America
Obama, Malia, 113, 319
Obama, Michelle, 60, 64, 103
  activism, 116–122
  early life and background, 104–105
  first lady, 107–112, 122–125
  political campaigns, 105–107
  social media, 112–116
  See also Let Girls Learn Initiative; Let's Move Campaign; Reach Higher
Obama, Sasha, 113, 319
Obama Doctrine, 35, 252, 253
Obama For America (2008 OFA), 91–92
Obama Foundation, 122, 124, 187, 319, 321, 322, 323

Obamacare. *See* Affordable Care Act
Obergefell v. Hodges, 180–181
  See also Same Sex Marriage
Operation Odyssey Dawn, 254, 257. *See also* Arab Spring; Gaddafi, Muanmmar; Libya
Organization for American (2012 OFA), 91–93

Paris Climate Accords, 199, 261, 277–284, 318. *See also* Climate Change; Intergovernmental Panel on Climate Change (IPCC)
Pelosi, Nancy, 90, 96, 185, 190
Permanent Campaigns, 91–93
Philippines, 304–309. *See also* Duterte, Rodrigo.
Pivot to Asia, 252, 253, 290, 304, 309. *See also* China
Power, Samantha, 254
Presidential Proclamations, 75, 76, 79, 80
Primaries, 41, 105, 191, 193
Public Opinion Polls, 11, 30, 93, 104, 106, 188,
Pulse Nightclub Shooting, 209, 214, 216, 218, 221, 222, 224. *See also* Gun Control; Mass Shootings
Putin, Vladimir, 294–299, 302, 319. *See also* Russia

Quayle, J. Danforth, 28, 41

Reach Higher, 112, 116, 119, 120, 122. *See also* Obama, Michelle
Reagan, Ronald, 4, 10, 12, 15, 51, 67, 90, 93, 157, 181, 192, 195, 201, 202, 206, 207, 213, 260, 268, 318
Reid, Harry, 90, 140, 168, 185
Republican Party, 75, 78, 79, 81, 89, 90, 95–98, 106, 140, 145, 152,

153–155, 156, 162, 164, 168, 169, 170–174, 176, 178, 181, 187, 188, 190–197, 198, 201, 212, 268, 269, 283, 318. *See also* Tea Party
Rhodes, Ben, 256
Rice, Susan, 256
Ricci v. DeStefano, 171
Roberts, John, 167–168, 172, 175, 177, 178–179
Rouhani, Hassan, 261–262. *See also* Iran Nuclear Deal
Romney, Mitt, 58, 59, 60, 89, 212
Roosevelt, Franklin D., 4, 11, 12, 79, 155, 160, 169, 172, 278, 296, 322
Roosevelt, Theodore, 4, 7, 11, 12, 13, 26, 75, 82, 152
"New nationalism," 153–154
Russia, 35, 37, 95, 161, 197, 198, 258, 259, 289–290, 291, 303, 310
reset of relations, 197, 290, 293, 294–295, 296–302
See also Crimea; Putin, Vladimir; Ukraine

Same Sex Marriage, 30, 33, 107, 145, 173, 180–181
San Bernardino Shooting, 214, 228. *See also* Gun Control; Mass Shootings
Sandy Hook Shooting, 202, 208, 212, 214, 216–217, 218, 219, 220, 221, 223, 224. *See also* Gun Control, Mass Shootings
Saudi Arabia, 200, 255, 260, 263
Scalia, Antonin, 179, 181, 196
Schlesinger, Arthur M., 2–3, 5, 13
School Lunch Program, 118
Sessions, Jeff, 171
Shelby County v. Holder, 176
Social Media, 9, 16, 18, 104, 109, 112–116, 117, 118, 120, 123, 124, 187, 252, 258

Social Capitalism, 268, 272
Social Security, 155–156
Solyndra Bankruptcy, 272–273. *See also* American Recovery and Reinvestment Act
Sotomayor, Sonia, 169–172, 174, 195
Souter, David, 168–169, 173
South China Sea, 290, 304, 307–310. *See also* Australia; China; Philippines; Taiwan
South Korea, 121, 308
State Department, U.S., 62, 258, 291, 297, 298
Strategic Arms Reduction Talks (New START), 38, 161, 300
Swine Flu (H1N1), 207
Syria, 197, 199, 201, 234, 238, 241, 244, 246, 253, 257–260, 264, 300
chemical weapons ("red line"), 198, 252, 259, 297
Syrian National Council (SNC), 300
See also Al-Assad, Bashar; Arab Spring; Russia

Taiwan, 307, 308
Tea Party, 56, 192, 193, 194. *See also* Republican Party
Terrorism, 36, 105, 121, 198, 200, 206, 214–215, 222, 224, 234, 235–243, 244, 245, 246, 249, 291. *See also* Boston Marathon Bombing
Texas Wildfires (2011), 211
Trans-Pacific Partnership (TPP), 306
Trayvon Martin Shooting, 213, 224,
Truman, Harry S., 4, 8, 11, 12, 78, 80, 156
Trump, Donald, 5, 11, 17, 18, 19, 28, 40–41, 47, 63, 64–65, 69, 106, 107, 139, 141, 152, 161, 181,

Trump, Donald (*continued*)
    196, 213, 263, 274, 283, 284, 304, 317, 318–321, 322, 323
    executive orders, 77, 82, 94, 142, 277
Tunisia, 253, 258

Ukraine, 37, 95, 197, 257, 295, 296, 299
United Kingdom, 256, 305. *See also* Cameron, David
United Nations (UN), 121, 254, 256, 261, 262, 278, 308
United Nations Convention on the Law of the Sea (UNCLOS), 308–309
United States v. Windsor, 180
Upper Big Branch Mine Disaster, 208, 210, 216, 217

Vietnam, 13, 158, 305, 307, 308

Violence Against Women Act, 39
Voter Identification Laws, 176

WikiLeaks Scandal, 253
Wilson, Woodrow, 4, 154, 155, 213
Wood, Diane, 169–170
World Trade Organization (WTO), 303

Xi Jinping, 281, 303, 306. *See also* China; Pivot to Asia; South China Sea

Yanukovych, Viktor, 296. *See also* Ukraine
Yemen, 253, 255, 260, 303. *See also* Arab Spring

Zhou Enlai, 317, 324
Zimmerman, George, 211. *See* Trayvon Martin Shooting

CPSIA information can be obtained
at www.ICGtesting.com
Printed in the USA
BVHW032104090322
631125BV00004B/59